# RELENTLESS
# PURSUIT

# RELENTLESS PURSUIT

*My Fight for the Victims*
*of Jeffrey Epstein*

## Bradley J. Edwards

### with Brittany Henderson

GALLERY BOOKS
New York   London   Toronto   Sydney   New Delhi

Gallery Books
An Imprint of Simon & Schuster, Inc.
1230 Avenue of the Americas
New York, NY 10020

First Gallery Books hardcover edition March 2020

GALLERY BOOKS and colophon are registered trademarks of Simon & Schuster, Inc.

For information about special discounts for bulk purchases, please contact Simon & Schuster Special Sales at 1-866-506-1949 or business@simonandschuster.com.

The Simon & Schuster Speakers Bureau can bring authors to your live event. For more information or to book an event, contact the Simon & Schuster Speakers Bureau at 1-866-248-3049 or visit our website at www.simonspeakers.com.

Interior design by Davina Mock-Maniscalco

Manufactured in the United States of America

10  9  8  7  6  5  4  3  2  1

Library of Congress Cataloging-in-Publication Data has been applied for.

ISBN 978-1-9821-4813-3
ISBN 978-1-9821-4815-7 (ebook)

*Papa, I miss you. You are my guide every day.*
*Your selfless leadership lives on forever, through all those*
*you taught and influenced during your lifetime.*

# CONTENTS

## AUTHOR'S NOTE

I N WRITING THIS BOOK, THE protection of our clients and other victims was paramount. For that reason, several names have been changed to protect the identity of certain individuals who wish to remain anonymous. Additionally, we simply could not include all the meaningful histories of the many survivors we interviewed over the years. For those reasons, we have included composite characters in this book—namely, Allison, Savanah, and Seloh. Through each composite character, we were able to share the experiences of more than one survivor of Jeffrey Epstein in a way that both protects privacy and allows for a better understanding of the circumstances surrounding the breadth of Epstein's abuse and the history of those he preyed upon.

Finally, with regard to the many conversations that occurred between Jeffrey Epstein and me that are detailed herein, the quotations represent the essence of the words spoken during such exchanges to the very best of my recollection.

# PROLOGUE

MY PURSUIT OF JEFFREY EPSTEIN on behalf of his victims became my personal life's mission. Jeffrey Epstein was an intellectually gifted sociopath with unlimited wealth who lived an unconventional and virtually unconstrained life. The rules he—and those in his fold—lived by were his own. The problem was that his rules didn't account for laws.

Epstein had amassed extensive political and worldly connections. His friends included a former United States president, the current U.S. president, leaders of foreign countries, the greatest scientists on the planet, some of the wealthiest men in the world, and even a member of the British royal family.

But his wealth and connections weren't what put him on my radar. It was his lifestyle that did. For decades he used his tremendous fortune to sexually exploit women and girls, some as young as fourteen years old. The more I learned, the more determined I was to bring his manipulation and abuse to an end. When he was finally discovered by law enforcement, his money and connections bought him out of serious trouble. He was able to negotiate an agreement with the United States government that essentially immunized him from the federal sex crimes he'd committed against dozens of children. Even more offensive, the government worked with Epstein to keep the immunity agreement concealed from the victims he had abused.

One victim, Courtney Wild, hired me as her lawyer to make sure her rights as a crime victim of Jeffrey Epstein were protected. At first, that sounded as if it should have been easy. It was anything but. Over the course of eleven years the investigation had taken me all over the United States and beyond. I had represented more than thirty victims in lawsuits and claims against Jeffrey Epstein, multiple personal lawsuits, and an unprecedented pro bono case that itself spanned more than a decade. In the end, however, justice was finally served. Epstein was arrested. He was incarcerated for only a month before he escaped responsibility once again, this time by committing suicide in a federal correctional institution in New York.

Had it not been for some very courageous women, there is little doubt Jeffrey Epstein would have continued to harm young girls on a massive scale while globetrotting with his dedicated followers. He was the master of his universe, ruling through manipulation and absolute control. After years of being pursued, fighting one legal battle after another, he was eventually captured. Still, he managed to stay in control—by choosing the way he left his universe behind.

Even though he died, the story of Jeffrey Epstein's crimes should not. I believe I owe it to my clients, the brave women who came forward to seek justice, and the good people who risked their privacy and safety to help us hold Jeffrey Epstein accountable to share what really happened during this time in history.

# ONE

# THE BEGINNING OF THE END

I T WAS SATURDAY, JULY 6, 2019. I was in Naples, Florida, with my wife, Terry, and our three sons, Blake, Cashton, and Austin, enjoying the Fourth of July holiday weekend with several other families from our hometown of Fort Lauderdale. We spent the day hanging out at the hotel pool and throwing a football around until suddenly black clouds came out of nowhere and filled the sky. Within minutes, a lightning bolt shot down and thunder drowned out the lifeguard whistles as everyone was asked to evacuate the pool area. We corralled the children and ushered them inside.

Cooped up in a hotel room, the kids were bouncing off the walls, and the adults wanted a break. One of the other dads and I volunteered to take all the kids somewhere to let them run off their energy. We loaded up two cars with ten children ranging from four to fourteen years old and went to the local bowling alley.

As soon as I parked, my phone rang. It was my law partner Stan Pottinger. Making a concerted effort not to let anything disrupt my family time, I didn't answer and shoved my phone back in my pocket. It was still raining so hard you could barely see. The kids and I opened the car doors and made a run for it. We quickly realized we were not the only ones in town with this idea. The alley was packed. And loud. The kids immediately dashed to the counter. While I was trying to pay for the shoes and lanes, my phone kept ringing. Stan again. I thought to myself, *This is strange. He never does that.* Still, I couldn't answer at the moment.

"What size shoes do you need?" asked the clerk. Most of the kids, excited to get bowling, just started yelling out shoe sizes simultaneously.

"I don't know what my shoe size is," shouted my friend's four-year-old daughter, Callie. I placed my phone faceup on the counter while lifting Callie in the air to show the clerk her foot so that he could take his best guess at her size.

"Your phone is ringing," Callie said. I looked down. It was Stan again. This had to be important. After I helped Callie get her shoes on and find a lightweight bowling ball, I asked the other dad to watch the kids while I made a quick call.

Before I could dial, Stan called again. I ducked into the quieter bar area to answer. "Are you okay?" I asked as I pulled the phone to my ear.

Stan, in his typical very calm voice, said, "I just got a call from the FBI. He's in handcuffs. They arrested him an hour ago coming off his jet from Paris."

Jeffrey Epstein, infamous billionaire and my longtime archenemy, who until now had gotten away with international sexual abuse against hundreds of young women and girls, was in custody.

At that moment, a million thoughts shot through my mind. I didn't say anything for a good five seconds, unable to figure out which one I wanted to turn into a question. "No kidding," I finally replied. "Who arrested him? What did they charge him with? Have you seen the indictment? Has it been reported?"

Stan continued with what little information he had. "The indictment is sealed," he explained. "I don't know who the victims are, but he's charged with sex trafficking. His first appearance hearing is Monday. Because some of our clients are known victims and may be witnesses, the FBI is trying to alert them to the arrest before it leaks to the press. Hopefully that won't happen before we get to them, but you should call them as soon as you can." He was right—bowling would have to wait. Our clients should get the news from us, and as soon as possible. I hung up with Stan and immediately called my associate attorney, Brittany Henderson, so that she could help me begin sharing the news with all of our clients.

The first client I called was Courtney Wild. "No way. I don't believe you," she said. After that, all I heard was crying, years of emotions pouring out. "I have to see him in handcuffs. I won't believe it until I do. I want to be at the hearing on Monday. If I have to drive to New York, I will! We need to be there," she exclaimed.

"One way or the other, we will be," I assured her.

Before I could reach out to anyone else, I received an incoming call from another client and victim, Olivia. Her voice was shaking, "Jeffrey Epstein was arrested. The FBI just called me. I can't believe this day has finally come."

When the next call came, I figured it was a client, but it was a reporter from the *New York Times*, and within seconds, I discovered that he knew more than I did. "Why did they raid his New York mansion?" he asked. I didn't know they had. I wasn't interested in wasting time on the phone speculating, so I let all the other unidentified calls go to voice mail.

I spent the rest of the night talking with clients, one after another. For more than ten years, we had been through so much together. I was more than just their lawyer. By this point, I served in the role of trusted friend and oftentimes therapist. After hours of trying to answer as many questions as possible, I finished the last client call and sat on the hotel balcony, staring at the water and reflecting.

*The day has finally come. Jeffrey Epstein is in custody. But this is not over. This is a world-class heavyweight fight and Jeffrey Epstein is not someone you can just sucker-punch and think you've won. The government has to keep swinging until they finish him off, because if he gets a second to recover, he will. And if he does, he will make them pay. He will make everyone who took this shot at him pay.* Those thoughts made sleep impossible that night.

———————————

The next day, Sunday July 7, Courtney got on a plane from West Palm Beach, Florida, to New York City. I drove back from Naples to Fort Lauderdale and flew to New York Monday morning. We knew the courthouse would be crawling with reporters, which made Courtney nervous. As an Epstein victim, she'd been unfairly labeled and mischaracterized by certain members of the press, which meant that, unable to tell the good ones from the bad, she distrusted them all.

While we hoped to avoid the press altogether—at least until everyone got their bearings—we knew that was not going to be possible. Courtney rode in one car with Michelle Licata, another Epstein child sex abuse victim, whom Courtney had never met before that day. I went separately in another. We thought if we didn't show up together, we could probably get into the courthouse without a media siege. To some extent, the strategy worked.

As I approached the lawyer's entrance to the Daniel Patrick Moynihan United States Courthouse at 500 Pearl Street, I could see the sidewalk lined with cameras. It was raining, so I used my umbrella to shield my face as I scooted behind the reporters, who were waving their microphones while frantically scanning the perimeter of the building in search of victims or their attorneys.

I made it all the way to the courthouse steps unnoticed before a member of the crew working on an Epstein-related Netflix series recognized me. "Brad, where are your clients?" he called out. I ignored the question and made my way up the courthouse steps. Just then, at least twenty reporters who had covered the Epstein saga over the years started shouting my name, all following with different questions. When I didn't answer, one called out, "Come on, Brad, give us something. Are you relieved that he is in custody?" I turned to the crowd and responded to the calls for comment with one line: "Better late than never."

Once inside the federal courthouse, I called Courtney and told her where to enter to avoid reporters. With most of the press standing guard at the front, Courtney and Michelle were able to enter through a side door.

Both were smiling from ear to ear as they waited in the security line, which I could see through a glass-plated window inside.

After moving through security, Courtney walked up to me and gave me a hug. Reporters noticed us and approached, although they were respectful when I waved them off and walked with Courtney and Michelle toward the elevator.

We got off on the seventeenth floor. The hall was filled with people. It was standing room only in the courtroom, and a long line had formed outside where the bailiff was deciding who was going to get in and who was not. "Will we be able to get in?" Courtney asked.

"Yes," I told her, "because of you, we will get in. You won't be denied your right to be at this hearing." She smiled, realizing the truth in that statement. The Crime Victims' Rights Act (CVRA), a federal law Courtney and I had litigated for years to enforce, explicitly gave her that right.

We walked to the courtroom door and the bailiff asked that we go to the end of the line that extended the length of the hall. I told him, "I represent these two victims." The bailiff responded, "Right this way," and escorted us into the courtroom, where he sat us in the special row designated for victims and their attorneys.

Members of the press comprised most of the gallery; they turned around, staring at us. Some of the reporters were friendly, familiar faces, like investigative journalists Julie Brown of the *Miami Herald* and Vicky Ward. Others, I had never met. Regardless, any reporter who was able to make eye contact asked if we would stick around afterward for an interview. We ignored all of the inquiries. The thought of Jeffrey Epstein walking into the room in handcuffs was so unbelievable that none of us could think past that.

Courtney, nervous, looked around the courtroom, trying to take it in. While a first appearance hearing is not usually terribly exciting, she had been waiting for this scene for almost fifteen years. Her abuser was in custody. Even though his arrest was not directly for crimes he had committed against her, this day was evidence that her voice, long disregarded, finally mattered.

After a half-hour wait, Judge Henry Pitman entered, and everyone stood. The tension in the room thickened. As the court came to order, the surreal nature of the moment set in. It was like no other feeling I had ever experienced, in or out of a courtroom, and I could tell Courtney felt the same way. Everything seemed to be happening in slow motion.

After the judge took the bench and we all sat, Courtney whispered to ask who everyone was. At the table for the United States were prosecutors Alex Rossmiller and Alison Moe, along with two FBI case agents, all of whom Courtney had previously met. At the defense table sat nationally renowned white-collar criminal defense lawyers Marty Weinberg, Reid Weingarten, and Marc Fernich. The gallery was full, and the jury box was packed with additional press members and courtroom artists (no cameras are allowed in federal court, so artistic sketches are the only images released to the public). Everyone was in position, motionless. There was complete silence as the United States marshals walked to the side door of the courtroom that connected to the inmate holding cell.

All eyes were fixed on the door. Federal officers opened it and walked in first. Then came the moment everyone had been waiting for. Dressed in a navy blue federal prison uniform, Jeffrey Epstein entered the courtroom.

He looked reasonably fresh, considering that he had spent the last forty-eight hours in a jail cell. As he approached his table, he still had his typical confident air, although his normal strut was slightly less arrogant than usual. But still, something about him, even in a jail uniform, made him seem more important than everyone else in the room.

As he sat down at the table with his attorneys, he scanned the courtroom. Based on what had led up to this moment, I had to wonder if he was looking for me, suspecting that I was the person behind his arrest. In any event, given our long history, he no doubt knew I would not have missed this hearing for anything. But at the moment, he had more important problems. He never looked back again.

Within seconds of sitting down, Epstein turned to Marty Weinberg, his counsel, and appeared to whisper one of his typical wisecracks. I'd seen that facial expression too many times to miss its nature—it was the one he made just before unleashing a perfectly executed one-liner that reset the mood of everyone in the room. I could only guess at this one, probably something about how his prison cook did not quite measure up to the five-star traveling chef he employed.

The hearing was short. It was only an arraignment—a reading of the government's charges to the defendant, which is a right the Constitution affords all people charged with a crime. As it ended, Judge Pitman informed the attentive audience that the next hearing would be held immediately in Judge Richard M. Berman's nearby courtroom. Eager to learn whether Epstein would be let out on bail, our small group left the courtroom and stayed together, steering clear of reporters who were trying to corner us.

I ran into Marty in the hallway. "Brad, why are you here?" he asked.

"Why do you think?" I replied. We exchanged respectful smiles and walked in opposite directions.

A row near the back of the gallery in Judge Berman's courtroom had been cleared for the victims and their lawyers, so we took our seats. Soon, the U.S. marshals turned toward the side door, and all eyes followed. So did utter silence. As in the other courtroom, Epstein, unshackled, walked in seeming as though he was still on top of the world. But knowing him as well as I did, I could sense his irritation.

Jeffrey Epstein, accustomed to sitting on his throne, hated nothing more than having a room filled with people whom he considered to be insignificant staring at him like some type of caged animal at the zoo. He was a lion who, when free, would be king of his jungle, with a hit list including all of those people in the audience who now dared to look at him. But he was also an actor on his best behavior, with one objective: to impress the federal judge who would determine his fate and consequently the fates of many others.

Judge Berman heard from the prosecution first. Assistant U.S. Attorney Alex Rossmiller revealed that hundreds, if not over a thousand, photographs of nude young women had been confiscated from a secret vault in Epstein's mansion—a vault that had been sawed open by the FBI after its court-approved search. This was the first indication I had gotten that Epstein had no idea his arrest was coming. When a search warrant had been executed on his Florida mansion fourteen years earlier, he had been tipped off and had sanitized his house before the FBI could find much of value. There was no way he would have left behind those photos for the FBI to snag if he knew they were coming for him.

Rather than proceed with the bail hearing, Epstein's attorneys requested a postponement so that they could more thoroughly prepare their argument for why their client deserved to be released. The court agreed to a few days' delay, and with that, Mr. Epstein was escorted out the side door of the courtroom, back to his cell.

Courtney had seen what she thought she would never see—Jeffrey Epstein in a prison uniform. "It still doesn't feel real," she kept saying as we moved from the courtroom to the courthouse lobby.

When Courtney, Michelle, and I tried to leave the building, we realized that there was no way to get to our car without encountering the press. As soon as we exited, cameras were put in our faces and questions started flying fast, at all three of us: "How do you feel now that he's in custody? Do you think he'll stay? Will the government let him off again this time? Don't you think he'll buy his way out of this? Brad, how did you finally get him arrested?"

We had a plan to get to our car, which was parked around the corner. Courtney and Michelle walked ahead of me while I stayed back answering as many questions as I could while walking. The reporters and cameramen, moving backward in front of me, occasionally tripping, were frustrated that I didn't hold a press conference and brief everyone. Some, of course, were downright mad. Reporters continued stacking up in front of me, still walking backward while I walked faster, trying to make it to our getaway driver. One reporter backed into a light pole and fell down, and like dominos, two cameramen fell on top of him, cameras and mics flying. Once I saw that no one was hurt, I used the pileup as my chance to get to our SUV, now waiting at the corner.

In the ensuing hours after getting away, we got constant media calls and emails demanding our reaction. Rightfully so. The public had a legitimate interest in the case. It was crucial to us that everyone understood the importance of the event. At the same time, Courtney and Michelle did not want their privacy invaded. We decided to do a brief interview with ABC News, to be aired on *Good Morning America* and *World News Tonight*. It was the right idea because it gave Courtney and Michelle a long-awaited chance to share their feelings with the public on their own terms.

Courtney was happy with the day's events, and seeing her finally feel some satisfaction made me happy, too. On somewhat of a high, she agreed to do one live interview the next day, this one with Gayle King on *CBS This Morning*, a show she loved watching.

After the ABC taping, Courtney and I got into the SUV and went back to the hotel. The day was a whirlwind, so this was the first time we really got to talk. I explained that, in reality, nothing eventful had actually happened. Epstein appeared in court, but the issue of whether he would get bail and be released was yet to be resolved. There would be another hearing where the court would make that determination, and I thought the likelihood of bail was a close call.

"Does it matter whether he gets out on bail?" she asked. "They're putting the case together anyway. And he had so many victims—the government can't lose." As the words were coming out of her mouth, I could see the wheels turning in another direction. She was, rightfully, second-guessing that thought.

I finished it for her: "Bail is a make-or-break decision for the case. His ability to do what he has done for so long is contingent on his ability to control everyone around him. He has this immense, nearly absolute control over his victims, his employees, his co-conspirators, and his friends, many of whom are rich and powerful. Everyone is afraid of him. If he stays in jail, he loses his control. He'll be as powerless as you or me. More victims will come forward and the case will get stronger. His employees and co-conspirators will turn on him so they can stay out of jail. His friends will distance themselves and likely help the prosecution. Stripping him of his freedom deprives him of his greatest asset: his total control of everyone. Plus, if he gets out and sees that things aren't going his way, he'll escape from New York one way or the other. One thing I can tell you for sure: he will never go to trial."

She was concerned. As she thought more, for some reason she had second thoughts about doing the Gayle King show. "Do I have to do it? I thought it was a good idea, but I really don't want to now," she said.

I told her, "It's your choice. If an interview helps get something done you want to accomplish and you feel comfortable with it, then do it. Otherwise, don't."

Despite her affinity for Gayle, she decided not to go on, so I canceled. The producer was not happy with this, to say the least, and asked if I would go on alone.

I thought it through. *Epstein is in jail, but maybe not for much longer. Once he's out, everyone is going to hide. We need the case to get stronger, and fast. More victims need to come forward. I need to invite them to call the FBI.* I called the producer back and said, "Okay, I'll do it."

The next morning, I was live on *CBS This Morning* with Gayle King, Anthony Mason, and Tony Dokoupil. It was the right show for the task at hand. I got four minutes on air to lay the case out generally and call for other victims to come forward, which resulted in many more victims almost immediately contacting the FBI.

When I got back to Florida that night, Courtney called and said, "I want to go to the bail hearing. When is it?"

"It's Monday, July fifteenth. Brittany and I will fly back up to New York with you," I told her. Brittany Henderson had been working with me on Epstein cases for five years.

---

The scene at the courthouse in Manhattan on the fifteenth was similar to the scene a week earlier. The media presence was maybe even greater. I sat between Courtney and Annie Farmer, a victim who was represented by David

Boies. During the hearing, the government revealed that another safe they had opened inside Epstein's New York mansion contained loose diamonds, stacks of cash, and an expired Austrian passport with Mr. Epstein's photo but a false name and Saudi Arabian address. This was a bombshell. When that was announced, I happened to look over to the reporters in the jury box and saw one mouth, *Holy shit*, recognizing that this was evidence that Epstein had a decades-long, premeditated getaway plan.

Epstein was offering to put up $500 million as collateral, which he claimed was his entire net worth, although those of us who knew him believed that amount was grossly understated. Regardless, it was a lot of money and a sign that he desperately wanted out. There was only one known circumstance in life he couldn't cope with, and this was it. Extended time in prison for him was impossible. He knew that this bail decision by the court was a matter of life or death.

The hearing was coming to an end and Judge Berman asked if any victims were in the courtroom and wanted to speak. Courtney and Annie, who had never met before that moment, briefly conferred across me, only a few feet behind the chair where Epstein sat. They both decided this was their time to speak. In fact, each saw it as her duty. Neither had come to the hearing to say something, but they both stood up. Epstein didn't turn around. He had effectively silenced his victims for decades. And now, when he had no control over them, and no warning, they were about to give the court their opinions on whether he should be released.

Annie spoke first. She leaned in and explained that she "had the misfortune" of meeting Jeffrey Epstein when she was very young, alluding to his assault on her at his New Mexico ranch. Her message was clear and powerful. She told the judge that Epstein needed to stay in jail because his wealth, privilege, and notoriety would make it difficult for other victims to come forward if he was free.

Then I introduced Courtney. As I stepped up to the podium, I glanced at Epstein. He stared straight ahead.

Courtney came forward next and was even more direct: "I was sexually abused by Jeffrey Epstein starting at the age of fourteen. It's a public case, and he's a scary person to have walking the streets." She urged the judge to keep him in prison "for the safety of any other girls."

Judge Berman did not rule on bail that day, which indicated to us that he needed to carefully deliberate on the decision.

We walked out of the courthouse and were mobbed by reporters. David Boies and I approached the microphones staged on the steps of the courthouse. We answered questions while Courtney, Annie, Brittany, and Stan stood behind us. One of the photographs that would be most widely circulated in the days to come was one of all six of us at that short press conference. Brittany, who was roughly the same age as Courtney, was even mislabeled as an Epstein victim rather than a lawyer for the victims.

After a few minutes, we walked down the steps, hoping our impromptu press availability would stave off a swarm. It didn't. Courtney had not come to New York to appear before a distrusted media. She was there to see that justice was served, and in that respect, she had already done her part. She and Brittany pushed through the crowd of reporters and Brittany hailed a cab. We all essentially dove inside. Because we had just dodged a huge crowd of paparazzi who were still calling out to us and surrounding the car, the taxi driver just assumed that we had to be important, maybe even famous. He spent the entire drive back to the hotel asking questions and trying to take selfies with us to text to his family and friends.

By the time we got back, my email inbox was full. Each television network was pushing for us to appear. Going on one would mean the others would get offended. After all, that's what had happened the week before, when Courtney only spoke with ABC.

Stan said, "You guys have been fighting this thing for ten years and nobody in the press wanted to listen. These events have turned that around. You can't complain that they don't get the facts right when you are the team who has the facts, but you don't want to make the media rounds. I understand your philosophy about not wanting unnecessary publicity, but we are at a crossroads here. The case either gets stronger now or it weakens. The press is key. If you hold a press conference and invite the media in general, you can satisfy everyone at once." His words were convincing—now that Jeffrey Epstein was behind bars, we had a real shot at getting victims to contact the government and help them win their case. It finally felt like the right time for the world to be told about the journey we had taken over the past decade.

I agreed to a one-hour press conference the next day at the Andaz 5th Avenue hotel in midtown Manhattan. The room was wall-to-wall reporters. "Just be careful what you say, Brad," Stan warned. "Talk about what you know. The press can be tricky."

I said, "I'm just going to try and answer their questions."

There was no script. Brittany, Stan, Courtney, and I sat at a table. I then spent more than an hour laying out the summary of the history of the case, dispelling false rumors, setting the record straight on certain commonly reported mistakes regarding the current case, and making a plea to the public to call the FBI with any information. The press, accustomed to lawyers speaking in meaningless sound bites and avoiding answering real questions at all costs, seemed pleasantly surprised by our candid and thorough presentation. Before we left, Courtney read a letter she had written to other victims, again urging them to call the FBI. It could not have gone better. We, as a team, did our part.

———————

In the same way people remember where they were when JFK was shot or when the planes hit the Twin Towers on 9/11, I will never forget my exact location when the court ruled on Jeffrey Epstein's bail. On July 18, two days after our press conference, Brittany and I were sitting at the Starbucks on Glades Road in Boca Raton, where on more than one occasion I had secretly met with Jeffrey Epstein. Knowing that the judge would be making his ruling any second, we were anxiously going back and forth with predictions until finally the first article popped up on our phones. Epstein's bail had been denied. It was a surreal moment. Throughout the years, we had become conditioned to the wrong decisions being made, in favor of Epstein.

In making his ruling, the judge cited, among other things, the heartfelt testimony given a week earlier by Courtney and Annie. Epstein would be in jail until trial, which would be at least a year away. But I knew he'd be in jail much longer—and, more important, I knew he knew that, too. Epstein was never getting out.

When the hearing ended, we were still sitting at the table when Stan called to debrief us on the reaction from the courtroom. I put him on speaker, and he asked us, "What do you think?"

In that moment, I reflected on what many victims had told us about the importance of sex to Epstein's survival. As one of those victims, Johanna, had said, "He needed to have three orgasms a day. It was biological, like eating."

I knew the answer immediately: "He's dead."

Three weeks later, he actually was.

# TWO

# THE HEARING HEARD 'ROUND THE WORLD

O N JULY 23, 2019, I was on a Disney cruise in Alaska with my family when I got a series of text messages from Brittany telling me it was urgent that I call her back. I did. She had just received a call from a trusted source of ours that Jeffrey Epstein was found in his cell, semiconscious, with injuries to his neck. "He [speaking of our source] is saying either Epstein attempted suicide or his cell mate tried to kill him," Brittany told me.

"What's his cell mate saying?" I asked.

"He's apparently saying he never touched Jeff and that he just tried to help him when he saw that he was hurt," she explained.

"Tell me about the cell mate," I inquired, wanting to know more before I could form an opinion with the little information we had available.

"He was a cop. Arrested on charges of kidnapping and killing four people during a drug deal he was involved in," she explained, exhausting the details she had been told.

"Sounds like a suicide attempt to me. If he tried to kill him, Jeff would be dead. At the very least, it would be obvious that there was an attempted murder. The biggest threat to Jeff is himself. If everyone lets him use this cop roommate of his as a decoy, he'll be gone before we know it." I paused between thoughts. "Jeff isn't going to make it in there. He doesn't want to," I reasoned. "Has it been reported yet?"

"No, but it will be any minute," she said, repeating what our source had told her.

Shortly after we hung up, the reports came in, with mixed suspicions of suicide and an attack by this muscle-bound dirty cop. Epstein was being placed on suicide watch where he would be monitored around the clock, further confirmation of my belief that he tried to kill himself.

I called Brittany back. "He's already made up his mind. It's just a matter of when he will try again. He'll make sure he doesn't fail twice. But he's going to have to wait until he gets off suicide watch, which could be never."

On August 10, 2019, the same source called me as I was stepping onto an early-morning flight home from New Jersey. I answered and he didn't even bother with hello.

"He was just found hanging in his cell, he's gone," he said in a melancholy tone.

"You're kidding. How did this happen? I thought he was on suicide watch," I came back.

"I don't know the details. I'll let you know when I hear more. It won't be reported for another hour or so," he finished before we hung up and I boarded my plane.

It turned out that Jeffrey convinced a psychologist to let him off suicide watch. Of course he did. He could convince anyone of anything, although this one was tough to swallow. He was the most notorious child molester on the planet. He had fallen overnight from a jet-setting billionaire who controlled everyone around him to a caged animal at the mercy of prison guards and lowlife inmates. All signs indicated a high risk for suicide. And if the circumstantial evidence was not enough, seventeen days after his arrival at the Manhattan Correctional Center, and five days after he was denied bail, he allegedly attempted suicide. Yet, just two weeks later, he was found hanging in his cell with a bed sheet tied around his neck.

How was I going to explain this to my clients? I called Courtney. She was as in shock as I was. It was a short conversation, as I was taking off. "How did they let this happen?" she asked over and over.

I sat back in my seat, trying to think back to the many conversations I had with Epstein. Many emotions came over me. Sadness was one. Anger was another—at him and at the correctional facility. They had one job; keep him alive. *How difficult is that?* I thought. My clients had been robbed of justice. Again. This is not how it was supposed to end. It took eleven years to get here, and one month for him to escape, this time forever.

On the plane, I hooked up to Wi-Fi and around mid-flight the articles starting coming in.

Rumors began to fly almost immediately about whether he was murdered or committed suicide. The general public was quick to call foul, stating the obvious in news articles, blog posts, and tweets. As more information poured out about Jeffrey Epstein every day, it became increasingly clear that Epstein's many powerful friends might be at risk and would have had reason to off him. There were even memes of Hillary Clinton dressed as a prison guard sneaking in to "check on" Mr. Epstein, implying that the Clintons played a role in silencing him. That particular theme got increased traction when it was revealed that among the items found during the search of Epstein's New York mansion were a large painting of President Clinton wearing "the blue dress" and red heels and a personalized note from Clinton to Epstein. Still, the autopsy concluded Epstein's death was a suicide.

The debate didn't end there, though. Epstein's brother, Mark, hired a private medical examiner to provide an opinion, who concluded that Epstein's injuries were more consistent with murder. Epstein's lawyers highlighted some suspicious evidence, such as the video cameras that should have captured those going in and out of his cell, which just so happened to not work on the day Epstein died. The security guards were allegedly both "asleep" and therefore neither heard nor saw anything.

Did some powerful person have Epstein murdered to avoid Epstein using whatever blackmail information he had accumulated over the years to lighten what was sure to be a hefty prison sentence? Or was he killed by intelligence agencies to prevent him from revealing top secret spy information?

During Epstein's one month in jail, he had become known throughout the country and well beyond as the most notorious of pedophiles ever to live. No pedophile is safe in prison, so to say he was not too popular with other prisoners would likely be a huge understatement. If being a pedophile were not bad enough, Epstein also pulled a trick similar to the one he had perfected during his Florida jail time. He hustled lawyers in to visit him all day long, occupying one of the few private meeting rooms most of the day and apparently emptying out the snack machine during these extended visits. Money was no issue for Epstein, so he could pay for lawyers to visit around the clock. I can't imagine that behavior increased his popularity. It was later reported that even the guards were unhappy with his entitled conduct. They, in turn, reportedly threw his meals on the cell floor.

Every day a new article would go to print, and the conspiracies multiplied. As Epstein's alleged connections to former presidents, Middle Eastern dignitaries, the British royal family, other billionaires, the CIA, and Mossad became known, his brother and lawyers made clear they believed it was murder, and that many people had motives. I personally believe he killed himself. He was a selfish, manipulative control freak who was never going to let the world ridicule him. When Jeffrey made up his mind to do something, he did it. He'd made up his mind weeks earlier, when he'd first attempted suicide. He was not going to fail the second time.

With Epstein dead, the United States Attorney's Office was left with no choice but to file a motion to dismiss the criminal charges against him. Judge Berman issued an order setting the hearing for August 27, 2019, and, recognizing the rights of crime victims to be present at these important events, he ended his notice of the hearing by stating, "Counsel for the victims and the victims will also be heard, if they wish to be."

I called Courtney, who was feeling robbed over the fact that Epstein had escaped justice again. I told her that victims and their counsel would be allowed at the hearing. "I'm going, and I want to make sure everyone who wants to be there gets to be there this time," she insisted.

I then began calling all my other clients before telling prosecutors Alison Moe and Maurene Comey (daughter of former FBI director James Comey) that I had many clients who wanted a chance to address the court at the hearing. "All of the victims who want to come should be able to come. The hearing is being held on such short notice, though, and it's very expensive to travel. Can you ask the government to pay for all who want to come?" I pleaded.

"The government has never done that before. But we will ask," responded the lead prosecutor.

"This case is not typical," I explained. "We fought eleven years for these victims and for the opportunity for them to address the court. This is the last hearing. The last chance. It will go a long way in making up for the injustice done in the past. It's the right thing to do."

Within the hour, I got a call back: "Please tell your clients that the government has agreed to pay for the travel and hotels of all Epstein victims who wish to attend." Courtney was ecstatic when I told her the news.

Brittany was on a family vacation with her fiancé, Jose, in Greece. When she got to her next port, she checked in, and I gave her the news. "I'm going," she said.

"It's in five days—you'll still be on your cruise," I reminded her.

She hung up the phone. A few hours later she called back. "I'm getting off in Croatia. I'm flying to Germany and then from Germany to New York. With the time change, I can make it. I'll fly back and meet my family in Greece after the hearing."

I paused for a moment. Sensing that this meant I thought that she was crazy, she said, "Give me a break, Brad. You wouldn't miss this for anything in the world. You've worked for these girls for more than ten years to give them this chance, and I've worked my entire legal career for it. There's no way I am missing this. I'll be there." She was right. I would have done the same thing.

———————

There was already so much media attention that the day before the hearing the location was moved from Judge Berman's usual courtroom to the oversize ceremonial courtroom at the Foley Square courthouse. The change in location made the media suspicious that this would be more than a mundane dismissal of criminal charges. Since an objective for most of our clients was to be a part of the hearing without being cornered by the media, I ignored the hundreds of media inquiries about whether any victims were showing up.

On August 26, I arrived in New York and got to the hotel where Jay Howell, an attorney known in many circles as the godfather of crime victim advocates and a close friend who had also represented Epstein victims for years, was already waiting for me. Brittany arrived soon after, and the three of us started fielding calls from Epstein victims flying in from all over the world. They had concerns, most of which dealt with their fear of being filmed or photographed before or after the hearing.

That night, Jay, Brittany, and I went to the U.S. Attorney's Office and spoke with the prosecutor about allowing the victims to enter and exit the courtroom without having to encounter the press outside. She agreed and we mapped out a plan. We would just need to get everyone to the U.S. Attorney's Office without being seen and they could take the interior bridge over to the courtroom, avoiding the public altogether.

The next morning, I walked close enough to the Foley Square courthouse to see the crowds gathering, and to locate where the press was camped out looking for victims and attorneys. I called Brittany and let her know that the route we'd mapped out the night before was clear. She and more than a dozen of our clients (and several other victims who were not our clients but whom we looked after that day) got to our meeting spot undetected. Once all of them were safely inside the U.S. Attorney's Office, Brittany, Jay, Sigrid McCawley of Boies Schiller & Flexner, Stan, and I made our way toward the courthouse, periodically stopping to address questions from reporters who were lining the streets leading toward the entrance.

We met our clients inside and walked to the courtroom door. The hallway was crawling with people. We were immediately taken into the massive courtroom, where nearly an entire side of the room was reserved for victims and their attorneys. This experience would have been overwhelming and stressful for any one of the victims alone; however, the fact that they all walked over together and had each other's support seemed to ease their nerves.

The judge's law clerk expressed that Judge Berman had been concerned the courtroom was so large that there might be too much empty space. It was the opposite. There were people from wall to wall, and many in the hallway who could not get in because the courtroom was too crowded. This was the most powerful scene I had ever witnessed: dozens of victims of the same perpetrator, who had been abused in different parts of the world at different times, banded together as one strong, forceful voice.

I began to daydream for a second as I looked over to the table where Jeffrey Epstein's defense team sat. *I can't believe he escaped before he faced this; it just isn't fair*, I thought. While this was not the way we had hoped to finally solidify the rights of our clients to be noticed, present, and heard at important criminal hearings, it was still a historic moment that would impact the victims' movement forever.

Judge Berman took the bench. In his opening remarks he let everyone know that he was attuned to the importance of the rights of the victims. He addressed a *New York Law Journal* article that had been published the day before, written by Rebecca Roiphe, a New York Law School professor, and Bruce Green, an ethics professor at Fordham Law School. The authors expressed severe criticism of Judge Berman for inviting victims to the hearing, saying, "This is an odd moment for transparency in a criminal case" and not a time for victims to have a chance to speak. Of course, that was particularly offensive to me as a firm believer that without transparency, injustice is born.

Judge Berman voiced his opinion toward the authors. In addition to noting that the position in the article was insensitive to the victims as well as inconsistent with the law, Judge Berman also detected a possible hidden agenda. "It is my understanding that one of the authors of that article is himself counsel in one of the Epstein-related cases," he stated. David Boies, an attorney for several victims, later elaborated on that point, explaining that Professor Green was an expert witness for Alan Dershowitz, who had been an attorney for Jeffrey Epstein.

In defending his legally sound and historic decision to stand for the enforcement of crime victims' rights in this country, Judge Berman cited none other than my co-counsel, longtime friend, and former federal judge Paul

Cassell, reasoning, "Then District Judge Paul G. Cassell—who is now a law professor at the University of Utah and is regarded to be a noted expert in victims' rights—concluded that under the Crime Victims' Rights Act, victims have broad rights that extend to a court's decision whether to grant a government motion to dismiss under Rule 48. I completely share that viewpoint in these circumstances. . . . I believe it is the court's responsibility, and manifestly within its purview, to ensure that the victims in this case are treated fairly and with dignity."

Once the judge had set the stage, he turned to the United States, which was represented by prosecutors Comey and Moe. After the prosecutors announced their motion to dismiss, Marty Weinberg responded on behalf of the deceased defendant, Jeffrey Epstein. His argument had little to do with whether the case should be dismissed and more about his suspicion that Epstein had been murdered. Regardless of the cause of death, Marty argued that there needed to be an investigation into how the most high-profile inmate in the country could die like this.

Judge Berman called on me to approach on behalf of the victims. I approached first to address the court. Behind me stood a line of women, no longer teenagers, now ranging in age from twenty-five to forty-three years old. After expressing my regret for Jeffrey Epstein's death and the negative effect it had on bringing complete closure for my clients, I provided the court with some history regarding the Crime Victims' Rights Act case in which we had been fighting for the rights of Jeffrey Epstein's victims for more than a decade. Then I got ready to introduce the victims, who would address the court with their individual and extraordinary survival stories. There was no doubt who should go first.

"The first client that I have who is going to address your Honor is the one who walked into my office in 2008 asking just to be heard, Courtney Wild." I looked back from the podium and eleven years flashed through my mind as Courtney walked confidently toward the stand. Together we had sued and fought the U.S. government for violating her fundamental rights, and now she was finally able to exercise those rights.

Courtney spoke:

My name is Courtney Wild, and I'm a victim of Jeffrey Epstein. Jeffrey Epstein sexually abused me for years, robbing me of my innocence and mental health. Jeffrey Epstein has done nothing but manipulate our justice system, where he has never been held accountable for his actions, even to this day. Jeffrey Epstein robbed myself and all the other victims of our day in court to confront him one by one, and for that he is a coward. I want to thank the U.S. attorneys for seeking justice that has been long overdue, and most importantly, given us, the victims, our day in court to speak our peace and find some sort of closure. I feel very angry and sad that justice has never been served in this case. Thank you.

She set the right tone. Courtney perfectly paved the way for all twenty-three victims to get their chance to speak, and after hearing her, most of the victims who were on the fence about speaking decided to do so that day. While Epstein's abuses took place over three decades, every victim in the room found some part of the others' description relatable. There was an instant feeling of understanding among the victims. They were in this together.

After this meaningful event, we were escorted to the U.S. Attorney's Office to meet with Geoffrey Berman, the U.S. Attorney for the Southern District of New York. He expressed his gratitude for the cooperation of all the victims in the criminal case, his admiration for the courage it took to speak, and his regret about the way in which the case against Jeffrey Epstein had ended. The feeling in the room was intense solidarity, like nothing I may ever see again. I looked at Courtney. She walked over and gave me a big hug. While it was not exactly how we wanted it to end when we started out, I had to believe she was proud knowing that what was happening in that room, and everything leading to that moment, could not have happened without her unwavering determination and commitment to bringing Jeffrey Epstein to justice.

That is how it ended, but how did we get there?

# THREE

# WILD

I N JUNE 2008, I WAS thirty-two years old and had just started my own law firm in Hollywood, Florida. It was Friday, June 13, when I got a call from my mom's boss, Jay Howell. Jay was an attorney in Jacksonville, Florida, where I grew up. As one of the original founders of the National Center for Missing and Exploited Children, he was someone who had taught me what it meant to be a lawyer. He asked me if I had heard of Jeffrey Epstein. I had not.

Jay explained that he had been contacted by a lawyer who represented crime victims on a pro bono basis. She had been contacted by someone with the FBI and she referred the matter to Jay because he was the leading victims' rights attorney in Florida. Jay called me because the heart of the case was based in West Palm Beach and my office was nearby.

Jay said that he didn't have much information, other than that there was a twenty-year-old girl who had been sexually assaulted by a powerful man in Palm Beach around six years earlier. It was a criminal matter and this young woman needed an attorney. He'd just gotten off the phone with her and had given her my number. Her name was Courtney Wild.

Courtney called me and said she did not want to tell her story over the phone. I told her that if she wanted someone to talk to, she could come by anytime. "Thanks," she said before hanging up.

I had no idea whether she would show up or not. Less than an hour later, I heard, "Hi, I'm Courtney. I'm here to see Brad." Shawn Gilbert, my paralegal, walked her to the conference room, then came into my office to let me know Courtney was there. I was unsure what to expect. As I entered the conference room, Courtney stood up and confidently extended her hand to shake mine. Her grip was strong, and her big green eyes fixed sternly straight ahead. We sat and she cut to the chase: "I've been trying to get someone to help me. I finally got hold of Jay, who was great, and he told me you could help."

She wanted to start at the end. "I'm cooperating with the FBI against Jeffrey Epstein."

"Whoa." I stopped her. "Let's start from the beginning."

Courtney described her upbringing, unapologetically: "My dad wasn't around, and my mom had a problem with drugs." As a child, she would come home from middle school to find her parents and their friends strung out. Not feeling safe and not knowing what to do, she would often stay with friends. Yet she was determined to make it. When she was in eighth grade, she was in the school band, a cheerleader, and making excellent grades. But she had no money and as a result, not many clothes or personal belongings. Her only resource was sheer willpower, which she had in spades.

In 2002, when she was fourteen, Courtney was approached by one of her close friends, whom we will call Lynn, who told her that she could make two hundred dollars by giving a rich man a massage. That was more money than Courtney had ever seen. It was an easy decision, so she took a cab with Lynn over to the rich guy's house.

Jeffrey Epstein's house was on a cul-de-sac in the billionaire section of Palm Beach Island, not far from Donald Trump's Mar-a-Lago Club. Courtney was mesmerized as she was led by a household staff member into the kitchen of this mansion. Sarah Kellen, one of Epstein's trusted associates, then escorted the two girls upstairs into a bedroom where a massage table was set up.

A skinny young teen with braces, Courtney was sexually inexperienced. And she was nervous—very nervous. She had never seen, much less been inside, a house this big before. She had never been in the presence of some-one as powerful as the man she was about to massage. For that matter, she had never given anyone a massage. She had never gotten a massage, either.

She didn't even know what a massage was. All she knew was that an "old" man wanted one, and somehow Lynn got her this job that made so much money. All Courtney wanted now was to impress this man.

While she was standing beside the empty massage table next to her younger friend, an older graying man walked out of the shower wearing only a towel. He said, "I'm Jeffrey. What is your name? Nice to meet you." His greeting was warm. He smiled before extending his hand to shake Courtney's. She felt her anxiety disappear. He lay down face-first on the massage table.

During the massage, he instructed Courtney. "Rub my back. Work from the middle of the back up and the tops of the legs down. You always want the blood to circulate away from the heart." Jeffrey was teaching her the art of massage. At the same time, he was asking her questions about her family, her life, her grades, her school, her boyfriends, her interests, what she wanted to be when she grew up, what kind of car she wanted to drive. He was listening.

Jeffrey told her he was a brain surgeon, and that he, too, had come from humble beginnings. He said that he had amassed enormous wealth, which made him friends with the most powerful people in the world. He assured her that he could help her be whatever she wanted to be. What a concept that was to a young girl from the wrong side of the tracks. Just knowing that she was in the presence of somebody who might get her somewhere in life made her want to make him happy more than anything in the world. She wanted him to like her answers to his questions. This was the first person in Courtney's young life who had ever asked her any seri-ous personal questions at all, much less who actually appeared to give a shit about her responses.

She thought that whatever this guy had done to get where he was in life, it must have been right. Within minutes of meeting him, she already felt like he cared about her and he wanted to help. That's why she figured he was paying so much for a massage from someone who at the time wasn't even sure if she was massaging him or just tickling him.

Halfway through the massage, Jeffrey instructed Lynn to leave the room, which she did. What Courtney didn't know is that her friend was also receiving money—a finder's fee for bringing another girl to the mansion. As soon as Lynn left, Jeffrey rolled over onto his back and removed his towel. She didn't know what to do. She froze. But in his typically persuasive manner, Jeffrey told her not to worry, that this was normal, it was natural. He assured her that he was going to tell her exactly what to do, and that she didn't have to do anything she didn't want to. Courtney had nothing to compare this situation to, so she believed him. To the best of her understanding, it was normal that rich and powerful men got naked massages.

Jeffrey continued instructing her where to massage, starting with his chest. He closed his eyes and told her to pinch his nipples. Confused, Courtney complied. In an increasingly direct voice, Jeffrey kept telling her, "Harder, harder, harder." Jeffrey then grabbed himself with his hand and began to touch himself while Courtney was standing there pinching him as directed. As soon as Jeffrey finished, he hopped up off the table. True to his word, he paid her two hundred dollars in cash, and then he left her to find her own way back down the staircase.

To Courtney's dismay, Jeffrey's house was like a labyrinth, with multiple stairways. As Courtney would soon learn, the stairway that was used to shuttle high school girls to and from Jeffrey's bedroom was somewhat disguised. When she left his bedroom with money in her hand, she had no idea where Lynn was, so she scurried around the upstairs area, looking for the secret door to lead her back to where she had started.

There were so many doors up there, so many bedrooms; she didn't know who else was in the house, and she didn't want to overstep and walk in on what might be going on behind other doors. Still in shock from what she had just experienced, with self-preservation adrenaline rushing, she cracked open the door that was adjacent to a large painting of a little girl hanging in the hall outside the master bedroom. The girl in the painting appeared to be about four years old, looking back over her shoulder, wearing nothing but underwear that had been pulled down, exposing her untanned bottom. The painting had been made from a photograph of a girl Jeffrey would later claim was his goddaughter. Regardless, the nature of the painting combined with the "what the f***" kind of experience Courtney had just endured caused further confusion as she scrambled around looking for the door that would lead her out of the gigantic maze of a house.

As the seconds passed, she grew more conscious of her surroundings. She actually paid attention to the subjects of the many framed photographs lining the walls and sitting on every desk and dresser. Almost every frame contained a picture of a fully or partially naked young girl. There was one female figure, however, who was clearly older and appeared in many photographs, sometimes in the nude and other times with her clothes on. In the few photographs that did not contain naked females, this older woman appeared with Jeffrey alongside recognizably famous people. In fact, there was a photograph of Jeffrey, this woman, and the Pope sandwiched between two other picture frames containing the images of fully nude young women lounging by Epstein's swimming pool.

Trying to calm herself, Courtney kept thinking about how nice this guy had been to her, how he cared about her, asked her about things that felt good to share with someone, how he had come from basically nothing to all this. Jeffrey could help her. She knew that he could help her. But he had flipped over on that table and masturbated while forcing her to pinch his nipples, and now she was lost in the upstairs of his mansion, wanting to find a way back down by herself, a way that wouldn't require her to walk back into his bedroom and ask him for directions.

She realized that she wasn't just lost, she was trapped. Courtney was in a panic. As she cracked the next door open, she heard a voice that sounded like her friend laughing with someone else. What could possibly be funny at this moment? Did Lynn know what was happening? Was her friend laughing at her? Had Courtney been set up? Did Lynn think this was good? *Was* this a good thing? Was Courtney just overreacting to momentary disorientation? Was this whole experience totally normal? After all, she had been paid two hundred dollars. She was richer than she had ever been.

Courtney opened the door wider and saw there were stairs. The laughter was coming from the bottom. There was no one chasing her. In fact, there was no one else around. But the idea of seeing Lynn after what had just happened freaked her out. Every step down the stairs ratcheted up her anxiety a bit more until she opened the door at the bottom to find Lynn sitting at the fifteen-seat kitchen island eating cereal and chatting with Jeffrey's private chef about which was better, Froot Loops or Cheerios.

Courtney told her friend it was time to go. Before they could leave, Sarah Kellen walked in and asked Courtney for her telephone number. She told Courtney that Jeffrey liked her and wanted to see her again. The butler called for a taxicab to come pick up the girls. While they were waiting for it to show, the chef asked Courtney if she wanted a box of Froot Loops. Courtney said yes. Everyone had to know everything and the business-as-usual attitude convinced Courtney, at least for the moment, that Jeffrey was right. This was normal.

When the cab got there, the two girls walked down the long driveway past two Cadillac Escalades and a black Mercedes before hopping into the taxi. Courtney still had no idea what Lynn knew and didn't know about this man. As soon as the girls got into the cab, Courtney saw her friend counting money. That was the moment she understood that not only had *she* been paid two hundred dollars for giving the massage, but that *Lynn* had been paid two hundred dollars for bringing Courtney to the house. Courtney asked Lynn if she had ever given Jeffrey a massage. Lynn confirmed that she had had similar experiences with him.

Lynn, who had spent some time with Jeffrey and had bought into his philosophy, told Courtney that it was all totally normal. "This is what rich people do. This is how you become successful," Lynn explained. "They're only trying to help a bunch of poor trailer park kids like us who need a break in life. Look around you." To the untrained eye, she was right. Every house was bigger than the next. All of Palm Beach Island was filled with houses that had sprawling gated grand entrances, golden statues, and Bentleys in the driveways.

Lynn looked at her and continued, "Don't be mad at me. You should thank me. You can bring him girls, too. Any time you need two hundred dollars, you can give him a massage, or whatever that is, and if you don't want to do that, you can make two hundred dollars just by bringing him friends."

The girls lived in the same trailer park, so the cab drove them across the bridge from Palm Beach before turning onto Okeechobee and going down streets with hourly motels, old town houses, and other trailers. When they arrived, Courtney and her friend got out of the cab and went their separate ways. Courtney walked the dirt road home to her broken-down single-wide trailer, kicking cigarette butts and crushed beer cans along the way. No one was home. *Thank god*, she thought.

Courtney sat for a few hours trying to think about her life, everything that she had and didn't have, and everything that she had learned or seen in the last two hours. It was a lot to process for such a young kid. She reached in her pocket and pulled out the two crisp, folded hundred-dollar bills. She stared at the money. Maybe her friend was right. This was her chance. This was her opportunity. He seemed nice. What was the harm? She definitely didn't want to live in this trailer for the rest of her life. She definitely didn't want to be around her parents and their cracked-out friends.

The next day, Sarah Kellen called Courtney and asked her if she wanted to "work." Courtney knew what that meant. She told Sarah that she didn't have money for a cab, so Sarah sent the butler to pick Courtney up in a fancy black town car. The driver was named Juan, although the kids called him John. He told her he had worked for Jeffrey for years. Courtney didn't say a word, enjoying the nice new car on her way to beautiful Palm Beach Island.

On this trip, she paid close attention to everything. To Courtney, Palm Beach looked like it was out of a movie. The grass was greener than any grass she had ever seen. There were twenty-foot hedges lining the streets. Every car was nicer than the next and the people she saw were happy, wearing designer clothes while walking their well-groomed dogs. The teenagers were jogging or riding their shiny new bikes. And she noticed the half dozen landscaping trucks on the sides of the road with crews slaving away to serve the rich in the burning sun. These people, she thought in a flash, were the people who didn't make something of their opportunity. She didn't want to be one of them.

The slick black town car turned on El Brillo Way and headed west to the mansion's cul-de-sac. The gate opened on the left and John pulled into the large driveway that already had nine other fancy cars parked in it. The house looked like a hotel, white with a wraparound balcony. The driveway and the walkway leading to the house were paved with huge stones. There were two entrances that Courtney could see: the side entrance to the kitchen, which was the way she'd entered the first time, and the beautiful, grand front door.

Courtney wanted to know what was behind that front door. It was the biggest door she had ever seen. But John led her from the car to the side entrance and with every step she took, the big door got farther and farther away. Trying to take in as much as she could, she looked back toward the yard and saw another house that wasn't connected to the main house. She later learned that this was where the housekeepers and the butler stayed. Good lord, they had their own house! Even *that* house was five times bigger than the trailer Courtney shared with her parents and little brother. Even the "help" lived like kings. *This is why you're here*, she told herself. *You can live like this one day.*

When they walked into the kitchen, Sarah greeted Courtney like she was an old friend. Courtney looked to the right and saw a refrigerator that had to be eight feet across with two huge stainless-steel doors. There was a large stove, and on the back side of the kitchen island, she could see an opening into a large great room. She was so curious about what was through that door that she started to walk toward it, pretending to be lost and unsure of how to get to Jeffrey's sprawling bedroom. Sarah stopped her immediately and with a stern voice said, "This way." Sarah led her up the same hidden stairway and into Jeffrey's bedroom. After placing the massage oils on the table, Sarah said that Jeffrey would be there shortly. Then she left the room. Once again Courtney was alone.

This time Jeffrey came out of the shower naked, without even bothering to put the towel on. As he approached the table, he smiled at Courtney and gave her a little wink, signalling that it was nice to see her again. On the one hand, this felt strange and made her question what she was doing and everything that had led her to this moment. On the other hand, Jeffrey's smile projected sincerity and friendliness, both of which disarmed her enough to calm her nerves. That and, of course, the money. The hope of entering this rich universe. The thought of getting out of the pathetic trailer park where she lived. The thought of living a different, and better, life.

Jeff immediately began peppering her with more questions about herself. She was ashamed of her answers, most of which dealt with her parents and poor childhood, so she shaded some of her responses. Jeffrey asked her where she went to school, and she told him John I. Leonard, which was a local high school. He said, "I like you. This time, when you give me my massage, take your top off, and take off your shorts, too. It's a better massage experience for everyone. You'll see."

She knew that he was serious and complied. As she was massaging his back, she heard him begin to moan and thought, *Is this also normal? Is this the same thing that happened the first time, but I didn't realize it? Or am I hurting him?* She asked him if she was doing it right and he told her not to talk. He rolled over and demanded that she pinch his nipples. He exclaimed, "*Harder*," but she was pinching and squeezing as hard as she could. He kept saying "harder" over and over again, but she didn't know what more to do. When he couldn't get the force that he was looking for from her small fourteen-year-old body, Jeffrey reached down to touch himself and began to masturbate again.

This had happened last time. She was ready for it. *It isn't a big deal*, she kept telling herself.

Just as she finished that thought, he reached up and placed his hand on her right breast. "Take off your bra, it will be fine," he told her. She hardly needed a bra. She was nervous, but what choice did she really have? She was alone with one of the most powerful brain surgeons in the world, being paid in cash for just one hour of her time. She justified compliance—*What harm could really come from removing my bra?* She was embarrassed by her small A-cup breasts, but Jeffrey touched them softly and told her how nice they felt. As she describes it, Jeffrey Epstein was never mean to her.

---

There was more to the story, of course, and sitting in my office, she would let it slip out little by little during the interview. All in excruciating detail, yet it was necessary, both from her perspective as the client and mine as her lawyer. What was overwhelmingly clear was Epstein's manipulation. The hardest part for me was to listen to how he was able to employ his diabolical tactics on such a young kid who was already barely surviving against incredible odds. I was deeply frustrated that a grown man would constantly compliment a child in ways that got her to do things to him not meant for a child to do. As she continued to talk, my blood pressure rose. I found myself emotionally back in my former office as an assistant state attorney, wanting to personally make sure that he was prosecuted to the fullest extent of the law. This man needed to be stopped.

Courtney recounted Jeffrey's remarks telling her that her body was so pretty and that she had so much potential—not sexual potential, but human potential. The good stuff, the big stuff, the aspirational stuff. Coming from someone of his status and intelligence, those words boosted her confidence.

Courtney continued to describe how it began with Jeffrey, though she was defensive about how she could have been duped. Jeffrey had asked her *very politely* to remove her underwear. Before she knew it, he was inserting his finger inside of her with one hand, while touching himself with the other and telling her repeatedly to pinch his nipples harder. *Is this still part of the massage?*, she asked herself. She had never done anything like this before, but she found it easier to do as she was told, to comply with his wealth, power, and authority rather than to question it.

As soon as Jeffrey finished, he told Courtney to put on her clothes and walked toward the shower. When it was over, her money was always on the dresser. She never once had to ask.

I asked her to describe what she felt the second time after the massage. She took her money and put it into her ripped jean shorts pocket and walked out of Jeffrey's bedroom. As strange as the experience still was to her, she felt more empowered this time. She didn't feel trapped. She knew how to find the door to get out. She walked herself down the stairs, and this time it was she who struck up a conversation with the private chef. Courtney was important enough to have been in the room alone with the master of the house. She was important enough to ask for her own cereal, and to have it poured for her.

Moments later, Sarah walked in, and before she could say anything, Courtney announced, "I think I have a friend that Jeffrey would like. I was told that he would pay me if I brought them." Sarah told her she was right and gave Courtney Jeffrey's phone number to call when she confirmed the friend wanted to "work." *I've made it now*, she thought. Everyone on Palm Beach Island was a businessman or businesswoman who had started somewhere. Courtney was only fourteen years old, and in that moment, she knew she was on her way. This was her beginning.

The day after her second massage, Courtney went to the mall with Lynn, who was the only person on the planet she could talk to about her new "business." For the first time in her life, she could buy clothes. Up until this point, Courtney had relied on Goodwill or the Salvation Army, or, if she was lucky, hand-me-downs from other kids in the neighborhood. But that was a thing of the past as far as she was now concerned. Today, she could get her very own new clothes—anything she wanted. The same was true for Lynn, so the fact that they were experiencing this entreprenurial power together made each want it more.

As their business with Jeffrey continued, Courtney and Lynn compared notes, and oftentimes they found other girls together. The duo would approach girls at the mall, at school, in the park, at the beach, and anywhere else. Courtney's grades were no longer important. School was no longer important. She had new clothes and a whole new attitude. What was school for, anyway? To get a good job one day, right? She already had one, and she was her own boss. So was Lynn. Every day that Jeffrey was in town, Courtney or Lynn would be called by his team and asked if she wanted to work, or if she had any girls who did. Courtney and Lynn were working virtually around the clock, asking other teenagers if they wanted to get paid two hundred dollars to give a rich man a massage at his mansion in Palm Beach. Almost universally, their prospects agreed.

Courtney would accompany each new girl to the mansion—just as Lynn had accompanied her—and walk her up the narrow staircase and into Jeffrey's bedroom. Courtney wasn't the same scared girl she was that first time. Now she had confidence, power, and influence. And once she dropped the girl off next to the massage table in Jeffrey's bedroom, she had money.

Over the next two and a half years, Lynn delivered more than fifty girls between the ages of thirteen and seventeen to "work for Jeffrey," and Courtney delivered more than thirty. Lynn even created a flyer at her high school with a line of tabs at the bottom including her telephone number so that kids could call her if they wanted to "make $200." When Lynn or Courtney couldn't find anyone, they would just go themselves. By this point Courtney had gone so many times that she knew exactly what to expect, until, finally, she didn't.

As Jeffrey became more familiar with his girls, he pushed the sexual boundaries further. When Courtney was fifteen, she was jumped by some older girls in the trailer park and her braces got busted up. Her family had no money to fix them, and even though she had cash, she really didn't want to spend her money on dental work. During one massage, while Courtney was pinching Jeffrey's nipples as hard as she could, he took her head and forced it down on him. This was Courtney's first oral sex experience and it did not last long. While Jeffrey was holding her head down and she was doing the best job that she could, her braces were apparently getting in the way of his good time. He lifted her head up and told her so. She was sorry for not being better at it and he said it was okay, she just needed to work a little harder and find some more girls for him.

Sarah continued calling and demanding she bring more girls. What began as a seemingly cordial request was now a command. Courtney was *expected* to bring girls. She was told that if she didn't, she would disappoint

Jeffrey, which was certainly not something she wanted to do. This, she understood, was not just an expectation but a threat. Courtney was desperate. She was looking anywhere and everywhere to find other young teenagers to bring to his house. Jeffrey had a particular type, though. The younger the better, he would say. White. No tattoos. No piercings. No pregnancies. The girls had to look "pure."

Given these demands, Courtney was no longer regularly attending school. She was still living in the trailer park and was going to parties with older crowds. Innocent-looking fourteen-year-old girls who could keep a secret were not always easy for her to come by. On a few occasions, Courtney brought Jeffrey eighteen-year-olds. Without her even telling him their age, Jeffrey immediately told Courtney they were "too old" and turned them away. He had a keen sense of what he wanted and an equally keen sense of what he did not.

On one occasion, Courtney made a bigger mistake. Desperate for money, and not wanting to perform the sex acts herself, she brought an African American girl to his house. Sarah met them at the door and told them both to wait outside. Jeffrey came down himself. He took Courtney in the house and left the other girl outside. He handed Courtney two hundred dollars and said, "Do not ever do that again. Now get out of here." He said nothing more.

As their relationship went on, Courtney felt indebted to Jeffrey. At this point, she was seventeen years old and had a long history with him. What began as something awkward that she had questioned as perhaps not right had become something that her maturity told her was wrong. The problem was she saw no way out—not just because of money, but because of the relationship she had formed with Jeffrey. She did not want to disappoint the man who had become her friend, father figure, employer, and master. Still, if she was going to stick with his program—and she was—there were other problems to cope with. By now, it wasn't just her and Lynn who were bringing girls to Jeffrey.

Jeffrey's tactic of presenting each girl who performed a massage with the "opportunity" to bring other girls had created a pyramid scheme, or a spiderweb, of young girls, all constantly searching for other girls to bring. While the eighteen- or nineteen-year-olds were too old for Jeffrey's sexual appetite, they were not too old to recruit younger girls. With many girls in the area hungry for everything that Jeffrey had to offer, not least of which was the feeling of being important, there was abundant competition. To beat the competition, you had to do something special. And one day, that opportunity presented itself in a new way.

Jeffrey's sexual appetite was extraordinary. When he was in town, he would typically have three or four of these massages a day, each time with a separate teenager. It was harder and harder for Courtney to do anything to set herself apart, and at seventeen she was close to aging out. Still, Jeffrey seemed to appreciate Courtney and their long relationship. If she had any doubts about that, they dissipated on this one particular day, when Jeffrey called for her to work at his house. This time, he asked her to come alone.

Courtney honestly thought that it was going to be a discussion about how the quality of girls that she was bringing was not up to par—not young enough or not pure enough. She arrived at the house and the butler told her to go to the front. It was finally happening. She was now important enough to enter through the front doors. She smiled as she strutted up and knocked.

Jeffrey opened the door himself, something that he had never done before. Courtney's dreams were coming true, she thought.

She walked in to find a large lion sculpture, the highest ceilings that she had ever seen, a winding staircase, and a view of the swimming pool, where several young, tall, thin girls were sunbathing naked. Despite all she'd done in the last three years, she was shocked.

Jeffrey told her to follow him up the stairs, which she did. She entered the bedroom and on the bed she saw, for the first time, a beautiful young woman named Nadia. Nadia Marcinkova was a real model, and she looked the part. Jeffrey told Courtney that he had purchased Nadia from her family in Yugoslavia. She was part of his harem. After making introductions, Jeffrey got down to business.

He instructed Nadia to kiss Courtney and continued to direct all sorts of action between the two girls. He would push their heads together, tell them to undress each other, and while they were touching one another, he would touch himself next to them. Jeffrey told the girls to perform oral sex on each other in a sixty-nine position while he arranged himself above Courtney's head to have sex with Nadia. He did that until he had finished, at which point Nadia got up and walked out of the room, leaving Jeffrey and Courtney behind.

"That was amazing. It's just now hitting her what happened," he said after Nadia was gone, talking about how he and Courtney had just made Nadia feel so good. Rather than hand Courtney money and kick her out of the house, as usual, Jeffrey told Courtney to follow him to the steam room. They sat together while Jeffrey told her how special she was and how special they had both made Nadia feel. Once again, Courtney was assured that what she was doing was not that bad. She knew better by now. But she also needed the money, not just to build a future life but to maintain the current lifestyle she'd gotten used to.

By this stage, Courtney was using drugs, in part, if not primarily, to dull the experiences that she was engaged in. Her once-promising high school career was long gone. Her life was spent sexually servicing an old man on Palm Beach Island or bringing others to do it in her place. Still, he had always been nice to her. He had always given her the impression that he was looking out for her, and whenever she was having second thoughts, he went the extra mile to make her feel special and convince her that what she was doing was right for herself.

Epstein's manipulative control was strong, but as she got older and was of less use to him, he paid her less attention. She learned that she wasn't all that important to him in the end. While she was still bringing him girls, when she could find those suitably young enough, she was back to entering only through the side door. Then she was contacted by law enforcement and realized that Epstein's gig was up. In her heart, she knew what he had done to her and many others was wrong. Cooperating was her first step to do her part to make things right.

What I'd expected to be a thirty-minute meeting taken as a favor to a lawyer and friend had by now turned into a three-hour marathon of many interwoven tales. The patchwork of her young life was so incredible, all I could say when Courtney finished talking was "I want to help you in whatever way I can. What do you want to do?"

She told me that the FBI had approached her a year ago about their federal investigation of Jeffrey Epstein. She was cooperating with the United States Attorney's Office through what seemed to be a very long process. Recently she had tried to get in touch with her victim advocate at the FBI, but she was having trouble getting any real information.

Courtney wanted answers. She wanted answers to questions that were basic, and certainly no different from those that the victims I used to represent at the state prosecutor's office would ask. Was Epstein going to be prosecuted? Would he plead guilty? Would she have to testify at a trial? I told her that I could not imagine this case going to trial when she had described dozens of witnesses and victims who would inevitably also testify—a story that couldn't possibly be dismissed as having been fabricated and could not be won by the defense. Epstein would eventually have to plead guilty.

Still, she seemed agitated about the state of the investigation and, more to the point, the lack of information about it. In any prosecution she would likely be a key witness, and she understood all that this entailed: the enormous time commitment, the huge expenditure of energy, the replacement of ongoing life with a public airing of her past, the reliving of events she preferred to put behind her.

Most of all, she knew it included facing the man whom she had known so well, who'd turned her life upside down. For Courtney, this case was a very big deal, and to be kept in the dark about it was frustrating. The silence had suspended her life. It had kept her in a state of constant self-questioning. It held her back from moving forward with steps she now knew were right and healthy. It kept her a prisoner of her past—and of him.

I asked her if she had any written communications from the government and she provided me with letters from January and May of 2008 informing her that she had rights under the Crime Victims' Rights Act; that this was a long investigation; and that the FBI and U.S. Attorney's Office appreciated her patience.

Courtney's story was compelling. I felt for her. I told her I would help her. I really believed, as I explained to Courtney at the time, that it would be no problem for me to contact the U.S. Attorney's Office to find out exactly what was going on in what had to be a major federal investigation and indictment. Courtney left that day with my word that what she was asking me to do was no big deal and that I would make sure that this miscommunication, or noncommunication, from the government would quickly be taken care of.

I thought that this would be nothing more than one telephone call to the U.S. Attorney's Office. I mean, after all, why would the government be deliberately ignoring her? If it was true that they were, it was probably for a simple reason, like there were so many victims they just didn't have time to keep informing each one of every step in the process. Or even more likely, because the crimes that Mr. Epstein had committed against these children could result in a life sentence, the government was negotiating how many consecutive life sentences to give him and couldn't concern themselves with notifying the victims about a case that would never need to be tried because it would end in a guilty plea.

As it turned out, I was wrong. Very wrong. This would be the first time I was wrong in the Epstein saga, but it wouldn't be the last.

# FOUR

# THE CALL

I N MID-JUNE 2008, I PICKED UP the phone to call the assistant U.S. attorney on the case, Marie Villafaña, expecting to have a conversation in which she would confirm that the massive case was moving along as quickly as possible and would result in long prison sentences for Epstein and his co-conspirators. When I was a prosecutor, I would share everything with a victim's attorney because they had the right to know everything. So I expected this conversation to be an informative one. This was the second time I was wrong in the Epstein case.

It was unlike any conversation I ever had with a prosecutor. From the very beginning, Villafaña was guarded. I introduced myself as Courtney Wild's attorney, a former prosecutor, and someone who would assist her in any way she needed to ensure a successful prosecution in this important case. She only said, "Okay. Thanks for offering to help. The investigation is ongoing. I'll call you when we need anything from Courtney."

My dissatisfaction with the first call led me to call her again. I figured if she knew I was on the right team, she would appreciate having another advocate in the corner of the victims. Unable to reach her, I left a message and waited for a response. When she called me back a day later, I was on a vacation with my family in a little time-share motel in Pompano Beach that my father-in-law had rented for us. I had promised my wife, Terry, that I wouldn't work on this vacation. But when the "unknown" number appeared on my phone, I knew it was Marie and that I had to answer.

I kept her on the phone for thirty minutes, asking questions, trying to elicit any information I could. The more I asked, the less she gave. I finally told her that in addition to representing Courtney, I was meeting with Courtney's friends who were also victims. I understood that coordination was difficult, especially with so many victims, and assured Villafaña that I would help.

I paced around the run-down pool deck as I shared what information I knew. Villafaña explained that she was fully aware of all the information I had. She confirmed that there were many people involved, both in terms of criminal targets as well as the number of people prosecuting the case for the government. In fact, she explained that the case began as an investigation by the local Palm Beach Police Department, which was originally submitted to the Palm Beach County state attorney, Barry Krischer. But in 2006, because of the extent of some of the crimes, the case had been turned over to the FBI and the U.S. Attorney's Office.

Marie told me who some of Jeffrey Epstein's big-name lawyers were. I responded that they made this a dream case for a prosecutor—I was jealous of her opportunity. She had the chance to take down what had to be the most prolific sexual predator in American history. And she got to do it against some of the best criminal defense attorneys in the United States. I reminded her that she had dozens of victims who could all testify in the same case corroborating one another's stories, and that there was absolutely no factual defense. I told her I was all in if she needed any help. She told me thanks and that we would stay in touch. I had a lot to offer, yet she was not asking for my help. This was strange. Even given the typical way prosecutors ask for more information than they dole out, her apparent ambivalence about my assistance and utter refusal to share basic information with a lawyer representing her victims made me suspicious.

After the call, I made a public records request to the Palm Beach County State Attorney's Office in an effort to obtain the Palm Beach Police

Department's criminal investigation file. My paralegal, Shawn, checked on that request every single day for a week.

---

The day after my vacation ended, I met for the first time with Lynn, and then Marissa, another friend of Courtney's who had fallen victim to Epstein. Courtney had set up the meeting with Lynn and told her to trust me. Lynn did not trust anyone. She met me in a public park, and while I already knew all the relevant portions of her story, she went out of her way to shock me. Lynn was all about the shock factor. While she was only fourteen when she first "worked" for Jeffrey, she had been exposed to more than most kids her age. And even though she was no longer working for Jeffrey, she didn't leave the line of work. With one story after another, Lynn tried her best to get a rise out of me. While I admit I was learning things I had never known before—such as the inner workings and prevalence of "jack shacks"—I was unfazed.

After peeling through her layers of side stories, she reflected on her young son, who was playing on the playground in front of us, and said, "I would kill someone if they did to him what Epstein did to me." She was worried, though, that because of her other life experiences she would not be a sympathetic witness. She was also conflicted. She still liked many things about Jeffrey Epstein and spoke fondly of him. While I could not help her with that complicated conflict of emotions, I reminded her that she had been a child and not to worry about what other people would think. As I was leaving the park, she asked if I was sure I would help her after all I'd heard. In a way I think she wanted me to say no, so that she could brag that she was too much for me and so that she could avoid the conflict altogether. I told her that as long as she told me the truth, I would help her. This was good enough for her.

I then went to Marissa's house where she described her experience with Jeffrey Epstein. Unlike Lynn and Courtney, Marissa never brought any of her friends to Epstein. Marissa had a fascinating yet troubled background that led her to being influenced by her friends into going to Jeffrey Epstein's lair when she was only fourteen years old.

While Courtney and Lynn had strong facades, there was no hiding that Marissa had been damaged tremendously. At that moment, I realized something that I hadn't understood when Courtney had originally explained the scheme. While Epstein's victims had been lumped together in police reports, pleadings, newspaper articles, and other narratives, they are all strikingly different individuals. The only common denominators were their vulnerable ages and socioeconomic disadvantages, which a powerful, manipulative, and rich man was able to exploit.

When I got home from West Palm Beach that day, I immediately called AUSA Marie Villafaña—I couldn't wait to tell her the additional information I had gathered from the other firsthand accounts and descriptions of the predatory behavior that occurred at 358 El Brillo Way. But to my dismay, our conversation did not go as I had hoped. She was not surprised by anything I was telling her, except for the fact that I had met with Lynn.

Marie told me that she knew Lynn was a victim who was also enticed at a young age to recruit many other children for Jeffrey Epstein to abuse. Marie went on to explain that Lynn had not only refused to cooperate with the government but also in fact cooperated with Epstein and was represented by a lawyer hired by Epstein. We both agreed that the documentary evidence, and countless witness accounts verified Lynn's role as a victim of Epstein's abuse.

Despite three years of that abuse, Lynn had good reason to have given a favorable statement about Epstein to the FBI and to Marie a year earlier. While she was being paid as a sixteen-year-old recruiter for Jeffrey Epstein, Lynn got pregnant by her boyfriend. When the criminal investigation began, Lynn explained to me, the FBI went to her house. Epstein had tipped her off that such a day might come eventually and told her to call him if it did. Epstein had always looked out for her. In fact, months before she gave birth, Epstein learned from Sarah Kellen that Lynn was holding a baby shower in her single-wide trailer in the trailer park. On the day of the shower, two dark-tinted Mercedes Benz cars pulled up outside Lynn's trailer. In true Epstein fashion, he arranged for every item on Lynn's baby shower registry to be delivered to the party. His staff personally carried every item inside, making Lynn feel like a queen. He even threw in a silver Tiffany baby rattle for good measure. In addition to the gifts, he delivered the business card of a criminal defense lawyer, in case she was ever questioned.

Fast-forward a couple of months: FBI agents surrounded Lynn in her driveway with her baby in the car, blocking her in and preventing her from leaving. Lynn was still a child. A scared child. She was a brand-new mother and all that she cared about was her baby. She didn't know what to do.

She couldn't back up, and the agents were standing outside her car, so she drove forward over the rocks in her front yard, breaking her front fender and causing it to drag on the ground with sparks flying all over the place as she peeled away. Not knowing where to turn, she went directly to the office of the lawyer listed on that business card. She understood that her risk was next to nothing so long as she cooperated with Jeffrey. She had no real reason to conclude otherwise. After all, Jeffrey had always made her feel like the most special person in the world. She was one of his top girls. He even continued to pay her for each girl Lynn brought him while she was pregnant, which helped her financially prepare to be a mom. The supposed bad guy had always been nice to her and had supported her in tough times. The supposed good guys were chasing her around town, making her scared for her life, and had done nothing for her. This made her choice of whose side she was on pretty simple. I completely understood.

AUSA Villafaña said she understood, too, and knew most of it already. Still, any prosecutor hearing that a witness who had been uncooperative was now willing to cooperate should drop everything to get that interview. Marie checked with her office, which had no interest. I incorrectly chalked this up to the investigation being too large for her to focus on a small-time witness like Lynn, and figured she would get to it at some point.

# FIVE

# 23 VICTIMS

I N RESPONSE TO MY FORMAL REQUEST to the Palm Beach County State Attorney's Office, five Bankers boxes of investigative materials from the 2005 Palm Beach Police Department investigation showed up at my law firm. In order to determine how I was going to advocate for Courtney, I had to understand what had happened up to this point. I brought the boxes home and put them on my kitchen table. I went through every piece of paper twice that night. The first time I went through it I read every document but also created stacks all over my dining room, trying to place things in chronological order. The second time through, I was able to read the story in order from beginning to end.

The lead detective on the case was Joe Recarey. His excellent investigation uncovered twenty-three underage girls as victims of sexual abuse by Epstein. He had established conclusive evidence that the girls' accounts were true.

The Palm Beach police investigation started with a tip on March 14, 2005, from the concerned parents of a girl we'll call Tiffani. Tiffani had wads of cash that she could not explain. Her parents learned that she got the cash from a wealthy man in Palm Beach named Jeffrey Epstein, with whom they believed she was having a sexual relationship. This was actually not the first time the police had heard this story, but it was the first time it stuck.

Years earlier, a similar account of young women going to Epstein's house to give sexual massages surfaced, but a brief investigation revealed that the few who were identified were students at local colleges—arguably, in the view of prosecutors, consenting adults—and the file was closed.

This tip about Tiffani was different. She was only fourteen years old. Palm Beach detectives questioned her about the events, and she described in detail being brought over by a classmate, Kelly, to give a massage for cash to a wealthy Palm Beach man in his mansion. Kelly had known what was going to happen when Tiffani got there. Kelly had also known that Tiffani would be so impressed when she showed up at Epstein's house that she would do what she needed to do in order to make money.

When questioned by the police, Tiffani explained how the whole event had unfolded with this man who appeared to be approximately fifty years old walking out of his fancy bathroom asking for a massage that quickly escalated into her being ordered to straddle his back before he turned over and masturbated in front of her. Tiffani was then given two hundred dollars in cash, which in her mind made everything that had just happened better. She went downstairs and her cool friend from school high-fived her and told her if they did this every weekend, they would be rich. It was a story much like the one you have already heard, and which you will hear again. It was also a story that made Detective Recarey certain that this man needed to be spending the rest of his life in prison.

The Palm Beach police listened to this troubling account and wanted to speak with Kelly next. So they tracked her down, but she was very reluctant to talk because of her regular and close contact with Epstein. She was still actively rounding up classmates to sexually service him under the guise of giving a massage. After speaking with her, the police realized that this case was much bigger than the abuse of a few teenagers, which would have been bad enough.

Kelly told the police initially that she'd brought six of her friends, ranging between the ages of fourteen and seventeen, to Jeffrey Epstein's house. While in the back of a police car with tears streaming down her face, she reflected out loud that she had become "like Heidi Fleiss," a reference to the notorious madam to Hollywood stars.

The Palm Beach police assigned officers and detectives to the case to perform various investigative functions, including recording telephone calls and interviewing victims and witnesses. The detectives even conducted trash pulls at Epstein's home. To do this without being noticed by Epstein or the many members of his household staff, they contracted a local sanitation service to deliver Epstein's trash to the police department after it was picked up from his house, so that they could sift through for any evidence of what Tiffani and Kelly were saying.

The evidence they found gave new meaning to the phrase "One man's trash is another man's treasure." Among the items in Epstein's trash were his message pads—or more specifically, the carbon copies from old-fashioned message-taking forms that included the original, a yellow carbon copy sheet, and a pink carbon copy sheet. The messages showed everyone who was calling the house and leaving a message for Epstein or anyone else. It was obvious from even a basic review that there was a clear method for taking a message. Whoever answered the phone put the date, the name of the caller, the time of the call, the message that was being left, and a notation at the bottom indicating who in the house was taking the message.

Most of the messages that were confiscated were taken by the butler, who, in 2005, was a man named Alfredo Rodriguez. Other messages were taken by Epstein's various assistants, including Sarah Kellen and Nadia Marcinkova. Someone named Ghislaine Maxwell also took messages and was one of the few people other than Jeffrey who received messages. She was referred to in the messages sometimes as Ghislaine, and other times, by the staff, as Ms. Maxwell. The regular callers included Donald Trump, David Copperfield, Palm Beach politician C. Gerald Goldsmith, and former national security advisor Sandy Berger. Epstein's close friends, such as model scout Jean-Luc Brunel, left more detailed messages during that time period, which gave better insight into what Epstein was up to.

Aside from the famous people calling for Jeffrey, there were many messages from girls. Girls like Courtney, Lynn, Molly, Holly, and Rebecca would call with messages such as "has girl for tonight" or "wondering if she can work tomorrow." At least three girls a day were scheduled to go to his house, sometimes with little time between appointments. Sarah Kellen, for instance, left a message scheduling one girl to come at three o'clock and the next to arrive at four thirty.

The need for a constant flow of girls was clear from these messages: "Samantha hadn't confirmed Veronica for 11:00 yet, so she is keeping Becki on hold in case Veronica doesn't call back." "Becki is available on Tuesday. No one for tomorrow." "Becki is confirmed at 4pm. Who is scheduled for the morning? I believe Julie wants to work." All of those girls were later identified as minor children who were coming over to "work," which was code for giving sexual massages.

The PBPD continued to interview the victims. Each of them was between fourteen and seventeen years old. (Like Courtney, Kelly told the police that she once tried to bring a woman older than twenty, who was immediately turned away by Epstein as being too old.) Each was brought to the house with the enticement of making cash in exchange for what seemed to be a glamorous or at the very least innocuous one-hour massage, for a billionaire inside the largest mansion any of them had ever seen. All were nervous but feigned confidence as kids living in this oversize adult world.

Each teenager was led by someone whom she admired, usually a friend, up the stairs and into a bedroom with the promise that what would happen would not be bad and would lead to immediate cash. Once inside the room, their experiences were nearly identical, although the girls didn't know that the experiences of their friends had been the same as their own. At the time that each visited the house, she was made to believe she was the only one—and at her particular moment, she was.

At some point, not long after entering Epstein's room, the friend who was being paid to bring the new masseuse would leave and go back downstairs to wait in the kitchen. Whether it was Alexa or Veronica or Becki or Lauren, there was always a first time when she had no idea what to expect, when she knew only that her recruiting friend wanted to be a player in this glamorous atmosphere, which amplified the strength of peer pressure on the newbie to join in. By the end of each massage, each girl, in her different but similar words, described Jeffrey Epstein ordering her to remove her clothes and pinch his nipples while he masturbated. For those girls who returned a second, third, fourth, or fifth time, the escalation of sexual advances was also consistent in their experiences.

It was a slow pattern in which Epstein was somehow able to mark where he was in the game with each one of these girls, enabling him to pick up where he'd left off with her the very next time. Grabbing their breasts would escalate to digital penetration and the use of sex toys, which would escalate to oral sex and then to penetrative sex, to finally even threesomes with one of his traveling girlfriends, like Nadia Marcinkova. On a few occasions, Epstein got carried away and forced sex upon his teenage victim while she was resisting. But on those occasions, Epstein did the "fair" thing and paid $1,000 as opposed to the $200 or $300 going rate.

Every single one of these children identified by the police was paid for being subject to inappropriate touching, which was referred to by Epstein and his assistants as "work." At the end of the first "working" experience, one of Epstein's assistants, either Sarah Kellen or Adriana Mucinska, would take down the girl's phone number and make sure that it was not the telephone number of a parent. Each was told that she could come back if she wanted to and that she would be paid each time. Each was given the "opportunity" to bring others of similar age and be paid for recruiting.

As a former state prosecutor, I could not imagine an easier case to prosecute. These were victims who were telling consistent stories. This level of specificity could not be made up, especially since most of the girls didn't even know one another. It would be an impossible case to lose.

I continued to sift through the boxes in my living room. There were phone records of Jeffrey Epstein and Sarah Kellen showing that the numbers they were calling during this time period belonged to high school kids, many of whom were the same as those identified in the message pads. There were inventory lists from a search warrant that was executed on Jeffrey Epstein's home, including porn videos alongside high school transcripts of some of his victims. It is believed that all the photographs confiscated from the home at the time of the investigation depicted only young females who were over the age of eighteen; however, in deposition, Detective Recarey testified to the home having been sanitized prior to his investigative efforts. Given the frequency of his interaction with minors, there was still plenty of incriminating evidence left behind. There was proof that Epstein had rented a car for one of the kids while she was in high school. There was even a note from Epstein to his butler instructing him to deliver roses to one of the victims at the high school drama play. He was clearly a mastermind at making these girls feel special, and he had the resources to make them feel more special than anyone ever had before. But even his "thoughtful" overtures now amounted to evidence that left no doubt as to Epstein's true intentions.

Included in the boxes was an Amazon receipt in the name of Jeffrey Epstein dated September 4, 2005, for the shipment of *SM101: A Realistic Introduction* by Jay Wiseman; *SlaveCraft: Roadmaps for Erotic Servitude—Principles, Skills and Tools* by Guy Baldwin; and *Training with Miss Abernathy: A Workbook for Erotic Slaves and Their Owners* by Christina Abernathy.

I reviewed the documents contained within these boxes realizing that I had never even heard of a case with so much evidence. A life sentence seemed likely. Ten-year sentences were handed out regularly to older men communicating on the internet with people they thought were fourteen-year-old girls, even when the actual person on the other end was instead an undercover cop. Epstein was not only communicating with actual teenage girls but was also following through on the sexual acts. Isolating the sexual charges to Courtney alone would result in life imprisonment on a criminal sentencing scoresheet. With the number of victims who were known, if calculated properly, Epstein's conduct would score hundreds of years in prison.

The Palm Beach police did the bulk of their work in 2005 and 2006, uncovering twenty-three girls who had been underage when Jeffrey Epstein engaged in sexual massages with them. The ultimate decision whether to charge Epstein with a crime rested with the state attorney in Palm Beach

County, where the crimes were committed. The state attorney for Palm Beach County was Barry Krischer.

When the Palm Beach police brought him the preliminary investigative results, including credible evidence of regular sex abuse of minors occurring on El Brillo Way, Krischer green-lighted the investigation moving forward. Police Chief Michael Reiter and Detective Recarey put more detectives on the case and increased their investigative resources. As they chased down leads, they continued to discover more victims. Many more. With each victim came detailed accounts of serious sexual offenses.

The evidence they were collecting matched perfectly with the taped statements of the many high schoolers who were describing how they were lured to Epstein's mansion. Multiple victims under sixteen years old described a sexual grooming process employed by most known pedophiles—starting slow and easy and always making the victim feel everything is consensual. From the perspective of a detective trying to locate a witness, Epstein's method of paying girls to bring other girls made acquiring the identity of the next victim as easy as asking, "Who told you about Mr. Epstein?"

The victims gave accounts of Sarah Kellen arranging for the butlers to drive the girls home because they were too young to drive and how Epstein inquired about which high school they were attending. Not only did Epstein and his many associates know the ages of these children with whom he was scheduling massage appointments, but their youth was a requirement to the point that those as "old" as eighteen were often rejected. And not one had any massage experience. The case Recarey was building could not have been stronger. And he was reporting this to Krischer, who seemed enthusiastic about the progress.

That is, until Epstein's well-known lawyer, Alan Dershowitz, entered the fray. Dershowitz was a Harvard Law School professor who had developed a reputation for representing the most despised criminals in the country. He successfully represented Claus von Bülow, overturning his conviction for murdering his wife. Dershowitz was also on OJ Simpson's legal team, defending the double homicide of Nicole Brown Simpson and Ronald Goldman.

But by the time Dershowitz became involved in the criminal investigation, he had been a longtime personal friend of Jeffrey Epstein's who
claimed to consider Mr. Epstein like family and had been quoted separately
saying as much. In 2003, he had told *Vanity Fair* reporter Vicky Ward that
he was authoring his twentieth book and that "the only person outside of
my immediate family that I send drafts to is Jeffrey." The article went on
to say that as Dershowitz "was getting to know Epstein, his wife asked him
if he would still be close to him if Epstein suddenly filed for bankruptcy.
Dershowitz says he replied, 'Absolutely. I would be as interested in him as a
friend if we had hamburgers on the boardwalk in Coney Island and talked
about his ideas.'" That same year, Epstein donated millions to Harvard University, the same school where Dershowitz was a famed law professor. And
when Epstein got in trouble, Dershowitz was the first to come to his defense, labeling the little girls who were abused regularly by his buddy as
liars.

Krischer changed his prosecutorial mentality in the wake of his engagement with Dershowitz. He refused to charge Epstein with the lewd
and lascivious molestations that the police had conclusive proof Epstein
had committed. Krischer instead sought to empanel a grand jury, where select evidence could be presented to result in lesser charges being pressed on
Epstein. Police Chief Reiter was troubled by this and wrote a letter to his
once-friendly ally, Krischer, explaining, "After giving this much thought and
consideration, I must urge you to examine the unusual course that your office's handling of this matter has taken and consider if good and sufficient
reason exists to require your disqualification from the prosecution of these
cases." Shortly after this letter was delivered on May 1, 2006, Chief Reiter
contacted the FBI himself and demanded a federal investigation.

I could not think of a legitimate reason for Krischer's refusal to prosecute Epstein. The Palm Beach investigation even included taped interviews
of the girls in their childlike voices using little-girl words like "wee-wee" to
describe Epstein's penis. I had a feeling of overwhelming anger while reviewing this material. I had prosecuted evil people who had beaten, stabbed,
shot, and violently raped their victims in ways that, on paper, may have

seemed worse as singular acts of violence. But I had never seen someone premeditatedly orchestrate the type of crime Epstein had organized and get away with it for so long. What jumped off the page was the realization that this guy lived by his own laws. While I couldn't completely calm Courtney's anxiety about the status of the federal investigation, after looking at this evidence gathered by the state, and knowing that this information and more was now in the hands of the FBI and United States Attorney's Office, I felt confident telling her that everything was going to be fine. Jeffrey Epstein surely would be going to prison for the rest of his life. It was only a matter of when.

# SIX

# OFF THE RECORD

O VER THE NEXT COUPLE OF weeks, I checked in with Assistant U.S. Attorney Marie Villafaña as to the status of the federal case. Each time, her message was the same as that delivered to the victims in written correspondence: it was a major federal investigation, and everyone just needed to be patient. The message was consistent but getting old.

On Friday, June 27, 2008, my wife, two-year-old son, and I drove to Jacksonville to spend the weekend with my parents. The next day, I got a call from AUSA Villafaña. While we had established a cordial working relationship up to this point, we were not personal friends by any means, and it was certainly strange to get a call from her on a weekend. Throughout the conversation, I felt there was tension in her voice behind what she was saying—and not saying. My impression was that she was being constrained not by her own sense of prosecutorial limitation, but by an office policy or directive of some kind.

The main point of her call was to tell me that Jeffrey Epstein was pleading guilty to two felony criminal charges in state court on Monday morning at the Palm Beach County courthouse. One comprised three misdemeanor solicitations of prostitution; the other was procuring a minor for prostitution. (In Florida solicitation of prostitution is only a misdemeanor; three misdemeanor charges are the equivalent of one felony.) This message was odd to me for many reasons, not the least of which was that a federal prosecutor was calling me to tell me about state charges filed on behalf of victims I didn't represent. I told her that as a matter of course, I would have my law clerk go to the hearing to watch. For good measure, before hanging up, I confirmed with her that the charges Epstein was pleading to were state charges *only* that were not related to any of my clients, who were all part of the federal case against him.

That Monday, June 30, 2008, Jeffrey Epstein showed up to the Palm Beach County Courthouse with his team of high-priced lawyers from different parts of the country. I was not there. However, video, along with the transcript of the hearing, makes the events of that morning indisputable. Judge Deborah Dale Pucillo, a judge with an excellent reputation, presided over the proceedings. When it was time for Epstein to enter his plea, Assistant State Attorney (ASA) Lanna Belohlavek approached for the state of Florida, while Jeffrey Epstein and his lawyers walked to the front of the courtroom on the other side.

Judge Pucillo announced that Jeffrey Epstein would plead guilty to two felonies that carried "twenty-one point five months in the Department of Corrections as the lowest permissible prison sentence." The judge then confirmed that Epstein's highest level of education was high school before making her way to questions regarding the Florida Science Foundation—the company in which Jeffrey would be employed during his jail sentence. Epstein's attorney Jack Goldberger informed the court that the Florida Science Foundation was a 501(c)(3) corporation that Jeffrey Epstein formed to do charitable work. When asked how long the corporation had been in existence, Epstein himself responded, "Fifteen years." He went on to explain that the corporation had funded more than fifty science programs in Florida and around the country, boasting recent grants to Harvard University, the "Neuro Science Institute of California," and the Massachusetts Institute of Technology.

After a conversation among Epstein's attorneys, the prosecutor representing the state of Florida, and the judge was held off the record, Judge Pucillo allowed a sealed envelope presented by Goldberger to be attached to the plea agreement, with no explanation to the audience sitting in the open courtroom as to what it contained. The judge then went back on the record and found a sufficient factual basis to support the plea before asking if all of the victims were in agreement with its terms.

It is impossible to know what went through ASA Belohlavek's mind, or the mind of any federal prosecutor who was sitting in the room that morning when the judge confronted the state with this very direct question about victim notification. The judge could have been told, and without doubt should have been told, any of the following information in response to her question: between the state and federal investigations, forty or more underage children had been identified as victims so far; the offenses Jeffrey Epstein committed included sex trafficking of minors; several of the victims had attorneys who were regularly inquiring about the status of the criminal case; the victims had recently been told to be patient because it would be a long investigation; and in fact, *none* of the many victims had been properly notified of this hearing, which was a violation of their rights as crime victims—they all had a right to be present and be heard.

Instead, without much hesitation, ASA Belohlavek answered Judge Pucillo's question, basically stating that she believed they had. Under the false impression that all identified victims had been given notice of the hearing and had just elected not to show up—a very unusual occurrence—Judge Pucillo accepted the plea negotiation.

After the hearing, my law clerk reported back that Jeffrey Epstein was sentenced to eighteen months in jail, followed by twelve months under house arrest, for the state crimes. Judge Pucillo made sure Mr. Epstein understood that he was also being registered as a sex offender and was to have no contact with any minors. From the hearing, Jeffrey Epstein was taken into custody at the Palm Beach county jail.

## SEVEN

# EMERGENCY

A FTER LEARNING ABOUT EPSTEIN'S GUILTY plea for the state felony charges, I contacted AUSA Marie Villafaña. Now that Jeffrey Epstein was going to jail for some short period of time on those state charges, I asked when we could expect the federal indictment on the crimes committed against all the victims identified by her office, including my clients. She said she still couldn't tell me anything about that, but as I pressed, she urged me to write a letter to her office concerning the importance of the federal prosecution. That statement troubled me. Why would I need to write to her office to state the obvious?

Regardless, on July 3, 2008, I wrote a letter to the U.S. Attorney's Office explaining that Jeffrey Epstein was the most dangerous child molester in modern history, a man who had probably abused more than a hundred children, according to facts known to anyone who had investigated the case for more than a minute. I followed my letter with a telephone call and demanded to meet immediately with the U.S. Attorney's Office on behalf of my clients. Marie only said that she wished she could tell me more, but she couldn't. She did mention that there were ongoing discussions with Epstein's lawyers. "Settlement discussions? Plea negotiations on the federal case?" I asked. She repeated that she wished she could answer that but she couldn't. This was frustrating, to say the least.

I spent my weekend at the office trying to unravel this cryptic conversation for Jay Howell, the lawyer who introduced me to Courtney. I looked over the letter that Courtney had received from the FBI citing to 18 USC § 3771, the Crime Victims' Rights Act, or CVRA. The CVRA, which was enacted in 2004, provides basic statutory rights for all federal crime victims, including the right to be protected from the accused, the right to timely notice of all public hearings, the right to be heard at any such hearing, the right to confer with the government in the case, and the right to be treated with fairness and respect.

By now, it was clear that the only way we were going to find out what was happening behind the scenes was if we filed something with the court. I wasn't sure what needed to be filed, so I entitled the pleading, "Victim's Petition for Enforcement of Crime Victim's Rights Act, 18 U.S.C. Section 3771."

I explained that my client was a victim of federal crimes committed by Jeffrey Epstein when she was a minor child because he flew from New York to Florida for the purpose of engaging in sexual contact with her. I was now under the impression that potential plea discussions were happening between Epstein's attorneys and the government, yet the U.S. Attorney's Office was refusing to keep me or my clients informed of the process. Truth is, I had no idea at that moment exactly what the Crime Victims' Rights Act was meant to accomplish or what exactly needed to be filed to enforce a client's assumed rights under the statute. I just knew that in order to protect Courtney, I had to give it a shot. When I finished my petition, I decided that I would hand-deliver it to the courthouse on Monday morning and, in light of what I suspected was taking place behind closed doors, ask the court to hold a hearing immediately.

Before that day, I had only practiced law in state courts, which meant I had never even been to the federal courthouse. I walked inside and could barely tell the security guard why I was there or who I was going to see, but he eventually directed me to the clerk's office. When I arrived, there was no one around except for a woman behind the last window. I told her I had a case to file. She said okay and asked me for a copy of the pleading.

When I handed her my petition, she looked up at me as if to say, *Why are you still standing there?* I told her, "I need a hearing." She said that the judge would send out a hearing notice if a hearing was required, but that most of the time, in federal court, there weren't any hearings. "This is an emergency, I need a hearing now," I declared. She left the room, I assumed to talk to her supervisor, since she was gone for a while.

When she came back, she said, "This doesn't even say 'emergency' on it, so it won't be treated like an emergency." She put the pleading down on the counter, and before she could say another word, I snatched it up and walked to the other side of the room, where pens were dangling from little metal chains. I handwrote the word *Emergency* at the beginning of the title and walked it back to her. "Now it's an emergency," I said. She started laughing and told me she had never seen that done before. She went to the back room again before returning to tell me that it would be filed as an emergency, but that didn't mean I would get a hearing that day.

My filing wasn't disregarded. The case was assigned to Judge Kenneth Marra, who took it seriously. He issued an order immediately directing the government to respond to our petition within two days, and directed us to reply the day after we received the government's response. He set a hearing for that Friday.

---

When I got back to my office, I had a message from a lawyer in Utah who said that it was very important I call him back. When I did, he asked if I was the lawyer who had just filed the case under the CVRA in Florida. He said he had been called by a friend of his, Jay Howell, who had alerted him to the filing. I said yes, and he said, "I would like to help you."

I told him, "Thank you, but I think I have it covered," and he reminded me that the first pleading filed in the case had the word *Emergency* handwritten on it—as if to say that it looked like I could use his help. That lawyer was Paul Cassell, and he was right. We soon became a formidable team and the best of friends.

During that conversation, Paul gave me his impressive résumé. He was a former assistant U.S. attorney who had clerked for Supreme Court Justice Antonin Scalia. Then, after spending years as a federal judge, he left to dedicate his career to representing crime victims and teaching law at the University of Utah. After hearing his credentials, I told him that I would love his help. In fact, Paul and I collaborated on the reply brief that week, which anyone would notice was of slightly better quality than the original petition.

------------

I picked my clients up at Courtney's house on the morning of the hearing, July 11, 2008. We sat on one side of the courtroom. On the other side was Assistant U.S. Attorney Marie Villafaña and the government's appellate lawyer, Dexter Lee. Just behind them, sitting in the front row, were a man and a woman in plain clothes who clearly had something to do with the investigation. They were the two primary FBI agents on the case, Jason Richards and Nesbitt Kuyrkendall.

Judge Marra took the bench and asked me to approach the podium. I began the hearing: "Your Honor, as a factual background, Mr. Epstein is a billionaire who sexually abused and molested dozens and dozens of girls between the ages of thirteen and seventeen years old. And through cooperating victims, that evidence can be proven. Because of his deviant appetite for young girls, combined with his extraordinary wealth and power, he may just be the most dangerous sexual predator in U.S. history."

I told the judge that we believed the government had been secretly negotiating with Epstein, which was forbidden by the CVRA. I sat down and Dexter Lee stood up and said: "Let me update the Court on the status of various matters. The agreement to defer prosecution to the State of Florida was signed and completed by December 2007. . . . [Epstein] ended up pleading guilty on June 30, 2008, to two charges in state court, and he was sentenced to a term of incarceration of 18 months, with another 12 months of community control after the completion of his sentence, and he is currently incarcerated as we speak." It was only then, in response to my argument, that the judge and I—and more important, my clients—learned *for the very first time* that our understanding of Epstein's imminent plea negotiation was incorrect. The situation was much worse. There was not going to be any federal plea by Epstein at all, of any kind. The federal investigation into his crimes had been brought to a close and the federal case was already over. The ball game had ended without anyone being in the stands to see it.

Even as the government was explaining this, it was still quite unclear exactly what they were saying. I wasn't the only one confused. Judge Marra also had no idea that the government had worked out a secret non-prosecution agreement *nine months* prior to this day and had hidden it from the victims in hopes of helping Jeffrey Epstein make all of his criminal problems go away at the same time, unnoticed.

Judge Marra turned back to me and asked what I wanted him to do, considering that the emergency we believed existed—the stopping of an imminent secret plea deal—was no longer an imminent concern. He sent us all into the hallway to talk. AUSA Dexter Lee tried to explain to me in some cryptic legalese that the procedure I had invoked was incorrect and that we should discuss whether the pleading needed to be withdrawn and some other process initiated. AUSA Marie Villafaña stood there not saying much. She seemed upset with what was happening. The FBI agents stood in the corner of this little breakout room grim-faced and not saying a word. After the work they'd put into the investigation, I could only imagine their sense of betrayal by the U.S. attorney as well.

As we left, I turned to Lynn, who had been quiet since we walked into the courtroom. "Where's Jeffrey? I thought I was going to see him today," she said.

Before I could begin to answer, Courtney interrupted: "What the f***? It's over?"

We left the courthouse that day and I wanted to explain to my clients what was going on, but it was impossible because I didn't understand myself.

The government had concealed everything from my clients and was only now providing bits and pieces when compelled to do so. "They intended for it to be over without you knowing. That is what we learned today. But don't worry, it's not over," I assured them.

The non-prosecution agreement—called an NPA—was a document that protected Epstein from being prosecuted by the federal government for crimes he committed in Florida.

Now that I knew it existed, I requested a copy. It would seem that the government would hand this document over to us, but instead, they objected, still fighting hard to prevent the victims from knowing the truth. A few days later, AUSA Marie Villafaña came to my office. When she showed up, I didn't know what to make of her. I had just learned that Jeffrey Epstein and his army of reputable lawyers had conspired with the U.S. Attorney's Office to immunize Epstein for hundreds of sexual offenses against minor children. Now the prosecutor who had failed to warn me in prior conversations of what was actually going on, and who by all appearances was the lead prosecutor on the case, was at my office for a personal meeting.

I learned a lot about Marie Villafaña that day. She was the first person in her family to go to college. She had decided when she got her first job at the U.S. Attorney's Office that she was going to work in public service forever, either as a U.S. attorney or a federal judge. She was loyal to the office, and that loyalty prevented her, despite how upset she was, from telling me all what she wanted to tell me.

Her main message that day was that she understood what Courtney had been through and appreciated why she was upset. Marie made no excuses and did not try to dissuade me from pushing forward on behalf of the victims.

Marie was concerned about how the closing of the case would make her look, but not more concerned than she was for the victims, many of whom she knew had been deeply harmed. She and I talked for more than an hour. By the time she left, I felt in my gut that if she had it her way, she would have prosecuted Epstein and his co-conspirators. She did not cave in to the NPA because she was weak, but it seemed that her loyalty to her superiors left her without a choice. Listening to her, I got the distinct impression that she would be loyal to her office even to her personal detriment.

On August 21, 2008, the court ordered that the victims could see the NPA, as long as they signed an agreement not to disseminate it publicly. It sounds as ridiculous now as it did then. The victims whose rights had been extinguished through this document were now required to keep it confidential.

The agreement was a seven-page document signed by Jeffrey Epstein, several of his lawyers, and Marie Villafaña on behalf of U.S. Attorney Alexander Acosta. On September 24, 2007—nine months before Epstein's plea deal—this document had been signed, sealed, and finalized. While the agreement was relatively complicated, it could be broken down into simple parts.

First, Jeffrey Epstein and four named co-conspirators—Lesley Groff, Sarah Kellen, Adriana Ross (an alias for Adriana Mucinska), and Nadia Marcinkova—were granted federal immunity for all crimes they had committed between 2001 and 2007 in the Southern District of Florida (which runs from Fort Pierce to Key West, and includes Palm Beach, Fort Lauderdale, and Miami). As if that weren't strange enough, apparently the government and Epstein wanted to ensure that none of his pilots, butlers, assistants, attorneys, or other friends who may have been involved in his crimes were punished, either. To that end, a catchall phrase had been thrown in immunizing any "known or unknown co-conspirators" as well. For Epstein's part, all he had to do was plead guilty to the charges in state court that effectively labeled his victims as prostitutes, endure what would be a cakewalk sentence, and go back to life as usual.

It was a win on many levels for Jeffrey Epstein. His lawyers basically got to characterize him as a wealthy philanthropist who unknowingly had underage girls at his home—the poor guy was just trying to get a massage and he had no idea that these girls were minors. These were just regular "prostitutes" who had taken advantage of him.

There was one problem, though—surely some of these minors who were sexually abused by Epstein would file civil lawsuits against him, which could expose the criminal enterprise and risked exposing the existence of the NPA as well. The government and Epstein tried to head this problem off by adding a provision to the NPA where each of the victims would be provided a lawyer to settle all civil lawsuits for a set minimal amount of money. This was bizarre, as the government never involves itself in civil lawsuits. That is just not the function of the government.

Yet, for Jeffrey Epstein, they made an exception and decided to help him resolve his criminal exposure and any related civil claims all at once. If everything had worked as designed in the NPA, the criminal case would have gone away forever at that state court hearing on June 30, 2008, and all potential civil lawsuits against Epstein would have been wrapped up immediately thereafter for a nominal amount of money. Most important, nobody would ever even know about the existence of the NPA.

Unfortunately for Epstein and the U.S. attorney, by filing the emergency petition to enforce Courtney's rights and obtaining a copy of the NPA, Epstein and the government's secret agreement began to be exposed. And the plan started to slowly unravel.

# EIGHT

# A LIGHT SENTENCE

IN THE MEANTIME, EPSTEIN WAS beginning to serve his mandated eighteen-month sentence as handed down by Judge Pucillo for the two state felonies to which he had pleaded guilty. But Epstein's sentence didn't look much like that of a typical convict. A review of the inmate Visitor Information sheets for Epstein revealed that he was almost never alone. He was visited every day by a number of people, including regulars Jean-Luc Brunel, Nadia Marcinkova, and Sarah Kellen. He also had steady visits from lawyers and businessmen with whom he had close ties. One such guest was Arnold Prosperi, a convicted fraudster whose sentence had been commuted by one of Epstein's other friends—former president Bill Clinton.

Three months into his "jail" sentence, Jeffrey Epstein was approved for work release. This is a special benefit conferred on those inmates who are particularly well behaved and have earned the opportunity to work and be contributing members of society. Like the term implies, work release is supposed to consist of release from jail during the day for the inmate to go to a job, where he is constantly supervised. Epstein was a recently registered sex offender who spent so much time with his jail visitors that it was difficult to say whether he had earned the chance to be placed on work release. Then there was the fact that he didn't really work, even before being sentenced.

Yet Epstein had set up an office on Australian Avenue in Palm Beach, adjacent to his lawyer Jack Goldberger's office. Epstein registered his office with the state of Florida as a business known as the Florida Science Foundation, which was incorporated in Florida on November 1, 2007, shortly after Epstein had signed the NPA. The formalities ended there.

The Palm Beach County Sheriff's Office was paid more than $100,000 by Epstein for deputies to drive him to "work" and guard him while there. It was later discovered that sometimes those deputies made unauthorized detours to Epstein's house so that Jeffrey could make sure his mansion was functioning properly.

On a typical day, Epstein would walk into the Florida Science Foundation, a do-nothing company; talk on the phone to his various employees working at his numerous mansions around the world; send emails to his former and current girls, including victims of his sex-trafficking operation; and continue to arrange for women to be flown to him for sexual purposes. He even had a new email at the time—jeevacation@gmail.com. It was pretty apropos considering his jail time was by most standards a vacation.

At the end of the day, deputies would drive him back to jail for the night. Jail barely changed Jeffrey Epstein's daily routine.

During evenings in the jail, Epstein was not referred to as an inmate like everyone else. Instead, he was discussed in reports as a "client," and because he was, according to internal sheriff's office memos, "poorly versed in jail routine," the sheriff authorized that "his cell door be left unlocked and he be given liberal access to the attorney room where a TV will be installed."

Things got even better for him in July 2009, when his eighteen-month sentence was cut short by five months for "good behavior," and he was released to begin a year of "community control," or "house arrest." As you can imagine, he took great liberty with this variety of confinement as well. There was a constant influx of new women flying from all over to stay with him. When that wasn't enough, Epstein would just leave the house. Of course, that is inconsistent with the concept of house arrest, but if nobody was going to enforce it, did it really exist?

I was hearing all kinds of stories about his "house arrest." There was the time the Palm Beach police spotted him strolling the beach with no explanation other than confusion over what the parameters of this stage of his punishment meant. On another occasion, Palm Beach detectives stopped him miles away from his house and he explained that he was walking to work. Despite the fact that he was not in an area between his home and the office, the police officers were told by Epstein's probation officer to just give him a warning. Other times, the probation officer would show up and be told that Jeffrey was in another area of the house and the officer would take note and leave so as not to bother Epstein. On several occasions, Epstein left the state altogether. He was still thumbing his nose at the system, and I knew it. I was already determined to hold him accountable for his crimes, but as he continued to pompously exhibit his entitlement to live above the law, bringing him down became more of a personal challenge.

# NINE

# LET'S FIGHT

FROM AS FAR BACK AS I can remember, the world was only about competition. It wasn't just sports: I wanted to compete in everything, from school, to grades, to who could get to the front of the lunch line first. As important to me as the competition itself was the idea that the game was *fair*. I despised cheaters, bullies, or those who cut corners to get an advantage. While I never cheated to retaliate, my dislike of those who didn't play fair got me into more than my share of fistfights.

When I was really young, competing in sports like football, soccer, and basketball was my life. As I started getting older, the kids got bigger, and the competition became fierce. I didn't take losing well. My dad would tell me, "You don't have to like losing, but you have to learn how to lose." Those words were meaningless to me at the time. Losing hurt me to my core. When I lost, I would turn my focus onto the person or team that beat me. I would obsess over how I was going to get them back next time. I would single out one human being and tell myself that no matter what, he was never going to beat me again. Revenge, or at least avenging or erasing the loss, became an obsession.

My lifelong competitive nature was fueled by my dad. Dad knew how much I loved to win, which made him love coaching me and my younger twin brothers, Travis and David. I can still hear him telling me to "quit loafing" from the soccer sidelines, even though I was actually going full speed all the time. He would always push me harder, no matter what. My dad wanted me to maximize whatever talent I had, and help me realize I could always improve. He wasn't the only one pushing me. My mother's father, whom I called Papa, knew that I would outwork and outlast anyone. That was my real strength. Dad and Papa had their own ways of conveying their wisdom to drive me well past the point where most kids my age would succumb to the feeling of exhaustion. Just before I walked on the field or court, Dad would always say, "Kick ass and take names, and don't forget, the bigger they are, the harder they fall," his way of telling me there was no excuse for losing.

Predictably, Papa, a true realist who knew my weapon was my will to never give up, would follow Dad's words with "It's never over till the fat lady sings." Everybody loves a good comeback, and my athletic career was full of them. Of course, I never planned it that way, but anyone who says they don't get pleasure out of wearing a stronger opponent down mentally and physically is lying. Plus, every great battle has observable momentum shifts, and every great fighter can time his strategic attack to shift the momentum in the right direction at the end.

The earliest memories I have of Papa are from going to his house at four or five years old. Every time I went to see him and Granny, I would jump out of the car, run into the house, and leap over to his La-Z-Boy recliner, which was only five feet away from the door. My goal was to catch him off guard before jumping on his lap and saying, "Let's fight." I would try to fight him. He would tickle me until I laughed so hard it made me cry. He would always stick his finger into the space below my collarbone and pretend like it was stuck. It hurt so bad, but not bad enough to distract me from my own laughter. He would make me say, "Mercy," and promise to stop before he would remove his "stuck" finger. I would usually stop for about a second before attacking him again. I loved fighting Papa, and competing against him, and actually, any second I spent with him. I would give anything for one more fight in his lap in that La-Z-Boy.

As I got older, when we weren't playing, we were usually talking about sports. I vividly remember a talk I had with Papa on the way back from a tennis tournament. That talk shaped my life. I had lost to a faster, bigger, stronger player. Out of frustration, I complained that I wasn't tall enough, giving that as my excuse for losing. He told me something that I still tell my kids to this day: "You can't worry about the things you can't control. You are not always going to be the tallest, or the fastest, or the strongest, but you can always be the toughest and you can try the hardest. If you are tough enough and you try hard enough, you can overcome all of those other things. Every time you do anything, put yourself on the line and give it everything you have."

These words can be applied to nearly all life situations. When Papa first said them, he was talking about sports, but later he repeated them when talking about school and work. Nobody likes excuses or explanations for failure. Wasting energy on things out of my control was unacceptable. And the ultimate excuse, "I didn't try"—a cop-out many athletes mutter after a loss—is the most inexcusable. That's what he meant by putting yourself on the line—even if you lose, you still tried your hardest from beginning to end and the other guy was just better. No doubt strict adherence to these principles made me forever tougher.

---

When I went to college, I believed that I was going to be a professional athlete of some sort. I played on the University of Florida tennis team, but I also badly wanted to play football. So much so that I went to the football team meeting, where it became clear the Florida Gators had probably ten quarterbacks who were all better than me. Call me hardheaded or maybe even delusional, but that didn't stop me. I went to walk-on tryouts anyway and I made sure that I beat every single guy running the stadium stairs. I think that was the only drill I won. At five foot ten and 149 pounds, all I could do was show them that I was fast and hardworking and enjoy my two-day University of Florida football career to the fullest. It goes without saying that I didn't make the team.

It wasn't until my second year on the UF tennis team that I realized becoming a professional tennis player was about as realistic as playing on the UF football team. Wasn't going to happen. So now what?

My mom, who, after Papa, was probably the biggest influence in my life, worked as a paralegal for Jay Howell in Jacksonville. I had told Mom from the time that I was very young that if I wasn't going to be a professional athlete, I would be a lawyer, and because Mom worked for Jay, I thought representing children and crime victims was what it meant to be a lawyer.

You get to compete every day in law, so if I couldn't be on a field or on a court, then this was the best way to spend my life. From that day forward, I only saw myself in a courtroom. This also seemed like the profession where I could play a role in evening the playing field, where true fairness could be achieved, equally for everyone.

# TEN

# THE FUN BEGINS

I N AUGUST 2008, WHILE EPSTEIN was still in "jail," my clients exercised their right to reject the civil settlement structure proposed by the NPA, which allowed me to file separate civil lawsuits against him on behalf of Courtney, Lynn, and Marissa. From the very beginning of the civil cases, Epstein's lawyers fought us on everything.

Epstein was represented by Marty Weinberg, Roy Black, Guy Lewis, Michael Tien, Lilly Ann Sanchez, Jack Goldberger, Ken Starr, Jay Lefkowitz, Gerald Lefcourt, Alan Dershowitz, and locally by Bob Critton. This was a multimillion-dollar dream team of lawyers whose main defense strategy was to paper the cases to death. His lawyers filed objections to everything. They filed motions on every issue, and on every nonissue. I was quickly drowning in paperwork.

There came a point when Epstein's growing team of attorneys was forcing me to go to court in Palm Beach, an hour from my office, multiple times a week. The other days of the week, I was up there meeting with my clients, who were being followed by private investigators and called by old friends, acquaintances, teachers, and neighbors who had been interrogated by Epstein's investigators. His full-court press was taking a toll.

Courtney was working at a bagel shop when Epstein's investigators came in and demanded that she speak with them. They told her flat out that she should not prosecute any civil case against him. Needless to say, that left Courtney scared. Another time, she was stopped at the gas station by one of Epstein's people and boxed in while vague threats were made toward her about what would happen if she continued to pursue her civil claims against him. The best goons money could buy were out in force doing Epstein's bidding.

Paul Cassell and I were fighting against some of the highest-paid lawyers in the country. Paul didn't have any staff and I only had one paralegal and a law clerk. As for the lawyers on Epstein's payroll, they were supported by large law firms employing hundreds of other staff members and associates.

Regardless, we worked long hours to hold our own. Unfortunately, my non-Epstein cases were falling behind. Far behind. The Epstein cases were consuming so much time that it was impossible to do other work. I considered my options, of course. Some fine firms in town had tried to recruit me over the years, and if ever there was a time for that, it was now. But I wanted to do it on my own terms.

---

By the time I'd opened my own office in 2007, I had a wife, a one-year-old son, no income, and bills that didn't put themselves on hold while I tried to establish a law practice. Those days were rewarding, though. Cases would come in through friends at the police department, the state attorney's office, and social workers who were in touch with victims who had been shot, stabbed, or, in some cases, sexually assaulted. I represented these clients primarily against corporate entities who failed to implement appropriate levels of security, thereby providing opportunity for criminals to hurt my clients.

This niche was unique. Consequently, I was bringing in a lot of cases. More than I could handle; especially while working on this Epstein mess.

During the spring of 2009, I was at the gym—where I went from five to six o'clock every morning—when I was approached by a lawyer I had litigated against named Russell Adler. He had a reputation for representing sexual abuse victims. Russell was running the trial division at a fast-growing Fort Lauderdale law firm called Rothstein Rosenfeldt Adler (RRA).

Russell had recently won a $20 million case against a sexual predator, which naturally led to our conversation about the Jeffrey Epstein case and how much of my time it was consuming. I told him that the rest of my practice was starting to suffer. He wanted me to sit down with Scott Rothstein, the managing partner of his firm, to talk about what RRA could do for me to support my other cases while I continued to fight Epstein. There were more than fifty lawyers at RRA, many of whom were former judges, and on top of that, only the best lawyers around town were being recruited by that firm, or at least that was the impression he gave me.

Russell set up a meeting for me with Scott Rothstein in a steak house called Bova Prime located on the bottom floor of the huge skyscraper building in Fort Lauderdale where RRA maintained four floors of office space. The restaurant was owned by Rothstein himself. I wasn't given much information about Scott or RRA before the meeting, only what Russell told me, which was that Scott had been one of the best young trial attorneys in the area of employment law before parlaying those wins into multiple lucrative business ventures. Scott owned properties throughout Fort Lauderdale, both residential and commercial, including the famous Versace Mansion in Miami. He was even part owner of a vodka brand.

I arrived at Bova Prime and told the hostess that I was there to see Scott Rothstein. She took me upstairs to the second floor, where no one was apparently permitted to go except for Scott. She sat me at a large round table overlooking the entire restaurant. I had never seen Scott before and had no idea what to expect. I figured that since he was a lawyer running one of the most powerful law firms in Fort Lauderdale, he would be an older guy with white hair and glasses, dressed traditionally in a business suit. I knew from his reputation that just about the entire city was completely enamored of him.

I heard a loud male voice and peered over the railing into the main dining area. From my angle I couldn't get a good look, but from the sound of it, the man seemed to be greeting everyone like he was the mayor. I heard multiple people yelling out, "Scottyyyy," and then the sound of high fives. "I have an important meeting. Gotta go, love ya," the man yelled before walking up to the VIP area where I was sitting. He looked nothing like what I'd expected. He was in his forties, with spiky brown hair, wearing a bright purple suit and a massive watch covered in diamonds.

I didn't know what he knew about me or what Russell had told him. He sat down in front of me and cocked his head to the left. I thought that he was doing it intentionally in an inquisitive way, but this was actually the result of a peculiar tic. One of his eyes would also blink at the same time his head would twitch.

While I was prepared to answer all of his questions, the interview lasted barely two minutes. The only thing he asked me was what I expected my role at the firm to be.

Before Scott gave me the chance to answer, he proclaimed, "Russell says you're great. You'd better be. You're hired." He said not to worry about the salary because his law firm operated on the "system of fairness" and that if I made him money, he would treat me fairly. He quickly countered that with the statement that if I disappointed him, I'd have to see things his way and accept reduced pay. Sounded fair to me.

Before I could finish the conversation, he yelled over to the waitress to get him a martini, which she did. For a second, I thought that he was going to drink it right there, but then he got up, walked downstairs, and handed it to someone else, presumably to make them feel important. Scott was a master at making everyone around him feel important, and yet at the same time, everyone knew that no one was more important than Scott.

I called Russ and told him I was joining the firm, then took my paralegal, Shawn, to lunch at this little place called Mama Mia near our office in Hollywood. I told her we were going to join RRA. She was skeptical but agreed to come along. She believed in me. Prior to meeting me, she had worked for a big firm for twenty years. Even though she didn't want to go back to a place like that, she said she'd do it for me. And I certainly didn't want to go without her. I told her *we* had already been hired at RRA and that her meeting with the hiring staff there was merely a formality that she would have to go through before the first day of work.

That weekend, we loaded up more than sixty boxes of files and drove back and forth between our old office in Hollywood and our new office in downtown Fort Lauderdale. On Monday morning, we walked into the offices on the twelfth floor of RRA together. I remember noticing right from the beginning that everyone we saw seemed happy. It was a relaxed environment, with people talking in the hallways and sharing ideas. It reminded me a lot of the camaraderie I'd been a part of at the state attorney's office. To me, this was refreshing.

Shawn went in for her "interview" with Scott's assistant, Debra. I am sure Shawn asked more questions of Debra than Debra asked of Shawn. The truth was, Debra knew nothing about being a paralegal, and Shawn knew everything. By this point in her career, Shawn had even published a book about how to be a paralegal that was being used to teach students in law schools.

I expected Shawn to be as excited as I was when she came to my office after the interview. She shut the door and said, "I am so sorry, I told you I would go anywhere with you, but I will not stay here. It just doesn't feel right. But call me when you leave, because you will, and I will come back and work for you." She packed up her stuff right then and there and left the office without working one second at RRA.

I didn't really have any time to think about losing Shawn. There was too much work to do and I needed to quickly get acclimated to this new law firm so that I could finally take advantage of all of its resources. I immediately told Russell that I wanted to put a team together to go after Jeffrey Epstein.

Russell followed through. Right after I started, I held a meeting in the main conference room where ten other lawyers and two investigators attended to listen to the factual and procedural history of the Epstein civil cases. I then laid out my plan of attack for putting us in the best position to win.

At this point, I had not yet seen Scott Rothstein in the office. He was talked about by everyone, not only in the office but all over town, as this larger-than-life super lawyer whom all of the richest people wanted to latch on to. He was rumored to travel only by private plane or helicopter, with a hand in every growing business, all while also running the most powerful law firm in town.

Later that week, though, Scott convened a firm-wide meeting in the large banquet room on the first floor of the building. More than one hundred lawyers and employees piled in and waited for him to arrive. Everyone was talking among themselves when all of a sudden, straight out of a movie, both doors swung open, slammed against the wall, and he entered like an NFL linebacker at the Super Bowl. There was no introduction, no pleasantries; he just started yelling at the top of his lungs.

"Every law firm," he said, "practices law the same way. One firm files a motion, another firm files a motion. Someone files a complaint, another firm files an answer. That is not how we practice at RRA. When someone files a motion, I want you to chop their motherf***ing heads off. We are going to take over this town. We are going to change the way people practice law. I want everyone to be entrepreneurial. Anyone who comes to me with ideas about how to take over this place is going to be rewarded. Now everyone go and tear heads off."

He slammed his hand down on the table before skipping out of the room. As barbaric as it sounds, on some level I left feeling excited to work for this guy. The scene reminded me of my high school football locker room. Clownish as he may have been, Scott knew how to perform, organize, and most of all motivate.

Scott's energy was off the charts. With the resources of RRA, I was inspired to assemble an unbeatable team to do as Scott had just ordered—take off Epstein's head.

# ELEVEN

# THE TWO OF US

K NOWING YOUR OPPONENT IS THE key to winning. When I later found a 2003 *Vanity Fair* article called "The Talented Mr. Epstein," in which Jeffrey was quoted saying to reporter Vicky Ward, "Let's play chess. You be white. You get the first move," I knew that I was getting ready to play one hell of a chess game.

During my senior year of college, my roommate brought home a chessboard. He had played his entire life, and I'd never played before. In the beginning, I got killed. Game after game, no matter who I played, I lost. It's so easy to concentrate only on trying to capture your opponent's king when you first learn the objective. You forget that you have to make sure that your own king is protected before trying to attack. I still remember when I won my first game. It gave me the confidence to think that I finally understood the bigger picture. It really wasn't long before I was beating everyone. Not all of the time, but most of the time. The game was captivating, forcing my mind to think through layers of actions and reactions.

When I went to law school at Florida State University, I started going up against better players, including people who were on the university chess team. While studying abroad one summer in the Czech Republic, I bought a hand-carved chess set that I took everywhere (and still play on to this day). For a long time, I was infatuated with trying different openings, different combinations, different attack methods, and yet no matter how comfortable I got, there was always someone who knew exactly how to counter me. I realized that the infinite complexity of symbiotic move combinations didn't allow for anyone to ever solve the game completely.

That piece by Vicky Ward also made it seem as if Epstein believed there was some chivalry in combat. Ward even quoted Epstein's longtime multibillionaire friend Les Wexner to that effect. Wexner offered some insight into his friend's combative style: "Many times people confuse winning and losing," Wexner said. "Jeffrey has the unusual quality of knowing when he is winning. Whether in conversations or negotiations, he always stands back and lets the other person determine the style and manner of the conversation or negotiation. And then he responds in their style. Jeffrey sees it in chivalrous terms. He does not pick a fight, but if there is a fight, he will let you choose your weapon."

I had read Ward's article and the few others about Epstein that were available at that point so many times that I had memorized them—they were the only game footage I had of my opponent. To beat him, I had to understand him. I needed to be able to predict his tendencies, his offensive and defensive strategies. There was no comparison when lining up his resources against mine; he was the heavy favorite. Preparation, toughness, resilience, and a perfect balance of offense and defense could overcome the disparity. At least that's what I thought.

Unfortunately for me, until I got to RRA, my mentality just wasn't realistic. Epstein had so many pieces on his chessboard and so many resources that he could basically just make up the game as he went along. It wasn't until I had RRA's resources that I could finally sit at the table and start to trade moves with him. Now I would have to meet him personally to understand any more.

In April 2009, I took Jeffrey Epstein's deposition for the first time. Because I was now working at a big firm, and this was perceived to be an important case, another RRA lawyer went with me to the deposition—former Palm Beach Circuit Court judge Bill Berger. Berger had recently left the bench. He told me that he had been skeptical when Russell first told him the allegations against Epstein. After hearing my initial presentation at the firm, he quickly changed his mind. He felt it was important to show at this first deposition that our firm was not going to be outmanned by Epstein's arsenal of attorneys. I didn't care one way or the other if anyone went with me, and I didn't really know Bill, but the car ride there gave me a chance to talk out loud about what we might expect.

Typically, in cases like this where the evidence is strong that the defendant committed what amounts to criminal acts, there is a high likelihood that he will invoke his Fifth Amendment right against self-incrimination rather than actually answer questions.

Up until this point, Epstein's written discovery responses had contained primarily Fifth Amendment invocations with few nuggets of substantive information. He did provide the names of certain employees who had worked at his Palm Beach mansion for a period of time that included the years during which Courtney, Lynn, and Marissa were abused. In the beginning of this case, it seemed whichever lawyer was steering that ship still cared about compliance with the rules, at least on the face of things.

Not knowing whether Epstein was going to answer questions or not, I spent two whole days preparing for the deposition. Very little preparation would be necessary if he wasn't going to answer, but on the off chance that he did, I had to be ready. This was also the first time I would be meeting him in person, and I figured that he had underestimated me, so this might be my only chance to catch him off guard.

After all, who was I? There were many other Epstein victims who were represented by prominent local lawyers like Bob Josefsberg, a nationally recognized Harvard-educated lawyer and one of the most successful attorneys in Florida, and Jack Scarola, who was a respected lawyer in Palm Beach, where the cases were venued. Me? I was thirty-three years old and totally unknown on paper, except of course for my "Victim's Petition for Enforcement of Crime Victims' Rights Act," where I'd hand-scribbled the word

*Emergency* at the top. I saw this as a big advantage for me because I could fly under the radar.

I knew from the publicly available information on Jeffrey Epstein at that point that he was always prepared, and that he studied his opponents with the same meticulous attention to detail that I did. His preferred style of engagement—rope-a-dope—was also very similar to mine. I felt like this gave me tremendous insight into who he was and what potential vulnerabilities he might have.

What I had learned so far was that he approached every situation in the way most likely to disarm his opponent. On the one hand, he was always more prepared, yet on the other hand, he knew not to let his ego get in the way of a victory. By that, I mean he did not make an effort to overshare information in order to impress the others in the room. He, like me, cared only about the end result, and if that meant giving the false impression that everyone else was smarter than him or knew more than him, then that is exactly what he would do. He was intellectually dangerous.

I walked into that deposition with my game plan intact—I wanted to make Jeffrey Epstein believe that I was unprepared. The deposition was being held in a fancy all-glass office building with restrictive front desk security that required permission to access the elevators. Fully expecting to get off the elevator and walk down the hallway to Epstein's lawyer's office, I was casually talking to Bill about whether Epstein was even going to appear when the elevator doors opened up onto the second floor. I did not have one foot out of the elevator before Jeffrey Epstein appeared alone, standing three feet in front of me with his hand fully extended, saying, "Hi, Brad. Nice to meet you. I'm Jeffrey." He totally caught me off guard. In our first chess match, Epstein had put me in check.

Everything he did was calculated. He wasn't just saying hi. He put me in a position where I had no choice but to shake his hand the way I would to begin a professional or friendly relationship. The last thing on this earth I ever wanted to do was be his friend. I wanted to hate him. I wanted to disarm him and start this relationship on my terms. Instead, we started it on his.

Epstein looked me right in the eyes. He gave me a lopsided smile and said, "I'll see you in the room." He acted like we were old friends. I walked down the hallway thinking about whether I should have anticipated that opening gesture, or whether he was really showing me more respect than he would others. There was actually part of me that thought I had done something to earn his respect and that it should somehow be meaningful to me because of who he was. Of course, this was just Epstein doing what he did best—manipulating.

It's crazy to think that we took this deposition while Epstein was technically still in "jail," spending twelve hours of his day down the hall from the deposition room at the Florida Science Foundation. He invoked the Fifth Amendment in response to hours of questions. He read a long, prepackaged script that was constructed to obstruct the deposition.

Unbeknownst to me, Bill was texting Russell Adler during the deposition, explaining that Epstein was making a mockery of the deposition process by invoking constitutional amendments in response to every question. Russell came over to meet us for lunch and we discussed that the law in Florida suggests a plaintiff may be entitled to an "adverse inference" against a defendant who invokes constitutional protection. (In some states, the judge will prohibit the plaintiff's lawyer from telling the jury it should consider the defendant's "taking of the Fifth" as a sign of guilt or liability, while other states allow the plaintiff's lawyer to make that argument, called an "adverse inference.") I suggested to Russell that going through all the factually intensive questions that I had was more detrimental than it was beneficial. Epstein was paying close attention to every word and learning what we knew and what we did not know from my questions.

If we continued down that road, it would have only enabled him to better prepare for trial. My suggestion was that we had already gained sufficient advantage through his Fifth Amendment invocations and whatever adverse inference to which we might be entitled. We should spend the rest of the deposition asking the questions that would likely increase the punitive damage award against him if he continued to refuse to answer. Russell agreed.

As soon as everyone settled back into their seats, my first few questions were along the lines of whether Epstein was aware while he was sexually molesting each little girl that this was someone's daughter and whether he was remorseful for sexually abusing certain named fourteen-year-old girls. Epstein went from very calm to tellingly irritated. His lawyers took the position that he had no real choice but to refuse to answer the questions and that I was now taking unfair advantage of that fact by inserting these salacious questions into the record.

They began to angrily object. They threatened to terminate the deposition if I continued to ask those types of questions. This only prompted me to ask even more inflammatory questions until Epstein removed his microphone and walked out of the room. He never came back. What had started with his version of a handshake had ended with mine. I was back on the chessboard.

---

After that deposition, Epstein's harassment of our clients amplified. One client was working as a dancer at a club when one of Epstein's investigators bought a dance from her and told her his affiliation just to make it clear that she was being watched. She was later fired from that job, and then fired from her next three jobs without explanation. Another client was followed into the Fort Lauderdale airport, where a private investigator boarded her airplane and kept eyes on her all the way to New York. When she got there, the investigator followed her, videotaped her, and took photographs of her all over New York City. Those photographs were later shown to her during her Florida deposition to remind her that Epstein was always watching. Epstein's aggressive tactics were distracting, to say the least. If we were forced to play defense during the whole case, without making any offensive moves, the game was going to be over very soon.

Our clients were scared. Their worlds were caving in on them. It seemed like every day a different friend, boyfriend, ex-boyfriend, or former employer was calling one of them to complain about being approached out of nowhere by an investigator trying to dig up dirt on her. The investigators were asking these people, many of whom had been out of our clients' lives for years, about any questionable activity in which our clients had ever engaged, including drug use or even skipping school. Each time a client received one of these uncomfortable calls from an old acquaintance, she would call me, asking, "Why are they doing this to me? They are making everyone hate me for involving them and I haven't involved anyone. How does Jeffrey Epstein even know who this person is? Can we stop them from doing this?"

For a stretch, I was getting some version of this call from multiple clients, multiple times per week. And Epstein wasn't only humiliating and intimidating *my* clients: he was doing this to all of the victims who were bringing civil lawsuits against him. When the criminal investigation first began, one of Epstein's high school student victims was even told by one of Epstein's top recruiters, "Those who help him will be compensated and *those who hurt him will be dealt with.*"

Epstein employed new intimidation tactics constantly. He was able to get away with it because he used his lawyers as buffers. In reality, his lawyers would hire and pay the investigators, but all of the action was being puppeteered by Epstein himself. When Epstein's investigators overstepped, and Epstein was confronted with the overaggressive scare tactics, he immediately acted as if he had so many lawyers doing so many things that he was totally unaware of what was going on. He would promise to not let it happen again. A week later, a new batch of investigators was unleashed, and the harassment would ramp up again.

No matter what side you are on, there is strength in numbers. With that in mind, I created a list of victims I had discovered through my work and research who were not represented by other attorneys. We worked with our current clients and witnesses to gather and comb through high school yearbooks, circling pictures of other young girls who had been taken to Epstein. We then ran background searches on them before I instructed my investigators to track each of them down and take statements. Sometimes I went with them and knocked on the doors myself. We couldn't waste any time. If we did not locate the witness first, Epstein's investigators would. And when that happened, the witness or victim would be scared into hiding forever, a situation we encountered more than once.

# TWELVE

# THE GIRLS

I N MAY 2009, WE LEARNED via PACER (Public Access to Court Electronic Records) about a civil lawsuit filed against Jeffrey Epstein on behalf of someone who went by the pseudonym Jane Doe 102. The complaint stated that she was recruited as a young teenager when she was a spa employee of Donald Trump's Mar-a-Lago Club in Palm Beach. The person she said recruited her was not another minor child, but Epstein's top assistant and longtime girlfriend, Ghislaine Maxwell. Before that complaint was filed, we had scant information about his activities when he wasn't in Florida. We also didn't know whether his powerful friends were aware of his exploits. This victim and her lawsuit changed that.

If Jeffrey Epstein was running his elaborate scheme to fuel his sexual appetite in Florida, then logic would dictate that he was doing the same thing everywhere else he went during his frequent travel around the world. The Jane Doe 102 complaint gave us confirmation and exposed the breadth of his sexual appetite. Unlike the others identified by the FBI, Jane Doe 102 flew on Epstein's airplane and visited his other homes. She had been to his house in New York, which was one of the largest town houses in Manhattan; his ranch in New Mexico, which he'd purchased from the governor of New Mexico and which included its own airplane runway; his apartment in Paris; and his own private island in the U.S. Virgin Islands, Little

Saint James, nicknamed Little Saint Jeff's. She had traveled the world with Epstein and was a true insider with much more knowledge of the structure of his organization than the others.

Perhaps most important, Jane Doe 102 named Ghislaine Maxwell as being deeply involved in the criminal activities. Logically, we knew that some adult was at the top of the pyramid having recruited a child for Jeffrey, but before now we didn't know who that adult was. Jane Doe 102 described Maxwell approaching her at Trump's Mar-a-Lago and inviting her over to learn massage therapy. When her father dropped her off that night, she was sexually abused by both Maxwell and Epstein, who finished by telling her that she had "lots of potential." The complaint alleged that she was given "hundreds of dollars" for the day, which was much more than she was making at Mar-a-Lago.

Jane Doe 102 then described essentially becoming an underage traveling sex slave trained by Maxwell to perform sexually on Jeffrey Epstein daily. She claimed not only to have met Epstein's close friends but to have been lent out for sex with many of them. While they were not identified by name, they were described as politicians, academics, businessmen, and even royalty. As suspected, Epstein's criminal enterprise reached far beyond Palm Beach.

Jane Doe 102 traveled all around the world and saw Epstein engage in sexual acts with girls from many different countries. She alleged that Maxwell participated in the same activities and was the master recruiter. She even recounted one of Epstein's friends sending him three twelve-year-old girls from France who spoke no English as a birthday "gift," just so he could sexually exploit and abuse them before they were sent back to France the next day.

Jane Doe 102 described the photographs of nude girls that covered the walls of Epstein's homes in New York City, Palm Beach, Santa Fe, and the Virgin Islands, many of which were taken by Ghislaine Maxwell and at least one of which was a nude photograph of Jane Doe 102 herself. She explained that the abuse got so bad that she was finally forced to flee the country in 2002. She was sent to Thailand by Epstein and Maxwell with instructions to locate a young girl whom Epstein was considering to become one of his sex slaves. Jane Doe 102 instead left Thailand and went to Australia, where she hid out from Epstein and Maxwell for more than a decade. She thought she was safe until she received a threatening telephone call in 2007 from Epstein himself, telling her not to cooperate against him in any investigation. She was important to the clients I represented and she was the key to taking Jeffrey Epstein down.

I needed to meet Jane Doe 102.

The problem was I didn't represent her. She was still hiding halfway across the world, and her attorneys were guarding her closely. I would have to be patient and, in the meantime, keep tracking down other local victims. We located more than twenty women. One by one, I heard the ways in which time spent with Jeffrey Epstein rather than living a regular high school life left lasting scars.

Each went through an experience that started with teenage excitement and typically ended in humiliation. While Epstein made all of them feel special during the grooming process, most of them would eventually realize that he was a predator who had stripped them of their self-esteem and rearranged their values through manipulation. To cope, many of his victims turned to drugs. Others, depleted of all self-worth, submitted to abusive relationships or degrading professions. In story after story, these now young adults broke down crying, whether in formal depositions or just speaking with me in informal interviews when asked to discuss the time when their adolescent lives collided with Jeffrey Epstein.

---

While most, but not all, of these girls who were sexually used by Epstein as teens felt victimized, every so often a former victim had a completely different outlook.

Allison was not the only victim who had expressed gratitude toward Epstein, but she was certainly the most extreme example. While she was twenty years old and had not seen Epstein in years, Allison was still deeply conflicted about her feelings toward him. It took me going to her house several times before she was comfortable enough to share the uncensored version of her story.

Allison was only fourteen when she met Epstein, but by that point she had been as desensitized to sex as a young teenager could be. Not only had she serviced Epstein, but she was hard at work recruiting other girls, as young as fourteen, to bring to Jeffrey.

Allison explained how she spent more time in taxicabs between 2002 and 2005, shuttling girls to and from the house, than she did in school. In fact, the only reason she even attended high school was because it was the perfect recruiting ground. She was beautiful, charismatic, and hungry to succeed in her new business venture with Epstein. She wanted to prove herself as loyal and committed. In return, Epstein referred to Allison as his number one girl. She didn't know that he referred to many others the same way.

When the police started to close in on Epstein, Allison had Jeffrey's back. Not only did she continue to recruit for him, but she went to her prior recruits to persuade them to agree to help Jeffrey by staying quiet. The police investigation was cramping Allison's hustle. But she was addicted to the life. When Epstein went to "jail," Allison began escorting in seedy establishments masquerading as massage parlors in the area.

Allison's dysfunctional work life was matched by the craziness of her home life. She would talk about sex even as an eight-year-old kid. By ten years old, Allison was so oversexualized that she told her fifth grade math teacher, whom we will call Mr. Jeffers, that she had just sent her mom out to give a blow job. When the teacher told Allison he was going to call the Department of Children and Families, Allison cried and begged him not to. He asked her to stay after school so that they could discuss what Allison was talking about.

Sitting behind his desk and across from a sobbing and crying ten-year-old little girl, the math teacher told Allison to come over to him. Allison hung her head and nestled in as her teacher gave her a hug to comfort her. "I won't tell, but then you shouldn't, either," her teacher explained. Allison agreed, still thinking that they were talking about her mom.

Allison confided to Mr. Jeffers that her mom was a prostitute and Allison answered the phone when her mom was working to make sure she didn't miss the next job. It felt good to get this off her chest. As Allison picked up her head with tears dripping off of her small, freckled nose,

Mr. Jeffers leaned in to wipe away the tears. He slid his hands down her back and lifted her up to place her on his left knee. "Remember, I won't say anything," he confirmed. "You can come back and talk to me, and only me, about your secrets."

For the rest of the school year, Mr. Jeffers would regularly ask Allison to stay after school. She and her teacher had "secrets." That was comforting to Allison. No one else in her class had these types of secrets. It made her special. She began to embrace the world of secrets. She finally felt like she had an adult who cared about her.

To prove she was more than just a telephone operator for her mom, after one of the long hugs with her teacher, Allison took charge and kissed him. She was in control, or at least that was what her fifth grade math teacher had very carefully led her to believe.

By the time Allison graduated from fifth grade, she had experienced what she believed was a sexual relationship with an older man and had mastered the scheduling of a sex worker—her mother—as well as the art and power of keeping a secret.

As if things weren't bad enough, during the summer between fifth and sixth grades, Allison was maturing. Her braces had been removed. She was beginning to develop. A normal summer outfit for Allison consisted of short jean shorts, a crop top that looked more like a bathing suit, and a pair of flip-flops—advanced for someone that age, but her dominating personality gave her such an influence over the kids around her, all of her friends quickly began following suit.

Allison turned twelve that summer. On her birthday, her dad, Manny, had a party for her and eight of her friends at the community pool in the trailer park where he lived. There wasn't any birthday cake, nor were there drinks for the kids, chips, or fancy Happy Birthday napkins; instead, her dad invited his two best friends, Forrest and Jesse, and brought a cooler full of Miller Genuine Draft bottles. Forrest had an eleven-year-old daughter, Savanah, whom he brought to the party, even though she had never met Allison or Allison's friends. Manny told Allison to be nice to Savanah.

Savanah was sitting awkwardly on her father's lap while the other girls were huddled by the pool. "Savanah, come over!" Allison screamed from the other side.

Savanah stood up from her father's knee and soon she was with all the other girls in the pool. "What school do you go to, Savanah?" Allison asked.

"I live with my mom and go to school in North Carolina," she said. "I'm just here visiting my dad for the summer." Those were the first words she had spoken all day.

"Now you hang out with us," Allison told her, immediately making Savanah feel welcome.

A few minutes later, the girls looked up to see the dads walking out of the pool area and to the trailer. Allison ran over to the cooler and grabbed three beers. She popped them all open before walking back into the pool, using the steps to make sure she didn't spill. She passed the beers around. "Drink fast. The old guys could come back any minute."

Angela, the only friend who did not live in a trailer, asked, "Aren't they going to notice that the beers are gone?"

Allison replied, "Of course not. They're too drunk already, and I know my dad. He's taking them inside to do drugs."

The girls passed around the bottles, taking swigs each time one got to them. Allison was watching closely, noting who was drinking and who was pretending. When the bottle got to Savanah, Allison put her fingers on the bottom of the glass as soon as Savanah tipped it back so that the bottle would stay pressed to her lips. "Drink more," Allison encouraged, "till it's gone!"

When Allison finally let Savanah release the bottle, it was empty. "That was awesome," Allison told her. Savanah, who already admired Allison by this point, winked as if to say, *Thank you for letting me into your world.*

Allison hopped out of the pool with all three beers and ran to the bin behind the bathroom to toss them out. A few minutes later, her dad came back with Forrest and Jesse—all three clearly hopped up on something.

They couldn't sit still. Each immediately popped open a new beer and began pacing around the pool, directing the girls to have chicken fights with each other. Savanah's dad, Forrest, demanded that one girl put Allison on her shoulders and fight against another girl and Savanah. Allison and Savanah were on top, face-to-face.

Allison started out by taking it easy on Savanah, until Savanah tried to grab Allison by her hair and pull her backward into the pool. Allison reached out with her right hand, grabbed Savanah's bathing suit top, and pulled forward to regain her own balance. But when Allison didn't let go, Savanah's top came off of the right side of her chest, exposing her breast completely.

"Oh yeah!" shouted Forrest. "Now we have a fight. Go get her, Savanah!" He cheered as he splashed the girls with beer. Caught up in the excitement, Allison put Savanah in a headlock and both girls started swinging at each other's faces ferociously. The others backed away and let them fight for a while until Allison took Savanah's head and dunked her underwater, where she held her until Savanah's father screamed for Allison to let her up.

As soon as Savanah's head resurfaced, she dove at Allison with a roundhouse punch that hit her just below the eye. Jesse jumped in the pool to break it up. The "party" was over. One by one the girls began to grab their things and walk home.

Manny, Forrest, and their two girls walked back to the trailer. While the dads drank, Allison and Savanah made up as they hung out in Allison's bedroom.

"Where did you get this?" asked Savanah as she stood up from the bed and walked over to grab a locked jewelry box that was sitting on the dresser.

"Do you want to open it and see what's inside?" Allison asked. Savanah nodded. "I'll show you if you take off your underwear. Don't worry, after you do it, I will, too." Savanah stood there unsure. To ease her in, Allison said, "You can just pull it down in the front."

Savanah flashed Allison and Allison smiled. "Good enough for now." She grabbed her key and handed it to Savanah so that she could open the box.

Savanah looked inside and turned immediately to find Allison laughing on her bed. "It's empty," Savanah said.

"I didn't say anything was inside," replied Allison. "Are you a virgin?" she asked, certain she knew the answer but wanting to hear it anyway.

"What does that mean?" Savanah asked.

Allison said, "It's when a boy puts his penis in you." Allison was expecting to hear Savanah say that was gross or no way or one of the responses Allison had received from her other friends with whom she had played this "show me yours and I'll let you see the stuff in my room" game.

Savanah instead whispered, "Has it happened to you?" It hadn't, although Allison was "too cool" to admit that. Since graduating from elementary school, she had met up on several occasions with some older boys—fifteen and sixteen—at the community park. There, she became increasingly "experienced," fooling around and letting them touch her. But she had not actually had intercourse.

"Of course I have," Allison lied, "with the older guys."

Savanah paused for an uncomfortably long time and stared at Allison. She believed she knew what Allison was saying because Allison had referred to the dads at the pool as the "old guys." Seizing on the connection, Savanah pulled closer and spoke in a softer whisper. "Then I can talk to you," Savanah said. "I've never told anyone, but I also haven't ever met anyone else whose dad did that to them."

Allison's mind was immediately racing. For once, she stayed silent.

"Are they going to make us do it tonight?" Savanah asked. "My dad did it to me the first time when I was really little. I think I was seven. A few months ago, he started taking me to his friend's house by my school in North Carolina and letting Jesse do it to me, too. My dad and Jesse dress up as girls when they do it to me. They did it to Jesse's daughter the day before we drove down here. Does your dad dress up like a girl? Is he mean?"

As confident and in charge as Allison always liked to be, she was unsure how to respond. She later explained to me how she thought to herself at that point, *I can't believe I let the conversation get this far. How do I tell her now that my dad hasn't ever done anything like that to me? . . . Wait, is my dad going to do this to me? . . . Is that why Savanah is here?*

She quickly put on a strong face. Even though she had not gone through exactly what Savanah was describing, Allison did now feel a connection that she hadn't previously felt.

Her dad was down the hall laughing loudly with Forrest. She could tell they were continuing to do drugs and get drunker. One thing Allison decided was that she and Savanah were not staying there. Savanah believed she and Allison had this bond, having endured the same type of abuse. While that wasn't actually true, Allison was taking no risk that it might become true.

Allison stood up and grabbed Savanah's hand, saying "Let's get out of here. Follow me." They both walked quietly out of the bedroom and left through the back door of the trailer to walk to the community park. When they got there, they found Chad and Joe, two of the older boys Allison had made friends with, drinking.

"We want a drink," Allison said.

John handed her two Natural Lights. "Take this, too," he said, handing out two white oblong pills.

Allison tossed one of the pills in her mouth and chased it with a sip of beer before asking, "What is it?"

"Xanax bars. They get you messed up faster," Joe told her.

"Exactly what I was hoping for. Here's yours, Savanah," Allison said as Savanah took the pill from her and followed her lead.

Before they knew it, the girls had each downed four beers. Allison turned to Savanah and said, "I dare you to kiss Joe."

Joe was cool. He was a sixteen-year-old who drove a black 1988 Mustang 5.0 with no muffler that he had rebuilt himself in the garage next to his trailer. Savanah, with clearly lowered inhibitions, gazed at Joe, almost daring him to do it. Joe leaned in and grabbed Savanah's face as he pecked her on the lips.

"What was that?" Allison asked. "I said kiss him, like this." She jumped into Chad's arms and made out with him.

Allison had this way about her that made Savanah want to do anything she said. For the rest of the summer, Allison and Savanah hung out with Chad and Joe, driving around West Palm Beach and getting drunk. The girls were bound together by secrets. Savanah left Florida at the end of the summer to go back to North Carolina.

———————

Allison spent the next two years spiraling further and further into the world of sex and drugs as she watched her mom work the streets day in and day out—just as she had for Allison's entire existence. With her confident personality, Allison started to outgrow coordinating her mom's escorting schedule.

At Allison's middle school graduation party, she met a girl named Carol. The two girls spent the night drinking together. When the keg ran dry, Carol pulled out a one-hundred-dollar bill and yelled to her friend's dad, "Go get us another keg."

"Where did you get that money?" Allison asked.

"An old guy in Palm Beach. He'll let you give him a massage for two hundred dollars, cash."

"What do you have to do for it?" Allison responded.

Carol just looked at Allison, not directly answering the question. "Do you want to make money?"

Allison's eyes lit up. "Of course." She wanted nothing more in this world than to make money. Her own money. The girls partied until the early morning. When they were leaving, Allison turned to Carol and said, "Are you ready?"

"Ready for what?" Carol responded.

"To go to the guy's house to get the money," Allison reminded her.

While Carol wasn't nearly as ambitious as Allison, she needed money, too, and wasn't passing up this opportunity. Carol went back inside to use the house phone. She pulled a napkin out of her purse with a telephone number and the name Sarah Kellen written on it.

Allison stood there listening to half of the conversation. "Do you have work for me? It's not just me, I have a new girl for Jeffrey," Carol explained. "Today? Okay, four o'clock is fine."

"We're going today?" Allison asked. Carol nodded. A huge smile spread across Allison's face. "What do I have to do again? Give this guy a massage?

I've never given anyone a massage. What should I wear? Where is his house? How do we get there?"

Carol held out her hand as if to stop Allison from talking. "Don't worry, you're going to be fine. He doesn't care about what you wear. You can wear what you have on."

Allison went home and lay down in her bed, but not before setting her alarm for three p.m. When she woke up, she heard a car horn honking outside. Allison looked out the window and saw Carol waving from a yellow cab. She ran outside and jumped into the taxi, barely able to contain her excitement.

"Where am I going?" asked the cabdriver.

Carol responded, "Let me look for the address, it's El Brillo or something like that, on the island."

The cabdriver cut her off: "Let me guess, 358 El Brillo Way?"

"That's it!" Carol confirmed before the cab headed east.

Allison had never been to Palm Beach Island. The closer the cab got to the house, the stronger the butterflies grew in her stomach. The taxi parked in the driveway and Carol told the driver that she would be right back. She walked up to the house while Allison sat in the cab, as instructed. The fare was $11.69. Within seconds, a striking blonde walked up to the car with a twenty-dollar bill and handed it to the cabdriver as if this was something that she had done a million times.

Allison had been gazing up at the massive house from the back seat of the taxi. She was mesmerized. She stepped out of the cab and continued to stare. In that moment, she knew that no matter what happened in that house, she was all in. This house and this experience represented all that Allison ever wanted.

An hour later, the same cabdriver was sitting in the driveway as Allison and Carol exited the kitchen door. Unlike most of the girls leaving Epstein's house after giving him their first "massage," Allison could not have been happier. While her experience in the room was no different than the others', her reaction certainly was. "That was awesome," Allison said. Carol told her to just let her know when she wanted to go back and she would call Sarah.

Carol didn't know that Allison had already left her number with Sarah and even told Sarah that she expected a call the next day. Carol had served her purpose for Allison. Now nothing was going to stand in Allison's way.

Allison went home to her mom's trailer that night, about a mile east of where her father lived. It wasn't as roomy as her dad's, but it was closer to Jeffrey's house, and the park was full of childhood friends that Allison had already targeted in her mind as "masseuses" for Jeffrey. Plus, Allison had left her mother's telephone number for Sarah, knowing that her dad might get suspicious of a call from an adult-sounding voice.

When Allison walked into her mom's place, her mom was sitting at the kitchen counter. Allison pulled up a chair next to her and pulled out four folded fifty-dollar bills from her jean shorts pocket and began counting. Her mom took a long drag from her cigarette and laid it down on the ashtray before asking, "Where did you get that?"

Allison smiled. "I do my own thing now."

Allison walked to her bedroom. She lay on her bed, staring at the ceiling, thinking just how easy it had been to make this money and how there was so much more where that came from. Her mom had brought her up in a very unorthodox way, but it had prepared her exactly for this.

Allison just needed to bring Jeffrey one girl and she would be off to a good start. It had to be someone who wouldn't chicken out—a sure thing. Someone she could bring immediately to prove to Jeffrey that she was a better recruiter than anyone else. She racked her brain, going through everyone she'd grown up with. It had to be somebody who needed money. It had to be someone who wasn't going to think that going over to some old man's house to "massage" him was too crazy or scary. It needed to be someone who had already experienced pain. Someone who might actually see this strange experience as a good escape from ordinary life.

"I wonder what happened to Savanah," she thought. Allison hadn't seen the girl in more than a year. The last she heard, Savanah's father, Forrest, had died. There was actually suspicion that he had been killed, but that was probably just a drunk story Allison's dad had told her. She did remember that her dad said the funeral was in Florida, and that he had gone.

Allison picked up the phone. "Dad, remember your friend Forrest? You went to his funeral, right? Where is Savanah?" Her dad explained that Savanah had been arrested and was now in summer school at the Pace Center for Girls, a local center for troubled kids. After school the next day, Allison took a cab to Pace and waited for her old friend to show up.

Allison stood behind a tree watching as kids filed down the stairs of a bus. When she saw Savanah, she ran at her at full speed. Savanah lifted her head to see this flash coming out of the corner of her eye. Before she could really react, Allison had her in a bear hug and was spinning her in circles. "What's up, bitch? It's been a long time." Both girls were so excited to see each other, they were jumping up and down.

"What are you doing here?" Savanah asked.

"Look, I'm not going to get mad at you for not telling me you moved back to Florida or for not tracking me down, but I got us all set up. Wanna make two hundred dollars? Meet me at Lakeside at ten a.m. tomorrow and be excited." Lakeside was a trailer park that both girls knew well.

Allison called Sarah as soon as she left Savanah. She told Sarah that she was ready to work again in an hour. Sarah told her there was an opening and to come over. That afternoon, when Jeffrey was on the massage table and instructed her to remove her panties, Allison did so without pause. "I have someone new for you tomorrow morning."

Jeffrey opened his eyes and smiled at Allison. "Very good. Now pinch my nipples," he said as he closed his eyes again.

The next morning, Allison was at Lakeside in a taxi thirty minutes early, at 9:30 a.m. So was Savanah. "Get in, you're about to have the time of your life," Allison told her. She talked it up the entire ride. Savanah was about as excited as she could be, although with her usual emotionless face. You could never tell how Savanah was feeling by looking at her. She was almost a zombie going through life. But if Allison said to do it, then she would never turn it down.

Allison showed herself up the stairs and into the bedroom, with Savanah following closely behind. It all happened in such a hurry; Savanah didn't have time to think, much less ask any questions. Allison walked into the bedroom and within seconds had stripped completely naked and told Savanah to do the same.

When Jeffrey emerged from the shower and walked toward the massage table, there were two naked fourteen-year-old children waiting to rub him down. Allison led the way and Savanah followed suit. While Jeffrey was pressing a vibrator down on Allison, he was commanding Savanah to pinch his nipples harder. No matter how hard Savanah squeezed, it wasn't hard enough. He kept telling her over and over again to keep squeezing harder. Before Jeffrey finished, he was irritated. Savanah was pinching as hard as she possibly could and it still wasn't enough.

Jeffrey wiped himself with a towel and hopped up from the massage table. "Your money is on the table," he said as he walked toward the dresser.

"See you tomorrow," Allison said arrogantly. She grabbed both stacks of money, handing one to Savanah. The girls got dressed and Allison led the way back down the stairs and out the door.

This was the last time Allison would see Savanah for a long time. Jeffrey typically only paid one finder's fee for the first time a new girl was brought, so Savanah didn't have much of a purpose for Allison after that day.

From that point forward, if Jeffrey was in town, Allison was there, either with a new young girl in tow or, on the occasion when she couldn't find anyone, by herself. Allison didn't have the patience for massage. When she went alone, she would sit in front of Jeffrey with her legs spread so that he could read the morning newspaper while looking over to catch a glimpse of her straddled in front of him. In her mind, it was the same two hundred dollars. She didn't think that she needed to pretend to be a masseuse to earn it. She just gave him what he wanted, whatever that might be on any given day.

As the years went on, Allison stayed the course. She was on call until Jeffrey was arrested. Jeffrey called her himself and told her the news. "You have nothing to worry about," Allison told him, "thank you for everything. You have always been good to me. If I can help, I will."

By the time I learned Allison's story, I had already spoken with many victims. Allison wasn't the first to say that her time with Jeffrey wasn't so bad. But she was the first to give such a glowing testament to his positive contribution to her life.

Allison thrived off of what Jeffrey Epstein did to her. For years, she remained in the sex industry and credited Epstein with catapulting both her confidence and her "career." She was proud of the woman she had become and she always appreciated the role Epstein played in her life.

But then there was Savanah. Like Allison, Savanah didn't get involved in the criminal investigation or any of the civil lawsuits. But unlike Allison, she felt severely damaged by this experience. At twenty-seven years old, she was sitting on the couch with her husband, breastfeeding her newborn for the very first time, when she started to cry uncontrollably. As her child latched down on her nipple, the only thought running through her mind was Epstein repeating "Pinch my nipples" and her overwhelming feeling of inadequacy. Savanah couldn't do it. She couldn't breastfeed her son. The flashback from that day began playing over and over in her mind. Savanah was able to put the incestual abuse by her father behind her, but one morning at Jeffrey's house was destroying her ability to nurture her child.

# THIRTEEN

# THE CIRCLE

ONE MAJOR ASPECT OF PUTTING the case together was understanding the perspectives of the different victims. Their stories were sure to be powerful at any trial or any future prosecution of Jeffrey Epstein. But he knew the victims' stories and had plotted his attack on them already. We needed other, more neutral witnesses to tell us what they knew about Jeffrey Epstein. Speaking with those witnesses would coincidentally have the effect of causing Epstein's social and business world to fold in on him the way he constantly tried to do to anyone who opposed or tried to expose him. Deposing or taking statements from Epstein's closest friends and associates would be my next focus.

While Jeffrey Epstein was flagrantly engaging in illegal sex with minors, abetted by many assistants and staff, surely not all of his friends or acquaintances were aware. But at the same time, his acquaintances, whether involved or not, were likely at least a bit suspicious that something unusual was going on. It seemed that every second of every day Epstein was either engaging in sex or encouraging his victims to bring him new prey. How big was the enterprise? How many victims were there? Who was involved? Which witnesses would be brave enough to come forward and tell the truth?

To answer these questions, I began seeking information in summer

2009 from many of Epstein's onetime reportedly close friends, including Donald Trump; David Copperfield, the magician; Leslie Wexner, owner of Victoria's Secret and the Limited, among other enterprises; modeling agent Jean-Luc Brunel; hedge fund mogul Glenn Dubin; Bill Clinton; and director-producer Paula Heil Fisher; as well as Epstein's assistant Sarah Kellen and his girlfriend Ghislaine Maxwell.

The first of Epstein's powerful friends to answer our subpoena in a meaningful way was Donald Trump. We served him in 2009 in the Trump Tower in New York City. His lawyer, Alan Garten, called in response to tell me that while Mr. Trump would appear for a formal deposition, it was not necessary. He would make Mr. Trump available for me to interview within the next few days.

True to his word, we set up a time to talk by telephone that week. Mr. Trump called me at exactly the time he was supposed to, said that he'd heard I had questions about Jeffrey Epstein, and asked me how he could help. Mr. Trump explained that he was a business acquaintance of Mr. Epstein's from many years earlier. He said that the two of them had attended many of the same events and parties, but that he was not as close with Epstein as the media had made it seem. I reminded Mr. Trump that he had been quoted in a 2002 *New York* magazine article by Landon Thomas Jr. stating, "I've known Jeff for fifteen years. Terrific guy. He's a lot of fun to be with. It is even said that he likes beautiful women as much as I do, and many of them are on the younger side. No doubt about it—Jeffrey enjoys his social life."

Mr. Trump explained that when that article was being written, Epstein had called him and explained that he needed people to say nice things, so he asked Trump if he would attribute the quote—written by Jeff himself—as his own words. Seeing nothing wrong with that and having been asked for the favor long before the allegations of Epstein's abuse had surfaced, Trump agreed.

Trump did say that he always saw Epstein around younger girls, but to his knowledge, none were underage. He said Jeffrey was not secretive about his lifestyle, and whether it was at a party, a private event, or a public event, there were always multiple young women at Epstein's side. I asked about a rumor I had heard that Mr. Trump had expelled Epstein from the Mar-a-Lago Club for trying to take home a member's fifteen-year-old daughter. He paused before saying that something along those lines happened but that he could not recall the exact details and instead referred me to his Mar-a-Lago manager, Bernd Lembcke. (Mr. Lembcke would neither confirm nor deny the rumor.)

Mr. Trump explained that he had not spoken with Mr. Epstein in years. The last time he remembered seeing Epstein personally was when he had gone to Epstein's house in Palm Beach one day for a business meeting before Epstein's legal troubles came to light. Mr. Trump looked outside and saw young women, who Epstein explained were part of a mentoring-type program that he was involved in, which Mr. Trump thought was a bit odd. He quickly said, "The guy was always strange. Even back when I ran into him more, I never really liked him." He then gave me names of some other people that would know Epstein's propensities better, so I jotted down the information to follow up. Before I finished the interview, Mr. Trump told me to say hi to his lovely daughter Ivanka, who had apparently just walked in the room. He then talked about her for a few seconds before saying I could give him a call anytime and he would try to answer my questions if I came across anything else of interest.

In 2015, I was working a class action case on behalf of sixty-five members of one of Trump's golf clubs in Palm Beach against the Trump Organization. That April, I flew to New York to take Donald Trump's deposition at the Trump Tower. At the end of his deposition, I reminded him of our 2009 conversation regarding Jeffrey Epstein and asked if we could discuss it again. We went to his office and talked. He framed most of the information he had about potentially relevant leads as rumors that he had heard over the years. Still, his rumors were helpful. He maintained that his relationship with Epstein was primarily centered on business, which, because of the circles in which they traveled, resulted in them running into each other at social gatherings on occasion.

The conversation turned to the class action case that we were there to talk about and why it should be resolved. Before we left, he yelled to his son Eric to settle the case. Eric should have listened to his father but didn't—that case went to trial in August 2016 and we won.

Over the next few years, I spoke to several other witnesses who told us that they had been introduced by Jeffrey Epstein to Donald Trump. Some had seen him at Epstein's office, others at one of Epstein's homes, at parties or social events, and even on Epstein's plane. In fact, Epstein bragged to certain young women in his life about how he had bailed Trump out of bankruptcy and how Trump was indebted to him. None of them knew whether there was any truth to that claim, but given Epstein's life it seemed believable to them.

In 2019, I saw video from 1992 of Epstein and Trump together, suggesting that Epstein and Trump were closer social friends than I had been made to understand during my discussions with Trump. However, whether Trump was ever a closer friend than he let on was really of no concern to me. None of the people I interviewed who had met Trump through Epstein ever claimed that Trump had engaged in any improper sexual activity at all, nor did they say that he was around when minors were present. More important, he was one of the only people who didn't resist talking with me about Epstein and instead provided helpful, often corroborating, information (couched as rumors) that I used to focus my investigation on some of the people "rumored" to have more knowledge.

---

Leslie Wexner, owner of the Limited Brand and Victoria's Secret, was by all credible accounts Jeffrey Epstein's mentor, friend, and the source of Epstein's wealth. My sources had told me that Wexner held the key to knowing exactly who Epstein was, who protected him, and what his weaknesses were. By any objective measure, their mysterious relationship was an odd one.

They met through a mutual friend, insurance mogul Bob Meister, in the mid-1980s. At the time, Epstein—a college dropout from Brooklyn, who had been fired from his job as a math teacher at the Dalton School in New York in 1976, and left a five-year stint at Bear Stearns in 1981 after an

SEC insider-trading investigation—was rumored to be a high-end financial bounty hunter, tasked with recovering money stolen from the government and wealthy individuals. There were also whispers that he was associated with the CIA, Mossad, or another intelligence agency. Whatever Jeffrey Epstein was or was not before he met Les Wexner, Wexner was intrigued.

Before long, Wexner turned the management of his billion-dollar fortune over to Epstein. Wexner even gave Epstein his eight-story town house at 9 East Seventy-First Street on New York's Upper East Side. While Epstein claimed J. Epstein & Company, the wealth management company he founded after leaving Bear Stearns, managed the fortunes of clients with net worths that were each more than a billion dollars, he never left his fingerprints on any public trades, which makes this doubtful. The only publicly known client of J. Epstein & Company was Les Wexner.

Until at least 2006, Epstein managed and controlled Wexner's finances and personal life. Epstein would also brag that he scouted models for Victoria's Secret. There was some truth to that, in the sense that Jeffrey used his connection to Wexner to enhance the credibility of his model scout pickup line in order to grope models. (In October 2014, we uncovered a police report from Santa Monica, California, alleging that Epstein posed as a scout in order to lure an aspiring actress to his hotel room and sexually "manhandle" her. Nothing ever came of that report.)

The deposition of Wexner was a big pressure point for Epstein, and I knew it.

We served someone affiliated with Wexner with a subpoena for Wexner's deposition outside his office in New Albany, Ohio, in the summer of 2009. Within an hour I received a call from his New York attorney, Stan Arkin, who was screaming into the phone with every other word an expletive because he didn't want his client dragged into this case. This was the exact opposite response to the one I received from Trump's lawyer. Arkin complained about some technical deficiency with the subpoena. (David Copperfield's attorney had done the same thing after I served Copperfield a subpoena outside one of his magic shows in Las Vegas; regrettably we never were able to depose Copperfield due to a number of legal and logistical roadblocks.) I am not sure that I ever understood what Arkin thought the problem was because all that I heard was f***, f***, f***. Either way, by the end of that call he set a time to come meet me and other lawyers representing some of the victims in Florida. It was obvious I had hit a nerve.

Once in Florida, Wexner's lawyers made it clear that Wexner intended to avoid having his deposition taken at all costs. Whatever his relationship had been with Epstein, a deposition was going to be embarrassing. He contended to have been an Epstein victim from whom Epstein stole hundreds of millions of dollars and offered to provide a road map to Epstein's money if we ever needed to execute a judgment. After hours of talking, Wexner's lawyers were effective in convincing the other lawyers representing plaintiffs against Epstein that Wexner's help behind the scenes would be of greater benefit than his testimony. We reluctantly withdrew the deposition subpoena in exchange for Wexner's promise to help. This was a bad deal for us. I knew it at the time, but figured we had found a pressure point and would come back if we needed to.

———————

During that summer, another witness was coming into focus as perhaps the most important of all: Ghislaine Maxwell. There was a wealth of publicly available information regarding the mysterious death of her well-known, wealthy father, Robert Maxwell, who drowned after "falling" from his mega-yacht, the *Lady Ghislaine*, in November 1991. Robert Maxwell was known to have links to many international intelligence organizations, including MI6, the KGB, and Mossad. In fact, at least six heads of Mossad attended his funeral in Israel, and the eulogy was given by Israeli president Chaim Herzog. The most popularly reported theories relating to Robert Maxwell's death are either that he committed suicide that night, or that his involvement as a superspy for Mossad got him murdered. Ultimately, his death was ruled an accident. (These suspicions are strikingly similar to those surrounding Epstein's death. Coincidence?)

Regardless, whether Epstein's connection to Ghislaine Maxwell had anything to do with Epstein's rumored intelligence agency affiliation, she was crucial to understanding his sexual deviancy. Ghislaine was the one woman who, by all appearances, Epstein treated as his equal. They had typically presented themselves as boyfriend and girlfriend; sometimes she even referred to him privately as her husband. They were a strange, inseparable pair.

An elegant woman with a British accent, Ghislaine had short dark hair and captivating, warm facial features. She was, and I am sure still is, a chameleon, able to blend in with high and low society as it suits her. She could sit at a dinner table having the most sophisticated conversation with a brilliant scientist and an hour later attend a burlesque show and make the raunchiest joke in the aisle. Everyone described her as fun, funny, and crass—as open-minded as she was intelligent. Her circle in London included the highest-powered businessmen and members of the British royal family. But after losing her father, Ghislaine was heartbroken. She was also broke after it was learned that her father had stolen nearly $900 million from employee pension funds—one of the largest frauds of its kind. Humiliated, Ghislaine fled London for the United States soon thereafter. Because her media tycoon father had been connected to the world's most powerful people, she grew up with an impressive list of friends. Later, she expanded on the Rolodex her father created for her, becoming close with the likes of Prince Andrew and President Bill Clinton.

To fully appreciate Ghislaine's importance to Epstein, some background is necessary. At the height of their relationship, Maxwell had everything that Epstein needed, and he had everything she wanted. She had connections; he had money. By all public appearances and witness accounts, they were inseparable for almost two decades. They slept in the same bed and traveled together on private planes all over the world.

By the summer of 2009, when I was deciding who to subpoena, I had also been contacted by a former New York City police officer who had spent significant time researching and investigating Jeffrey Epstein and his friends.

The former police officer spent most of the time stressing how important Ghislaine was. This was no surprise, of course. During the Palm Beach Police Department's criminal investigation of Epstein in 2005, her name was mentioned as someone the police wanted to speak with. From the messages that had been confiscated in the infamous trash pulls, we learned that callers were leaving messages for Maxwell as if she lived at the house during a time when high school girls were regularly being shuttled there. As soon as the criminal investigation began, however, she became a ghost. She completely distanced herself from Epstein. This looked like someone with a guilty conscience; even more reason to track her down. But she had her connections and Epstein's financial resources, so she was able to make herself difficult to locate.

We learned through other sources that she was a close friend of Bill Clinton's. If that was true, then surely she would attend the 2009 Clinton Global Initiative Annual Meeting at the Sheraton New York Hotel and Towers. We hired investigators to get into the event and serve her with a subpoena for her deposition, which they did. To say she was upset about being publicly served at this function is an understatement. She had a profound determination to avoid her deposition, both before and after being served. Unlike in most cases, when Epstein was involved, serving witnesses with subpoenas didn't mean they would acquiesce to having a deposition taken. It just meant new strategies to avoid the deposition would begin. And such was the case with Ghislaine.

---

While wrangling with Ghislaine over setting a date for her testimony, we continued finding and serving other members of Epstein's inner circle. Another character with valuable information for our case who could not deny his long-standing relationship with Epstein was Jean-Luc Brunel, a model scout and owner of Karin Models, which later became the MC$^2$ modeling agency. Jean-Luc was considered one of the most talented scouts in the business—he had discovered models such as Christy Turlington, Sharon Stone, and Milla Jovovich. But he also was rumored to use cocaine heavily and had a history of soliciting sex with the talent. He had been banned from his modeling agency in Europe for being included in the scandalous 1999 BBC *MacIntyre Undercover* report, an investigation into modeling agency owners who preyed on teenage girls. Jean-Luc was revealed as one of the most egregious perpetrators of the bunch.

After the release of the devastating report, a group of agency owners retreated to the Caribbean for a meeting to figure out how to deal with it. Jean-Luc allegedly showed up at this crisis management meeting with—yes, you guessed it—a teenage model. The reaction from his colleagues was by all accounts utter incredulity.

Though he still had an unusual eye for talent, after the scandal he had little money, and without money he had no way to pursue his passion. Enter Jeffrey Epstein. Jean-Luc had something that Epstein wanted, and Epstein had something that Jean-Luc needed. The symbiosis that made Epstein effective was once again in play.

Ghislaine met Jean-Luc in the 1980s when she was working with her father. She later introduced Jean-Luc to Epstein in New York. It was a match made in some sort of messed-up heaven. Epstein eventually agreed to fund Jean-Luc's new modeling agency, and Jean-Luc continued to do what he always did: find new girls. The Palm Beach police captured a message memorializing the naming of $MC^2$ Model Management in the trash pull conducted at the house. The agency was named to give credit to Epstein as being the Wizard of Oz behind the curtain—E (Epstein) = $MC^2$.

We tracked down Jean-Luc in New York City with the help of other $MC^2$ employees who had informed us that the agency brought many young foreign girls into the United States. No surprise to us, most were housed at 301 East Sixty-Sixth Street, in the apartments owned by Dara Partners, a company co-owned by Mark Epstein, who rented eight to ten units to his brother, Jeffrey. Employees of $MC^2$ told us they were paid to help obtain visas for the young girls living in these apartments. Those employees later quit after learning that the work some of the girls were doing was not limited to modeling.

$MC^2$ employees told me where I could find Jean-Luc in New York City to serve him with a subpoena. Sure enough, Jean-Luc was hailing a taxi, right where his employees told us he would be, when our investigator approached him. When the investigator attempted to introduce himself, Jean-Luc turned around and put his hands behind his back for handcuffing, believing he was being arrested. Our investigator spun him back around, announcing, "You aren't being arrested. Just take this subpoena." Jean-Luc, too, would eventually wiggle out from his deposition date, but he was also under Jeffrey's control so we should have seen that coming.

---

In our continuing efforts to obtain hard evidence, we also served subpoenas on Epstein's current and former employees. Up until this point, the only documentary evidence that we had was from the trash pulls conducted by the Palm Beach Police Department in March, April, June, July, September, and October 2005. Those in Epstein's inner circle were unbelievably loyal. So loyal that almost everyone who had worked for him showed up at their depositions with an attorney paid for by Epstein, including Epstein's former housekeeper Juan Alessi and his wife, Maria Alessi; housekeeper Louella Rabuyo; pilots Dave Rodgers, Larry Morrison, Larry Visoski, and of course Sarah Kellen and Nadia Marcinkova.

In fact, Sarah Kellen and all of Epstein's pilots were represented by Bruce Reinhart—a lawyer who had been a supervisor at the U.S. Attorney's Office in the Southern District of Florida when Epstein's lawyers were negotiating his non-prosecution plea agreement. Reinhart left his government post in October 2007 and opened up his law firm at the same address that would later house Jeffrey Epstein's Florida Science Foundation.

The depositions of the pilots were important because they could identify the individuals who flew on Epstein's different airplanes with him. The individuals on the flights could have been witnesses or they could have been victims. Regardless, the pilots had powerful information that could incriminate their boss.

This was particularly true of Larry Visoski, who, despite having worked for and known Epstein for nearly two decades, claimed to have no idea that Epstein had placed various boats, properties, and cars in Visoski's name. In fact, Visoski maintained he had no idea what Epstein did for a living, how he made his money, what type of business Epstein conducted, or even the circumstances surrounding the assets that were placed in Visoski's name. This know-nothing testimony was capped by the fact that Larry Visoski's wife was also employed by Epstein and yet he claimed not to know what she did during her employment. Visoski came across as someone who would have literally gone down with the plane for Jeffrey Epstein.

All of Epstein's pilots were subpoenaed to appear for deposition on two consecutive days, and I requested that each bring all of his flight manifests to his deposition. Since none of these employees had thus far showed up with the documents we'd requested, I didn't expect much. But, to my great surprise and satisfaction, Dave Rodgers complied.

Rodgers brought a passenger manifest with him that listed the travelers on each of the flights that he piloted from 1995 to 2007. The flight logs confirmed many of our suspicions, including the veracity of key allegations against Epstein made by Jane Doe 102.

The flight logs made it clear that Epstein was always flying with a loyal crew consisting primarily of young women and girls, and many times also with passengers who were powerful, wealthy, and connected businessmen, industry leaders, and political figures. According to the logs, Bill Clinton had flown on more than twenty flights with Jeffrey Epstein and Ghislaine Maxwell. We finally had our hands on a great piece of previously unavailable evidence. Evidence that gave us insight into Jeffrey Epstein's habits—where and with whom he frequently traveled.

---

In July 2009, Jeffrey Epstein was released from "jail" and placed on house arrest in his mansion located at 358 El Brillo Way in Palm Beach. I knew this was going to make our job harder, especially coupled with a personal injury I was soon dealing with. On August 28, 2009, I had emergency back surgery after herniating a disk and fracturing several vertebrae in my back during a flag football game. This was when I realized at the ripe age of thirty-three that getting old sucks. Even catching footballs with a bunch of lawyers was now too much for me.

For the brief period while I was laid up, the cases went on without me. On September 2, 2009, I missed out on a deposition of Epstein taken by Spencer Kuvin, an attorney representing another victim. A videotape of the deposition was released and showed up in the press and online almost immediately. Seconds after Epstein had been sworn in as a witness, Kuvin's first question was "Is it true, sir, that you have what has been described as an egg-shaped penis?" There *was* a description in one of the police reports by a fourteen-year-old victim of Epstein's genitals as being "egg shaped," but Spencer didn't provide that or any other predicate for his question. I didn't really miss much because Epstein stood up and left the room immediately after that one question. More entertaining, and probably more valuable than the deposition itself was the *Opie and Anthony* radio show where the hosts poked fun at the one-question deposition. It's definitely worth a listen.

Back in the real world, the doctor told me not to work for at least two weeks. I followed his instructions for about four days. After months trying to serve Jeffrey Epstein's brother, Mark Epstein, with a subpoena for his deposition, we finally had done so and I was not going to miss it just because I was recovering. I was actually pretty impressed with the creativity of our process server. He pulled his car up very close to Mark Epstein's car outside Mark's New York apartment. He then told the doorman that he had hit the car, so the doorman went to notify Mark. When Mark came outside to see the "damage," he was handed the subpoena, and we were in business.

On September 21, 2009, I flew into LaGuardia Airport in New York with no bags, still unable to carry anything because of the surgery. Russ Adler flew up separately and met me at the deposition with all the materials I needed.

Before we sat down in the deposition, Mark Epstein's lawyer Mark Cohen took me into the hallway to tell me how upset Mark was that he was being dragged into this case, and warned me not to ask family-related questions. During the deposition, Mark never smiled. He acted as if I were there trying to put *him* in jail. In typical fashion for witnesses under Jeffrey Epstein's control, Mark had a case of amnesia and could not remember the simplest of things.

He didn't remember when he saw his brother last or how many times he had been on the airplane or anything about his brother's business success. He knew that his brother had accumulated tremendous wealth and assets over the years yet gave the impression that it was through some unknown magic trick. Maybe David Copperfield made the money appear out of nowhere. The only thing Mark did remember was flying on Epstein's plane with Donald Trump, although even that description was suspiciously vague. While Mark had the chance to help, he didn't. We would need to look elsewhere.

# FOURTEEN

# THE HOLY GRAIL

EPSTEIN'S MANEUVERS TO OBSTRUCT MY efforts to infiltrate his clan could not save him forever. On August 7, 2009, I took the deposition of Alfredo Rodriguez, one of the former butlers at Epstein's Palm Beach property. Alfredo was the only person from the Epstein camp who did not either invoke the Fifth Amendment or show up with a lawyer paid for by Epstein. This was our first real opportunity to obtain truthful information from an insider.

In his deposition, he told us that during the couple of years—2004 and 2005—he worked at Epstein's house in Palm Beach, underage girls came to the residence every day Epstein was there. Rodriguez testified that the activity upstairs involved sex toys and devices of various kinds that were found in the room after Epstein received his massages. Also noteworthy, Alfredo observed that Epstein did not hide his sexual activities from his houseguests.

One houseguest that Alfredo named in particular was Alan Dershowitz, whom Rodriguez said was Epstein's personal friend. He testified that Dershowitz would sit by the pool, sipping wine and reading books or stay inside while the local Palm Beach girls were upstairs servicing Epstein. That Epstein did not suspend his sexual abuse of girls when Dershowitz was in the house struck me as important. Epstein's routine was so fundamental in his life that he refused to break from it even when the person he would eventually employ as his criminal defense attorney was around. I now knew that if we could identify the people who were not on Epstein's payroll—his traveling companions, close friends, and houseguests—we would then have credible witnesses to strengthen our cases and destroy Epstein's defenses.

Prior to Rodriguez's deposition, I read in one of the investigative police reports that he had claimed to have a list of the underage girls who had been to the house. I understood that despite having been subpoenaed to produce that information to the grand jury during the 2006 criminal investigation, Rodriguez failed to produce the document. So during his deposition I hoped to determine if this list was real. When asked, he confirmed that Ghislaine Maxwell did, in fact, keep typed lists on her computer of the names of girls who would come and give massages. Alfredo was eventually fired from the job by Ghislaine. But before he left, he told us, he printed the lists from Maxwell's computer, which included all of the people in Epstein and Maxwell's Rolodex as well as the names and telephone numbers of the girls who frequently visited the Palm Beach house. Rodriguez claimed that he didn't have it anymore. I sensed he was lying.

When we left Alfredo's deposition, I handed him my business card with my cell phone number on it and told him to call me if he remembered anything else. Sure enough, a day later, I got a call on my cell phone. The voice on the other end said, "This is Alfredo. I have something for you. It is what you were asking about, but much better. It is the Holy Grail." I thought this important piece of evidence was just going to fall into my lap. Boy, was I wrong.

Alfredo explained, "The book that I printed from Ms. Maxwell's computer? I have it." I told him that was great, I would leave the office immediately to get it from him, wherever he was. As I started to thank him, he said, "Bring fifty thousand dollars. Cash."

Alfredo looked like a butler. He talked like a butler. He had this mysterious, raspy, soft voice as if he was always talking in a whisper and everything he said was either a secret or confirmation that he was keeping one. This particular conversation was no different.

I actually thought that he was joking about the money demand, so I laughed and asked him again where he was so that I could come and pick up the Holy Grail. He jumped back in. "It's the golden ticket. Everything you will ever need. Epstein and Maxwell's little black book. It contains the names of many underage girls and others who are involved. You don't understand how big this is." Realizing he was serious, and not wanting to lose my shot at the book, I told him I would get back to him.

As soon as I hung up, I went to find my investigator Mike Fisten. I told Mike everything that Alfredo had just said. Mike looked at me like I was crazy. He had been a homicide detective for twenty years and this ransom for evidence was a first even for him. He had his doubts about the offer. Nonetheless, I called Alfredo back with Mike on the line and told him I was thinking about what he'd said. I asked him why he thought anyone had to pay for information that was subpoenaed by a criminal grand jury, and which we had also subpoenaed for his civil deposition. I reminded him that he had failed to produce it earlier, as required by law, and now was trying to sell it for $50,000, which was a crime.

Alfredo, in that covert, slow drawl said, "There are two reasons. First, when I was fired, I thought they would kill me. This was my insurance policy. If I ever disappeared, my wife would know it was Ghislaine and Jeffrey. Second, at this point, it is my property. I own it. It has value. It would be like me having a Mercedes-Benz. Just because you asked for it by subpoena, you think that I should hand it over to you."

I said, "The Mercedes-Benz example doesn't work. And if anyone was going to die right now, it would probably be me, not you." Mike Fisten was looking at me like I was out of my mind. He wanted me to tell Alfredo we were paying him and then just show up and take it. That idea seemed fraught with problems.

Alfredo told me to meet him in Miami and that I would have to first open my trunk and show him the money. No lie, he was describing a scene out of some old mobster movie.

Mike and I talked about how to do this. We decided that we would tell Alfredo to meet us at a restaurant and show up before Alfredo got there.

Mike would sit in one booth and I would sit in another close enough that Mike could record the conversation in a public place. If Alfredo didn't agree to produce the document without any payment, we could turn the whole thing over to law enforcement. I did some research to confirm that we could legally record the conversation, which we could do so long as we were in a place where Alfredo didn't have a reasonable expectation of privacy. I called Alfredo back and told him where he could meet me. He rightly didn't believe that I could have come up with the cash so fast, so he wanted to postpone the meeting until I could prove I had the cash. His condition was nonnegotiable.

The next day I contacted the FBI, asking, "Hypothetically speaking, if someone was served with a federal subpoena in both a criminal case and a civil case and they had valuable information that they failed to deliver, and later they told me that they had it all along but would only turn it over if they were paid fifty thousand dollars in cash, would you be interested?" I was made to repeat this to an assistant U.S. attorney, who said this sounded like an obstruction of justice.

I didn't tell the prosecutor the identity of the person who claimed to have the information, and I didn't give her any hints. I just wanted to be sure the office was going to be interested in prosecuting the case if I did this. I wanted the evidence, but I also didn't want to get Alfredo in trouble if I could avoid it. This guy was fired from his job with Epstein for calling the police when a sixteen-year-old showed up at the house to collect her money and he mistakenly reported her car in the driveway. The police showed up and he told the officer, who was already suspicious of this little girl in the driveway, that girls like that were coming to the house regularly.

Everyone from Epstein's former friends to witnesses was reluctant to give us any honest or relevant information. Alfredo was the first person who had shown up and testified to what everyone knew was just the truth.

Looking for ways to avoid turning Alfredo in, I went to the white-collar criminal defense attorney at RRA, Marc Nurik, and told him the entire story. He thought we should hire an outside attorney—preferably a former

U.S. attorney—to provide an opinion defining our legal options. We hired Kendall Coffey.

Kendall was the U.S. attorney for the Southern District of Florida who had famously prosecuted one of the most notorious drug-trafficking charges of all time against Willie Falcon and Sal Magluta. The evidence in that case was overwhelming, yet the jury returned a not-guilty verdict. Rumor was that, in an apparent effort to drown his sorrows, Kendall went out to a strip club, drank too much, and bit a stripper. Weeks later, he found out that the jury had been bought. The foreman had been paid $500,000 to influence the verdict. It didn't matter at that point that Kendall should have won the case; now he was in trouble for the stripper incident. Regardless of these bizarre events, he was now running a well-respected law firm in Miami and fit all the criteria needed to deal with our situation.

I told Kendall the details and he agreed to turn around an opinion letter within a day or two. It was long, but the letter basically informed me that I could meet with Alfredo to continue to persuade him to do the right thing, but that I could not pay him, which, of course, I already knew. The conclusion was that I did not have to go to the authorities at this moment, but could meet with Alfredo to try to get him to do the right thing and turn over the evidence.

I drove to Miami with Mike and made calls to Alfredo on the way to arrange the meeting. At the last minute, Alfredo changed the location from the restaurant to his house. We would no longer be able to record him there, and I didn't trust him at this point—least of all at his own home—so we turned around and went back to Fort Lauderdale. I called the U.S. Attorney's Office again, this time without conferring with anyone from RRA.

I met the next day with the FBI and continued to work with them through controlled telephone calls to Alfredo, setting him up on the obstruction of justice charge. I was torn. I liked Alfredo. I actually felt sorry for him.

After he was fired by Epstein, Alfredo had tried to get jobs with other wealthy people, but was unable to for two reasons. First, he had apparently violated the number one rule of being a butler by revealing what was going on inside the house, even though he felt he was doing the right thing. And second, he had worked for a man who was a now-notorious sexual predator.

The combination made Alfredo unemployable. He saw the sale of this phone journal as his only means of survival. He had also given us the most helpful information in the case even before turning over what he called the Holy Grail. He was a good man who did the right thing. Mostly. But now it looked as if he'd gone past that point and left me with no option.

I lost a lot of sleep due to being a confidential informant against Alfredo. After I made a few calls that were recorded by the FBI, the case against him was so strong that there was really nothing else that the prosecutors needed. The only thing left was for me to set up the purchase of the documents. I went up to the FBI's West Palm Beach office to make that phone call. I was instructed to tell Alfredo that I was having someone named Paul meet him at a hotel in Miami. I had two agents sitting next to me reminding me to keep it a short conversation and only set up the buy.

Even with those very strict instructions, I gave Alfredo one more chance to do the right thing. I told him that I had the cash, but I didn't do these kinds of things, so I was sending my fixer, who did. To the dismay of the FBI, instead of just telling Alfredo to go to the hotel, I told him again not to commit this crime. Alfredo responded with something along the lines of "I know that this is a federal crime, but you should look at this like you are helping put my daughter through college." He went on for minutes explaining how he was so determined to do this despite knowing it was a crime.

I didn't sleep for one second that night. Still, I felt my conscience was clear because I had tried so many times to stop him from going down this road.

The next day, Alfredo met "Paul"—who wasn't the law firm employee that I had described but was instead an undercover FBI agent. I had spent twenty or more hours cultivating this relationship with Alfredo and helping the government get this "Holy Grail." The FBI told me that the mission was successful, so I called AUSA Marie Villafaña to get a copy of the document. She told me that not only could I not have it, but she didn't think that the government was ever going to turn it over to me. Major plot twist. It never occurred to me that I had needed to extract a specific agreement from the government to share a copy of something I already had a right to see.

I devised a different plan. Alfredo was being charged with obstruction of justice, so we served a subpoena on his criminal defense attorney, Dave Brannon, requesting a copy of the phone journal. Brannon complied on the same day that the subpoena was served. It is pretty ironic that I had worked so hard and risked so much for the government, yet still I had to get the document from Alfredo. In fact, he was more cooperative and reliable even in custody than the government ever was on anything.

This document really was the Holy Grail. It was ninety-seven pages of typed names and phone numbers, including nearly one hundred victims of sexual abuse listed in the document under the heading "Massage," with certain designated geographical locations including Florida, New Mexico, New York, and Paris. Many of my clients and their telephone numbers were listed—including those of Jean-Luc Brunel, Ghislaine Maxwell, Donald Trump, Les Wexner, and Alan Dershowitz.

In addition, as he had promised me, Alfredo had circled the names of others who he claimed were involved with or had knowledge of the sexual molestation operation. I wasn't in the room when the FBI takedown occurred, so I am not sure to this day of the discussion they had deciphering Alfredo's handwritten marks on the document. But several of the names of those I had suspected and whom I had subpoenaed months prior were circled.

Alfredo Rodriguez pleaded guilty to obstruction of justice and was freed on bail. Coincidentally, Alfredo's case was in front of Judge Marra—the same judge presiding over the still pending Crime Victims' Rights Act case that I had filed back in 2008. Judge Marra entered an eighteen-month suspended sentence after Alfredo promised to cooperate with the government. Alfredo took this court document showing his guilty plea, put it in the front seat of his truck, and drove toward Miami. Before arriving at his house, he stopped at an apartment complex.

Unfortunately for Alfredo, this was an apartment complex under surveillance for an operation targeting the running of guns and automatic weapons from South America. Alfredo walked out of the apartment carrying two AK-47s and multiple magazines of ammunition. He was arrested by FBI agents in the parking lot. Knowing that he was in big trouble, he explained to the agents that he was coming from the courthouse, where he had just pleaded guilty and he was cooperating in a major sex-trafficking operation. While the agents knew about the case and saw his court documentation on his front seat, this was not enough to convince them to let him walk.

During this new investigation, the agents also confiscated numerous guns from his home. This whole ordeal was an immediate violation of the probation that he had been placed on only hours before, resulting in a five-year prison sentence. Alfredo was never given a chance to cooperate with the feds against Epstein because of these new charges. Even Judge Marra commented on the disparity in Alfredo's receiving more prison time for having possessed the Holy Grail than Epstein received for committing crimes against the people in the document itself.

More concerning for me was the fact that I learned of Alfredo's arrest in the newspaper. You might think the FBI would have called to let me know that the man against whom I was a confidential informant pleaded guilty, then immediately bought assault rifles and ammo to do God knows what to God knows who. Because they arrested Alfredo before learning what he was going to do with the artillery, they didn't think warning me was necessary.

# FIFTEEN

# THE NEW BERNIE MADOFF

B Y OCTOBER 2009, WE WERE putting pressure on Epstein from every angle. We had subpoenaed his friends and high-powered connections, deposed his employees, and uncovered his private travel information, including his flight logs. We were giving him a taste of his own medicine.

One morning, I went to the twelfth floor of RRA and the war room where we were keeping the files related to Epstein. My lead investigator, Mike Fisten, was normally on that floor, but he wasn't in his office. Mike and the files were missing. Something was off. I called him on his cell phone, asking, "Where are the files?"

"Scott had us wheel them to his office," Mike responded.

"Why?" I inquired.

"We weren't given any information; just that it was urgent that all of the Epstein files be brought to his office. He sent his bodyguard down to the war room to load them on a cart and take them up. I went up there when they were delivered," Mike explained.

This made no sense to me, but Scott was the boss and could certainly say where the files were going to be kept. Scott did have extreme paranoia about security. Maybe with all the intense activity, especially given my FBI cooperation with Alfredo and the implication of other powerful people whom we now knew were frequent travelers on Epstein's jet, he wanted to provide maximum security. But even if that was the explanation, why wouldn't Scott discuss it with me first?

After our first "interview," Scott had spoken to me on only two occasions. The first time I was eating lunch in Bova Prime when he walked by my crowded table, shouting, "Have you gotten that pedophile yet?" loud enough to make sure that the entire restaurant heard him. The second time, I was standing in the hallway outside my office talking to Russell Adler when Scott asked, "How's that case with that pedophile going?"

Despite Scott's quirks, I appreciated the resources of the firm and the way Scott was in his own world and let me do my thing without much interference. With this unannounced move of my files, though, he changed that. I went to Scott's office but didn't have an appointment, so I couldn't get in.

I went to Russell's office. He was at his stand-up keyboard, looking past his monitor out the window at the Fort Lauderdale skyline. "Russ," I started, but only got that one word out before he interrupted, talking a mile a minute, which was a normal tempo for Russ: "Brad, what's up, man? We have all kinds of great stuff going on. You're a rock star, the next great trial lawyer. Scott is taking notice. He's personally reviewing your Epstein cases. He's really busy with his other businesses, including the Qtask computer software that he's working on, but he had Fisten and the guys bring him the files. You're rising to the top fast. With that case, everyone in America is going to know you."

Still skeptical, I asked, "I don't understand, what does any of this have to do with my files being in Scott's locked office?"

Russ fired back: "Before Scott was the power-broker businessman that he is, he was the best trial lawyer around. He wants to try the Epstein case with you personally. This is a huge deal. He's personally all in. Imagine what you're going to be able to do with these cases with literally unlimited resources."

For a second, this thought excited me. My mind drifted to Scott following me into a courtroom where Epstein and his tribe of high-priced lawyers had to sit quiet, taking the wrath of my closing argument. We had assembled *all* of the evidence. Epstein's famous political friends testified and were forced to tell the truth in the face of irrefutable proof and a judge threatening perjury charges against all of them. Even Clinton suddenly understood the common definition of "sexual relations" and testified against his pal. Not only did the jury decide that all of Epstein's money would go to the many victims he hurt, but the judge ordered Epstein and his buddies to be removed in handcuffs. Epstein's hundreds of victims cheered. Finally, justice.

When the daydream faded, reality set back in. My files were not accessible. Scott was not accessible. His office was like a sealed vault with multiple layers of protection to keep everyone out, including me.

This was not an exaggeration. In order to get into Scott's office, you had to tell his assistant that you wanted to meet with him and wait outside the door. She would then let you through a door into a room with a private elevator on one side and another series of doors on the other. Once you were granted permission to enter one of those doors, you were trapped in an area where only Scott could let you through a corridor into his office. He had an enormous twenty-five-foot conference table and a desk with six computer screens that rose on elevator platforms out of the mahogany. The upholstery on his office furniture was Ferrari leather. Now my case files were in Scott's secret compound, and I had to try to figure out how to speak with Scott.

Scott claimed to have an open-door policy each Tuesday, which he called "Talk to Me Tuesday," but, inevitably, those meetings would get delayed into "Whine to Me Wednesday" or "Try Me Again Thursday" or "Go F*** Yourself Friday." This kiss-ass meeting scheduling process was bullshit and wasn't worth the time it would waste. I didn't have that time to burn. I just continued to do what I was doing. I decided that trying to talk to him about the physical files wasn't worth the trouble. Most of the materials were stored on the computer to which I had access, or their contents were in my head at this point, so I resorted to alternative options.

On October 23, 2009, a week after he took the files, I got an email from Scott demanding that I and three other attorneys, including Russell Adler, report to his office immediately. I didn't go. I was not happy with him. He'd had my files in his office for that long and hadn't said a word to me about it. It wasn't that he didn't have the chance to, either.

Days earlier he had called one of his firm-wide meetings. He sent an email demanding every lawyer report to the firm's barroom—a glass-enclosed alcohol-filled bar on the twenty-second floor of our office building. It was not a small room, but it was tight with forty or more lawyers crammed in. Scott walked in twitching and holding a martini. He was noticeably irritated.

He began frantically pounding numbers on the oversize conference phone on the table, connecting the RRA Boca, Caracas, and Miami offices so that he had everyone's attention.

Once they were on, he slammed his martini on the table, spilling most of it on himself as he cocked his head to his favorite position before launching into a nonsensical tirade at full volume: "I've built the most successful f***ing firm in Fort Lauderdale, maybe the United States. You lazy f***s are just coasting. The numbers suck. What the f*** do you assholes do all f***ing day? Money doesn't sleep, you f***s. I can fire all of you right now and am close to doing it and just shutting this firm down. You have no appreciation for what has been given to you—this opportunity, you're just going to coast until I fire you. I will do it; I haven't decided whether it will be one at a time or all at once. I built new offices for half of you. And you repay me by doing nothing, sitting around with your thumbs up your f***ing ass. Get the f*** out of here and go do something to show me you want your job—for those of you that don't know what I mean, go make me some goddamn money."

His rant ended with him stumbling, clearly drunk, and holding the conference phone in his hands, screaming into it like the *Scarface* scene where Tony Montana yells at Sosa. After we went back to our floor, another lawyer who was infatuated with Scott told me that we really should feel more gratitude for Scott. I remember thinking, *Are you kidding? That guy is a lunatic.*

Now, less than a week after his tantrum, Scott was demanding that I go to his office along with three other lawyers. I could not imagine why, if three other lawyers were there, I also needed to be there. I had work to do and frankly didn't have time for Scott Rothstein. His flamboyant drill-sergeant, football-coach style might have had a certain amount of charm at first, but it had grown old. So, I ignored him.

Apparently this was unprecedented. No one ignored Scott, which I learned that very day when his assistant, and Russell, and Marc, and Scott, frantically continued to call me to get me to the meeting. I was in the office, and now ignoring them was becoming more time-consuming than just going. I eventually answered the phone for Russ. He knew what to say to make me move: "Brad, get up here. It's about Epstein."

When I got there, I found four others in the room, including Scott, and at least one lawyer on the phone. Scott was standing over nine boxes of Epstein files and silenced everyone as I walked into the center of the room. Providing no context whatsoever, Scott, seeming like he was on some sort of stimulant, shouted, "Brad, just the person we need—we need an answer quickly."

"About what?" I asked, really wanting to ask much more but also knowing it was not the time to overstep, especially since everyone in the room knew I had been intentionally ignoring all of them for the past fifteen minutes.

"You don't need to know anything. I have a simple research question about structured settlements. I need a simple answer," he said impatiently.

Russ jumped in. "This is important, everyone, let's get an answer," taking the spotlight off of me.

Scott continued: "Guys, I need you. You are the smartest in this firm, and we are the best firm in town. We are close to something monumental. You do your magic and get me an answer and I will do mine. There is no time to waste. Go back to your offices and send me the answer." It was obvious this question was the most important thing in the world to Scott.

We all walked out of Scott's fortress together. As soon as the door shut behind us, I turned to Russ. "What is going on?"

"Scott's talking to people only he has access to. Not only Epstein's people but his rich friends who we know were involved. They want to settle the case for hundreds of millions," he explained. "Confidentiality is everything for them, though. The victims will likely structure their settlement monies." I knew that if the clients ever decided to settle the cases, a structured settlement would make a lot of sense. Structured settlements are essentially tax-free annuity payments that grow over time and are common for these types of cases. "The structured settlement statute in Florida has a provision that requires court intervention if the victims ever transfer or sell the structure, which would destroy confidentiality. Scott wants to assure the bad guys that this isn't going to come back to haunt them one day," Russ said, justifying the urgent "research project."

I called Paul Cassell, the former federal judge and legal genius working most closely with me on all Epstein-related matters, and did my best to run through everything. It made as much sense to him as it did to me. He had the same questions I did. "Hundreds of millions of dollars? Who was involved in settling this? Clinton? Trump? Wexner?" he speculated. I had no answers. The concept was not far-fetched at all. I'd always assumed that billionaires (and politicians who relied on billionaires for survival) probably communicated directly with each other in ways that I wasn't aware of. Scott was very politically tied in, too, having just hosted John McCain at his home for a fund-raiser—he had a wall lined with photos of him posing with famous politicians who would answer his call at any hour.

After hours of research, even after all his "answers" were in, Scott gave us nothing in return. Russ would only say that Scott was working on it, but that Scott would not tell him much either.

Later that week, it became obvious this was not the only project Scott was working on. He sent out a firm-wide email that also needed an immediate answer. The firm had an important client being represented in a white-collar criminal matter related to wire fraud. He had questions about countries that would accept the client and not extradite him back to the United States while the criminal matter was being negotiated.

Of course, I knew RRA had top-notch criminal defense lawyers. But I never really thought about the conversations that went on between criminal clients and their lawyers. I guessed this was a normal ask from a criminal to the law firm he employed to maintain his liberty. Still, Scott's email left me uneasy. It didn't matter much to me—I didn't practice criminal law, nor did I have any immigration experience to know which countries didn't have extradition treaties with the United States. I ignored it. Later that day, a thorough response to that email came back—RRA's expert immigration attorney, Sara Coen, replied to all with her well-reasoned legal analysis. In short, her answer was Morocco. There was no extradition, and a wealthy client could live a decent life while the good lawyers at RRA went to work defending him against these federal financial crimes.

The following Saturday, on Halloween, just before I took my kids out trick-or-treating, I got a call from Russell, who said he had something urgent to talk about. I walked into my backyard with the phone to my ear. "You sitting down?" he asked. "Scott is in Morocco. There's money missing from our firm trust account. He didn't tell anyone he was leaving." My mind was racing. *Did he go to Morocco to deliver money to that major white-collar criminal client? Why would that be a big deal—oh, because the money he was delivering was coming from the firm trust account?*

"Why are you calling me?" I asked naively. "Does this have something to do with Epstein?"

"I don't think so. Nobody can get a hold of Scott," Russ said. "We don't think he's coming back. We don't know much, but we've confirmed that RRA does not have a white-collar client that needs to know how to abscond to a safe-haven country to avoid prosecution," he continued. "Scott is the client." When we hung up, I was still a little baffled, and thought it must be an exaggeration.

Terry and I put on our Superman and Superwoman costumes after dressing our boys as little superheroes. We walked the neighborhood, going door-to-door for candy. I waited until we got home to try to tell Terry about the call. She cut to the chase. "You're already spending too much time thinking about the possibilities. If it was as big a deal as Russ is making it, then it would be all over the news. Figure it out on Monday," she said.

When I went to work the following Monday, lawyers at the top of RRA were all huddled in corners. No one seemed to know what was really happening. Stuart Rosenfeldt called a meeting downstairs in the same banquet room where Scott had given his motivational speech during my first week at RRA. Not only for lawyers; for the whole firm, every employee. He confirmed what Russell told me on Halloween. Scott was gone and was not coming back. He had taken so much money from the firm's trust account that Rosenfeldt thought the firm would probably have to close and file for bankruptcy. This news was surreal. Without knowing more, there was no way to make sense of it.

RRA had never struck me or anyone else as a "normal" law firm, but the abnormal things about it never suggested to me that the firm was just a house of cards. In fact, by reputation, appearance, and the quality of the work and capabilities of most people in the firm, the opposite was true. It wasn't as if you saw gangsters walking the hallways. Well, not the obvious kind, anyway.

To be fair, there *were* two convicted felons who worked for Scott, one of them a former Italian Mafia associate, but both employees were only document runners whom I was told Scott was giving a second chance in life. Every day there were also at least four uniformed Fort Lauderdale police officers walking the hallways as if they were patrolling the Federal Reserve.

Any place where uniformed police officers are routinely on duty would not strike a normal person as a place where you'd expect to find massive criminal activity. Bank robbers, in my mind, did not normally hide out in a police station. What's more, there was a good explanation for uniformed police to stalk the halls of the firm.

Prior to my joining, an RRA partner named Melissa Britt Lewis was tragically murdered. It turned out the murderer was the husband of Scott's assistant Debra Villegas. Scott would explain to anyone who asked about the police presence that he was never going to allow another one of his "family" of employees to be harmed the way that Melissa had been. He could afford the extra security, he said, so he would do it in her honor.

That Monday after Halloween, all everyone did was sit and talk about the unfolding drama. After Stuart told us about Scott running to Morocco, at least half of the people in the room dissolved into tears. I promptly returned to my office, thinking there was nothing I could do to alter this new reality other than to figure out where I'd go if the firm really did go out of business.

In the days that followed, as word got around, I received calls from several law firms in town asking if I wanted to join them in the wake of whatever was going on over at RRA. I needed some advice about where to go. I was pretty gun-shy about going to another big firm. I called a friend of mine who had a lot of connections and he advised me to see a lawyer whom I had known only by reputation. The lawyer's office was directly across the street from RRA, so I went over without an appointment and told the receptionist I needed to see Bruce, it was an emergency.

Bruce Rogow was a law professor and a lawyer's lawyer. He was known to have the ability to handle any situation. I think he had argued more cases before the Florida Supreme Court than any other lawyer alive. I'm sure I was talking too fast to make sense, looking for a magical piece of advice, when he took me into his conference room.

Bruce sat back in his chair and after listening said, "This is very amusing."

I tilted my head and said, "What part?"

"I heard Scott Rothstein owns a Bugatti. I heard he etched his initials into the leather seats, and I wonder how difficult it would be to change his initials to mine," he said. "I don't understand why you think this is a problem. You have a great reputation, and you don't need to go to another firm out of desperation. Do you like the people you're working with over there? I know Steve Jaffe, Seth Lehrman, and Matt Weissing, and they're all good lawyers. You should talk to them about starting your own law firm. You're all going through this emergency, which means you'll work faster than you would in normal circumstances."

I went back to RRA and told Steve Jaffe I wanted to talk to him. We agreed to set a breakfast the next morning at the Floridian on Las Olas Boulevard. The meeting turned out to include me, Steve Jaffe, Gary Farmer, Matt Weissing, Mark Fistos, and Seth Lehrman. Russell Adler heard about it and came by, saying if we were starting something new, he wanted to be part of it. The problem was, he was a close friend of Scott's and a named partner of RRA. Whether he was involved in Scott's problems or not, it would be next to impossible for us to explain his joining us.

As soon as Russell sat down, we started grilling him about what was going on with Scott. As much as we all liked Russ and appreciated his bringing us together, we explained why we couldn't be associated with him going forward. He said he understood, and I think he genuinely did. We left breakfast after I had explained to the guys that Bruce Rogow recommended we start our own law firm. We agreed we would pick up the conversation the next day and that I would take the lead on securing a place to have the meeting.

Then we all went back to RRA and worked. I tried to catch up on my other cases to make sure my clients knew I was on top of things and to make sure the judges on my cases knew it, too.

I was working at about six o'clock that night when, facing my computer screen, with my back to the door, I saw a reflection of someone entering my office. A male voice told me to take my hands off of my keyboard. When I turned around and looked up, there was a guy wearing all black with the letters FBI on his shirt. I assumed he was the only agent there. *Why did he single me out?*, I wondered. *Epstein has to have something to do with this.*

I lifted my hands from the keyboard and moved toward him. I walked slowly out of my office, confused, to find FBI and IRS agents everywhere. They had swarmed the building. By the time I got down to the lobby, there were dozens of RRA employees huddled together, all prevented from leaving the building. The agents were upstairs confiscating all of the firm's files, documents, and computers—absolutely everything that held information. They kept us there for three hours or so before letting us leave and telling us we were not permitted to come back. Not that it mattered. By now, there was nothing to come back to. Everyone seemed panicked, but I felt relieved. At least this was not Epstein's personal attack on me.

That night, the RRA firm hired Kendall Coffey to represent it. It wasn't just the biggest news story in town, it was the biggest in the country. There were videos of the raid on national television, with Kendall doing his best to try to explain that only Scott Rothstein, and few if any others, had knowledge of the crimes that were said to have been committed. He even walked the news crews through the office to show how secluded Scott's office was from everyone else's. It was a nice try, I suppose, but this scandal was now beyond normal crisis management. In good times and bad, Scott Rothstein was a larger-than-life personality whose footprint could not be denied. The only thing missing was his moral compass. As it turned out, he had been running the largest Ponzi scheme in Florida history, and second-largest Ponzi scheme in United States history, trailing behind only Bernie Madoff.

Outside the Joe DiMaggio Children's Hospital was a statue of Scott. The firm name was on display at the American Airlines Arena, where the Miami Heat play, and on the Long Key Park Garden of Relection for Crime Victims in Davie, Florida. Bova Prime was his restaurant, he owned the Versace Mansion, and Fort Lauderdale was his town. Overnight, he went from the most popular and powerful man in South Florida to the most destructive and hated criminal in our small-town history.

Just when I thought I had heard it all, I learned that the cases I was litigating against Jeffrey Epstein had been used in the final chapter of Scott's Ponzi scheme just before its implosion. The premise of the scheme was to tell investors that he represented victims of sexual abuse or sexual harassment who had received large settlements that would be paid out to the victims over a period of time. For a significant payment, the investor could acquire the rights to the long-term payouts of the settlement. For example, Scott would tell an investor that an abuse victim received a settlement that would pay her $20 million over the next ten years, but that she would prefer to receive a one-time lump-sum $5 million payment immediately. The investor would then pay $5 million and acquire the rights to $20 million over time. What the investors didn't know is that these were not real cases or settlements at all. Instead, they were just made-up stories living in Scott Rothstein's mind.

At the end, Scott's wealthy investors had become suspicious. Several investors had hired attorneys, wanting to verify that the cases in which Scott was offering the opportunity to acquire settlements were real. Of course, none were real, but Scott was unwilling to give up that easily. He was desperate for new funds to keep his Ponzi scheme afloat. Scott needed a case with sensational facts that fit into the framework of his stories about settlements for sexual abuse and sexual harassment victims. As luck would have it, just as his scheme started to fall apart, Scott found the perfect cases right at his fingertips. Enter the legitimate lawsuits that I was litigating against Jeffrey Epstein, which Scott, unbeknownst to me, showed to investors to try to convince them that all the other stories he was peddling were legitimate.

The only difference between Scott Rothstein and Jeffrey Epstein was the consequences that each faced for his crime. Scott was soon to be treated as he should have been. Epstein had been given special treatment, but I wasn't done with him yet.

# SIXTEEN

# THE FALLOUT

Prior to my joining RRA, Epstein definitely felt he had the advantage over me, and maybe that was true. He was intimidating his victims, having his lawyers bash them in public by filing motions to expose embarrassing things in their lives and past history, from petty theft, to drug use, to abortion. You name it, he exposed it. What's more, his lawyers kept us on the defense, forcing me into the courtroom on nitpicking discovery motions nearly every day. We were on our heels with his rat-a-tat-tat maneuvers. But that had all begun to change. Once I got to RRA, I'd been able to put on a very aggressive offensive, and Epstein was frantically defending.

As soon as he found a way to plug a hole we'd poked in his defense, we opened up another. The momentum had been shifting quickly. We'd served subpoenas on his friends and ex-employees to force them to testify under oath to what they had seen him do and say. We obtained crucial documents from his pilots and ex-butler.

Knowing that his most powerful weapon was his ability to control everyone in his employ through his vast wealth, we'd decided to attack his money directly. We filed a motion to freeze millions of dollars of his assets, citing the fraudulent transfers he had made to his chief pilot, Larry Visoski. We were cornering him. He had no way out. I thought in those days we were only a few moves away from checkmate. In order to get out of the traps we'd set, Epstein needed a big break. And thanks to Rothstein, he got it. Somehow, he always seemed to wriggle away just as the legal noose was tightening. When RRA imploded, he was able to do it again.

Practicing law during this time was not easy for me. The FBI had confiscated my files, including my computer and my digital notations in the Qtask system. With my case information gone, I found myself attending hearings and arguing motions without the benefit of documentation, an assistant, or even a formal law firm behind me. That was my life on a typical morning. In the afternoons, when my new partners and I weren't busy looking for office space to open our new firm, Farmer, Jaffe, Weissing, Edwards, Fistos & Lehrman, I was going door-to-door to tell my clients what had happened and explain their choices. Telling them their law firm had been labeled a criminal enterprise was not fun.

According to the rules, I had to tell them they could remain with RRA—which had at this point been forced into bankruptcy, with the managing partner of the firm under investigation for running a $1.2 billion Ponzi scheme. Or they could stay with me and the new firm I was opening with five others who had also been at RRA. Or, of course, they could find a new law firm altogether and not deal with the headaches of RRA and those of us who'd been there. I had a good relationship with my clients; not one of them left me.

In November 2009, we opened the new law firm. I went to the U.S. Attorney's Office in Fort Lauderdale and let them know that it was important that I get the remainder of my files back from the FBI heist. They finished their review that day before helping me load the boxes into my car. After a month, I was finally able to get back to work. Or so I thought.

In December 2009, I set up a lunch with my friend Earleen Cote to let her know I was doing fine. Earleen had been my boss from 2004 to 2007, when I first left the State Attorney's office for private civil practice, so she was particularly invested in my professional success. She'd been worried about me, since the new firm was working around the clock to get off the ground. During lunch, I got several calls from a telephone number I did not recognize. I finally answered to hear a process server tell me he had something for me to sign. I told him where I was, and he came to meet me. I figured it was probably something related to the bankruptcy proceedings with RRA, but instead, it was a message from Jeffrey Epstein. Not just any old message, but one that arrived in the form of a thirty-six-page complaint filed in Palm Beach County court. Jeffrey Epstein was now suing Scott Rothstein—no surprise there—but also my client Lynn, whom Epstein had abused, and *me*.

Epstein made outlandish criminal allegations against me. He first alleged that the three of us formed a criminal enterprise and conspiracy to defraud him. None of the Rothstein fraud had anything to do with me, Lynn, or the legitimate cases that were being prosecuted against Epstein. Epstein knew that, but he also knew that this was an opportunity to attempt to pressure me into abandoning my cases, including the CVRA, a case that exposed him to possible criminal liability and another prosecution. He had cover for his outlandish complaint, too, since there had been nine boxes of files related to him in Rothstein's office when Rothstein left for Morocco.

In the complaint, Epstein alleged that I had forged judges' signatures, conducted various kinds of illegal discovery including wiretaps, and formed a criminal enterprise in which I had directed Scott Rothstein on how to mastermind the RRA Ponzi scheme. On its face, the complaint was a joke. Earleen and I both laughed out loud as we read it. Frankly, it was confirmation that Epstein knew I was winning. But because he was able to hire respected lawyers, they added credibility to the false allegations. His lawyers disseminated the complaint to the press at a time when Scott Rothstein was the most hated lawyer in Broward County, the state of Florida, and a good part of the country.

People were reading the complaint against me at the same time that Scott's statue was being removed from the hospital, millions of dollars in donations were being returned by various charities, and Scott was coming home from Morocco to begin cooperating with the FBI. The fact that he came back was a surprise to many; evidently it was not out of a respect for law or the goodness of his heart. According to rumors, some of the victims he'd duped in his Ponzi scheme, particularly a few less-than-upstanding citizens, were threatening to mail Scott some of his beloved relatives, one body part at a time, if he didn't come home with their money.

When he returned to the U.S., Scott brilliantly defended himself by playing a role only he could. The media was following him around every step he took, and instead of hiding out, he made himself conspicuous. He was eating at restaurants all over town. The media would ambush him with questions and without faltering, he would explain, "The FBI has made a terrible mistake, but the truth will soon come out."

But there was more to his act than met the eye. While he was all over town with everyone he could see, he was wearing a wire for the FBI and trying to nail the bad guys he had worked with throughout the years. One of them was named Roberto Settineri, a reputed Sicilian mob boss wanted in Italy for attempted murder. Scott convinced Settineri to help him destroy documents and launder $79,000 for him. Apparently, it had not occurred to the man that Scott was recording their conversations. Settineri was arrested.

The court initially sentenced Scott to fifty years. In order to shave some time off his sentence, he even had his own uncle arrested. It wasn't an entirely fruitless strategy. His cooperation got him into the witness protection program and a drastically reduced sentence, which likely would have ended up at around seven to ten years.

With most crooks, cutting a deal with prosecutors and the courts to reduce a prison term would be considered a smart move, but Scott blew even that one. He started strong, giving weeks of sworn testimony in civil cases and countless hours of interviews to authorities, resulting in the arrest of all of his former co-conspirators and other criminals he knew. He put so many people in jail he probably could have reduced his sentence further, but then, he contacted his wife, Kimmy, and told her where he had hidden a 12.08-carat yellow diamond—an asset he had intentionally failed to disclose to the FBI.

Kimmy found the stone and had her friend sell it to Patrick Daoud of Daoud's Fine Jewelry in Fort Lauderdale for $175,000. But that didn't work out very well, either. Daoud was arrested, in part for lying about his role in the scandal, and was represented in criminal proceedings by a local legal legend named Fred Haddad, who would later become one of the lawyers representing Epstein in the case he had filed against me.

Daoud was sentenced to ten months of house arrest and two years probation for obstruction of justice, while Kimmy Rothstein was sentenced to eighteen months in prison and her friend was sentenced to three months in prison and three years of supervised release.

Because of his concealment of the diamond, Scott's fifty-year sentence was not reduced, and he will be serving his prison sentence for the rest of his life. The word on the street was that he was able to remain in the witness protection program during his time in prison, but who knows how much that is worth these days.

In addition to Scott Rothstein, the remaining two named partners at RRA—Stuart Rosenfeldt and Russell Adler—also served time for crimes related to Rothstein's operation. Russell Adler was also represented by Fred Haddad, who was able to keep him out of jail for a while. The government initially investigated Russell for being one of the main co-conspirators in the Ponzi scheme, but ultimately only had evidence related to campaign donations. It took them years to even file those charges. Once the government gave Russell his options and he realized that taking a plea was in the best interest of himself and his family, he didn't back down like everyone else with their tail between their legs. That was not Russell's style.

Instead, he threw a going-away party at Prime Cigar and Wine Bar in Boca Raton. The back room had a table with a black-and-white tablecloth that had jail bars on it. The pictures on the wall were of other people, mainly Italian wiseguys, who had thrown parties before going off to jail. You would think that someone going to jail wouldn't have a very big turnout because for the most part, everyone wanted separation from everyone else who was at RRA and was being charged with a crime. But in true Russell Adler fashion, his party was full of doctors, lawyers, judges, and friends sending him on his way to Pensacola to do his two-and-a-half-year sentence.

In total, more than two dozen people were arrested in connection with

Rothstein's Ponzi scheme. The firm CFO, Irene Stay, was charged with conspiracy to commit money laundering and to defraud a financial institution for her role in overseeing the accounting functions of the law firm. Broward Sheriff's Office lieutenant David Benjamin was arrested and charged with conspiracy to commit extortion and violate civil rights in federal court, and Detective Jeff Alan Poole was jailed for conspiracy to violate civil rights. RRA's general counsel, David Boden, and Richard Pearson, an investment banker who worked in the same building as RRA, were also arrested in relation to the scheme.

Michael Szafranski, Rothstein's financial advisor, was arrested and sentenced to two and a half years in prison after pleading guilty to wire fraud, in addition to having to pay $6.5 million in restitution to the victims. The number of people who went down with that ship was high and the extent of their crimes was investigated in a no-stone-left-unturned manner for years. As the extent of the fraud and the number of people involved became more obvious, Epstein used each arrest as leverage to give credence to his suit against me. Remember, he alleged that I was Rothstein's main conspirator.

As an interesting aside, Roger Stone was the lawyer in the office next to mine during my first few months at RRA. While he didn't go to jail because of the RRA Ponzi scheme, and for the most part kept to himself, he was convicted in 2019 in connection with his work for President Donald Trump for allegedly communicating with Russian operatives. Their relationship dated back many decades, and he is apparently the first person to have encouraged Trump to run for president in 1998. It really is a small world.

# SEVENTEEN

# ENTER JACK

A FTER AN ARTICLE ABOUT EPSTEIN'S lawsuit against me ran in the *South Florida Sun Sentinel* newspaper on December 10, 2009, I got a call from a local Palm Beach attorney named Jack Scarola, a trial lawyer I had known from his representation of other Epstein victims. As soon as he got on the phone, he declared in his deep, booming Shakespearean voice, "I see Epstein has published a fairy tale in hopes that it will intimidate you. It would be my distinct honor to represent you. Once we dismiss his action, I would enjoy nothing more than to prosecute the very valuable malicious prosecution case you will have against him and the lawyers that signed their name to that piece of paper. Do not get distracted." I accepted his offer.

Epstein's attack did not end with the lies that he spread in this public complaint where he cast me as the criminal mastermind behind the Ponzi scheme. A few days later, I was contacted by the Florida Bar informing me that Epstein had filed a bar complaint against me. I knew that Bruce Rogow had represented lawyers in bar actions, so once again I called him. He referred me to a lawyer in Palm Beach named G. Michael Keenan who was confident that the bar complaint would be dismissed. But Epstein's tactics were annoying, to say the least. And expensive. Keenan's legal fees were more than $20,000 when the complaint against me was indeed dismissed, which was just about $20,000 more than I had to my name at the time.

Epstein brought to bear the same massive resources against me as he had used against his victims. The time and money required to defend myself from a bad lawsuit was only part of his attack. He also immediately put my family and me under surveillance. Then he served subpoenas on the RRA trustee to obtain all my files related to him, including all the emails I had ever sent to anyone involving him while I had been working at RRA. And then there was the RRA bankruptcy case, which was a mess with nearly every lawyer in town seeming to play some part in it. There was no way to avoid this massive distraction.

Despite Jack's offer to represent me, there were many pieces of the Epstein lawsuit against me that Jack couldn't handle because he didn't know the facts well enough. This forced me to personally appear in bankruptcy court, where the RRA fiasco was being handled, on a regular basis.

I should not have had much to worry about with Epstein's transparently false lawsuit and harassing legal moves against me. Clearly, I had not made the molestation up as part of a Ponzi scheme. The fictional lawsuit he filed was nothing but a ploy to discover my privileged files, find out how I was pursuing him, and try to scare me out of doing my work. This seemed utterly obvious to me, my counsel, and everyone else. Everyone, that is, except the one person who mattered: the bankruptcy judge.

Judge Raymond Ray was being inundated on a daily basis with RRA-related litigation. He seemed to believe that anyone ever affiliated with RRA was already guilty. More of that supposition would raise its ugly head later, in a big way, but at the moment, what mattered was that he ordered RRA to turn over to my new law firm all the emails ever written to or from me or Scott Rothstein so that I could determine whether the communications in each email were privileged and therefore protected from disclosure to Epstein's counsel. I reminded Judge Ray that to allow Epstein to subpoena all of my work product and attorney-client privileged information would be to turn the entire legal system on its head. Judge Ray directed me to start by reviewing every email before making arguments about why I thought each one was privileged.

Of course, all of the emails were privileged because every single one of

them related to the cases I was pursuing against Epstein on behalf of Courtney, Lynn, and Marissa. Epstein knew this. Everyone in the courtroom
knew this. The judge probably knew this, too, but he didn't seem to care
how time-consuming this project was going to be for me, at a time when I
was trying to start a new firm and keep my investigation on track.

The next thing I knew, 27,500 pages of emails showed up at our law
firm on a CD. When we realized the magnitude of this project, requiring us
to individually analyze every single email, which would not only waste time
but would also be expensive, we returned to the court and asked for help.
The judge hired a special master, a former judge named Robert Carney. Carney seemed to be overly impressed by Epstein's powerful legal team and to
assume that anyone who had been accused by anyone else of being involved
in the Ponzi scheme was guilty until proven innocent. This despite the fact
that the only person throwing me into that category was a convicted criminal. Jeffrey Epstein was conducting an obviously contrived sideshow of
smoke, mirrors, and shiny objects, but it was working.

We asked Judge Ray to have Epstein pay to print the 27,500 emails that
were on the CD in order to have them delivered to our office for review.
One of Epstein's lawyers, Lilly Ann Sanchez, "offered" to have her law firm,
Fowler White Burnett—a blue-chip Miami law firm with a hundred-year
reputation—make the copies rather than cause Epstein to incur the expense
of a third-party copying service. Carney liked that idea. "Are you kidding?"
we asked. "You're going to have Epstein's attorneys, who are not allowed to
see these documents before there is a determination about which are privileged, print the documents themselves?" Talk about the fox guarding the
henhouse.

Despite the outrageousness of this screwball offer, and over our strong
objection, Special Master Carney supported that process. He flatly told us
that he would recommend it over our objection. In a vain effort to provide
at least some protection against Epstein's attorneys improperly keeping a
copy of all these privileged materials, we drafted a very particular order allowing the court to keep jurisdiction to impose sanctions if Epstein's attor-

neys retained any copies of the documents on the CD. The court entered the order, but we knew a piece of paper from a judge would never stop Epstein.

Special Master Carney then provided the CD to Epstein's legal team at Fowler White. Epstein's lawyers made hard copies of all 27,500 pages of documents and delivered them to me before allegedly returning the CD to Special Master Carney. This was supposed to ensure that Epstein's counsel never accessed any of these documents.

My new law firm now had 27,500 pages to review and log, which cost us hundreds of hours of time and who knows how many thousands of dollars. This was exactly the distraction Epstein wanted. And, while running me around the track, he continued on a second front to relentlessly attack the girls he'd victimized, using his investigators to intimidate them. Nearly every day, while I was combing through stacks of old RRA emails, I was also getting calls from my clients saying that Epstein's private investigators were harassing them. They were scared Epstein was coming to get them.

I knew Epstein was winning and I was losing. I just didn't know how bad it was. That I would find out soon.

# EIGHTEEN

# HOW THE FIGHT
# BECAME A WAR

ECAUSE THE RRA DEBACLE CAUSED me to lose momentum and time,
I had to narrow my attack. Of the various depositions I served on witnesses but did not yet take before RRA dissolved, Ghislaine Maxwell was the
most important. So I began working with her lawyer to reset her deposition.
Ghislaine was represented by Cohen & Gresser, the same New York law firm
that represented Jeff's brother, Mark Epstein, so I had good reason to think
she and Jeffrey were still in close communication.

Ghislaine was still under the original subpoena that had set her deposition for late 2009, so she could not avoid it altogether, though her lawyers
delayed setting a date by trying to establish all kinds of parameters, in particular a restriction on the questions that could be asked about her sexual
relationship with Jeffrey Epstein. Even though we didn't agree to that term,
we ultimately agreed on some level of confidentiality and set a deposition
date. Once I locked that in for May 2010, I focused on securing a deposition of model scout Jean-Luc Brunel as well.

Both of these witnesses were soft spots in Jeffrey's armor. I knew it and
he knew it. Ghislaine had been around him for two decades, knew his secrets, and could not credibly deny all of them. Jean-Luc had a public reputation, documented by the BBC and CBS's *60 Minutes*, for engaging in

sexually abusive conduct against young females of which Epstein was also accused and was still one of Epstein's closest associates. Getting those two witnesses set did not stop us from continuing to pursue others.

As discovery continued in Courtney's case, I took the deposition of Epstein's butler Janusz Banasiak on February 16, 2010. This was the butler who was present at the Palm Beach house when the search warrant that led to Epstein's arrest was executed in 2005. True to form, Banasiak showed up with an Epstein-paid lawyer, but he seemed decently honest about what he knew. Banasiak revealed that Jean-Luc Brunel had been staying at Epstein's house the week prior to this deposition in February 2010. He also confirmed that Jean-Luc was still one of Epstein's closest friends.

The next day was reserved for Jeffrey's deposition. Epstein's lawyers were successful arguing that his deposition should not be taken separately for every case against him, so there were seven lawyers slotted to ask him questions. I was first up. I arrived an hour early to set up and see how Epstein arrived. Who drove him? What car was he driving in?

Epstein arrived at his deposition in a black Suburban. It looked like the driver was Banasiak. Epstein stepped out in gray slippers, jeans, and a collared shirt turned up to cover his neck. He didn't see me in my car parked at the other end of the lot. Jack Goldberger pulled in within seconds of Epstein arriving and they entered the building together. I got out of my car and walked quickly to take the elevator with them. Jack Goldberger said hello. Epstein did not. He just stared with his steely, squinty eyes and pursed his lips. It was a look I had not seen before but one I have seen many times since. His eyes lasered through me. Just before I was convinced that he was trying to kill me with his eyes, he lifted the left side of his lips to smirk, as if to convey that he controlled the temperature in the room.

I exited the elevator first and checked in before walking down to room 4—the largest room at the court reporter's office, set up with a video camera at one end shooting down the table at the deponent's chair with a blue screen background behind it. Along each side were six chairs, most of which would have been empty in a normal deposition, but today every chair would be occupied.

Other than the videographer, I was the first in the room. I set my brief-case on the table in front of the chair closest to where Epstein would be sitting and started unloading the documents that would be deposition exhibits. I stacked everything up in order alongside my yellow legal pads and six pens. One by one, the other plaintiff attorneys filed in, choosing chairs at the table, each with a stack of exhibits. By this point, all the other law firms representing victims expected me to take the lead.

Epstein's legal team then came in, together, and sat on the opposite side of the table. He had five lawyers there that day. Once everyone was situated, Jack Goldberger walked in and took the last chair on the other side of the table, directly across from me. Epstein walked in behind him and took his seat at the head. He surveyed the room and grabbed one of the microphones to pin to his shirt. He looked at me, and I locked eyes with him.

He softened his look and said, "Janusz said you were nice to him. Thank you for that. I appreciate it." Was this his way of trying to soften me up? That wasn't going to happen.

As soon as he sat, the court reporter asked him to raise his hand as she swore him in—which in layman's terms theoretically means the witness must tell the truth. A witness who is being asked questions about his criminal behavior has another choice, and that is to invoke his or her Fifth Amendment right against self-incrimination. The typical way to invoke is simple—the witness simply replies, "I invoke the Fifth." But Epstein never did the typical.

And so we started.

"Mr. Epstein, how long have you been sexually attracted to underage minor females?" I began.

"Are you kidding?" he responded.

After objections and an invocation of his rights to remain silent, I rephrased. "Would you consider yourself addicted to sex with minor females?"

Rather than simply say, "I invoke the Fifth," Epstein responded, "You know, Mr. Edwards, again, I want to be very respectful. As the current U.S. attorney has described your law firm as a criminal enterprise and part of one of the largest frauds in Florida's history, it has been reported that your firm has fabricated multiple cases against me in order to fleece unsuspecting investors out of millions and millions of dollars, so unfortunately at this time, although I would like to answer that question, on advice of counsel I will have to refrain and assert my Fifth, Sixth, and Fourteenth Amendment rights." He and his legal team had apparently decided to inject a nonresponsive and self-serving monologue in order to dilute the power of his invocation, and to irritate me.

I had designed the questions and physically positioned myself at the table in order to evoke as much body language from him as possible, since he was on video and I knew he wouldn't provide much in the way of substance. While he continued to read through his script and assert a variety of constitutional rights to avoid answering, his facial expressions gave me some insight into his mind. While his prepared speech was frustrating, it was not something that would play well with the judge or a jury, especially once it could be shown that it was just more bluster to deflect from his guilt.

I asked him about his friend Jean-Luc Brunel. He looked at me as if he didn't understand my question, then asked me to spell the name, implying that he had no idea who Brunel was. After I spelled it, he looked at the video camera again as if I had asked some crazy question about someone he had never heard of. I then said, "[Jean-Luc Brunel] was at your house last week, does that remind you?" He hadn't realized that Banasiak had testified to that. With this question, he likely believed I had surveillance on him. He stared in a way that told me just how caught off guard he was. I asked again, "Are you acting like you don't know him?" This time he reverted to his safety blanket and read from his script.

For the first time, he was off-balance. He knew I had done my research not only on his background but also on everyone he was associated with, to the point that I now knew who his houseguests were. Of course, I didn't know half as much as he thought I did, but I made the most of what I did know.

He looked disarmed and nervous about the information I had accumulated. During a break, all the other lawyers left the room. Epstein stayed. So, of course, I did, too. The only other person in the room was the court reporter.

We stared at each other, less than three feet apart, sizing one another up. It was uncomfortable. His gaze relaxed, though, and he tried to once again change tactics. "I like Lynn. I don't like that she's having to go through this," he admitted. Lynn was someone whom he'd only known when she was between the ages of fourteen and sixteen, when she would go to his house to service him for sex or bring him other children to do the same. He liked her because she brought him so many girls, and because she liked him. And his way of trying to convince me that he was a good guy and not the blatant liar who was just caught on tape pretending not to know who Jean-Luc Brunel was, was to tell me that he liked Lynn. This was his second big mistake that day.

Once the other lawyers filed back into the room and sat down, I resumed the questions. "Do you know [Lynn]?" He responded with a facial gesture into the camera to impress that he had no idea who she was, before reciting his scripted invocation.

"When we were in the room today, didn't you look at me and say, 'I like [Lynn]'?" I continued.

Despite the fact that only minutes had passed, he responded, "I don't remember. I don't know. Sorry," as his lawyers were stunned and began objecting to the questions. They had not been in the room when Epstein casually made this admission to me. However, the court reporter, who had been there, could not believe Epstein would have the candid conversation she'd just heard, then get on the record and act like he had no idea what I was talking about. We asked her to sign an affidavit about the conversation and subsequent perjury. She did that. And she was ready to testify about Jeffrey perjuring himself.

I took her affidavit to the Palm Beach State Attorney's office, which refused to take it on. I was told that Jeffrey Epstein was far too powerful to prosecute for something as petty as perjury. Apparently, only the powerless can get charged with lying under oath.

Less than a month later, Jeffrey was deposed in the case he'd filed against me personally, and he decided to try to get revenge by ramping up his attack on me and Lynn. Rather than making his already obnoxious Fifth Amendment invocations, he enhanced his creativity. In response to practically any question, he would incorporate his disparaging and false claims of my supposed involvement in the Rothstein Ponzi scheme into his answer, and now also dragged Lynn in, too. For example, when my lawyer, Jack Scarola, asked him why he was suing my client Lynn, he responded, "[Lynn] is part of a conspiracy with Scott Rothstein, Bradley Edwards, creating—excuse me—creating fraudulent cases of a sexually charged nature in which the U.S. attorney has already charged the firm of Rothstein, a firm of which Bradley Edwards is a partner, was a partner, with creating, fabricating malicious cases of a sexual nature, including cases with respect to me, specifically, in order to fleece unsuspecting investors in South Florida out of millions of dollars." While this didn't get him far, Epstein kept up with these antics for what I can only imagine to be his own amusement.

Jean-Luc Brunel's deposition was up next. He would have no choice but to bury his buddy Epstein—I had too much on him for him to lie his way out of things. The day before the deposition I got a message on my voice mail from his attorney—who was paid for by Jeffrey Epstein—saying that Jean-Luc had to fly to France for an emergency. Of course he did. And he had no plans of ever returning to the United States.

I filed another motion for sanctions, telling the judge about the lie that had just been created by Brunel and all the reasons that we knew it was a lie. On the one hand, I kept being railroaded and prevented from taking these critical depositions. On the other hand, this was evidence that Epstein was vulnerable. He couldn't fend off my attack forever.

There was an occasion in early 2010 when Jeffrey Epstein and I were at an office for another deposition and he called me into a private room. He sat and pointed at the chair across from him. I sat. He leaned back and crossed his foot over his leg. "How long is this going to go on, Brad?" he asked.

"Till it's over, I guess," I shot back.

He didn't flinch. He said, "I think you know now, Brad, that you and I are a lot more alike than you originally thought. I'm not talking about our behaviors, but our approach, you know?" Before I could put much thought into that, he immediately followed it up with: "There is a difference, though, and I haven't put that difference in motion. The difference is that I have unfair power at my fingertips. I hired a former MMA champion who is out there in the hallway, and I have access to all of the resources in the world. You don't even know who all of my friends are. I haven't employed my resources only because it wouldn't be a fair fight. I, like you, am all about being fair, so I am trying to be fair with you. I suggest you start doing the same with me and let's figure out a way for everyone to walk away."

This was an art that Jeffrey Epstein had mastered. He was the best ever at making you believe that he was being the most fair, the most honest, the most revealing, the most exposed, as if he literally had nothing to hide. But he revealed things about himself he wasn't aware of. Just before he was going to say something totally untrue that he wanted you to believe, he would preface it with an explanation of why you should believe the next thing to come out of his mouth.

It was obvious, for instance, to anyone looking at the facts that he targeted underage girls for sex, yet he wanted desperately for me to believe that he was really the victim of their opportunistic behavior. In an effort to gain my confidence and resolve cases more favorably for him, he would say things like, "Listen, Brad, I am going to play my cards face-up for you," while motioning with his hands, turning them palm-up in the air.

He did this before making a small concession: "I have never denied that these girls came to my house, but I was lied to about some of their ages, I was taken advantage of. I am certainly not asking for anyone to feel sorry for me, only to be treated fairly, the way I treat everyone. You can ask the girls, I was always fair, the same way I am being fair to you. I am going to continue not to use the resources at my disposal because that would not be fair. But I expect you to start being fair to me."

Simply saying he wasn't going to use his power was, of course, a veiled threat that he would use it. Despite that and everything else I knew about him, there was a part of me that was influenced by the words. Not necessarily because I believed him, which I didn't, but because fairness has always been a soft spot for me, a principle worth taking risks to achieve. He was a master manipulator, and he proved that to me time and time again. Jeffrey played dumb to curry favor, and right at his calculated moment, he pursed his lips and gave sharp retorts with the appearance that they were off the top of his head.

His real genius was his ability to read his adversary. He was able to exploit his opponent's values because of the careful attention he paid to both the strengths and weaknesses of the person sitting on the other side of the table. With me, he recognized that I was a competitor but that fairness was a pillar of my personality. Because he was able to identify that, he wanted very much to demonstrate at every stage that he, too, held fairness as a cardinal principle. This would be the quality he constantly tried to exploit. Jeffrey Epstein was a sociopath, and the advantage he gained from the fact that he operated without a conscience was tremendous.

Epstein had an uncanny ability to keep his lies straight and so give the impression he was never lying. He was always in charge, and when he needed to make that clear, he would. Any time he offended me with one of his tactics, he would quickly blame it on someone else, such as a lawyer. But I knew there was no detail that he did not direct. He was responsible for moving every single chess piece on his side of the board. When he thought he was caught red-handed lying or acting in a way that would cause him to lose credibility, especially in taking an offensive move, he would immediately and believably give the impression that there were so many layers between himself and the person performing the act that he wasn't even in the same state as the house with the chessboard. Whether it was in court statements about me or my clients or aggressive investigative moves, he acted as though he had no idea who was sitting at the chair moving the pieces.

The rich and powerful are responsible for and preoccupied with so many important things that they delegate many tasks, therefore they might indeed be unaware of something done on their behalf. That concept made his claims of innocence somewhat believable. But I knew nothing was done on Jeffrey's behalf without his knowledge.

There was something about him—an inexplicable charisma—in every encounter I had with him that made me want to like him until I remembered all the reasons I knew I had to dislike him. Jeffrey Epstein was an enigma. An enigma that I would have many more occasions to study. But if I let my guard down and let him go on the offensive, he would destroy my clients, the cases, and me. I needed to constantly make him play defense. In order to keep him playing defense, I had to keep trying to infiltrate his inner sanctum to remove his control. This was his weakness.

Two weeks later, my law partner Steve Jaffe and I had another meeting with Epstein and his lawyer. He and his lawyer were on one side of the table and Steve and I were on the other. I immediately looked at Epstein and stated, "We have a real fundamental, philosophical disagreement between what is right and what is wrong."

He leaned back and smiled and said, "No, we don't." Before I could say anything else, he got very serious. The most serious I had ever seen him. Playing nice had not worked, so he decided to change things up. He said, "You are being way too aggressive. You're misunderstanding the power differential here. You even sent investigators onto my property dressed like ninjas. If you keep coming after me the way that you are, I am telling you, somebody is going to get hurt."

Make no mistake, this was a threat. I knew that I needed to be more careful. However, backing off was not an option.

————————

Without missing a beat, we tracked down a woman named Maritza Vasquez in Miami who was a former employee of Jean-Luc's Epstein-funded modeling agency, MC². In June 2010, my investigator and I knocked on her front door. When she agreed to talk to us, I called a court reporter to appear at her house immediately and take a sworn statement, not knowing if we would ever get another shot at her testimony.

While Maritza had met Jeffrey Epstein on only one occasion, she was very familiar with the inner workings of Jean-Luc Brunel's modeling agency. She had known Jean-Luc for years. She had been hired by his prior modeling agency, Karin, as a bookkeeper in 1998. She remained with Karin until the formation of MC$^2$ in 2003, at which time she continued to work for Brunel at the new agency.

Maritza confirmed what we knew—that Epstein and Brunel were close friends, Brunel was living in Epstein's apartment at 301 East Sixty-Sixth Street, and Epstein was financing MC$^2$. Maritza knew that young models were staying in the apartments owned by Mark Epstein and rented by Jeffrey in New York City. She described Jean-Luc as a cocaine addict with an insatiable appetite for young girls.

Maritza told us that Jean-Luc would bring teenage girls with him to Jeffrey's house and that Jean-Luc would arrange young girls for Epstein when he traveled to places such as Ecuador. She explained how the modeling industry has historically provided easy access to teenage girls who would enter the country without their parents and without supervision. Maritza believed that the only reason Jeffrey Epstein was involved in MC$^2$ was because of access to the girls; that was the only similarity between Jean-Luc and Jeffrey.

Her statement made me pay even closer attention to Jean-Luc because I now knew that Epstein had a direct pipeline to young girls through the cover of a modeling agency. I was hot on Jean-Luc's trail and ready to expose him as one of Epstein's biggest enablers.

While Jean-Luc was important, Ghislaine was still at the top of my list. Just before I was about to board the plane to New York in July 2010 for Maxwell's deposition, I received a call from her attorney explaining that Maxwell's mother was very ill, so Maxwell was leaving the country, with no plans to return to the United States. Sound familiar? I prepared a motion for sanctions against her, given that my travel was already booked and I had spent so much time preparing. To avoid the drama, Maxwell agreed to pay all the costs associated with my troubles, which she actually did—her attorney sent me a check. But I was still enormously bothered by the fact that she could just get on a plane, leave the country, and claim she was never returning. Mainly because on some level—every level—I knew it wasn't true.

Shortly after she had successfully ditched her deposition, I was in my kitchen and saw a copy of the August 2010 issue of *People* magazine lying on the counter. Inside was a large spread featuring Bill Clinton walking his daughter, Chelsea, down the aisle at her wedding on July 31. I picked up the magazine to read further because I knew Clinton was one of Epstein's close friends. I looked at the picture of the father and the bride, briefly scanning the page beyond Bill and Chelsea. *Holy shit*, I thought. Who was front and center on the aisle? Ghislaine Maxwell. As it turned out, she didn't leave the United States forever. For all I knew, she hadn't left at all. But there was an important tell in this move by Epstein, too: Clearly he *really* didn't want me to talk to Ghislaine.

We knew Bill Clinton had been on Jeffrey's private plane many times and that Jeffrey had subsequently been busted for sexual contact with minors, pleaded guilty, and gone to jail. Still, his former lover, and closest advisor, was invited to Clinton's daughter's wedding. How odd. I've never said or thought that Bill Clinton did anything wrong in connection with Ghislaine, Epstein, or their airplane rides, but by all appearances Clinton had helpful information. I couldn't help but wonder why he wouldn't pick up the phone and tell us what he knew?

# NINETEEN

# MARISSA

W E HAD QUESTIONS FOR CLINTON, but didn't have time to chase every lead. We were back in the office, trying to piece the intricate details of Marissa's case together, as it was set to go to trial first.

The court had ordered that the case be mediated, which happens in every case to give the defendant the chance to make a monetary offer and the plaintiff to accept or reject that offer. For Epstein, mediation was just another opportunity to play games. I had prepared Marissa for it. Our mediation took place on April 5, 2010. Rather than make an offer, Epstein wanted Marissa to walk away from her case to avoid further invasion of her life. It was Epstein's way of gauging her courage. We walked out without hesitation, not allowing Epstein to get a good read. I believed then that we were actually going to get Epstein to a trial. From my perspective, trial was the only way to go in Marissa's case because it would expose his organization.

During the final preparations for trial, which was set for July, Epstein started to realize that he might not win this game of chicken and got worried. On June 28, 2010, he filed a motion practically begging for another mediation. We resisted it, knowing that trying the case would accomplish more in the end. But, at Epstein's urging, the court ordered a settlement conference to take place on July 6, 2010, at the federal courthouse in Miami with ninety-two-year-old federal magistrate Judge Peter R. Palermo. Marissa was resolute; she was not going to settle for anything. There was no amount of money that could take her off the course to trial.

In light of our belief that Epstein was using this second settlement discussion as a means to intimidate her, we filed a motion on June 30 to ensure that she would not be forced to come into contact with Epstein at the settlement conference, in keeping with the no-contact order that had been entered at his plea hearing on June 30, 2008. Taking the matter very seriously, Magistrate Palermo issued an order the very next day requiring the no-contact order to remain in full effect and directing Epstein to arrive at the federal courthouse earlier than Marissa with instruction that the parties would be dismissed separately from the settlement conference at different times. With these parameters in place, we were feeling better about our required attendance at the conference.

On July 1, 2010, just five days before the scheduled settlement conference, I got a frantic call from Marissa. "Brad! They're trying to kill me!" On her way to the grocery store, she noticed that an Infiniti SUV was following close behind her. When she left, the same SUV began tailing her in a much more aggressive manner, causing her to run off the side of Haverhill Road in West Palm Beach. It didn't take much to run her off the road because she was a relatively novice driver. I knew that because I'm the one who taught her how to drive in a parking lot in Palm Beach so she could pass her driver's license test. Nevertheless, she was scared.

When she finally got home, the guy who had followed her was parked across the street in front of her house, intermittently flashing his high beam lights into her home. Now Marissa and her grandmother were terrified. Marissa's one-year-old daughter huddled into her mother's arms, trembling. Never mind a trial—Marissa thought that she was going to be killed for standing up to Epstein for too long.

I told her to call the police while I called Mike Fisten. By the time the police arrived, they actually found Epstein's investigator sitting in his car in the driveway and told him he had to leave her private property. In true Epstein form, the investigator just went back to the other side of the street, into the public space, and kept his lights shining through Marissa's window. Realizing that the police weren't going to do more, my investigator parked his car between Epstein's investigator and the house, blocking the headlights. In fact, Mike positioned his car so he could shine his own headlights into Epstein's investigator's car. At the end of the shine-off, Mike was left with no choice but to take Marissa to my office in the middle of the night before checking her into a hotel where we could keep her safe. We drafted a motion to inform the court of Epstein's intimidation, which we would file the next day.

As Mike was leaving the hotel where he had just dropped Marissa off, he saw Epstein's investigator walking into the hotel, looking for her. We called Marissa and had her walk down the back stairs while Epstein's investigator was waiting in the lobby with my investigator. We were finally able to help her escape from that hotel into the car with another one of our investigators, who then took her to another hotel and watched her for days until the mediation was set to begin.

Even though Marissa was now in a safe location, she was afraid for the safety of her daughter and her grandmother. Her entire attitude had changed, for good reason. She now wanted the case to be over at all costs. Lynn and Courtney were already scared to death, and knowing what Marissa was going through was frightening them as well. Both were calling to ask if Epstein was coming after them next and whether they were in danger. We told Lynn and Courtney to be in Miami with us on the day of Marissa's settlement conference. That way we knew they would all be safe.

We had been excited that a trial would finally make many of the details about Jeffrey Epstein public, which would increase the likelihood that others would come forward. But by now, all three girls had experienced serious forms of his intimidation, and all three were ready for the fight to be over.

Our clients were frightened when we arrived in Miami. When we entered the federal courthouse, because of the no-contact order, we were taken to a private elevator that I didn't even know existed, despite having been to that courthouse many times by now. When we got out of the elevator, we were greeted by Judge Palermo's assistant, who looked at Marissa and promised to personally make sure that she didn't have to see Epstein. Marissa was still scared, but she was also comforted by the precautions that Judge Palermo and his staff had taken.

When Judge Palermo came into the room to introduce himself, we quickly warned him about Epstein. Honestly, we didn't have much confidence because we felt that no one could actually influence Epstein. He did whatever he wanted, whenever he wanted, and no judge or anyone else was going to change that. Judge Palermo must have sensed our skepticism of him and related it in part to his age because he sharply responded, "You don't have to worry about me being intimidated. Manuel Noriega sat right there in the same chair where Mr. Epstein will be sitting. And don't think for a second that I am going to get worn out by this process. Last year, when I was ninety-one, I did ninety-one push-ups every day. This year, I do ninety-two." As he finished the last word, he dropped to the floor right there and began doing push-ups just to prove the point. His grit reminded me so much of Papa that I knew he was right for this job.

Knowing what was at stake, Palermo conducted the opening statement of the settlement conference sitting at his desk in his office with Epstein and his attorney sitting directly across from him. Marissa, Paul Cassell, Steve Jaffe, and I were in the conference room that connected to Palermo's office. In order to speak to all parties at once while ensuring that Marissa did not have to see Epstein's face, I sat in the doorway between the conference room and the office, with Paul behind me and Marissa inside the next room at the opposite end of the table—she was close enough to hear but far enough to feel safe.

Judge Palermo made it clear right out of the gate that he would not tolerate any potential intimidation, which was why he'd positioned the parties as he had. Epstein's attorney immediately attempted to interject, but was met by Judge Palermo holding his hand up to stop the attorney from talking. Palermo didn't say a word. He put his head in his hand and paused for an uncomfortable period of time. Steve quietly asked if I thought the judge had fallen asleep. After at least thirty seconds, Palermo looked up, straight at Epstein, who was sitting four feet in front of him. "I've read the recent motion that the plaintiff filed in this case. I understand that certain events unfolded resulting in the lawyers having to take this girl away from her child and her home. I'm thinking about throwing you in jail." Epstein looked amazed. He couldn't believe that someone would speak to him that way. Judge Palermo was dead serious. For the first time, Epstein looked like he knew he wasn't in control. Everyone in the room sensed that this wasn't going to end well for him.

There came a point when Epstein said he was making a good-faith effort to settle Marissa's case, but that it didn't make sense for him to do so unless Courtney and Lynn settled their cases, too. No doubt Epstein planned to use this as another reason to try to postpone the trial. But this move was predictable. We called our investigator, who was waiting outside with Courtney and Lynn, and told him to bring them to the front of the courthouse. When I walked back upstairs with them, Judge Palermo had a big smile on his face.

Palermo got all three cases settled. Courtney, Lynn, and Marissa were relieved, and my law partners were happy, but I was disappointed. I had put so much time into getting ready for this trial, and now it was gone. Most people thought I won that round, but I didn't see it that way. Still, while Epstein thought it was over, I was not about to let it go.

As a consolation, in preparing for Marissa's trial, we had found two additional victims who were going to testify as witnesses. When Courtney, Lynn, and Marissa's cases settled, on July 6, 2010, these witnesses became clients who wanted to pursue their own claims against Epstein. So we picked up where we'd left off, immediately filed a lawsuit for one of the women, and went at him again.

# TWENTY

# GAMING THE
# SYSTEM, AGAIN

I N JANUARY 2011, I GOT a call from Reichart Von Wolfsheild, a genius computer programmer and engineer who had developed the data management program Qtask. Qtask was used to keep track of the many pieces of information a law practice must use—from files, pleadings, depositions, conversations among team members, and evidence, to calendars, client contacts, emails, and letters. Qtask was also the software company that RRA had used to store case-related information. Rumor was that the firm had even invested in the company. When RRA imploded, all of Scott Rothstein's investment assets, and presumably those of the firm, were seized by the government and subject to forfeiture.

Because of the relation to RRA, Qtask, Reichart's software company, was a prime target of the government. The bankruptcy trustee then attacked Qtask as the storage system of information likely to include Ponzi-scheme-related evidence. It was a shame because Reichart—who wasn't involved in the firm's dealings, illegal or otherwise—was an innocent entrepreneur. He didn't deserve the headache.

Nonetheless, the bankruptcy action dragged Reichart in to defend the confidentiality of the program's users. The government wanted his software company to turn over confidential information derived from the database, which Reichart couldn't allow or else every client he had would have pulled out for fear of similar forced disclosure. Reichart spent a lot of money protecting this important user data, causing his product to practically be killed during the proceedings. Still, he was a good and honest guy who would have died fighting for his product and what he thought was right.

I had followed the attacks on Reichart in Judge Ray's bankruptcy court. Since I was also being attacked, we were in the same boat. By the time Epstein invited Reichart to his island, Little Saint James, in January 2011 for a scientific brain-trust meeting he was hosting, Epstein also knew all about Qtask. Epstein's lawyers had asked me many questions in my deposition about the program and especially about the projects that I had stored in Qtask related to Epstein. This program basically contained all the most secret investigative information that I had on Epstein, and Epstein knew from the RRA bankruptcy proceedings that Reichart was the protector of that information. Epstein also knew that if he could get access to my Qtask projects, he would know everything that I knew—or didn't know—about him, enabling him to very easily defend against my attack.

While Reichart knew of me as a trial lawyer at RRA, and was aware that I was litigating a case against Jeffrey Epstein, he had no idea about the substance of that litigation. Nonetheless, Reichart was an honorable person and Epstein had underestimated his loyalty to doing what was right. So, when Epstein invited Reichart to his island, Reichart accepted the invitation in order to do a reconnaissance mission.

Reichart wasn't back for a day before he reached out to me through his lawyer, a mutual friend named Rob Buschel, to tell me about his visit to the Caribbean island where Epstein hosted various scientists and mathematicians. He gave me a full download.

Reichart isn't like a normal person. He has an extraordinary mind and remembered every single detail from the entire trip. Other people at this event included Nobel Prize winner Murray Gell-Mann, Ron Reisman of NASA, actor and financial wizard Brock Pierce, Caltech biochemist Frances Arnold, and journalist Dan Dubno. As soon as Reichart introduced himself to Epstein, he was cornered about the true reason why he was invited.

In Epstein's typical way, he attempted to befriend Reichart by telling him, "You and I are connected in a weird way, through the RRA litigation." He then asked him, "Do you know Brad Edwards? He's a problem for me. To resolve this problem, I filed a lawsuit against him to throw flak at it." Epstein told Reichart that his plan was to just continue throwing knives at this "Edwards problem" with the intent to derail the cases that I had filed against him. To facilitate his master plan, Epstein was requesting information and data to which he knew he wasn't entitled, similar to my emails he was trying to get. To further this goal, Epstein asked Reichart directly how he could obtain the information that I had accumulated on him, which was stored in RRA's Jeffrey Epstein Qtask project. He wanted to know whether he should subpoena it from Reichart directly.

More important for my purposes, Reichart reported to me that Epstein actually talked openly about sex and about girls on the island. Epstein shared that he liked young girls, but not "children," which Reichart interpreted Epstein to mean prepubescent. Epstein attempted to justify his philosophy that age is inconsequential, explaining that he simply wanted girls who were physically developed but were as young as possible. To Reichart, it appeared that Epstein was a "cult leader"—the many girls around him appeared to follow him and respect his "cult."

Epstein told Reichart that he targeted very young girls, and that before he got in trouble, he hadn't cared about their ages. Reichart described him as a lion that wanted to prey on girls who were, according to an old definition, "nubile," or, as Epstein put it, "the youngest-looking girl with breasts." Epstein said that he was now aware that people were watching him, so he was not going to be caught with an underage girl again, at least not in the United States, where it is illegal to touch them. At the same time Reichart felt that Epstein was not sorry in the least for his past sexual interactions with underage girls.

In fact, Reichart said, other than complications that arose from the law, Epstein seemed to see no problem on any level with his previous activity that landed him in legal trouble. In an attempt to minimize what he'd done in the eyes of others, Epstein would say to a *New York Post* reporter in February 2011 that his sexual interactions with minors were no big deal. He told the reporter specifically, "I'm not a sexual predator, I'm an 'offender.' It's the difference between a murderer and a person who steals a bagel." To Epstein, the law was wrong. Not his ways. But he knew getting caught again would not be as easy to get out of. The next "bagel" he stole would be much more costly.

Epstein spent most of his time with Reichart talking about formulaic systems that might be invented to "get young girls." Epstein expressed the view that women were "a life support system for a vagina." So, he wanted to discuss the statistical analysis of the marketplace and new ways for finding girls. He admitted that he knew nothing about computers but he thought the internet might hold the key for meeting volumes of young females in a short time.

A lot of the information Reichart provided I was already aware of. Epstein knew there was not a thread of truth to the lawsuit he filed against me and was using it to try to get information to which he was not entitled. He saw me as a major problem that he needed to shut down, both to eliminate any trouble from his prior conduct and to ensure that he could continue to go about business as usual. Epstein's arguments that my RRA emails were relevant to his fake lawsuit were an old tune at this point. The weak points only confirmed what I already understood: he was trying to get inside my private work product, my thinking, and my strategy in order to effectively map out his moves against me.

Reichart verified something else I suspected: Epstein was not going to stop his sex abuse or change his thinking about girls simply because he had been caught in Palm Beach and jailed for a few months under a cushy deal. He couldn't stop. This was his way of life. It was what drove him. Now he was just looking for more sophisticated and technologically advanced ways to find more girls and pursue them with less risk. The only thing jail had taught him was to be more careful and not get caught.

Reichart was on my team, but Epstein had no idea, so I was not about to blow his cover. Reichart's information would have helped with the judge presiding over my case, but the facts would come out eventually, so I decided to use his information in other ways.

With Reichart confirming Epstein's desire to discover what I knew about him, there was no doubt in my mind that Epstein had kept a copy of my entire trove of emails when they were turned over to his lawyer (supposedly for benign copying purposes and nothing more). We had warned Special Master Carney that this would happen.

Improperly having my emails wasn't enough. Epstein wanted everything he wasn't supposed to have. He wanted to find a way to get into my Qtask files, where I had stored my most valuable information about him. This was the reason he'd brought a computer programmer to his island: to figure out how to steal the most secretive part of my files and work product, including all the information too sensitive to put into emails. It would have been a smart move had it worked, but it didn't. Reichart couldn't be bought by the bad guys.

# TWENTY-ONE

# THE ISLAND

OTHER THAN WHAT WE HAD learned from the media, Reichart had provided the only information that we had about Jeffrey Epstein's private island, Little Saint James, which Epstein referred to as Little Saint Jeff's. While Reichart provided a full description of what he saw, he didn't have access to the entire island during his stay, and he didn't experience what we came to understand was going on behind the scenes.

Over the years, I interviewed at least half a dozen clients who were part of the fuller story of what happened on Little Saint Jeff's. Some had been to the island only once and others had been many, many times. Each had her unique stories, but all of them had a common thread: sex.

Seloh was one of Epstein's eighteen-year-old female invitees. She recounted her story to me, which encapsulated what I came to learn was a typical island "adventure" for a newcomer. She was an aspiring model in New York when she was recruited to meet Jeffrey Epstein, a wealthy financier with boundless connections who convinced her he was able to fulfill her most ambitious dreams and catapult her into the professional modeling life that she had always wanted.

After a few visits to his mansion in New York, and a few "massages," she was invited to his island along with several other young women in 2007. She was flown from Teterboro Airport in New Jersey to Saint Thomas on

Epstein's private Boeing 727 jet. After landing in Saint Thomas, she was taken by Epstein's private helicopter to Little Saint James. Once they arrived, Seloh and the three other similarly aged girls who had flown over with her stepped off of the helicopter into paradise while the island staff grabbed their bags. The girls walked barefoot toward the main house. Sculptures and statues lined the pathway up to an open structure. The girls were greeted by the regular crew—Ghislaine Maxwell, Jean-Luc Brunel, Nadia Marcinkova, Sarah Kellen, and, of course, Jeffrey Epstein.

Seloh was shown to her room: a beautiful, spacious cabana with one king-size bed. She walked out to the main outdoor area where everyone was gathered. "Go explore," said Ghislaine in her British accent to Seloh and the others, whom she referred to as "my children." Nadia led Seloh and her new friends down the steps and through an enclosed tunnel, where they encountered a small turtle that they took turns taking pictures with. This was a world that none of these girls had ever experienced.

"What do you want to do next?" asked Nadia.

One of the other girls responded, "Well, what are our options?"

To which Nadia replied, "Anything you can imagine," as she ran back up the stairs and toward ATVs parked on the beach.

Almost as if the whole thing was staged, Epstein was sitting atop one of the ATVs at the front of the line. Each girl jumped on her own ATV. Epstein looked back at the line of girls and yelled, "Follow me!" as he tore off through the sand. Seloh and her new friends followed.

They drove along the purest, cleanest-looking water Seloh had ever seen to their left, and past the intricate architectural structures that filled the island to their right. Seloh had only ever dreamed of seeing a place this beautiful; it was like somewhere from a postcard or in a movie. The experience was exhilarating.

As they approached the main house on their way back, Jeffrey—who was still leading the caravan—slammed on his brakes while going full speed and turned sharply to the right, causing his ATV to spin in dramatic fashion. Each of the women behind him stopped to admire his expert handling of the machine. He stepped off the ATV and said to Nadia, "Take everyone to the kitchen. I'll see you later." He then walked away.

Everyone knew that Nadia Marcinkova held the role of Jeffrey Epstein's girlfriend at the time. She was always around. You see, he had his favorite girls, but there was a difference between a "favorite girl" and his "girlfriend." First, it was Eva Andersson, then it was Ghislaine Maxwell, and now it was Nadia Marcinkova. Anyone who reached girlfriend status had also proven a commitment to a lifetime of allegiance and unwavering friendship. He once famously said that when a relationship is over, the girlfriend "moves up, not down" to friendship status.

Nadia walked Seloh and the other girls to the main house, where dinner was prepared. Everyone on the island, except for Jeffrey, ate together. The girls sat at the table talking while Sarah sat distantly in the background, scanning the room as if to assess the liabilities and assets. Jean-Luc walked over to pet Maxwell's Yorkie, Max, at the same time. Jean-Luc then tackled Ghislaine into the nearby chair before he engulfed her in one of his playful hugs. To Seloh, Jean-Luc and Ghislaine seemed thick as thieves.

Periodically throughout the day, each of the others had disappeared after Ghislaine or Nadia told them Jeffrey wanted to see them, but Seloh had yet to be summoned for private time with Jeffrey. After dinner, she retired to her room. As she grabbed her phone to check her text messages, there was a knock at the door. It was Ghislaine: "Jeffrey wants to see you now." Seloh walked over to the grand master bedroom. As she approached the door, she was nervous, but she didn't know enough to be too nervous. At most, she thought this would be a "regular" massage, which was sure to include having to pinch Jeffrey's nipples while he masturbated, but by this point, she was accustomed to that.

She opened the door and saw Jeffrey standing sternly in his white bathrobe in front of her. He pointed to the other side of the room, where there was a bar, and instructed her to turn around, bend over, and hold it. Seloh walked slowly toward the bar. When she got there, she turned back to look for Jeffrey and saw one of Jeffrey's other girls walk out from behind him.

The girl was dressed in all leather with a leather whip in her hand. "Remove your clothes," she said.

Seloh complied. Her thoughts spun. *I have no way out. I have no choice. I'm on an island in the middle of the ocean. WTF.* Before she could get very far: *crack.* She felt the straps of the leather whip smack against her bare bottom.

Jeffrey then instructed, "Put it on." His girl attached a harness containing a plastic dildo across her waist. Seloh turned around to see what was going on. As she began to turn, Epstein sternly warned her, "Do not turn around. Keep your hands on the bar." Reminding herself that she didn't have any other option but to comply, Seloh did as instructed. The girl approached and within seconds, Seloh felt something thrusting inside of her.

While periodically being whipped, she thought, *This hurts. What am I doing? How do I get out of here?* She opened her eyes and peered to her left to see Jeffrey smiling wryly while masturbating. As he held himself, Jeffrey spoke only and directly to the other girl. "Do you love this? Is this turning you on?"

"Oh yeah," she replied as she continued thrusting from behind Seloh.

"Seloh, grab your clothes. You can go," Jeffrey said with glee. Looking back just before she left the door, Seloh saw Jeffrey and his other girl go at it in the middle of the room. She thought, *What just happened? How does everyone around me think this is normal? Is this what I have to do to get where I need to go? Do I have any choice?* Calming her nerves, she realized that, at the moment, there was no choice. If she ultimately resisted, her career and life could be ruined. She convinced herself that this was normal and to just be happy and thankful.

The next morning, she played volleyball on the beach with Jean-Luc. Ghislaine yelled for another girl who was on the island that day, Natalie, to follow her to Jeffrey. Seloh immediately had flashbacks to the night before, realizing in that moment that Ghislaine controlled the rotation of Jeffrey's daily routine.

On the last night, Seloh was sleeping peacefully in her bed, not having seen Jeffrey for the entire day. She woke up to feel an erect penis inside of her from behind and Jeffrey's left index finger over her lips as if instructing her to *shhhh*. "I don't want to do this," said Seloh.

"Yes, you do. It's okay," he said. "The only thing that I ask is that you don't tell my girlfriend that I'm sleeping here." While Nadia obviously knew Jeffrey was engaging in sex with every other female who was around, she had one rule, and that was that he did not sleep in the same bed as another woman. But that didn't matter; once again, Seloh had no choice but to go along with it and ultimately to categorize it as her new normal.

The next morning, everyone met for breakfast. Seloh found her seat at the table. Without turning around, Nadia, hearing him approach, said, "Where did you sleep last night?"

Seloh, looking past her to Jeffrey, saw Jeffrey hold his index finger over his lips. He responded, "In the cabana—you were snoring." Seloh immediately felt enormous guilt. But she knew what everyone else knew—Jeffrey was in control. The only way to survive was to live under Jeffrey's rules, which were very clear.

Among them, say nothing.

# TWENTY-TWO

# IT'S NEVER OVER

I N LATE 2010 OR EARLY 2011, a reporter named Sharon Churcher from the *Daily Mail* called me saying that she wanted to meet with Virginia Roberts and asked if I could find her. I had figured out that Virginia was Jane Doe 102 because her name appeared repeatedly on various pieces of evidence that I had obtained. From questions her lawyers had asked during the Jane Doe 102 lawsuit, I also knew she had been lent out for sex to others. To me, she held the key to unlocking another level of Epstein's depravity.

I needed to speak with Virginia, so if some dogged reporter was willing to take a chance traveling across the world to knock on her door, I was happy to share what I knew. I passed along the few leads that I had to Sharon, who quickly tracked Virginia down in Australia. Sharon went to see Virginia and called me after interviewing her for two days. She told me Virginia wanted to be involved in the CVRA case. Finally, someone from Epstein's inner circle wanted to talk, and wanted to help.

After her interview with Churcher, Virginia called me herself. I explained the CVRA case, which was still in the discovery phase as we attempted to uncover documentation to prove that Epstein and the government actively concealed the NPA from the victims. We discussed how the goal of the case was in line with her own—to put Epstein in jail. She'd heard Epstein had attacked me personally with a bogus lawsuit. She knew he would attack anyone, which is why she had escaped from him the first chance she got, during a trip to Thailand nine years earlier.

At Epstein's direction, Virginia had been dispatched to Thailand to pick up a young girl, interview her, and let Epstein know if she was "qualified." But after having been used as a sex slave for years, Virginia saw the trip to Thailand as a way to free herself from the invisible chains of sexual servitude.

Epstein paid for Virginia's coach ticket to Thailand and for her hotel in Chiang Mai during the trip. Rather than meet the little girl for Epstein, she recognized her chance to escape—she went into town and met a guy from Down Under who fell in love with her and promised to take care of her. She married him days later, hopped a plane with him to Australia, and never looked back. She hid in Australia for nearly ten years, during which she had three children. That she had left the United States—the only country that she had ever known—in order to escape Epstein gave further credence to her story.

Virginia explained that she had been recruited by Ghislaine Maxwell. Maxwell had escaped being held responsible for any of Epstein's transgressions in any way up until this point, but that could all change after Virginia. Virginia began traveling with Epstein and Maxwell and became part of what she called their "dysfunctional family."

If she wasn't servicing Epstein, Virginia was being made to service one of his high-powered friends, and if she wasn't servicing someone at Epstein's direction, she was working for the organization, which meant hunting down girls to bring to Epstein. Maxwell was the one who knew what Jeffrey liked, which meant she was the one who taught Virginia the skills she needed in order to keep him happy. Those skills included how to act in front of important and powerful people, how to dress, how to hold her knife and fork, and, of course, how to please him sexually.

Because of her upbringing, Virginia was a prime target. She had been abused at an early age, was a runaway many times over by thirteen, had multiple run-ins with the law, and was a school dropout. Not to mention, she was stunningly attractive.

On Virginia's initial call, I asked her to provide proof of some of her allegations, including her dramatic escape from Epstein into a new life in Australia. She scanned and sent me the envelope with Maxwell's directions and cell phone number as well as the travel and hotel receipts from Thailand charged to Epstein's card.

Not long after, Virginia showed me a photograph of herself as a seventeen-year-old girl wedged in between Ghislaine Maxwell and Prince Andrew, a photo that she described as being taken by Jeffrey Epstein in Maxwell's apartment in London. Of all the people she claimed to have been introduced to and made to have sex with, the Duke of York sounded the most preposterous. Yet here was a picture of the two of them arm in arm, smiling like a happy pair out for the night—though he's twenty-three years her senior.

I hung up the phone and thought about all the things Virginia had told me. None of it was surprising, but all of it was confirmation of an extraordinary sex abuse enterprise that went far beyond what was uncovered in Florida. We knew Epstein was addicted to sex with children and had assistants scheduling multiple appointments per day with different girls. He traveled all the time, all over the world, with the same assistants, some of whom were named co-conspirators and who clearly knew what he was up to. The "Holy Grail" from Alfredo Rodriguez listed female names and telephone numbers from numerous locations around the world under the heading of "massage" in the exact same way that it listed the names of many underage girls under the same title for Florida. It only made sense that his sex addiction was not confined to Florida.

While there had not been any evidence of Prince Andrew spending time at the Palm Beach house while little girls were upstairs with Epstein, witnesses had confirmed that Epstein and the prince were close friends.

I studied the evidence Virginia sent me, namely her photos and Thailand hotel information bearing Epstein's name. Virginia took off from New York to Thailand on September 27, 2002, and arrived there with handwritten instructions to call Maxwell on her cell. According to Epstein's personal flight logs, Epstein and Maxwell took off from JFK in New York on September 21, 2002, on his Boeing jet on an extended trip to Africa with numerous passengers, including Sarah Kellen, Nadia Marcinkova, the actors Chris Tucker and Kevin Spacey, six U.S. Secret Service agents, and the object of their attention, former president Bill Clinton. Yes, while Virginia Roberts was being flown to Thailand on Epstein's dime, Epstein and Maxwell were traveling with Bill Clinton to various countries in Africa.

Upon returning from Africa, President Clinton commented via a spokesperson to *New York* magazine reporter Landon Thomas Jr.: "Jeffrey is both a highly successful financier and a committed philanthropist with a keen sense of global markets and an in-depth knowledge of twenty-first-century science. . . . I especially appreciated his insights and generosity during the recent trip to Africa to work on democratization, empowering the poor, citizen service, and combating HIV/AIDS." Years later, I learned more about the close bond President Clinton appeared to have with Jeffrey Epstein on that Africa trip. According to eyewitnesses, including my client Chauntae Davies, who was only twenty-three years old when she traveled to Africa with the duo, the men exchanged somewhat crass jokes about women more than they discussed the solutions to major world problems.

In addition to Prince Andrew, Virginia told me the identities of other individuals whom she was lent out to, and who would have information that was valuable and relevant to both the CVRA case and in my personal litigation against Epstein.

Because Epstein had based his malicious lawsuit against me on the allegation that I had attempted to take the depositions of powerful people who he claimed had no knowledge of any relevant information, such as Alan Dershowitz, David Copperfield, Bill Clinton, and Donald Trump, Virginia's account of her experience was very important. Jack Scarola called her, and with her consent, tape-recorded a conversation. She explained that she was frightened for her safety and limited in what she would say on the recording, but she confirmed that these powerful and connected friends of Jeffrey's would have very relevant information if they were under oath and told the truth.

Getting them to tell the truth under oath would be difficult, which made Virginia, who was willing to share what she knew, even more important.

# TWENTY-THREE

# YOUR MOVE OR MINE?

THINGS REALLY STARTED TO HEAT up between Jeffrey and me on a more personal level around this time, in early 2011. In response to the lawsuit that he had filed against me in December 2009, I had, of course, filed a counterclaim for malicious prosecution. My malicious prosecution case had been ongoing for more than a year, but the facts that we had uncovered had now changed the game. It was becoming obvious to anyone paying attention that his claims against me were both frivolous and calculated with a purpose of making me go away for good.

I was getting closer to blowing up his whole organization when he sued me out of desperation. He had no facts on his side, but he did have unlimited resources. I had been closing in on him and he had used the legal system to knock me off. But now, I was back on offense and Virginia gave me more confidence. With few pieces left on his chessboard, Epstein's lawsuit—and him with it—were finally in trouble.

But Epstein wasn't going to make it easy. He was determined to dispose of me. To carry that out, his main law firm continued to curry favor with their billionaire bully client. One of his lawyers demanded to meet in person, which I did. It was a short meeting with a clear message that Jeffrey Epstein was a powerful person who would financially destroy me and my family if I continued with my counterclaim. I quickly ended the meeting, telling him, "Tell Jeffrey these types of personal threats don't make me want to back down, and I don't forget any of them."

After the meeting with his lawyer, I was furious. All I could think about was how I was going to devote even more effort into putting Epstein in jail. This was now a war and I was preparing to ramp up the pressure. Almost sensing that the personal threat through his lawyer was going to elevate my attack, Jeffrey Epstein called me himself at my office the next morning. I was surprised by his call, but maybe I shouldn't have been. He said he had heard I was mad at him, and that he didn't blame me. He wanted to assure me that the message had not come from him, and that he was personally going to "take care of it."

From one day to the next, he went from threatening my livelihood and my family through a conduit acting on his behalf to personally conveying to me that his legal team had acted out of turn. I knew that no move was ever made by Epstein's lawyers without his approval, but I also knew it could only help to play along. This was a typical mobster move where wise guys would shake down an adversary and then swoop in the next day and offer protection to that adversary for a fee.

Still, once he thought I understood that he was really a good guy, he couldn't help but deliver his message, his way. He said that while his lawyers had miscalculated their last move, it would be "best for everyone if we all just walked away from the situation." In a flash, he reverted back to his threats. He then out of nowhere told me that he knew that one of my former law partners at RRA was "f***ing a prostitute." *So what?* I thought. *Why would I care about that?* He went on to tell me that in addition to having sex with her, my former RRA law partner had police officers threaten that she needed to leave the state of Florida. His "people" were telling him that this RRA lawyer and the goon cops who were involved were going to be arrested for it and that his "people" were looking into the conduct of all the lawyers at RRA—not just those related to the Ponzi scheme.

This time, he was sending a different message. He was saying that he would do whatever was necessary to shut down an embarrassing and problematic lawsuit against him, and that he was powerful enough to be provided highly confidential government information hot off the press. While he was apologetic for the actions of his lawyers as his agents, he verified that he was still in a position to have access to people and information that should make me nervous.

After the call, I told my gumshoe investigator this story and asked what in the world Epstein was talking about. I was assured that there was no truth in it, and that, as my investigator put it, "He's just talking shit." Nobody I knew had ever heard this story about a prostitute or extortion by police, so he told me to write it off. But I didn't. The eerie confidence of Epstein's voice as he was telling me these details made my gut jump.

Was it possible that Epstein was still so connected that he was given top secret information on the RRA federal criminal investigation? My investigator reminded me that Epstein was a child molester and the FBI did not filter their investigations to anyone, much less a criminal of Epstein's caliber, but I stored the entire conversation away in a special file cabinet in my mind.

Sure enough, two years later, in May 2014, Stuart Rosenfeldt, a former named partner at RRA, was arrested for doing basically what Epstein had described. So were the cops that helped him. What's more, these investigative facts were highly confidential at the time he told me. They were investigated by the FBI and a tightly constructed U.S. Attorney's Office, and yet Epstein knew virtually every important detail.

I remember the day that Stuart Rosenfeldt was arrested. I was sitting with one of my partners, Steve Jaffe. We looked at each other and Steve said, "Holy shit." Epstein knew this years ago and we thought he was just making it up. Who was his source inside the government? From that point forward, I was careful to keep my investigative materials to a trusted few people, restricting even what I provided to the government.

After telling me he was firing his lawyers because they had threatened me, Epstein went back to the drawing board. This time, in April 2012, he hired lawyers from my own legal circle—Fred Haddad and Tonja Haddad Coleman, a father-daughter duo whom I had known for years. I had no doubt that our friendship and familiarity was precisely the reason Epstein had hired them. His goal was to send the message that he could infiltrate my personal connections whenever he wanted.

This was not a new concept. During the federal criminal investigation of Epstein—the case that had ended with his cushy jail term—he had hired former U.S. attorney Guy Lewis and a former assistant U.S. attorney in the Southern District of Florida, Lilly Ann Sanchez, who had continued relationships inside the office, in order to ensure that he had a direct line of communication with the supervisors in charge of prosecuting his case. He'd also hired Republican heavyweights Ken Starr and Jay Lefkowitz to make sure that he could get "off campus" meetings with the then sitting U.S. attorney Alex Acosta. Hiring friends of those who would be making decisions was the strategy. This time, it hit closer to home, though. He was hiring acquaintances of mine.

This move sent a powerful, multilayered message to me. On the one hand, he was hiring someone who was friendly to me and who would therefore treat me fairly, the way he knew I prided myself on treating others. He wanted me to think that he wasn't a bad guy. But it was also his reminder that he could use his money to turn friends against me.

Tonja was, at the time, a local lawyer who had primarily practiced criminal defense law. Her husband, Tom, had been my supervisor when I was a young prosecutor at the state attorney's office. Her father, Fred, was a respected trial lawyer who had for decades built a reputation for trying any case at any time, regardless of how badly the deck was stacked against him. The fact that his name was on the pleadings also made this hire more threatening to me.

Epstein was stepping it up a level.

(I would find out in early 2018 that Tonja and Fred had never even received the boxes of case files that Epstein's old law firms had maintained over the years. The files remained in the possession of Epstein's main law firm, Fowler White, until 2018, when they were obtained by Epstein's trial counsel who had eventually replaced Tonja and Fred. This fact underlined beyond a doubt that the hiring of the Haddads was what it appeared to be:

an intimidation ploy. It annoyed and disappointed me, but intimidate me it did not.)

This one-on-one lawsuit with Epstein was consuming too much time. The distraction from my pursuit of Epstein in the CVRA case was unavoidable. He used the lawsuit as his vehicle for harassment, and because of the "litigation privilege"—a legal concept that allows parties in a lawsuit to say whatever they want about each other, whether true or false—he could say anything in the course of legal proceedings and suffer no consequences for it. And I would get stuck having to defend against each falsehood.

I couldn't sue him or his lawyers for lying about me. There was no effective redress. I simply had to keep litigating against him. Only if I could keep fighting to the end—and win—could I escape from this vindictive suit. Still, I saw the positive: yes, his lawsuit against me gave him a legal vehicle to carry out threats of harm, but it also gave me a legal vehicle to keep digging into his crimes with the goal of, one day, exposing those bad acts to law enforcement.

This was no ordinary lawsuit, though, because he was no ordinary adversary. Epstein hired investigators who camped out outside my house. That caused me to hire my own investigator to watch his investigators.

On one occasion in 2011, my investigator Mike Fisten found out through the private investigator community that one of Epstein's hired henchmen believed he had uncovered information about me that they could finally use as blackmail. They had discovered that rather than driving home every day after work, I was actually driving to a woman's house in Weston, Florida. They had placed a homing device on the bottom of my car and tracked me driving to this "secret rendezvous" every night. I laughed. My investigator didn't. I assured him that his intel was wrong. Regardless, Mike said he needed to check my car to locate the tracking device. He found nothing.

As we were standing by my car in the parking garage, Steve Jaffe pulled in his silver Infiniti M37. Steve drove the same make and model as I did at the time. Then it hit me: I looked at Mike and said, "Get the f*** out of here." We walked over to Steve's car and Mike began searching under the bumpers. Steve got out, really confused.

They had placed the tracking device on Steve's car. Idiots.

———————

In addition to bothering me in the physical world, Epstein was employing psychological warfare in the courtroom. I had told him during one of our telephone calls that paying me money, alone, was never going to settle our case. I reiterated that before I ever settled anything, he would have to admit that he fabricated the entire case against me. If he didn't do that, then I could never get him prosecuted—everyone would think whatever I said was made up as part of some civil litigation. I should not have told him that. He used every word he learned to his advantage.

Knowing my position, he would file "proposals for settlement" with the court, offering to settle my case for hundreds of thousands of dollars, knowing that the case wasn't about money for me. But what he also knew was that my refusal to accept a payment was something he could leverage into greater threats. Because of the way the law works in Florida, if I declined his offers to settle, went to trial, and obtained a jury verdict 25 percent less than the offer I had rejected, I would be responsible for paying his legal fees. Anyone want to take a guess at how many millions those were?

To help you appreciate the gravity of this settlement proposal maneuver, let's hypothetically say that Epstein offered to settle for $1 million. If a jury returned a verdict in my favor in the amount of $700,000, that might look like a win. In fact, the jury might think they had done me a favor. But in reality, because that amount was at least 25 percent less than his $1 million offer of settlement, which I had rejected, I would be responsible for Jeffrey Epstein's legal bills, which by the time of trial would exceed $10 million. Imagine the power he would have wielded with a $10 million judgment over my head for the rest of my life.

This power was not lost on him. Going forward, he would continue to increase the monetary offers using this tool, knowing that I would turn them down on principle alone. This allowed him to offer a lot of money with no risk to him and a growing risk to me. Each time, he increased the chances that one day, he would have me and my family in a position to beg him for financial forgiveness. That was a risk that made everyone around me nervous. The advice from everyone I cared about and respected was to just end this personal battle and accept one of these offers and move on.

But that would allow him to win, which was not an option. I had big plans for Mr. Epstein, and taking his money without forcing him to admit that his allegations against me were false was not going to happen.

In response to one of the last proposals, I might have even set a record for the fastest rejection. I responded via email with my rejection of the proposal in less than a minute. Almost immediately, Epstein called me, laughing. But we both knew that this was a high-stakes game where there would be one big winner and one big loser—both of us were so dug in at this point that we couldn't have it any other way.

# TWENTY-FOUR

# THE RAT

By JUNE 2012, EPSTEIN WAS running out of tricks and had nothing left to do by way of the law. After years of defending me, my team had amassed the evidence that proved his lawsuit had to be dismissed as a fraud. Once that happened, I could really prosecute my case against him for malicious prosecution. But there was more. Epstein was not going to abandon his action without taking Scott Rothstein's deposition. That would be his only chance to tie me in to the Ponzi scheme.

Many depositions had already been taken during the three years since Epstein filed his lawsuit against me. He took depositions of investors in the RRA Ponzi scheme, all of whom verified what everyone knew—that they didn't know me, I didn't know them, and I had nothing to do with Scott's Ponzi scheme. But now, it was time to talk to Scott Rothstein himself, who by this time had been in prison for two years. All of us lawyers had to gather together in the U.S. Attorney's Office while Rothstein joined us on the other end of a Skype connection, testifying from inside a witness protection unit against an all-white backdrop that gave no hint as to his location.

Epstein's last hope for his lawsuit against me depended entirely, and ironically, on the word of a convicted fraudster. I can't say that no part of me was worried before the deposition began. I had no idea what Scott would say. I had hardly spoken with him while I was at RRA and had no communication with him since he had emptied the firm's trust account, run off to Morocco, returned after being threatened, flipped on international Italian mobsters, and sent some of his friends to jail.

The first thing that struck me when I saw Scott in June 2012 was that the twitch that I told you about earlier was completely gone. I guess prison was less stressful than managing a $1 billion fraud.

Scott explained in great detail how he started the Ponzi scheme in 2005 and continued its operation through November 2009. He was able to run it for that long because he created a legitimate law firm as its front with many excellent lawyers. He described having a dozen or so co-conspirators, people who were aware of the crimes that he was committing and helped him, to some degree, to pull them off. Having been incarcerated, Scott was certainly in no mood to hold back on ratting out those who'd been involved with him.

Because Epstein knew that Rothstein had tried to use my cases against Epstein to commit his fraud, Epstein and I, in a sense, had a common interest in getting to the truth behind it. But this was a complicated problem for Epstein. He wanted to know the facts, but at the same time, he didn't want to exonerate me. This was tricky because the facts did indeed exonerate me, and he knew it. So how could he walk that tightrope?

Since Epstein had set Rothstein's deposition, I thought there was a chance he'd paid him to lie. Epstein certainly had the money to buy that kind of testimony, and what risk was it to Rothstein to take it? This was, of course, the guy who had hidden a 12.08 carat yellow diamond from the FBI even after he'd been caught running the second-largest Ponzi scheme ever. I figured Epstein would convince Scott that he, Epstein, could make a legal maneuver to shorten Scott's sentence or even make it go away. Anything was possible.

My case relied on one piece of testimony that was totally unpredictable: Scott Rothstein's: If Scott lied and said that I was involved, I would have to spend the rest of my life trying to prove my innocence.

Epstein's attorney Tonja Haddad Coleman took the lead questioning Rothstein. She went into the detailed workings of the Ponzi scheme and had Rothstein admit that it was conducted inside a law firm where I was working. But she didn't want to let him speak too much about my noninvolvement, so she didn't elicit those answers. Instead, she left things muddy enough for an observer to draw their own conclusion about my possible involvement. This was, of course, mildly infuriating.

On cross-examination, Jack Scarola gave Rothstein the opportunity to testify freely about me through questions I had written out for Jack to ask. Rothstein explained from his bunker that I was a victim of the scheme. He apologized for hiring me into the law firm that he knew was crumbling beneath him. He then verified what everyone already knew: he had hardly spoken with me, and his improper, illegal, and sensational pitches to investors about how he would capitalize on Epstein's crimes were concocted by him alone—without my knowledge. While I was dedicating my time to the prosecution of my cases, including those against Epstein, unbeknownst to me (and *most* of the other lawyers in the firm), Scott was running a massive fraud. The truth of my noninvolvement in the Ponzi scheme was now on the record. Rothstein's testimony killed any chance Epstein had of proceeding with his baseless claims.

On August 16, 2012, Jeffrey Epstein had run out of legal rope and filed a voluntary dismissal of his lawsuit against me. The deposition of Scott Rothstein had been his last Hail Mary pass. I was finally going to be able to focus on my malicious prosecution case against Epstein and my investigation of his sexual misdeeds.

# TWENTY-FIVE

# GOOD VERSUS EVIL

O N JULY 17, 2013, the Third District Court of Appeal in Florida issued an opinion in the case of *Wolfe v. Foreman*, a case that I wasn't involved in but that had a legal impact on my own case against Jeffrey Epstein because it addressed the central legal issue in my case. I was actually on a cruise ship in Alaska with my wife, my former boss Earleen, and Earleen's husband when I first saw the opinion. I was scrolling through a random legal digest when it jumped out at me.

I couldn't believe my eyes. This court held that the litigation privilege Jeffrey Epstein was relying on as a safe harbor to attack me prevented me from continuing to litigate my case against him. The court basically announced that malicious prosecution no longer existed in Florida. My case against Epstein was a case for malicious prosecution. In other words, this one decision single-handedly eliminated my entire lawsuit against Jeffrey Epstein. It was no later than six o'clock in the morning when I finished reading and called Earleen. Maybe I was misunderstanding, I thought. Nope. Earleen confirmed my fears. A court in Miami had essentially ruled that malicious prosecution was officially abolished.

I was worried.

Seeing an opportunity to exploit this, Epstein made a good move. He filed a motion for summary judgment and asked Judge Donald Hafele, the judge presiding over my case, to throw it out based on *Wolfe v. Foreman.*

Let's rewind for a minute. Back in 2009, I had actually moved to recuse Judge Hafele, who, coincidentally, was the same judge who presided over Courtney and Lynn's state court cases against Jeffrey Epstein. The reason for that motion was simple. I had moved for the court to allow punitive damages to be assessed against Jeffrey Epstein on behalf of my clients. Punitive damages are usually allowed in cases where the conduct of the defendant is intentionally harmful. Since Epstein's conduct as a serial child molester was certainly that, I assumed the court would grant this request without even a hearing. Instead, Judge Hafele held a long hearing in which he focused on the character of the alleged *victims* rather than the behavior of Epstein.

I was taken aback by this one. During the hearing, Hafele agreed with Jeffrey Epstein's counsel, stating:

> Now, balanced with that [plaintiff's burden of proof] is the obvious concerns for the court in terms of trying to, on the one hand, not expose the alleged victims to unfettered invasions of their privacy, but at the same time recognize that the allegations here and the nature of the facts that have been developed thus far are quite different than what would be a rape case by a stranger, different from a sexual assault case on a one-time basis by a stranger or someone known to the victim. *Here we have elements of prostitution that are ingrained in the facts of the case.* While I understand the privacy nature of sexual activity, when we have cases like this—I think as Mr. Critton aptly pointed out, without trying to be disrespectful to the alleged victims—*we're not necessarily dealing, as far as the information known to date, with what would otherwise be considered tra-*

*ditional or normal high school–aged women* relative to the things that went on here as contended by [Lynn] in her statement.

Judge Hafele was new to the Jeffrey Epstein cases and I had never appeared in front of him before. He ultimately granted my motion for punitive damages but hinted that it was a close call. *A close call?* Child molestation was borderline something that should be punished? What alternate universe was I in?

This was unsettling to me. Because of his words, I filed a motion the next day formally asking Judge Hafele to step down from these cases and allow a different judge to take over. Judge Hafele denied that request and remained on the girls' cases.

Now, five years after Epstein filed a fake lawsuit against me and I had to sue him back, Hafele was the judge on *my* case.

On May 19, 2014, Judge Hafele granted Epstein's motion against me, which effectively got rid of my whole case against Jeffrey Epstein. Regardless of where anyone's pieces were on the chessboard on that day, the board was flipped upside down. It was as if I had him in check with nowhere to go and suddenly, he reversed the board and checkmated me.

It didn't end there.

Epstein asked the court to make me pay his attorneys' fees, since he'd in effect won the case that I had brought against him. The court granted that motion, too. The only way that I could avoid paying Epstein $10 million in fees (which, big surprise, I definitely did not have) was to overturn Judge Hafele's decision on appeal. Epstein held this over my head. This was the first time Epstein's threats against me had become a reality. He was finally in a legally supportable position to financially destroy me and there wasn't much that I could do about it. I was vulnerable and I knew it. It finally hit me that the bad guy could actually win.

He called me to say, "I told you that you should have walked away from this. I never wanted to do this to you. I told you fighting me was not fair. You and your family are now bankrupt. I'll give you one last chance to walk away. Really walk away. Do not ever pursue a case against me again. And the CVRA case must end. Now. If you appeal this decision, I can't help you anymore. You will have made a decision to self-destruct, but don't say I wasn't fair."

Against Epstein's advice, I filed my appeal.

TWENTY-SIX

# WHOSE SIDE ARE YOU ON?

I PROVIDED VIRGINIA ROBERTS'S INFORMATION TO the FBI, and on July 5, 2013, FBI agents interviewed her at the United States Consulate General in Sydney, Australia, to inquire about her time with Jeffrey Epstein. This interview sparked something in Virginia that she had tried for years to suppress. In the summer of 2014, she moved back to the United States. She did this because of how important the CVRA case was to her. She felt compelled to come home and fight not just for herself, but for all of Epstein's victims. She didn't know Courtney, but she loved what Courtney stood for and wanted to join in.

In addition to becoming a force in the CVRA case, Virginia wanted to see Epstein criminally prosecuted. Since she was a victim in many other jurisdictions, prosecution seemed like a reasonable goal given the extent of the crimes that had been committed against her. Remember, she had unique, often eyewitness information about how widespread Epstein's crimes really were. She came to America with her family for the sole purpose of continuing her crusade to bring her perpetrators to justice and help other similarly situated crime victims in any way that she could. When she arrived, we met to discuss how best to go about achieving her goals.

Shortly after our meeting, I received an entirely unexpected telephone call. I was at home in bed at eleven thirty on a Friday night when my phone rang. As soon as I said hello, the voice on the other end went into a windup that eventually became familiar.

"Let me introduce myself," the caller said. "My name is Stan Pottinger. I'm sure you get a lot of crazy calls about this subject matter—Jeffrey Epstein—but hear me out. I have a civil rights practice in New York. Before that, I was the assistant attorney general for the Civil Rights Division at the Justice Department in Washington. In addition to my own current work, I sometimes work on cases with David Boies. I've been contacted to represent one of the victims of Jeffrey Epstein and have told David about it. We understand that you're the expert and we don't want to reinvent the wheel. I'm calling to see if it makes sense to work together."

I asked him whether he represented a client who was victimized in New York or in Florida, and he told me Florida. I then told him I would keep it in confidence, but if he said the name of the victim, I would probably know her situation. When he identified the victim, I walked out on the balcony of my room and explained, "I'm not sure where you got your case from, but you have a problem. Your client was represented in the previous underlying litigation, and while she may not have liked her attorney [not me], or the representation she received, I know for a fact that she signed a settlement agreement with Jeffrey Epstein already." Stan explained that this was not his understanding, but he would check it out and get back to me the next day.

His call set off a bunch of suspicions for me that something was wrong. Sure enough, I got a call from him around the same time the next night—I must have forgotten to tell him that midnight on a weekend was not my preferred time to talk—but I stayed on the line. This time, his approach was slightly different. In the past twenty-four hours, he said, he had confirmed what I had told him. He felt confident that I knew all the characters involved here, and if he was going to get involved in any of this litigation, working with me was probably the best way for him and his colleagues to go.

I didn't know Stan, but I knew David Boies by reputation and found the thought of working with him intriguing. He was actually one of the lawyers who had unknowingly helped to shape my legal career. When I returned to Florida from my time studying abroad in the Czech Republic after my first year of law school, I had three weeks to kill before going back for my second year. My dad hooked me up with a law firm clerkship through a fishing buddy of his who was an admiralty lawyer in Jacksonville.

Having hired me only as a favor, the firm made it clear to me on my first day that, considering my lack of skills, they had no use for me. But, wanting to help me out, they asked what kind of law I wanted to practice. I told them I wanted to be a trial lawyer. They told me there was a guy trying a case down the street for the next three weeks and said they would pay me if I wanted to go to court and watch him.

I went to the trial and sat in the back of a Jacksonville courtroom that was filled with stacks of Bankers boxes. David Boies represented an electricity company called Florida Power & Light, which was in a contract dispute. I was the first person to arrive at the courtroom every day and watched everything he did for three weeks.

I still remember a few things about that trial. Boies's cross-examinations were very short, with a clear point to every question. I also remember a tactic he used repeatedly. When a witness was answering a question in a way that was not favorable to his client, David would start the next question by saying, "Let me make sure that we are communicating," and rephrase the question and steer the witness onto a totally different topic—one more favorable to his position. It was brilliant. I stole that device, among other things, from David's style.

Watching how he took over the courtroom solidified my view that this was exactly the type of lawyer I wanted to be. I told David this story fifteen years later, thinking he would be able to put a face to this person who was sitting in the back of the courtroom every day and say, "Oh, yeah, I remember you, too." He had absolutely no recollection of me (although he certainly remembered the case; I had to go back to law school before the trial was over, but apparently he lost). In any event, I found it cool that now, years later, maybe he wanted my help.

On our second late-night call, Stan thanked me for my help and told me that if anything ever came up, he would like to work with me and said David Boies would, too. He then asked me if I had anything else in the works against Epstein, so I told him a little bit about the current status of the CVRA case. This led to a long conversation about the breadth of the criminal enterprise headed by Jeffrey Epstein and my ultimate goal to overturn Epstein's non-prosecution agreement with the feds.

He then reminded me that he was the former U.S. assistant attorney general and that David and his law firm were well regarded by the U.S. Attorney's Office in New York and around the country. He said, "What you're doing is admirable. Your goal is to get Epstein prosecuted. But rather than try to undo this bad deal"—referring to the NPA—"isn't there anyone you represent who has traveled on Epstein's plane or been abused at any of his other locations?" I found the question unnerving, especially given the timing of his call and my current talks with Virginia. I'm admittedly quick to be suspicious, but my mind was racing.

The logic stacking up at that moment was simple. This powerful person who was closely associated with David Boies, one of the most powerful lawyers in America, had called me at midnight at my home, I suspected, under the pretense of representing someone whom I knew no longer had a case. And now, seemingly out of the blue, he'd asked a question the answer to which was Virginia Roberts. Hardly anyone knew that she was in the United States, and they certainly didn't know that I was talking to her. What were these two guys up to?

Epstein had scared Virginia into another country years ago and, but for the Sharon Churcher articles in the *Daily Mail* that came and went in 2011, Virginia had gone back into hiding. Was Stan working with Epstein? Was David? Had Epstein tagged Virginia's passport in order to receive a ping from the Justice Department if she ever entered the country? Despite these thoughts, which were a bit frantic, I told Stan that I had recently been contacted by Virginia Roberts and divulged parts of her story that had already been made public. But nothing else.

A couple of days passed, and Stan called again. "David and I would like to meet with you. How soon can you fly to New York?" I gave him a proposed itinerary. He told me to call him when I landed, and he would tell me where to meet them. Waiting until the last minute to figure out where to have lunch is not an unusual thing for people to do in New York, but given my lurking suspicions, I found it odd. It smelled like an Epstein setup.

I didn't have time to figure out a more elaborate solution to my worries, so I went to a local spy shop in Fort Lauderdale and asked for the best hidden recording device they had. They gave me a specialized recording device that looked like a USB flash drive and could make high-quality recordings up to four hours long.

Thinking that I was headed for a setup, I tried to remember any connections I was aware of between Jeffrey Epstein and his friends that might have tied him to David Boies's law firm. I looked through Alfredo Rodriguez's journal and couldn't find David. Next, I reviewed copies of the message pads that had been confiscated from the trash pulls at Epstein's house. I paged through calls from former national security advisor Sandy Berger, former United States senator George Mitchell, and movie producer Harvey Weinstein (more than a decade before he would be arrested on rape charges). I continued flipping through the messages and then, there it was—a call from David Boies. According to a message pad, he had called Jeffrey Epstein's house on February 25, 2005. There was no message associated with the call, only a handwritten note that someone named David Boies had personally called and left his cell phone number, asking that Jeffrey call him back. Was this a benign thing? A return business call to a business call placed by Epstein? Or was he, as I feared, Epstein's lawyer? A spy? There was only one way to find out.

I landed at LaGuardia and called Stan's cell phone for directions, as instructed. He wanted to meet somewhere where we could talk privately, without a lot of noise, so he suggested the Harvard Club. He said he was on his way and to tell the front desk when I arrived.

When I got there, I definitely was on unfamiliar turf. First, the concierge sent me to a coat room and the clerk took my backpack. I couldn't figure out why he wanted it. Club rules, of course: guests in the club were prevented from taking briefcases, luggage, or backpacks to their tables. This was definitely not a place for a public school kid from Jacksonville.

I had never met Stan, so I had researched everything that was publicly available about him before the meeting. He had worked on Wall Street for a while and was a bestselling author in addition to having had his early career at the Department of Justice in Washington. Notably, while he was assistant attorney general, Stan had cross-examined the associate director of the FBI, Mark Felt, in front of a 1976 federal grand jury, and discovered that Felt was "Deep Throat," the infamous secret informant of Bob Woodward and Carl Bernstein's during the Watergate scandal and a key figure in forcing the resignation of President Richard Nixon. Aside from Stan's professional information, I found out that he had political connections, and had dated women with public profiles like Kathie Lee Gifford, Connie Chung, and Gloria Steinem.

There were many media reports describing Jeffrey Epstein as this mysterious person with alleged ties to the CIA, Israeli intelligence, and political figures, and now I was meeting with this other mysterious person about whom I knew nothing. My gut kept saying I needed to be cautious. Stan could be a Jeffrey Epstein plant.

I showed up on time and Stan wasn't there. I continued to scan the room, making fun of all of these superior snobs in my head, waiting for an imperious attendant to either ask me what I was doing there or put me in a waiter's jacket and make me start serving hors d'oeuvres.

At this point, I expected to see Stan coming in wearing a vest and an attitude, but when he showed up, he had neither. Then again, wouldn't someone who *wasn't* stuffy be exactly the kind of person Epstein would have recruited?

Stan apologized immediately for having us meet in a club like this but said it provided privacy. Privacy was standard operating procedure for two lawyers talking about a case, of course, but I saw it differently: What was this meeting *really* about?

As we headed for a less formal dining area, suddenly I thought: *Oh no, the USB thumb drive recorder is still in my backpack.* If Stan was going to threaten me in this "place of privacy," I would have no evidence of it. Once again, my mind started racing.

We sat at the table and he launched into the purpose of our meeting. Still panicking, I told him that I needed to go to the bathroom. He must have been wondering, *What the heck is wrong with this guy? He's been waiting for me for fifteen minutes and* now *he has to go to the bathroom?* I walked back to the coatroom and dug through my backpack to find the recorder before heading back to the lunch table.

When I got back, I planned to force Stan to talk about his past before he could get into anything that he could use on behalf of Epstein. I asked him about Watergate and Mark Felt because, who were we kidding, that's cool stuff. He told me how, after his cross-examination of Felt, one of the jurors had asked Felt if he was Deep Throat. Stan stopped Felt from answering. He then walked up to Felt and privately told him that either he could answer the question, which he would have to do honestly since he was under oath, or Stan would withdraw the question as being irrelevant to the investigation. Felt's face turned white and uncharacteristically frightened before he immediately asked Stan to withdraw the question. Stan knew right then that Mark Felt was Deep Throat. He kept that secret for decades until Mark revealed his identity in *Vanity Fair* in 2005. Felt died in 2008.

I spent most of the lunch interrogating Stan about his past and present, making him comfortable, until he volunteered that he had known Epstein. He had worked with him briefly many years before. *Really?* Stan explained that after he'd left the Justice Department in Washington, he'd worked as an investment banker in New York, where a client introduced him to Epstein. They were not in the same firm, but the two of them had shared an office for a few weeks. He may have thought he was being candid and forthcoming, but all it did was ramp up my suspicions.

I asked if David knew Jeffrey, and Stan said as far as he knew, the answer was no. At this point, Stan really wasn't doing anything to dispel my concerns, since I knew that in the past David had left a private message for Jeffrey to call him.

Stan wanted to talk about Epstein, but I delayed that. When we finished eating, I told Stan it didn't make much sense for me to explain things twice, once to him and once to David, so why didn't we ask David to come join us? Stan suggested instead that we go to David's office. I got my backpack and we jumped in a cab to 575 Lexington Avenue. But this merely raised another red flag. David's office was in the same building as Jeffrey Epstein's main attorney Darren Indyke's office.

Darren Indyke had attended important hearings as well as my depositions of Epstein over the years. He wasn't a litigator, more like a fixer. Indyke had one client: Jeffrey Epstein. Now I was in a cab going to his office building in Manhattan. How many coincidences was I supposed to choke down before they were no longer coincidences?

In the building lobby, the two security guards knew Stan but asked for my driver's license. Stan signaled to the guards that I was okay, and they opened the electronic gate to let us in. Stan led the way into the elevator and up to the seventh floor. When we checked in, the receptionist said we were supposed to use a particular conference room, as if it had already been arranged. Stan had acted as if we were only meeting at the Harvard Club, yet he had *already* reserved a conference room at Boies Schiller Flexner? Again, it was odd.

I know that this seems crazy, but at that time, I was thinking that a conference room in a highly reputable law firm would be a strange place for Epstein to cause me bodily harm. So I had crossed his plans to kill me off the list. Still, with all I had been through, this had the markings of some larger plot that I must not have conceptualized yet. I couldn't figure out how he and Boies intended to piece it together.

Here's the other thing: I didn't even meet David that day. Stan told me that we were going there to meet him, but when we got there David was said to be tied up with other things.

In the conference room, Stan said he appreciated all that I had done for Epstein's abuse victims and that David and his partners only wanted to help. He asked me to tell him more about the CVRA and what Jeffrey Epstein did to Virginia in jurisdictions other than Florida. Instead of answering, I pulled out the message pads that I had in my backpack and went to the flagged page where David Boies had called Epstein's house in 2005. I put it in front of Stan and made the point that this call had probably been received between sexual massages that Epstein was getting that day from underage girls. It was clear from Stan's reaction, though, that he'd never seen this before and didn't know about it. He did confirm that the number was David's cellphone number.

I told him that this made me uneasy about the whole situation and I wanted to get to the bottom of whatever relationship there may have been between David and Jeffrey. Stan left the room for about ten minutes. During this break, I made sure that my recording device was still on. He came back and told me that David would not be able to meet with us. We spent the remainder of the meeting playing cat and mouse, neither learning much.

I left the office for LaGuardia very confused. If these were Jeffrey Epstein stand-ins, they had gotten no information from me. On the other hand, I really didn't get much information from them, either. I don't believe in coincidences, and had sufficient reason to believe that Stan, and perhaps David, was secretly working for the other side. However, these high-profile, powerful lawyers operating in the shadows on behalf of a large, successful law firm in order to contrive an elaborate plot to rope me in under false pretenses to frame me on behalf of a pedophile—that just didn't make sense.

I spent the airplane ride home writing down all the facts and separately all the "logical" conclusions I was drawing from them. By the time I had landed, I decided that Stan and David had to be on the right side with good intentions and that there was no grand conspiracy here after all. But man, they had certainly made me nervous. Or to be more accurate, Epstein had made me nervous. He was able to do that because he could control anyone, and I knew it.

# TWENTY-SEVEN

# BACK TO NEW YORK

ALTHOUGH I HAD NOT TOLD him that Virginia was in the country, Stan kept in touch, and expressed that he and David wanted to meet her. We set up a date in July 2014 for her and me to fly from Florida to New York for a meeting.

The entire plane ride up, I was picking Virginia's brain about the time she spent with her "dysfunctional family" from 2000 to 2002. She was confident that Epstein's New York butler Jojo Fontanilla would not only remember her but also cooperate with her against Epstein. She told me of a time before her eighteenth birthday when she was in Epstein's New York house in extraordinary pain. Jojo drove her, with Epstein and Maxwell, to a nearby hospital, where a medical team attended to her immediately. Jojo had been there for her then and always would be.

We spent three hours shuffling through hundreds of pages of evidence from the Epstein investigation. Before we landed, I asked her how she felt about tracking Jojo down to see what help he would give. She said she would do whatever it took to move the case forward. Our flight arrived at LaGuardia at noon. We had four hours to kill before our meeting with David and Stan.

We took a cab from JFK straight to East Seventy-First Street. As we walked toward Central Park, Virginia looked to the right and instantly reacquainted herself with the mansion that sprawled across nearly an entire city block. It was obvious that she had been there many times: she recognized every square inch of the place from the outside in.

The plan was for her to knock on the front door and ask for Jojo. Her fantasy was that he would come down the stairs and give her a big hug before saying he'd cooperate with her and thank her for coming and saving him from his indentured servitude. She believed he was a good person who would choose the right side over money.

As we walked down the sidewalk, coming closer to the door, she described the inside of the various portions of the house that we were passing. We approached the front door and saw video cameras outside. She described a video room where all the live images were monitored and recorded and stored for a certain period of time.

I told her to look down to avoid her facial capture by the cameras. As we walked under the main security bulb, she looked up, against my advice, and extended both of her middle fingers, hoping that Epstein would eventually see the footage. It was a double f*** you, impulsive and straight from her heart. But when I looked at her, she had tears streaming down her face and I knew we couldn't stop at the front door. We walked to the end of the block.

Virginia told me it was better for her to go to the door alone, and I agreed. I handed her the USB recording device and she put it in her top shirt pocket. I waited across the street and watched as she walked up to the giant front door and started knocking. I was standing behind a car in front of the public library, close enough to see her but far enough to not be seen.

A woman opened the front door. Virginia talked to her but did not enter. The interaction lasted about three minutes. The door eventually closed, and Virginia called me on my cell phone, unsure where I had gone.

She was still shaking when I met her at the end of the block. It had been more than a decade, and yet this building was so ingrained in Virginia's memory it caused her to have a physiological response when she came near it. Her reentry into the perimeters of Epstein's world had brought back the memories that had caused her to flee the country more than a decade earlier. But there was also another emotion at play. She told me that the woman said she'd inform Jojo that Virginia was there to see him. The woman had closed the door and then, after a few moments, opened it again and told Virginia that Jojo did not want to see her. The only person in the Epstein household she thought had a heart big enough and kind enough to come to the door had refused to see her.

Virginia understood that his doing so would have gotten him in trouble with his boss, but that did not matter, not now, not here. Right or wrong, she was genuinely surprised and disappointed by his snub. She was also relearning a lesson she'd learned many years before but, in the excitement of high expectations, had forgotten: in Epstein's world, money trumped friendships. While this was disappointing to Virginia, it was an important gesture for me to see. She was willing to go into the lion's den. It convinced me further of her credibility and determination.

Without my prompting, she asked, "How close are we to 301 East Sixty-Sixth Street?" This was the address of the apartments, which Maritza Vasquez had explained were where Epstein stashed his girls. I asked Virginia what she was planning to do once she got there. She said the girls would talk to her because they were going through everything that Virginia had gone through.

I told her that the only girl who I knew still lived there was Nadia Marcinkova. So, she went to the building and asked the doorman for Nadia. He was well trained when it came to the privacy of the residents of the 301 building. He said he could not confirm whether Nadia was there and that he would need to inform her of Virginia's credentials. He took the information, made a phone call, and then told Virginia that he could not help her.

With more time available before going to the Boies Schiller Flexner office, Virginia took me to other places in the city she had frequented, including the Victoria's Secret store where Epstein often took Virginia and other young girls to purchase lingerie. After this field trip, it was time for the meeting. We checked in at the front desk, but without Stan as an escort, access wasn't so easy. After taking our identification, which for Virginia was an Australian passport, security allowed us access to the elevators. It was still somewhat unnerving that this was the building where Darren Indyke, Epstein's personal lawyer, had his office.

We got off the elevator at the seventh floor and told the Boies Schiller Flexner receptionist that we were there. A few minutes later Stan and David both entered through the glass doors behind us. Virginia and I stood up. She had a way of not being impressed by anyone, and this was no different.

David led us into his large conference room. He was at the head of the table, but he had not sat for more than a second before Virginia started her spiel, thanking him for his help and telling him that she had stayed silent for too long. She told him that she was here to stop Epstein once and for all.

David, relaxed but methodical, listened to her patiently. He already had some background on Virginia, from Stan, and wanted to hear directly from her what she had experienced with Epstein and what her intentions were going forward. Knowing Boies's time was limited, Virginia kept her summary brief, not expanding much beyond what she had alleged in her original Jane Doe 102 complaint. That was enough to get David's attention. In essence, she was recruited as a teenager by Ghislaine Maxwell to be trafficked by Epstein. Now she wanted to be a part of undoing Epstein's non-prosecution agreement. I then chimed in about the mechanics of making that happen.

"It appears obvious Brad has everything well under control. Where do you see me fitting in?" David inquired.

I responded: "Epstein should be in jail. My goal is to put him there. He will do anything to stop me. He has a powerful team behind him and unlimited resources to go after me, and Virginia, and anyone who stands up to him. I'm going after him, but when he and his team fire, we're going to need a heavyweight legal team to counter their attacks. There will be plenty of room for you."

David reacted quickly. "Okay, then I'm in."

# TWENTY-EIGHT

# VIRGINIA

V IRGINIA WAS A POWERFUL WOMAN who would not scare easily or be bullied by anyone at this point in her life. She was a strong mother who was determined to set an example for her children by standing up to improve the lives of those who had experienced a similar misfortune. To appreciate Virginia's fortitude, I needed to know where she came from.

Virginia detailed it as well as she could. Her childhood was no fairy tale. In fact, from start to finish it was something out of a horror movie. At an early age, Virginia's parents put her in a girls' home that she couldn't tolerate. So she ran away—she boarded a bus in Palm Beach and went to Miami. She was a beautiful, tall, thin blonde with bright blue eyes who had not showered or eaten for days when a limousine pulled up next to the bus stop where she was sitting.

The man in the car rolled down the window and said, "You look like you could use a place to stay. Hop in." Adventurous, alone, and with nowhere to go, she hopped in. The sixty-three-year-old man introduced himself as Ron Eppinger. He treated this fifteen-year-old kid as his new girlfriend. He was a professional sex trafficker who imported women from Europe to pimp out as part of his escort service, called Perfect 10.

Within a month or so of Virginia's arrival, Ron learned that he had been noticed by the FBI. The federal investigation was focused solely on the international escort service that Ron was running, and it had not yet hit their radar that he was also coercing a fifteen-year-old into sex. Ron was scared. He didn't want to be caught, especially with Virginia. He drove her one night from Miami to Ocala, Florida, where he brutally abused her physically and mentally. She desperately wanted to escape, but she was afraid that he would kill her if she tried. She figured out that she had been stashed somewhere in a barn in the middle of the Ocala woods in northern Florida.

Ron needed to get rid of her one way or the other. Unbeknownst to Virginia, he was coordinating with someone to take her off his hands. In June 1999, Ron drove Virginia to Hot Chocolates nightclub in Fort Lauderdale and introduced her to a friend of the owner named David Kelmanson, who was involved in a seedy club scene. Kelmanson made her his so-called girlfriend. For a few weeks, Kelmanson showed her off at the nightclub and around town. Despite her age, she was able to hold her own in any crowd.

Virginia didn't want that life, but she was too afraid to escape Kelmanson and go to the police. She knew the police would have taken her home, where her parents would have rejected her, and with no money or place to live, she'd inevitably end up back in a troubled kids' shelter, which was, to her, worse than the streets. Virginia was stuck.

But now the FBI was hot on Eppinger's trail, which meant they were also hot on the trail of his friends. Virginia was in bed with Kelmanson one night when the Wilton Manors Police Department and the FBI burst through the front door. In June 1999, she was taken to the police station and, as predicted, her parents were called to pick her up. Her father came to take her home. This time, he didn't kick her out.

Virginia's father worked as a maintenance man at Donald Trump's Mar-a-Lago Club in Palm Beach, where he helped her get a summer job as a towel girl in the club's women's locker room. She couldn't change her past as a runaway, but she had a tremendous energy and drive to be successful. Working at the spa introduced her to the lifestyles of the famous and wealthy clientele she assisted on a daily basis.

Virginia went to the public library to get a book on massage therapy and brought it to work. She was reading it on her lunch break one day, sitting on a bench outside the Mar-a-Lago spa, when she was approached by a beautiful, charming woman who struck her as supremely important and elegant. Her British accent added to her allure. The woman showed an interest in the book Virginia was reading and wasted no time telling her that she could get Virginia a job with her billionaire friend who owned a house around the corner.

Virginia told the woman that she was just trying to learn, but really didn't know much about massage, to which the woman replied that she and her boss would teach Virginia anything that she needed to know. She handed Virginia the address and said, "I'm Ghislaine. See you tonight," presupposing that Virginia would show up.

Virginia ran to her father, excited. Someone thought she was important. This was her chance, and she couldn't let it slip by. Virginia had been beaten, abused, sexually assaulted, discarded, and told by the world that she would amount to nothing. Still, here she was, only sixteen, about to start working for a billionaire.

That evening, Virginia's father drove her to a palatial Palm Beach mansion on the water at 358 El Brillo Way. Too naïve to be scared, Virginia hopped out of the car and went to the door, ready to learn, to leave the past behind.

Ghislaine greeted Virginia and welcomed her into the house, which caused Virginia to boil with excitement. Every time she thought things couldn't get better, they did. She was pinching herself to remember that this wasn't just a dream. "Jeffrey has been waiting to meet you," Ghislaine told her in her soft, sophisticated accent. "Follow me," she said as she led Virginia up the stairs.

Virginia was taken to the bedroom to begin the massage, and Maxwell instructed her on every aspect from the location and placement of the oils to the length of time she would need to spend on each portion of the body, as well as the purpose behind every movement. Virginia paid close attention so that she could impress her new bosses as much as they had impressed her.

While standing on one side of the massage table, around the corner from the master bed, listening intently to Ghislaine brag about Epstein's brilliance and importance, Virginia saw someone emerging from the adjoining room, which, she would soon learn, held a shower. She turned to look and saw an older man who resembled Ralph Lauren walking in her direction wearing only a towel and a big, childish grin. "I'm Jeffrey," he said. He then lay down on the massage table.

Ghislaine and Jeffrey seemed almost giddy while asking Virginia questions about her life and her future, interspersed with Ghislaine's instruction on how to give a proper massage. Ghislaine wasted little time before stripping off all her clothes and telling Virginia to do the same. Ghislaine and Jeffrey made their movements seem so natural. It was as though this was the way massage was performed in the world of the rich and famous. Get with the program or get another job.

Virginia, embarrassed, first removed her white Mar-a-Lago uniform shirt and skirt. Maxwell and Epstein laughed to each other as they commented about how cute Virginia's Hello Kitty underwear was. Ghislaine picked up a bottle of massage oil from the table nearby. She gave it two big pumps and rubbed her hands together before placing them on Jeffrey's naked body. "Just do what I do," she said.

Virginia placed her hands on Jeffrey and followed Ghislaine's every movement. Together they worked down Jeffrey's back, and while Ghislaine spent time massaging his buttocks, Virginia glided her hands past, to the backs of Jeffrey's legs. Ghislaine placed her hands on top of Virginia's and pulled them back up. "It is important that you don't miss anywhere. If you skip around, the blood will not flow right," Ghislaine explained as she continued to guide Virginia's hands. The only thing calming Virginia about the fact that she was standing naked in front of two naked adults was the constant instruction from Ghislaine—reassurance that this was just a typical massage in their world.

Just when Virginia became comfortable with the motions, she heard Jeffrey begin to moan. At first, she couldn't tell if this was a sexual type of moan or a reaction to the pressure. Before Virginia had time to contemplate an answer, Jeffrey turned over and Virginia pulled both of her hands back and held them up in the air like two stop signs.

Jeffrey looked at her and smiled. Virginia stayed in that position, waiting for instruction. Ghislaine immediately placed both hands on Jeffrey's chest. "Like this," she said. "You want to push the blood away from the heart. Your turn." Virginia placed one hand on each of Jeffrey's pecs and began massaging in a circular motion. "Not in a circle," Ghislaine interrupted. "Push the blood away. Don't be afraid to use pressure." Virginia kept her eyes on Jeffrey's chest as she was rubbing. She could feel Jeffrey staring at her and could see his big smile from the corner of her eye. Jeffrey turned his head ever so slightly to look at Ghislaine. At the same time, Virginia peeked up. She saw Jeffrey wink in Ghislaine's direction and then close his eyes. "You're doing great," Ghislaine confirmed.

By this point, Virginia was over the fact that everyone in the room was naked. It wasn't the strangest situation she had ever been in. It was, however, the nicest room in the nicest house, and she was getting top-rank instruction in massage therapy. Or so she thought. Just as she was beginning to get her groove, Jeffrey reached his hand down and began stroking himself. He opened his eyes briefly, "You don't mind, do you?"

Shocked, and now realizing that this was not what she had hoped it to be, Virginia felt herself almost unable to respond. She wasn't going to let this ruin her chance, though. She just didn't know what to say.

Hoping to get more professional instruction and deflect from the activity that was going on below Jeffrey's waistline, Virginia asked, "What do I do next?"

Jeffrey and Ghislaine immediately laughed simultaneously the way two people do when they have an inside joke. "I know what he wants now," Ghislaine said. She walked away from the table and brought back a large white plastic instrument with a ball on top that looked like a back massager.

"What do I do with that?" Virginia asked. That question was also met with a short cackle from Jeffrey and Ghislaine.

Ghislaine extended her arm and Jeffrey grabbed the device and turned to Virginia. "You just keep doing what you're doing. This is for me to hold." Jeffrey turned it on low and dropped his arm beside the table, sliding the device between Virginia's legs and pressing the top against Virginia's inner thighs. "Doesn't that feel good?" Jeffrey queried.

Virginia wasn't sure what to think and definitely wasn't sure what to say. The situation had changed so many times since her father had dropped her off at the house—both in reality and in her mind. *What the hell is happening right now? How do I get out of this house?*, she thought to herself. Almost as if he could read her mind, Jeffrey whispered, "Everything is okay. This is going to be great for all of us."

This calming voice immediately convinced Virginia that despite the fact she had never experienced whatever was going on at the time, it was normal. Or as Jeffrey so confidently told her, it was okay. Those words resonated with her. Nobody was holding her down against her will, as she had suffered in the past. Nobody was berating her or screaming at her or telling her how worthless she was.

Jeffrey increased the intensity of the device and closed his own eyes before saying more sternly, "Now pinch my nipples."

Before Virginia could do anything, Ghislaine grabbed Jeffrey's nipples between her pointer fingers and thumbs and said, "Don't be easy on him. He likes it hard." She appeared to squeeze as hard as she could, while looking at Jeffrey's closed eyes and letting out a soft moan herself. Then she said, "Your turn."

Virginia grabbed hold of Jeffrey's nipples and tried to squeeze, although her hands were not quite as strong as Ghislaine's and the vibration from the device between her legs was distracting her. "Harder," Jeffrey demanded.

Virginia squeezed. "Very good," Ghislaine said with approval. Ghislaine then instructed Virginia to get on top and straddle Jeffrey until he finished.

Jeffrey invited Virginia to join him and Maxwell in the shower. Nothing about this was made to seem unusual. In fact, it was quite the opposite. Epstein and Maxwell worked together seamlessly, as if they had done this many times before. Even the washing-up process seemed standard.

Maxwell led the way toward the shower. "Follow me," she said. All three entered the shower, where there were two soaps, one in the shape of a penis and one in the shape of a vagina. "Now wash me off up and down," Epstein instructed. Virginia compliantly followed suit. After the shower, the three dried off. In front of Virginia, Jeffrey said to Ghislaine, "She's a keeper," as he walked to the other side of his master bedroom.

"You did great. He really loved you," Ghislaine told Virginia as she was putting her Mar-a-Lago polo back on. Ghislaine handed Virginia cash, "Can you come back tomorrow after you get off of work?"

"Of course," Virginia responded almost subconsciously, her mind still in a whirlwind. Ghislaine showed Virginia the stairway to get back downstairs and told her that Juan would drive her home.

Sure enough, when Virginia got to the base of the stairs, Juan was waiting. There was another woman in the kitchen as Virginia was passing through on the way to the car with Juan. She was a beautiful brunette with curly hair who looked up at Virginia with a soft smile and said in a British accent, "Hi, I'm Emmy."

"Oh, hi, I'm Jenna," Virginia responded, as that was the nickname she often used with friends. Unsure what to say but knowing it was rude to keep walking, Virginia said the first thing that came to her mind. "Do you work for Jeffrey?"

"Not exactly, but sort of," Emmy responded. "I'm Ghislaine's assistant."

"Oh, good," Virginia said. Feeling pressured by the fact that Juan had turned around to watch this conversation while also waiting with the keys in his hand, "Great. See you tomorrow." Emmy just smiled as Virginia and Juan left the house and walked toward the shiny black Suburban.

Virginia got in the back and told Juan her address. Not another word was spoken all the way home. When she arrived, Virginia's mom asked her how it had gone, and she said fine without saying much more. She spent the rest of the night in the bathroom of her parents' house, staring in the mirror and crying. What had just happened? Was everyone like this guy? *Every time I think I've escaped the jaws of abuse, another shark swallows me up. What do I do?*

He had paid her more money than she had been paid in her entire life, for an hour of her time. By the end of the night, she had decided that there was more of a future for her with Jeffrey Epstein than in the trailer parks of West Palm Beach.

---

By the time she was seventeen, Virginia told us, she was traveling around with a billionaire and interacting—mostly as a sex slave—with powerful people. She was also introduced by Epstein to some of the most interesting people in the world. While traveling with Epstein on his plane on February 23, 2001, Virginia convinced Matt Groening, the famed cartoonist and creator of *The Simpsons*, to draw a picture of Bart Simpson on Jeffrey Epstein's letterhead for her father. She still has the signed picture to prove it.

At the time she was traveling with Epstein and Maxwell, Virginia had a boyfriend who was relatively her age named Tony. He didn't ask many questions, even though he knew what was going on.

There did come a time, however, when the debauched lifestyle of Epstein's cultish world became too much for even a strong soul like Virginia. She recalled that when she was nineteen years old, after having been involved in the Epstein sex cult for two years, she was on the island with him and Maxwell when they made a new and surprising proposition to her: they wanted her to carry his baby. The duo told Virginia that she would be taken care of for the rest of her life if she would agree to give Epstein and Maxwell a child, although there were some strings attached. She would have to sign a contract agreeing that the baby was not her own, but the legal child of Epstein and Maxwell. This was the final straw for Virginia. She couldn't bear the thought of Epstein and Maxwell raising her child. She knew that she needed to escape.

While Virginia was the first to tell me about Epstein and Maxwell's baby proposition, she would not be the last. Two others who were propositioned with the same plan, and who didn't know Virginia, believed then, and told me they still do to this day, that they were the only ones who were asked to do this.

It was this particular perversity that made Virginia realize just how insidious the duo was and decide that she had to escape no matter the circumstances or the risk. She needed to find a place where she would be safe because quitting her "job" and returning to her old life in Florida was not an option. Based on everything she'd seen and heard she believed that Epstein and Maxwell would hunt her down. Because she was so involved in Epstein's trafficking operation and had accumulated knowledge of how it worked, who was in it, and the extent of their sexual abuse, she thought they would want to eliminate her, and if they decided to do that, she knew they could. She'd finally reached her "*no más*" moment. She was out.

Her knowledge of Epstein's capabilities—and her fear of them—echoed those voiced by Alfredo Rodriguez after he was fired and refused to leave without his "insurance policy" of a stolen copy of Epstein's black book of names and addresses. Indeed, many witnesses we uncovered expressed extreme fear of reprisal should Epstein ever learn they had shared information against him or Maxwell. Before meeting Epstein and Maxwell, Virginia was young and resilient. They had stolen the self-confidence and self-esteem that Virginia had managed to maintain even after being abused by Ron Eppinger and his dirty friends. Epstein and Maxwell broke her so badly that her personality crumbled to the point that she had to run as far away as she could. Escaping was survival for Virginia. But she would be back to get her revenge when she was ready.

The time had come. After having three children and spending a decade rebuilding her once-resilient personality, she was finally back in the United States and ready to fight. She saw the CVRA as her chance to seek justice. That was not her only mission, though. In addition to her strong desire to help overturn Epstein's immunity deal, she returned with an idea to start a charitable foundation where any money raised would go to help other survivors. One of the things that Virginia felt was missing was a well-known hub that could be accessed by phone or internet at any time from anywhere by a victim or survivor who needed shelter, clothing, or other necessities. She wanted to make sure that anyone who wanted to escape was able to do that through the resources that she could provide. The concept was inspiring. So, Brittany and I helped her incorporate and start her charity. Virginia named her organization Victims Refuse Silence (cleverly incorporating her initials).

Virginia now had a purpose in life and a never-say-die attitude to back it up.

# TWENTY-NINE

# NOBODY IS SAFE

FROM THE OUTSET OF THE Crime Victims' Rights Act case, Paul Cassell and I had requested copies of all the written communications between the government and Jeffrey Epstein's lawyers regarding the NPA, thinking that, like in any other typical case, there were probably half a dozen emails exchanged between the two parties. When the government spent half a decade putting up a huge fight to prevent the disclosure of the documents, Paul and I realized that there must be something unusual in there. Epstein filed formal papers with the court to intervene in the case so that he could help the government work against the victims to stop us from seeing the emails, too. These documents contained the key to our case.

Despite the government and Epstein working together against us, Judge Marra still ruled in our favor on June 18, 2013, granting us the rights not only to see the correspondence between the government and Epstein but also to use said correspondence to prove our case. On June 27, 2013, Epstein appealed Judge Marra's order to the Eleventh Circuit Court of Appeals in Georgia. Epstein's lawyer Marty Weinberg argued his (and the government's) position before the appellate court, and Paul gave a brilliant performance on behalf of our clients. After the argument but before the Eleventh Circuit decided, Epstein, sensing they would lose the argument, called me to discuss our personal lawsuit before switching gears and bringing up the issue relating to the emails with the government.

He explained that he hadn't been able to find any law on this idea, but that he had intervened in this part of the CVRA case and was wondering if it was possible to settle pieces of the case without resolving the whole thing. I asked him what he was talking about and he said that he wasn't offering to do anything, but just thinking out loud whether he wanted to buy a position in a lawsuit (where he would pay an agreed amount of money so that my clients would stop trying to obtain the emails and continue the case without that evidence).

"Do you want me to answer your question or skip ahead and answer what you're really asking?" I asked.

"I'm not sure I follow," he responded.

"Yes, you do—you want to pay for us to abandon our pursuit of the correspondence between you and the government and have framed it as whether it is permissible to pay for such a thing. I don't know whether its permissible or not, but regardless of whether that legal maneuver is allowed in any context, we would never accept it," I explained.

His question did mean one thing: these documents were as important as we thought they were.

As predicted, we won the appeal. On June 11, 2014, the Eleventh Circuit upheld Judge Marra's decision and required the government to turn over the documents, which consisted of hundreds of emails spanning the duration of the negotiation of Epstein's plea deal with the federal government. This prompted an unbelievable game of the government hiding the ball and refusing to produce documents in entirety. It took months for them to do so.

By October 2014, we finally had the universe of documents that we were going to get from the government. Before we could do anything with it, though, we needed to organize and read thousands and thousands of pages that had been handed over to us in sporadic, disjointed, and out-of-order document dumps over time. I had just finished a big trial. I was exhausted. But this project needed to get done. I sat down in the conference room with probably five Bankers boxes filled with documents, setting out on a mission to put every single piece of paper into chronological order.

Up to now, I had not really involved anyone from my office in this case. Other than the six months that I was at RRA, I did everything on my own, with extensive help from Paul Cassell on all legal pleadings. But with the way in which the government produced documents, it was like playing fifty-two-card pick-up. It was impossible for one person to put all of this into the order that my mind needed to see it in the short time we needed it done.

Out of desperation more than anything, I asked our brand-new law clerk, Brittany Henderson, who was still in law school, to help me out.

I explained the project and the purpose, and before I could even finish my explanation, Brittany was on top of it. She went and got tabs, her laptop, highlighters, yellow pads, and within seconds devised a plan to organize the documents for future purposes. We spent the next three days from sunrise to midnight in the conference room, taking only five or six hours to go home and sleep each night.

This wasn't just a matter of putting things into chronological order. Once the order had been established, we each read every single page from beginning to end, tabbing and labeling the significance of each and identifying what the government failed to produce. Our review revealed deep efforts between Epstein and the government to work out a secret deal with the goal of saving Epstein and his friends from prosecution, and to do that without the victims ever knowing what had happened. It was crazy.

At one point in time, the government was playing it straight, doing what it should, abiding by the law and legal process. By May 2007, the FBI had thoroughly investigated Epstein, which led to the United States Attorney's Office preparing an eighty-two-page prosecution memo and a fifty-three-page indictment against him, which was never filed. Shortly thereafter, on July 6, 2007, Alan Dershowitz authored a twenty-four-page letter along with Gerald Lefcourt on behalf of Epstein. In it, they explained that Epstein generously supported the Trilateral Commission and the Council on Foreign Relations, seemingly in an effort to curry favor with the government and make it clear just how important Epstein was. No coincidence, the letter also threw in that Epstein was one of the founding members of the Clinton Global Initiative, making his connection with Bill Clinton rather prominent.

And then, boom. All of a sudden, an honest investigation switched to the government and Epstein working together in concert, and in secret.

Before seeing the documents, we knew that the non-prosecution agreement had been signed by Epstein and the government on September 24, 2007. We also knew that until July 2008, the victims still believed that Jeffrey Epstein was going to be federally prosecuted. What we were now learning was just how much effort the government put into working with Epstein to violate the rights of his victims by keeping the NPA secret. After our review of the documents, we knew we could prove the victims' rights had been intentionally violated by the government.

As we were going through the documents, I would flip to one and say, "Oh my god, can you believe this?" It started to happen so frequently it seemed like we were talking more than reading. Every page was worse than the last.

These discoveries, while shocking, were not much worse than what I'd envisioned, and by this point in my career, I was not naive to the fact that money could buy corruption. But it was too much for Brittany to believe. I read one particular email aloud before I handed it to her. "Look, the prosecutor admits in this one that they had 'compiled a list of thirty-four confirmed minors.' They even said, 'There are six others, whose names we already have, who need to be interviewed by the FBI to confirm whether they were seventeen or eighteen at the time of their activity with Mr. Epstein.'"

Brittany grabbed the email and quietly began to compare it with the one in her other hand: "But wait, on September 15, 2007, AUSA Marie Villafaña emailed Epstein's lawyers that she had 'gotten some negative reaction to the assault charge with Sarah Kellen as the victim, since she is considered one of the main perpetrators of the offenses that we planned to charge in the indictment.' I don't understand. This doesn't make any sense. These emails were written nine days apart. The government says right here, in writing, that they had identified at least thirty-four minor victims. They had such an easy case. Why are they talking about some random assault charge against an adult? They wanted to charge Epstein with a crime he may or may not have committed against an adult instead of any of the crimes that he actually did commit against minors? One of his own co-conspirators? What about the victims? Why wouldn't they just charge him with one of the crimes that they prepared an indictment for? The crimes they can prove he committed? Why would they spend any time at all looking for other crimes?"

I looked at the emails and said, "Well, for whatever reason, it's pretty clear that instead of charging Epstein for a crime related to the minors, the government was trying to find a punishment that would be acceptable to Epstein and then back into that punishment with a manufactured charge."

"What?!" Brittany yelled in genuine disbelief. "Can the government do this? How can they do this? How can you just make up some random crime to charge someone with and completely ignore the fact that thirty-four children were actually sexually assaulted? What about all the real charges? What about all of the kids he hurt? Can lawyers get arrested for this?"

Before I could even start to answer her questions, she continued to read further down in the email about the Sarah Kellen assault charge: "The government wanted to construct a conspiracy around 'hearsay evidence that [Virginia Roberts] traveled on Mr. Epstein's airplane when she was under eighteen, in around the 2000 or 2001 time frame.'" From a place of increasing shock, Brittany said, 'Construct a conspiracy'?! There *was* a conspiracy! They knew that Virginia flew on the airplane when she was underage. Of course they knew why Virginia was on that airplane. What was there to construct?!"

I had seen this email before. I had felt the same feelings that Brittany was feeling. The whole thing had been shocking to me for six years by this point.

"What about the fact that she was actually being sexually abused when she was under eighteen?! Seriously, Brad, why would they have to construct a charge? There are so many charges for so many girls—for forty girls!" she blurted out, talking a mile a minute.

I replied, "Here, you'll love this one. On September 16, 2007, the prosecutor emailed Epstein's attorney and said, '[o]n an "avoid the press" note, I believe that Mr. Epstein's airplane was in Miami on the day of the [co-conspirator] telephone call. If he was in Miami-Dade County at the time, then I can file the charge in the district court in Miami, which will hopefully cut the press coverage significantly.' "

"Seems like the government really thought of everything they could to try to help Epstein get away with this. I just don't understand why," she said, exasperated.

I explained the best I could: "You're right. We can see what they want to accomplish—make this all go away for Epstein with as little consequence as possible. The problem they were having is that Epstein only committed very serious crimes against each of these minor victims. If they even attempted to charge a misdemeanor against him for one or more, the victim would get the chance to speak in court, which would likely blow up their whole plan because the judge would learn more about the real facts of the case and reject the plea deal. They needed a cooperative victim. The most obvious choice was one of Epstein's co-conspirators. To help the government out with this plan, you see the emails from Epstein's lawyers telling the government that when Epstein learned the FBI was attempting to serve important subpoenas on Nadia Marcinkova and Sarah Kellen, Epstein committed a physical assault against both of them to cause them not to cooperate. Those assaults could form the basis for misdemeanor charges on behalf of victims who would not provide the judge with information that could disrupt the plan to close the case. If we keep reading, I bet I can find the evidence that I'm talking about."

We kept working, and at two in the morning, I found the email proving my point in one of the last boxes. I handed it to Brittany. "Can you imagine what the judge would think if he ever saw that the AUSA told Epstein's attorneys, 'I will include our standard language regarding resolving all criminal liability and I will mention "co-conspirators," but I would prefer not to highlight for the judge all of the other crimes and all of the other persons that we could charge.'"

"Are you joking?!" she exclaimed. "The government worked with Epstein to make sure that the judge would never learn how many crimes and people they could charge . . . Seriously?!"

The amount of evidence was overwhelming, and her frustration only grew with each new damning revelation. I could barely get a word in.

But her comments were exactly the same as mine would have been had I seen these emails at the time when I was scribbling the word *Emergency* on the top of that motion in 2008. By now I was somewhat numb to the facts, although still angry and resolute. For Brittany, these were fresh wounds. She was "brand-new" mad. This was not just a first project for a young, soon-to-be lawyer. This was much more. The anger and frustration that she felt reviewing these documents inspired the direction of her legal career. She was now as committed to this as I was.

After hours of combing through documents, she finally came across something that shocked me. "Listen to this—Epstein's lawyers and the government put together a joint letter to a judge in Miami in October 2007 saying, 'the United States has identified forty young women who can be characterized as victims. . . . Some of those women went to Mr. Epstein's home only once, some went there as much as one hundred times or more. Some of the women's conduct was limited to performing a topless or nude massage while Mr. Epstein masturbated himself. For other women, the conduct escalated to full sexual intercourse.'" As she was expressing her shock over the fact that the "women" being referred to in this joint letter were actually minor children whom everyone knew Epstein had victimized, I remembered something that one of his lawyers had said to the media earlier the same year that the letter was written.

"Let me see your laptop for a second, I need to look something up," I said, as I grabbed her computer.

"I knew it. Here it is. Check out this article in the *Daily Mail* from earlier that same year. Just a few months before they jointly stated that Epstein had full sexual intercourse with victims, his attorney, Alan Dershowitz, was reported to have told the *Daily Mail* that 'Epstein had passed a lie detector test showing he was innocent of allegations' and that '[t]he financier had paid for massages, but had not engaged in sex or erotic massages with any minors.' It goes on to say that Dershowitz said that the girl who accused Epstein of forcible sex 'had a long record of lying, theft, and blaming others for her crimes.' " On its face, the letter appeared irreconcilable with those statements made that same year.

"How can he say that? This is unbelievable," Brittany quickly replied.

I came back to the central issue. "Let's not forget, the NPA was signed on September 24, 2007, before any of the victims were ever told that any type of agreement was even being negotiated. We need to figure out why. We know that the prosecutor emailed Epstein's lawyer that same day insinuating that they needed to discuss what she could tell the victims, but how long did this go on?"

She responded a few seconds later, reading from an October 10, 2007, email from Epstein's lawyer Jay Lefkowitz to then U.S. attorney Alex Acosta. " 'Neither federal agents nor anyone from your office should contact the identified individuals to inform them of the resolution of the case. . . . Not only would that violate the confidentiality of the agreement, but Mr. Epstein also will have no control over what is communicated to the identified individuals at this most critical stage.' "

This helped answer a crucial question. I said: "Well the one thing that we now know for sure is that the government complied with Epstein's demands not to notify the victims because on May 30, 2008—eight months after the NPA was signed—the government sent out a series of letters to victims saying, '[t]his case is currently under investigation. This can be a lengthy process and we request your continued patience while we conduct a thorough investigation.' That is the letter that brought Courtney to my office in the first place. We win this case on summary judgment," I told her confidently.

The review of these communications came directly on the heels of our meeting with Virginia. We now had the evidence we'd been looking for to strengthen our CVRA case—emails which revealed that the victims' rights had indeed been violated.

# THIRTY

# DERSHOWITZ

I N ADDITION TO EPSTEIN AND Maxwell, two other individuals surfaced in Virginia's account who seemed relevant to the CVRA case she was looking to join. Prince Andrew was one of them. That aspect of Virginia's story discussed how she was internationally trafficked by Epstein and Maxwell. Alan Dershowitz was the other. He was important because he was not only one of Epstein's attorneys when the unprecedented NPA was secretly crafted immunizing Epstein and all co-conspirators, but according to witnesses, he was also a friend and houseguest during time periods when Epstein was sexually abusing minors.

By late 2014, we had accumulated testimony and evidence of a personal relationship between Dershowitz and Epstein, but until talking with Virginia, the information we knew about Dershowitz didn't seem important to the CVRA case. Of course it was offensive that he would discredit Epstein's child victims to make sure Epstein stayed out of trouble. The fact that he so respected Epstein, a serial molester and abuser, was concerning. And it was beyond frustrating that he would not sit for a deposition so we could question what he saw during his relationship with Epstein. But, as close as it seemed he and Epstein were, nobody had ever specifically identified him to us as someone involved in Epstein's other lifestyle. Until Virginia.

In assessing how much detail the court needed to know about Virginia's involvement with Epstein in order to make a ruling on her ability to join the CVRA case as Jane Doe 3, we were extremely conflicted. Our focus was on the criminal acts of Jeffrey Epstein. We were not looking to unnecessarily expand the scope of the investigation or make the case messier than it already was. We felt, however, that we did need to explain to the court what made Virginia's account different from the current petitioners in the case, which was her frequent travel on Epstein's jet while she was undeniably underage, highlighted by her introduction to British royalty while a child, and her knowledge of one of Epstein's friends who also happened to be one of Epstein's lawyers at the time the NPA was devised. Virginia didn't just come in and out of Epstein's world through the side door of his Palm Beach mansion for an hour at a time like most of the other victims whose stories Judge Marra was familiar with. She traveled with Epstein and Maxwell for two years. She was intimately familiar with the inner workings of the operation and the expansive jurisdiction of the criminal organization. And through her accounts she offered a fuller explanation for why the sneaky deal was made to save Epstein.

There was another category of victim to be added to the CVRA case whose rights were not yet represented. These were the dozen or so individuals whom we identified as victims of Epstein's underage sex abuse but who, because the government elected to stop investigating and instead enter into this broad immunity agreement, were never formally identified by the government as victims. Before deciding to add Jane Doe 4 to represent the interests of that subcategory, we informed the U.S. Attorney's Office about her and several others who were similarly situated and who wanted to prosecute Epstein for the crimes he had committed. Because the government, having stopped its investigation, did not know their identities at the time the non-prosecution agreement was signed—or even eight months later when Epstein made his plea in state court—there could not possibly be any restriction against filing a new indictment against Epstein for those newly discovered crimes committed against these newly discovered victims. Right?

Despite our urging, the government refused to bring charges on behalf of these victims. While they would not commit to the position that Epstein's NPA was the reason they refused to bring those charges, they offered no other explanation, leaving us to believe they were using the NPA as cover to avoid prosecuting him.

We then felt strongly that it was important to join Jane Doe 4 at the time we moved to join Virginia Roberts, in the CVRA case. We decided to file the "Jane Doe #3 and Jane Doe #4's Motion Pursuant to Rule 21 for Joinder in Action" the day before New Year's Eve. We had hoped that the filing would go unnoticed, and it almost did, with the exception of one studious reporter.

On December 31, 2014, Josh Gerstein published an article in *Politico* in which he detailed the filing, focusing primarily on the allegations of sexual misconduct that Virginia had made regarding Alan Dershowitz, Prince Andrew, and Ghislaine Maxwell. Dershowitz was quoted in the article as saying that Virginia's allegations were "totally made up and totally fabricated from beginning to end."

Dershowitz's loud denial was not unexpected. We even expected for him to go on the attack against Virginia. What we did not expect was where he took his attack next. The first few days of 2015 were something straight out of a movie, one in which Dershowitz had decided to cast *me* as the villain.

# THIRTY-ONE

# RUNNING INTERFERENCE

I N JANUARY 2015, MY FAMILY TV set was turned on in my living room when my youngest son came running into my home office to tell me that my picture was on the screen and they were talking about me. I thought, *Cool, hopefully the public is finally taking notice of the importance of the CVRA case.* I could not have been more wrong. Alan Dershowitz was on CNN going berserk. Had I read his 2013 book *Taking the Stand: My Life in the Law*, this would not have been surprising.

He didn't just attack Virginia or her allegations, he turned his guns on Paul and me. Dershowitz went on one major national television network after another, fuming about Paul and me for allowing Virginia's allegations to be filed in a court pleading. He went on CNN, NBC, Fox, and MSNBC, repeatedly claiming that we should be kicked out of the legal profession— or worse—for believing our client. CNN was giving more airtime to Dershowitz than the network (or, for that matter, any other network) had ever given to the victims, so that he could impress that he had done nothing wrong, that he was merely Jeffrey Epstein's lawyer, and that Paul and I were the bad guys for believing Virginia.

On January 5, Dershowitz told CNN, "If they had just done an hour of research and work, they would have seen that she is lying through her teeth, that's why I'm going after them, their bar cards." He made so many threats about us that it was impossible to keep track. Dershowitz was trying to bully us. I spent the night fielding calls from friends, family, and other lawyers. I wanted to respond and go toe to toe on the facts, but my obligation was to my clients, including Virginia, and getting lured into a media battle would not be helpful to them. Still, we couldn't just ignore him.

In addition to his rants about Paul and me, he claimed that if Virginia believed the allegations she was leveling against him then she should be suing him for damages, which he claimed to want because it would give him a vehicle through which he could prove his innocence in court. But there was a major escape hatch in his "earnest" plea to be sued: the statute of limitations, which prevents such claims from being brought after a certain time period has passed.

By January 5, 2015, when Dershowitz was well into his public attack, David Boies, who had vetted Virginia's allegations, came to my office to consider how best to take Dershowitz up on his request to be sued by Virginia and his public offer to waive the statute of limitations. We decided I would send a simple, straightforward letter to Dershowitz asking him to make good on his offer to waive the statute by signing a one-paragraph agreement to that effect. Dershowitz never signed it, but that didn't stop him from continuing to publicly trash Paul and me.

The next day, I called Jack Scarola and asked him how quickly Paul and I could put together a defamation lawsuit against Dershowitz, since he would not stop attacking us. We sued Dershowitz that day—January 6, 2015. Jack was excited to represent us because he knew Dershowitz would now be unable to avoid having his deposition taken. But the filing of our lawsuit did not slow Alan down.

During his interviews, Dershowitz tried hard to control the narrative, but the public became less concerned about him and more focused on his client Mr. Epstein and the raw deal the victims received during the process. In addition to drawing negative attention to his client, Dershowitz also began encountering interviewers who started familiarizing themselves with the facts and asking him tougher questions about different aspects of his relationship with Epstein, including the topic of massage. On January 21,

2015, Dershowitz told the *New York Daily News* that he "never got a massage from anybody. It's made up out of whole cloth." Yet one day later, on January 22, 2015, he told Bob Norman of Channel 10 that he had a massage in Epstein's house but "kept my underwear on during the massage. I don't like massages particularly."

Because of Dershowitz, the entire Epstein story was now being thrust into the spotlight. People finally began noticing, and caring, about our CVRA case and the injustice of what the government had done in forgiving Epstein's unforgivable crimes against vulnerable children. If causing a distraction was the goal, it ultimately backfired. Dershowitz *finally* turned what had been a local story into national and even international news. After he made his first TV rounds, the reports started to circulate globally— Epstein was a politically connected billionaire who was investigated for receiving erotic massages from many underage females; he was now a registered sex offender; Dershowitz was one of his lawyers and longtime personal friends; as his lawyer, Dershowitz played a role in negotiating a non-prosecution agreement that immunized from federal sex offenses not only Epstein but also Epstein's named and unnamed co-conspirators; and now Virginia Roberts, one of Epstein's victims, was describing Epstein's traveling sex cult, which had operated for more than a decade throughout the country and even overseas and included some of Epstein's friends.

As that litigation continued, it began to consume a lot of my time. Dershowitz had further complicated things by filing a defamation counterclaim against us. In response, we filed a motion to dismiss his counterclaim. He didn't give up and instead filed an amended counterclaim, which we again moved to dismiss. And, while Jack Scarola was representing me, he didn't know the details the way I did, so most of the case-building for the lawsuit had to be done by Paul or me.

While the isolated facts leading to this defamation lawsuit were relatively simple, the lawsuit itself was more complicated. Basically, Virginia's allegations about being trafficked by Epstein and Maxwell included allegations regarding other people. Dershowitz claimed that Virginia was lying about everything and, more important, that we should have known Virginia was lying about everything when we allowed her allegations to be placed in the public record. Our lawsuit against Dershowitz was, then, not really about whether Virginia or Alan was telling the truth, but instead about what we knew or should have known about Virginia's credibility at the time the allegations were made. Still, there was no way to isolate that issue without delving into the underlying allegations and defenses.

Of course, in these types of "he said, she said" situations, it is rarely easy to know for sure exactly what happened between two people decades earlier. In most cases, though, we can ask the other witnesses who were allegedly there. In this case, the obvious witnesses who would know what had occurred included Jeffrey Epstein and his other named co-conspirators from the NPA. However, during their depositions, each of these witnesses hid behind the Fifth Amendment rather than answer questions.

Epstein was Dershowitz's friend and client, so Epstein's refusal to answer questions about Dershowitz on the basis that it would somehow incriminate Epstein certainly did not weigh favorably for Dershowitz. However, we could not place too much emphasis on that fact, since there were few questions in any proceeding for which Epstein didn't invoke the Fifth Amendment. With the only potential eyewitnesses all under Epstein's control, refusing to answer questions, the case became something of a credibility contest between Dershowitz and Virginia. We had vetted Virginia, both personally and through other attorneys and means.

The most seemingly outrageous claim she ever made was that she was taken by Epstein and Maxwell to London, where she was lent out to Prince Andrew, Duke of York, yet there she was with a photo of her with the Prince and Ghislaine, and Epstein's flight logs corroborated the trip. We also gathered as much information as we possibly could about Dershowitz, given his lack of cooperation with us. Despite our efforts, he had avoided giving us a deposition before now, but certainly his relationship with Epstein appeared closer than some of his statements suggested. We believed the facts and law were on our side.

Again, the gist of Dershowitz's public assault on us was that we had failed to check the truth of our client's claims, or even worse, knew her claims were false, before allowing her joinder motion in the CVRA case. But that couldn't be further from the truth. While these types of cases are rarely susceptible to absolute proof, we had certainly investigated Virginia's story and had good reason to allow her to assert her voice in court.

Dershowitz did not have the facts or the law on his side, but he had prepared a strategy for this type of situation that he had expressed many years before in his 2013 book. He wrote, "There's an old saying: 'If you have the law on your side, bang on the law. If you have the facts on your side, bang on the facts. If you have neither, bang on the table.' I have never believed that, but I do believe in a variation on that theme: If you don't have the law or legal facts on your side, argue your case in the court of public opinion."

At least we knew he believed in his own advice.

# THIRTY-TWO

# TITONE

SINCE THE BEGINNING, CALLS HAVE always poured in about this case. Most are from people who want to be helpful but don't have any real evidence or new information. But every once in a while, a more important, or at least interesting, call would come in. On February 25, 2015, I received one of those more interesting calls. It was from a lawyer who said that he represented someone I would be interested in speaking with, and wanted to make a personal appointment to come to my office. He wouldn't tell me who he represented over the phone. He insisted on meeting in person. And specifically on meeting at my office. He set the time for eight a.m. sharp.

Joe Titone was on time, dressed in a suit, and wearing a Kangol-style cap. He told me that he had been a politician and that his daughter was married to Adam Sandler. (That turns out to be true, and I can't wait to hear Sandler's song about how his name ended up in this book, of all places.) When Titone sat down, I still had no idea who he represented or why he was there.

Before he would tell me who he represented, he wanted to know, based on the information I had collected, whether I believed Epstein would ever be prosecuted. I told him I had no idea. Serious red flags went up. "Before we go any further," I said, "who do you represent?" He didn't answer. The conversation was going nowhere. Seeing that the meeting was going to end if he didn't identify his client, and seemingly exasperated, he launched into a tale that was one of those mixtures of fact and fiction that keeps you intrigued enough to listen.

He told me he represented a French guy I may have heard of, Jean-Luc Brunel. I was thinking, *I may have heard of him? Are you kidding me?* I had served him for a deposition, he had left messages for Epstein on the message pads offering a "2 × 8 year-old Russian girl," and had been a targeted witness of mine for years. He was one of Epstein's best friends, who stayed at Epstein's house and who had escaped his deposition with some lie delivered by a lawyer paid for by Jeffrey. Not only did I know who he was, but anyone who knew anything about Jean-Luc Brunel or Jeffrey Epstein knew that I knew who Jean-Luc was. Titone's comment made me even more suspicious about his reason for being there.

As he continued to explain why he represented Jean-Luc, I started asking questions. "Is he willing to give me a list of all the girls he knew Epstein had abused? Is he willing to turn over his photos of Epstein and the girls?" Titone backpedaled quickly, saying that he had only met his client once. They had mutual friends, including another French guy who owned property in Miami Beach and who had recommended Titone to Brunel. Titone told me that he had filed a lawsuit for Brunel against Epstein in Miami, in January, and that he needed my help in order to get it served on Epstein. I was trying to make sense of these comments and what I suspected was a different motive for the visit.

He's a practicing lawyer, and yet he says he needs *my* help effecting service on Jeffrey Epstein? Epstein was a registered sex offender who couldn't go anywhere in the world without telling various government agencies where he was at all times. And he had been successfully served with more than twenty lawsuits. Plus, hardly anyone in the world knew his day-to-day travel and living routine better than Jean-Luc Brunel. You're asking for help on this? Come on.

Then Titone dropped a timely bombshell. "My client has photos, lots of photos. With Epstein, and his friends. He tells me some even include young girls," he explained, immediately grabbing my attention. Of course, this was something I couldn't ignore. But again, what did he want from me? Surely it couldn't be help serving Epstein with a lawsuit.

It was probably more difficult to set up a meeting at my office and catch me at a convenient time than it was for Jean-Luc to figure out how to serve Jeffrey Epstein. Jean-Luc knew all of Epstein's staff, his travel companions, and even the doormen at Epstein's apartment complex in New York where Jean-Luc used to live, which, to the best of my knowledge, was still Jean-Luc's residence.

On the face of it, a lawsuit by Jean-Luc against Epstein was unlikely. "What did Jean-Luc sue Epstein for?" I asked. Titone then whipped out a copy of the complaint, which, including attachments, was more than one hundred pages long. I flipped through it. "So let me get this straight," I said. "Jean-Luc, who *60 Minutes* and the BBC reported was kicked out of his prior modeling agency in Europe for having sex with teenage models, is suing Jeffrey Epstein, his friend and pal who helped Jean-Luc get back on his feet? And the lawsuit claims that Epstein's molestation of children has somehow hurt Jean-Luc's reputation? I gotta tell you, Joe, this lawsuit makes no sense."

He shrugged. I continued: "I've been told that Epstein financed Jean-Luc's modeling agency so that Jean-Luc could import girls for Jeffrey and stash them at the apartments at 301 East Sixty-Sixth Street. I've taken a statement of a witness who has driven some of these girls to Jeffrey Epstein's home. After Epstein was arrested, Jean-Luc was one of the people who frequently visited him in jail. After his release, while he was on house arrest, Jean-Luc stayed at Epstein's home. The association you're saying damaged Jean-Luc was comprised of a series of choices made by Jean-Luc, most important his decision to lie in order to avoid his deposition. What is your cause of action?"

He answered, "Obstruction of justice." I asked him to explain. He said something along the lines of "Well, Jean-Luc knew of the suspicions that you had about Jeffrey Epstein and him. Jean-Luc claims that despite his past, he wasn't involved in sex with little girls. It was only Epstein. He knows all about that, and witnessed it on occasion, but he wasn't personally involved. When you served a deposition notice on Jean-Luc in 2009, he was finally going to get his opportunity tell the world under oath of his lack of involvement in Jeffrey Epstein's sex escapades. He wanted to testify. He flew to Palm Beach for that deposition and stayed with Epstein. He was anxious to provide information that was going to erase the cloud of suspicion that hung over him, but because of his lengthy relationship with Epstein, it was going to be damaging to his old friend. The night before the deposition, Epstein ordered Jean-Luc not to show up. Jean-Luc was told that his deposition would be canceled and that he should leave the country. Like everyone around Jeffrey, Jean-Luc knew he had no choice but to obey."

I still thought that this was another Epstein ploy. But I could not resist the urge to fall into whatever this trap was in order to find out what was really going on. I agreed that I would tell him where Epstein was so he could serve him if he would let me interview Jean-Luc. I had enough information to make me confident that I would be able to tell if Jean-Luc was lying. He was a very important witness. If there was even a 1 percent chance that he would cooperate against Epstein, it was worth the risk that I was being played. Titone told me that he would get back to me on that request and left the office.

I thought about the meeting. It was beyond strange, but if it was orchestrated by Epstein, it was smart. He knew that I identified Brunel as a key piece of the puzzle, a prized target, whose cooperation I would not be able to turn down no matter my level of suspicion. Epstein would be able to use my communication line with Brunel to learn what I knew and what I didn't and how close I was to having Epstein criminally investigated again.

I looked back at the complaint. One grown adult told another grown adult not to show up for a deposition. They were best friends connected only by the public exposure inflicted on each of them separately because of their penchant for teenage girls. And *this* was what supposedly drove them apart?

After I finished reading, I contacted our investigator and described what had just happened. My feeling was that for this to be a worthwhile move for Epstein, he had to get something out of it. What if it was more than just a means of communicating in order to relay back to Epstein what I knew and what I was doing to learn more? Was it possible that Joe Titone was a conduit carrying a bug to plant in my office? Our investigator instructed us on where to look and what to look for. We spent the better part of the rest of the day retracing Titone's steps from the time he exited his car to go into our office until he got back into his car to leave.

We found nothing, but I wasn't convinced. Jeffrey Epstein would only use the latest technology to bug us and certainly wouldn't do it in a way that ran the risk of getting caught.

I contacted Stan. He'd had government experience and had even prosecuted cases during his time at the Justice Department involving the illegal planting of recording devices. He agreed that Epstein was likely behind this.

Shortly after that meeting, other strange things started happening in our office. Important emails and documents that we would segregate on our hard drive would disappear. A bunch of our older files got corrupted. Our emails were hacked into more than once. I even asked Stan if there was a way that Epstein had done something to intercept our telephone calls or listen to our cell phone calls. Stan said that he knew of no private citizen doing it but the technology was out there and if anyone could pay to get hold of it, Epstein could.

Titone would, coincidentally or not, usually call after some important team meeting related to the ongoing Epstein litigation. I had suspected Epstein of wiretapping our cell phones years before when his team would somehow get information that was discussed only in private telephone conversations. To increase that concern, Epstein's extortionist complaint against me, in which he falsely claimed that I had been involved in the RRA Ponzi scheme, included the allegation that I had illegally wiretapped or bugged *his* house. This was concerning to me because Epstein's team were masters of accusing us of underhanded tactics that we had never considered using, as a way of deflecting attention from things they were doing themselves.

When Epstein would aggressively have investigators tail our clients, scaring the living daylights out of them and their families, before we could complain about it, Epstein would make false, crazy allegations that our investigators were hopping around his property dressed like ninjas. This history of false allegations elevated my fear that Epstein might have dispatched Titone to plant a bug.

One day I received a brown box in the mail with no return label. It looked sketchy. As I started opening it, I realized it had multiple layers. Each time I opened one, there was another. Nobody in my office knew a package was coming and it had no markings on it. I started to wonder if I should have an expert open it for me, or if we should even open it at all.

I carried this mysterious package over to Brittany's office and asked her jokingly if she would open it for me just in case. After a few minutes of ridiculous speculation about what could be inside, we finally took our chances and opened the smallest box in the package. What we found was a handwritten note next to a flip phone. The handwritten note contained instructions on how to set up the phone with a number to call once that was done. I immediately called the number and heard Stan at the other end. He told me this was how we were going to communicate on certain matters until we knew that my worries about Titone were needless. Anytime we had something particularly sensitive to discuss, including new witnesses, we would use this phone.

Was this Stan just being paranoid? Or would Epstein really concoct this whole elaborate plan to bug my office and wiretap our phones? It seemed risky even for him. But I guess it was better to be safe than sorry, so burner phones became a new way of life.

# THIRTY-THREE

# THE PLOT THICKENS

O UR TEAM WAS WORKING HARD to make sure we stayed focused on what mattered. Virginia Roberts had important revelations that should not be silenced. While Epstein and his entourage were looking to shut her down, she was determined to be heard. She was confident in the truth and in putting an end to Epstein's abusive clan who had chased her out of the country years earlier and no doubt had continued to leave a trail of victims in its wake. To accomplish her goal, she needed airtime on a major network.

We began putting feelers out and all were interested. Because ABC's Jim Hill was an adept investigative reporter who understood the complexities of the case far better than anyone else, and because Virginia really liked Amy Robach, the ABC anchor committed to the story, we chose ABC.

We met with ABC personnel prior to April 2015 when we flew with Virginia to New York for the taping of her full-story interview with Amy. David Boies's partner Sigrid McCawley, Stan, Virginia, and I worked with the ABC team to make sure they had everything they needed. Virginia's interview was powerful. The Epstein organization was finally going to be exposed. There would be no more abuse. Light was going to be shed on the expansiveness of the abuse. Moreover, ABC was going to publicize the sweetheart deal Epstein and his co-conspirators got in Florida and reveal how the government mistreated the Florida victims.

Amy was prepared, and Virginia's chemistry with her could not have been better. We were told on the set it was one of the best interviews anyone had seen and would air on *Good Morning America* first before airing on one of their longer platforms. After being strung along for weeks, we were finally told that because Virginia talked about her interactions with Prince Andrew, the network had to reach out to the British royal family and also to an attorney for Epstein since nearly the entire story discussed the inner workings of the Epstein sex-trafficking organization.

For some reason, both presented a problem for ABC. We were not told much, other than the network was scared that they would lose access to the royal family if they aired the interview. We were also told that Alan Dershowitz returned requests for comment by Jeffrey Epstein, and that whatever he said contributed to their apprehension to put Virginia on air. For whatever reasons, ABC never aired the interview, which deeply frustrated those closest to the story, including Amy and Jim.

(More than four years later, after Epstein's sexual abuse was widely reported by many other networks, Amy Robach was caught on a hot mic on set expressing her frustration over that lost opportunity: "I've had the story for three years. I've had this interview with Virginia Roberts. We would not put it on the air. First of all, I was told, who's Jeffrey Epstein. No one knows who that is. This is a stupid story. Then the Palace found out that we had her whole allegation about Prince Andrew and threatened us in a million different ways. We were so afraid we wouldn't be able to interview Kate and Will that also quashed the story. . . . I tried for three years to get it on to no avail. And now it's all coming out and it's like these new revelations. And I freaking had all of it. . . . Brad Edwards, the attorney, three years ago saying, like there will come a day when we will realize Jeffrey Epstein was the most prolific pedophile this country has ever known.")

Before, during, and after Virginia's interview with ABC, we were still dealing with the sideshow that Alan Dershowitz was creating. It wasn't all bad, though. As a direct consequence of him going on national news, more witnesses continued to come forward. People called from New York, Paris, New Mexico, and all over the world, helping us to build our case. As we were sifting through the calls about Epstein and his misdeeds, we were also now getting calls about Dershowitz himself. Most of them had nothing to do with any of the litigation that we were involved in, some were actually funny, some I wish I could forget.

A neighbor from Dershowitz's condo building in Miami called to recount in great detail how she would witness Dershowitz dress in a way to hide his identity while he walked the beach to look at topless girls sunbathing near their condo. Because of this behavior, the woman told Dershowitz's wife that he was a pervert. She claimed that in response Dershowitz got in her face and threatened her, forcing her to go to the police in fear for her safety. To confirm her account, we ordered the police report she said she filed. And there it was. She had told the police that Dershowitz said, "You don't know what I am capable of," and "You are going to be so sorry that you said that to my wife."

Other people telephoned to tell us how they had seen Dershowitz skinny-dipping on Martha's Vineyard. One Vineyard resident recalled walking up to a volleyball game where Dershowitz was playing nude.

Calls continued to come in fast and furious and some from very important witnesses, most of whom we went to meet in person, although because of the volume we didn't always get to everyone before the caller changed his or her mind about cooperating. Some people had information about not only Epstein or Dershowitz but also other powerful figures, and these callers were usually nervous.

On one occasion we heard from a former Harvard student who was living in New York. She told me how in 2004, a friend of hers had brought her to Little Saint James and Epstein was there with underage girls. She was very frightened to share the information, but ultimately revealed that she had been to Epstein's island twice. She wasn't only scared of Epstein but also of his very powerful friends. She knew of at least one heavyweight politician who was close with Epstein who had received erotic massages from young females provided by Epstein.

We talked several times. She wanted to share more but was scared to death. In most instances—in probably all but this one—I gained the trust of the various witnesses who came forward and could put them at ease. But this witness was different, perhaps understandably so. She had a career with everything to lose and nothing to gain, as she put it. Before I left Florida to meet her in New York, she called to say she'd changed her mind about co-operating. Realizing the importance of her information, especially as it corroborated generally the concept Virginia had advanced of Epstein lending his girls out to other powerful men, I sent an investigator to see her. Apparently, his approach was bad, and the witness called to tell me she was afraid for her life and never wanted to talk about this again.

While I have some educated guesses, I still don't know who the politician was. But over the years, we heard from numerous witnesses, including victims themselves, about various powerful friends of Epstein reaping the erotic massage benefits of that friendship, although it seemed most of those friends stayed clear of the girls who were underage.

––––––––

The summer of 2015 was the summer I nearly stopped sleeping altogether. I was coaching two of my sons' football teams, was embroiled in two personal lawsuits (suing Epstein in one that was still ongoing after six years, and Dershowitz in the other), and was also running a busy litigation firm.

In June, I was preparing for a long, fairly high-profile wrongful-death trial representing the husband of a pregnant woman who was hit by a drunk driver while she sat in a hotel cabana (yes, the car drove through the cabana), killing her and her unborn child. As with any case, I put all others out of my mind so that my total focus was on the trial at hand, although this was especially difficult to do. As I walked to and from the courtroom every day, I was frequently asked by lawyers and judges about the public assault Dershowitz had launched on me, the lawsuit I'd filed against him, my pursuit of justice for Epstein's victims, and how each was affecting the others. I made a conscious effort not to allow the hallway chatter to impact my trial.

After a very emotional three-week trial, the jury returned a verdict in my client's favor for $24 million. The verdict provided some justice for the family, which, as inadequate as it was given the terrible loss, was all I could help provide. Trials are emotionally draining, not only on the plaintiffs, but on the lawyers as well. To recover, I usually try to take a few days off afterward, but this time I couldn't. I had already lost valuable time. There was no choice but to immediately turn back to Epstein (and Dershowitz).

---

An important decision on my malicious prosecution claim against Epstein was scheduled to come down any day. There was a lot on the line. If the court decided in Epstein's favor and ruled that malicious prosecution was no longer a recognized claim in Florida (the *Wolfe v. Foreman* case referred to earlier), Epstein would almost immediately proceed to get a judgment against me in the millions of dollars. He and Dershowitz would then be in a great position to band together once again and go on the attack to finish me off.

While the appellate court had not ruled in my case, it did come down with a decision in a different case that raised the same issue. And the ruling looked good for me. The Fourth District Court of Appeal had disagreed with the *Wolfe v. Foreman* opinion that Epstein had used against me—the one that essentially abolished malicious prosecution as a claim in Florida. All of that legal jargon just meant that I was likely back in the game. Sure, there were some minor distinctions between the cases, but for the most part the central issue was the same—a person could be sued for malicious prosecution for filing a knowingly false complaint against another person, as Epstein had done to me. The tide had shifted heavily in my favor.

In light of that opinion, the trial court in my case ordered Epstein and me to attend a mediation in advance of any ruling from the appellate court. When a case is decided by a higher court that may change the outcome of other cases affected by the higher court's new decision, a trial court will often make the parties try to settle their differences, in light of the changed law, thereby hoping to avoid a long and expensive trial.

It was a strange time for mediation because, on the one hand, the trial court's order dismissing my case had not been overturned by a higher court. Thus, if a higher court upheld the trial court's decision in an appeal, it was I who would owe Epstein many millions as payment for his attorney's fees. On the other hand, in light of this new higher court decision on a similar case, the appeal in my case against Epstein looked as if it was going to go in my favor, in which case my malicious prosecution action would be reinstated. Given the egregious nature of his conduct against me, he would be the one at risk of losing big. This all created an interesting negotiating dynamic.

In every mediation that I had ever been in, the mediator sat at the head of a large table with one party on one side and the other party on the other. When we arrived at this mediation in Palm Beach, we found the mediator in the lobby and began walking to the large conference room where the parties would meet for the opening introduction and statements. Lining one side of the table were half a dozen lawyers representing Epstein. The seat at the head of the table, usually reserved for the mediator, who would command the room and run the meeting, was occupied. Leaning back in the mediator's chair, wearing a tie, one leg folded over the other, his hands intertwined on his lap, was Jeffrey Epstein. "Is this," he asked as we entered, "where I'm supposed to sit?"

The most startling thing about his presentation was not his preemptive move on the mediator's seat but the fact that he was wearing a tie. This had more meaning than anyone other than I would understand. This was a guy who was once quoted saying that he never *had* to be anywhere. He spent his life in sweatpants and monogrammed pullover sweatshirts, refusing to accept most societal norms. Yet here he was wearing a tie, feigning respect. But this was not a show of respect.

I looked at his tie a little closer and saw that it was extraordinarily short, extending just beyond the second button from the top. It looked like a seven-year-old's tie. He was giving the impression of respect while also making a mockery of the typical mediation or lawyer's attire. He loved to make fun of lawyers—how stupid they are, how they are always slaves to their clients. Making fun of the lawyer's monkey suit was just another of his childish jabs. Ironically—because I, too, wanted Jeffrey to know that he was not getting undue respect from me—I showed up in jeans and no tie.

The mediator quickly relocated Epstein and took his spot at the head of the table, with the lawyers closest to him and the clients—Jeffrey and me—at the end across from one another. The mediator started the same way that every mediator starts, by explaining the benefits of mediation and the unpredictability of trial. Before he began, Jeffrey and I locked eyes. Initially, both equally strong and almost simultaneously in response to what sounded like Charlie Brown's teacher in the background, we rolled our eyes at each other as if to say, *This guy knows nothing about either one of us, or what we have gone through to get here.*

Unconventionally, before any of our lawyers could speak, I said, "We don't need to spend any more time. There is nothing that anyone is going to say in this room that is going to change the mind of anyone else who matters in this room. I speak for myself, and also, I know in this regard, I speak for Jeffrey as well. If any differences will ever be resolved between the two of us, lawyers are not going to help."

Before I could finish, Jeffrey chimed in, "I agree."

The mediator asked what we recommended. I stood up and said, "We'll be back."

Jeffrey and I got up and walked to another room. Entering, we saw a table to the left with drinking glasses lined up. Jeffrey turned to me and said, "We should just start breaking the shit out of all of these glasses and make everyone think we're killing each other." I laughed. We sat at the small table in the room across from one another for thirty minutes or so.

There was this unspoken understanding we had with each other: after I truthfully answered one of his questions, it was his turn to do the same. He knew which witnesses I had spoken with, and also hinted that it was unlikely many of those people would give me any more information. I reminded him that I could still subpoena those I had already interviewed for trial. "Like you did with Jean-Luc?" he retorted.

"Speaking of Jean-Luc, I hear he's suing you. What's that about?" I took my chance to test whether that lawsuit was an Epstein concoction.

"It's stupid," he said with a dismissive poker face. He shifted the subject. "What about Ghislaine, are you going to leave her alone?"

I replied, "Only if you tell me everything I want to know about what you did, where you did it, and who you did it with. If you won't tell me, I'll ask Ghislaine. She has to know, since she's probably the one who created you."

We traded off this way while approximately a dozen lawyers who did not like one another sat awkwardly in the room, waiting for one or both of us to emerge. We got nowhere. The meeting ended with Epstein saying that he knew I wanted him to be arrested. "Since that will never happen, Brad, I strongly suggest we be done with each other. You drop all the cases and just go away," he said.

"We will continue to agree to disagree about how this is going to end," I responded quickly, and got up to leave.

"Is this the Brad Edwards negotiating method?" he said as he laughed and rocked back in his chair before rising to stand. Before we left the room, he said, "Let me think about this and I'll be in touch. Don't you think we should throw at least one of these glasses at each other before we leave the room?" getting me to laugh one last time.

We walked back to the main mediation room together and announced that we had not been able to resolve the case, or anything else, for that matter. But there was one more surprise before Epstein's team left. Just then, the process server we had hired to serve Jeffrey Epstein for another deposition walked in and served a subpoena on him. His lawyers were furious, yelling that they would seek sanctions for us using a mediation to get Epstein into a room where we could serve him with a subpoena. Jack and I just grinned as we left.

---

Epstein called a week later. "We need to resolve our case," he said, speaking about our personal lawsuit. He continued, "But this Dershowitz thing is making things complicated for me. I don't care about him, but it drags me in. It needs to be resolved, too. And all of the cases involving me need to be resolved." The last comment was his way of saying that he wanted to find a way to settle the CVRA case, but he knew it was risky for him to say that directly, so he chose those words carefully. "I'm always honest with you. I always fight fair with you. I never use my full resources against you, but it is getting to a point where you are leaving me little choice."

"I will not talk to you about the CVRA case," I told him first.

"Understood," he said.

"With Dershowitz, I want you to be honest with me and answer some questions about him and others," I said as a condition precedent.

"What do you want to know?" he offered.

"Tell me the names of all of your friends who had sex with your girls," I asked first. When he didn't respond, I sensed that maybe that question overstepped his invitation. So I rattled off a series of narrower questions: "How many of your friends did you send Virginia Roberts to? Was Alan Dershowitz one of those friends?"

"I can't answer any of these questions. You know that," he said.

"If you're not going to answer these basic questions, then I don't see us getting anywhere," I finished.

"For now," he responded before abruptly hanging up.

Epstein always had the ability to resolve all of the civil cases with the exception of the CVRA. But he could not bring himself to do so on my terms. The civil litigation was what gave me subpoena power and the ability to investigate and take depositions. He could have stopped all of that by paying plaintiffs for the damage he caused. But he didn't.

At several points, he made offhand comments about finding the litigation interesting and equating it to a complex chess game. He enjoyed the "offense and defense of it all." These types of comments, coupled with the knowledge that he had the financial ability to end any one of these "games" instantly, made me think that in some Br'er Rabbit "don't throw me in the briar patch" fashion, he wanted to be discovered. No doubt, he did not want to be punished, but he loved letting the world know that he made his own unconventional rules and that the laws of our society did not apply to him.

Now, though, he was getting nervous. Not only was I discovering a lot more information than he wanted me to know, but the Dershowitz thing had amplified the public attention on his activities in a bad way. The situation was running the risk of crossing over from the game he liked playing, where people would admire his unconventional lifestyle of constant erotic massages, to people paying close attention to the details, which included illegalities that could not be forgiven. He didn't want me to continue to investigate him, track down or subpoena witnesses, or collect more incriminating information, yet he also did not want to give in to my demands that would allow him to avoid those things.

It was hard to pin him down on why he was so hardheaded. He seemed to know that dragging out these cases, which were becoming more of a problem for him by the minute, ran the risk of exposing other crimes he had committed in other jurisdictions. In fact, we talked about that. But when I would tell him why he needed to resolve all cases on my terms, he would end the conversation abruptly, sometimes hanging up without much warning and other times making sure to tell me why he thought my proposed resolutions were not "fair" to him. He and I clearly had a different understanding of the word.

# THIRTY-FOUR

# SIDESWIPE

V IRGINIA WAS MAD ABOUT THE things that Dershowitz had been saying about her, but she was more hurt and offended by what Ghislaine Maxwell had said.

While Dershowitz was preparing his public tirade on Paul and me, Maxwell issued a statement on January 2, 2015, claiming not only that the allegations made by Virginia against her were untrue, but that Virginia's claims were "obvious lies and should be treated as such." In Virginia's mind, Maxwell had been like her mother for a period of her life. To call Virginia a liar was an attempt by Maxwell to use her status to invalidate Virginia. This was devastating.

On September 21, 2015, Virginia filed a defamation claim against Ghislaine Maxwell, claiming that Maxwell's statement to the press contained, among other things, three deliberate falsehoods: 1) that Virginia's sworn allegations "against Ghislaine Maxwell are untrue," 2) that the allegations have been "shown to be untrue," and 3) that Virginia's "claims are obvious lies."

In the initial pleading, Virginia was represented by Boies Schiller Flexner, as Paul and I didn't want our litigation with Dershowitz to interfere with Virginia's claim against Maxwell. Not being able to sign the initial pleading against Maxwell irritated Paul and me. Paul and I spent our lives representing crime victims, which is what made us want to stand behind Virginia for all the obvious reasons. Maxwell's and Dershowitz's respective attacks on her credibility had already slowed down the charity we had helped her create, Victims Refuse Silence. She was a powerful voice for survivors and her voice had been stolen. We wanted to help her retrieve it. The sooner we could put this mess with Dershowitz behind us, the sooner we could help.

In our absence, David assigned Virginia's case against Maxwell to the partner whom he trusted the most on these topics in his Fort Lauderdale office, Sigrid McCawley. Known to us as "Superwoman," Sigrid figures out how to build forty hours into each twenty-four-hour day. She is as genuine as any person you have ever met and can intellectually compete with anyone. More important, she is a master at identifying what is right and what is wrong. She, too, had vetted Virginia.

Virginia's lawsuit was the first direct attack on Ghislaine Maxwell, Jeffrey Epstein's right-hand woman during the 1990s and early 2000s. By 2015, Epstein and Maxwell had drifted apart. He had replaced her as his main girlfriend several times over, because she was way too old for him.

Regardless, Maxwell was someone with information that could harm Epstein and expose a part of the criminal organization that had not been revealed extensively at that point—namely the hundreds of victims who existed outside of Florida. Epstein believed Maxwell's statement about Virginia being a liar was "really stupid." (In 2018, he told me so.) Either way, Maxwell's gaffe initiated another intense legal battle that was going to draw Epstein back in, which meant the other side would fight hard. It wasn't going to be easy. But we had a client as tenacious and resilient as they come.

# THIRTY-FIVE

# STARBUCKS

I N THE FALL OF 2015, I was sitting at lunch with Brittany and another of my law partners, Seth Lehrman, when I got a call on my cell phone that showed the incoming number as 0000000000. I had never seen a phone number come up like that, so I walked outside and answered.

"Brad, it's Jeffrey. Let's meet face-to-face."

When I asked him why, he responded, "I want to see if there's a way for us to finally get divorced from one another." This was his way of implying that he wanted to find a way to resolve all cases that involved him, including those where he was not an actual party. The call told me he was concerned. It was one thing when he was being sued and could control the legal defense team. But with these ancillary lawsuits, where his activities and relationships were the primary subjects but he was not fully in control, he knew there was a possibility of real disaster.

We arranged to meet the next morning at a Starbucks in Boca Raton. Yes, this is highly unusual. We were both represented by lawyers. But things between us were far beyond anything lawyers could fix. In fact, every time our lawyers were involved, it only made things worse. Some small part of the coffee shop conversation could be classified as confidential settlement discussions, although the reality is that it was just gamesmanship, part of an eight-year legal chess game between a genius sociopath and me, a lawyer in the business of playing legal chess against bad guys.

I showed up to the Starbucks first and found a table against the wall with my back to the bathroom, facing the front door. Epstein, punctual as usual, appeared wearing his customary gray sweatpants and blue suede slippers with the collar turned up on his monogrammed polo. He took some cash out of his wallet and placed it and his phone on the center of the table where I was sitting and asked me if I wanted anything while he walked to the line to order a drink. He came back to the table and said, "Do I need to count the bills in my wallet?" The funny thing is, while he was at the counter, I had my phone in my hand and I was thinking that I was sure he had some device on his phone that could just steal all my data. Maybe he did. I'll never know.

We talked for an hour about our philosophical differences, our factual and legal disagreements in the various cases, and our understanding that no matter how bad things ever got we would always keep open this direct line of communication. Jeffrey had a charisma that made you want to engage with him on many topics, and I suspect that I would have been able to re-solve important issues with a version of him that likely had existed at some earlier time in his life.

Unfortunately, while he was creative in his problem-solving and could grasp my position and perspective on things, he was difficult to persuade because he felt the law was beneath him and he was beyond the rules that govern the common man. He thought that he was actually invincible. He basically said as much. The fact that our legal system had reaffirmed this idea in his experience only made him more confident in his twisted ideology. He loved to name-drop to let me know how important and protected he was. He had justifications for his diseased behavior that stood between us and prevented us from seeing eye to eye on anything of major importance.

The more we talked, the clearer certain things about him became. He was a very torn soul. He wanted to resolve his legal problems, all of which stemmed from his sexually deviant behavior, but he didn't really want to change his behavior. He rolled his eyes every time I mentioned the age of consent because the arbitrariness of that concept annoyed him. Knowing we disagreed on that topic, Jeffrey instead got down to business.

He threw out several ideas on how to resolve all of the civil cases. Instead of simply making a settlement offer, which was the traditional way to resolve a civil lawsuit, Epstein always had to make it more complicated. He wasn't very specific, but he pontificated about buying a house for someone and holding a mortgage that he would forgive, or giving a gift rather than couch it as a settlement so that he could display his generosity, or placing funds in trust for someone's children. Without much response from me, he explained why he couldn't resolve cases on the creative terms he had just finished outlining. I think he was hoping I would disagree and jump at one of his wacky solutions so that we could then be on the same team in his strangely concocted, unorthodox global settlement plan.

When I transitioned the conversation to more of a traditional civil settlement format with specific dollar amounts he would need to pay to adequately make up for the damage done, he ranted about how people take advantage of rich people and on principle he would not let that happen. He then drifted into this fantasy land where he was somehow the victim being made to pay unworthy plaintiffs his hard-earned money. I remember bringing him back to the choices he'd made that had put him in this predicament.

"You escaped what would have been a life sentence for anyone else on the planet. Your money and connections saved you from jail. Your current problems and the things that make you mad at me were all caused by you— not only your initial acts but also the choices you've made to allow these cases to continue," I reminded him.

He responded by saying, "I'm only trying to be fair. I never said I was a victim, but I don't want to become a victim. I will resolve cases in a fair way but not pay excessive money to people who I did not hurt."

"You say 'fair,'" I answered, "like it's an objective term and you're the only person who knows its meaning. Your perspective on everything has been clouded by your money and all that your money has created for you.

It's saved you so far. I don't understand why you're going to stubbornly allow it to bring you down." This was not the only time we had a version of that conversation. Whenever I said something that sounded like I was lecturing him, he gave me a condescending look until I stopped, after which he'd try to take the conversation to a specific point of contention in some litigation.

Regardless, he now desperately wanted all of the cases related to him in any way to be settled and done, but rather than suck it up and settle them, he could not help negotiating backward to a point that precluded any resolution. Getting the best deal possible was always, in the end, more important to him than eliminating his risk altogether. It was like he knew what he should do, but just before he committed to doing it, he would pull back, almost recognizing that once the attention was off of him and he no longer had any risk of getting caught, then his way of life would not be as much fun.

For the most part, I sat across from him and watched him change positions and personalities from one second to the next, presumably hoping I would come around to his way of thinking. He loved to make jokes that were particularly inappropriate for the situation while he thought out loud about possible resolutions to these serious cases. On this occasion he said something along the lines of "Brad, let's put our heads together and figure out how we can *massage* the narrative to make it more fair to me," before staring at me and pausing. Then he added, "My kind of massage, of course." These types of childish statements were irresistible for Jeffrey. He would snicker afterward, expecting a reciprocal laugh.

While at the Starbucks that day, Jeffrey looked at me and said, "You know, some of what Virginia is saying isn't right."

"What part?" I asked.

"Didn't Virginia say that she and Ghislaine had a threesome with Prince Andrew over in Ghislaine's apartment in London?"

He was clearly trying to embellish to make her appear incredible. I looked at him quizzically and corrected him, "No. She didn't say anything about a threesome, but now that you bring it up, she did say that she was with you and Ghislaine at the apartment in London when Prince Andrew came over and stayed the night. You instructed her to entertain him. There's even a picture to prove most of that."

He said, "There's a problem. Now I remember. She said she took a bath with Andy. If I could show you how small Ghislaine's tub was in that apartment, it would be tough for two people to fit in there." This seemed like a weak point to force.

"How about the threesomes with you and Ghislaine where Virginia was made to dress up as a Catholic schoolgirl and sometimes in latex outfits," I said. "That certainly doesn't seem far-fetched given that Juan Alessi [Epstein's former housekeeper] testified about Ghislaine's sex toys and we know you particularly enjoy the schoolgirls in uniform."

He smirked. "Does Ghislaine look like my type to you? Don't you know me better by now?"

He loved to make comments like that, clearly poking fun at the fact that he was attracted to young girls, a category into which Ghislaine did not fall.

Noticing that he wasn't gaining any ground with me, and seemingly deciding that our fact-by-fact sparring wasn't working out so well, he switched gears again: "Look, I know what you really want. You're not settling cases for fair offers because you're angry. Angry with me. I understand. You want me to give you answers and to stop making you chase everyone around because you can't get what you're looking for. I think you know I want to tell you the answers. My lawyers just won't let me. If we can get everything over with, I'll make you a deal. I'll give you straight answers to every question you can ask for a whole day. In fact, the only other person that probably will want the same deal is Marie Villafaña. I'll give you four hours of questions and I'll give her four hours of questions. I'll answer everything. Then we are done. For good."

"Marie?" I said.

"Yeah," he said. "I know y'all talk. I'm sure she still has a hard-on for me." As soon as the words left his mouth, he snickered and raised his eyebrows, and said, "Maybe I should choose my words more carefully. Regardless, what does it take to get everything behind us? You have this thing going on with Dershowitz. I don't really give a shit about it, but it pulls me in. My time is very valuable. These things waste a lot of my time. If it can be over, I want it over. The CVRA I don't care about. I've been assured that nobody can do anything about that deal and that the case will eventually be thrown out of court."

He went on, "So other than Dershowitz, all we have left is our case, right? You have nothing else that you're bringing against me, do you?" I confirmed that, *at that time*, the answer was no. "Let's resolve our personal case. Once I prove that I will be fair with you there, then you can consider resolving these other matters," he said, not expecting a response. And not getting one. He then explained his mathematical logic for the proposition he was going to suggest as a way to resolve our personal case. Of course, he said he was trying to find a solution that might take into account our differing opinions on what the word *fair* meant.

Our case against each other had still not been decided by the Fourth District Court of Appeal. He calculated his chances of winning at the Fourth at around 50 percent. He then tried to convince me that his chances at the Florida Supreme Court were at least 90 percent based on prior Supreme Court precedent. He cited a legal case off the top of his head, explaining the facts and the holding of the case as well as the application of those facts to the facts of our case. His analysis was not that crazy.

I brought up another case that defeated the argument he was making, as it was more squarely on point and would be more persuasive to the court. Familiar with that case, without hesitation, he said, "Yeah, but that case is yellow-flagged," which is a term used by lawyers when researching cases to indicate that there has been some disagreement or distinction by another court involving a topic within that case. Why did Jeffrey Epstein know about yellow flags? He talked confidently, like he believed he was a lawyer— and not just any lawyer, but the smartest lawyer on the planet. Inside, I was laughing at the fact that he had to be the only non-lawyer in the world who has ever talked about a case being yellow-flagged.

"Listen, Brad, that yellow flag is actually there for the same reason that your case is going to be rejected by the Florida Supreme Court," he continued, trying to convince me. That part of his argument was wrong, and while he had already considered it and knew the case well, he was much less convincing in his explanation of its inapplicability. "Either way, I want to make this fair," he continued. "You pick a number. I don't care what it is. Whatever amount you're comfortable with. You can put it in a trust account. I'll put five times that amount in. Winner at the Fourth District takes all. I told you, I'm always fair with you. Five-to-one odds in your favor is as fair as it gets." I didn't say a word in response. He thought he had just resolved that case, because he said so, and to him his idea was gospel. He continued, "All right then, now it's your turn. Figure out a fair way to get Dershowitz done and let me know." With that, he stood up. So did I.

I walked out of the coffee shop first. He followed. I waited in my car as he walked down the sidewalk to his black Suburban. I didn't see him get in the car because it was around the corner, but I knew that he only had one way out and I wanted to see whether somebody had driven him there or he had come alone. I didn't think that he saw me or knew where I was parked, or even knew what car I was driving. He passed behind my car, driving with a female passenger. For the record, I was never close enough to get a good look, but I didn't think she was underage. I pulled out, leaving enough space between our cars so he would not see that I was following him. There was only one exit in the parking lot. Instead of taking it, he turned into a dead end area—a place where I could not possibly follow him. So I changed my plan and turned to leave.

As soon as I committed to the exit, he pulled his car back around behind me. I looked in my rearview mirror and he waved. It was a statement as to who was chasing whom. It was also symbolic of the fact that the game board can change at any moment. When you think you are on the attack, you can instantly find yourself on defense. When you think you are winning, in a split second you can be behind. I think this was true for both of us.

In that moment, I thought back to a quote that Jeffrey claimed as his life motto: "Know when you are winning." It was one of those times when you're looking at the board and it's really anybody's game. The way it looked to me, we both believed we were winning.

———————

Not long after this meeting, on November 12, 2015, the Fourth District Court of Appeals ruled in my favor. The court reversed Judge Hafele's ruling and brought my malicious prosecution case back to life.

Almost immediately, Epstein called my office to congratulate me. I reminded him that his mathematical assessment of a 50 percent win was now a zero and asked him to recalculate what his chances were at the Florida Supreme Court. He explained that his prior calculation had built in the assumption that he had already lost at this appellate level, so his assessment was the same.

I reminded him: "You know, you told me a story about your belief that people took advantage of you because you were rich. You gave me the example of somebody installing lights or light switches at your house and wanting to be paid one hundred thousand dollars for doing so. While I think you were implying that your victims were asking for more money than they deserved, you were looking in the wrong direction. It seems to me that it's your lawyers who are taking advantage of the fact that you're rich. Anyone telling you that you have a ninety percent chance of winning at the Florida Supreme Court is lying to you. That is, unless you know something that I don't know."

I threw that last line out there to see if he would give me some hint that he had somehow bought off the Florida Supreme Court. I didn't really think it was possible, but I figured that if it was, Jeffrey Epstein would be the one to do it.

Reflecting back to his original proposition from our coffee shop meeting, I said, "If you believe there is a ninety percent chance that you will win, do you want me to pick a number and you put up nine times as much?"

He quickly responded, "No, that wouldn't be fair to you because for it to be worth it to you, the number you choose is going to be too big. It will still be meaningless to me, so I don't care, but I don't take advantage of people. Plus, if you would still do this given the risk to you on the chance you lose, then that tells me someone is probably putting the money up for you as insurance, which wouldn't be fair to me."

Again, we hung up agreeing to disagree and waiting around to see what was going to happen next.

# THIRTY-SIX

# BACK IN THE SPOTLIGHT

O N OCTOBER 15 AND 16, 2015, Jack Scarola took Alan Dershowitz's deposition at his attorney's office in downtown Fort Lauderdale. Jack is an excellent interrogator with a one-gear bull-in-a-china-shop style. His best attribute is the uncanny precision with which he speaks. Dershowitz was represented by probably ten lawyers, at least four of whom were in the room. His primary lawyer was Tom Scott, a former U.S. attorney who incidentally had been in charge of the U.S. Attorney's Office when Ron Eppinger, Virginia's early trafficker, was charged back in 1999. He had signed the indictment to prosecute Eppinger. In some indirect way, the arrest of Eppinger and his prosecution freed Virginia from her first abuser.

No matter the precision of the question that Jack would ask, Dershowitz simply took the question mark at the end as his opportunity to say whatever he wanted to say. The deposition ended with an agreement from all counsel that made it clear that any continuation of questioning would require the presence of a special master to maintain order. Before the next deposition, the judge presiding over the case, Tom Lynch, appointed Special Master Ed Pozzuoli, managing partner from the law firm Tripp Scott, to serve in that role.

Ed was a hard-nosed commercial litigator who had represented some of the biggest investor victims in Rothstein's Ponzi scheme. He had a reputation for being objective, honest, and, most important, someone who could not be influenced or starstruck.

While Jack is a strong questioner, Dershowitz was able to escape being cornered by him, not only by giving his nonresponsive answers, but also by his superior knowledge of the underlying details of the relevant facts. This included important topics such as his relationship with Jeffrey Epstein, Virginia's relationship with Jeffrey Epstein, and the places and times when their worlds could have collided. For that reason, our team agreed that I was best suited to take Alan's deposition the second time around. Dershowitz might still wiggle, but my command of the record gave us the best chance to keep him in line. Anticipating Dershowitz's objection to my conducting the deposition, I filed a notice of appearance on behalf of Paul, who was also a plaintiff in the case. Surely I could take a deposition on behalf of my own client.

The second half of Dershowitz's deposition was set for December, but just days before it was to occur we received a call saying that Alan had broken his arm and would need to reschedule. Nobody ever made the connection between having a broken arm and not being able to answer questions, but I would have to wait until January 13, 2016. Virginia's deposition was set to occur the day after Dershowitz's, with the special master presiding over both.

I had prepared thoroughly for Dershowitz's deposition and planned to use about 80 percent of the information that I had uncovered. I decided to save the best 20 percent for trial. We all filed into a large conference room in the law office of Tripp Scott, the firm where Ed Pozzuoli worked.

The room had a twenty-five-foot table. Our team was on one side, and on that day included Sigrid, representing Virginia Roberts; Paul Cassell; Brittany; Jack; and me. On the other side sat Tom Scott and Rick Simpson, representing Alan; and Ken Sweder and Darren Indyke, representing Jeffrey Epstein. The head of the table was reserved for the deponent, Alan himself, and on either side of Alan were the court reporter and Ed, our special master, whose job it was to make sure Alan answered questions responsively.

As mentioned earlier, Alan had staked out an extreme position that was difficult to defend. Essentially, he had said Virginia was lying about everything, and because she was lying about everything, Paul and I should have known it. The problem with such an extreme stance was that there was no believable way to sustain it based on the available evidence. Right out of the gate, he couldn't avoid his close relationship with Jeffrey Epstein, which meant he could not continue his broad proclamation that Virginia's story was made up from "beginning to end" or "out of whole cloth." Virginia had undeniably been trafficked by Epstein, which was the crux of her allegations. While his strategy was vehement denial of anything Virginia had ever said, I tested him on whether Virginia was a liar when she said she had met Prince Andrew. While he tried not to answer the question, he ultimately could not credibly deny it. "Was Virginia Roberts lying when she said she was paid to have sex with Prince Andrew?" I inquired.

Rather than call her a liar on this point, he reverted to another attack on Virginia's character. "If she was paid fifteen thousand dollars to have sex with Prince Andrew at the age of seventeen in England, she would be guilty of prostitution." His answer was an attempt to deflect from another credibility point going up in Virginia's column that would further refute his entire defense that Virginia had made everything up.

I didn't let him off the hook. "My question is, was she lying when she says she was paid to have sex with Prince Andrew?"

Trapped with nowhere to go, he responded, "I have no idea."

No matter how much evidence supported any statement Virginia had ever made, Dershowitz would not concede. On the most basic gimme, I asked, "Was she lying about knowing Jeffrey Epstein?" Rather than just admit that Virginia was truthful on that point, he responded, "On the basis of the objective evidence, she *probably* wasn't lying about the simple fact that she knew Jeffrey Epstein, yes."

At other points, when Dershowitz was faced with questions that he could not credibly deny, he found a way to evade answering the question altogether. For instance, was Virginia recruited by Ghislaine Maxwell when she was a minor? Was she molested by Jeffrey Epstein? Did she board and travel on Epstein's airplane while she was underage? Was she identified by the FBI as a victim of sex trafficking? Clearly the answer to all of these questions was yes. But to admit it would be to admit what we all knew— Virginia had not made up everything from "beginning to end" or "out of whole cloth" as Dershowitz had claimed.

Dershowitz refused to answer any of these questions on the basis that doing so would infringe upon his attorney-client privilege with Jeffrey Epstein. He claimed multiple privileges during his deposition—the attorney-client privilege, work product privilege, and even some joint defense privilege that he claimed to have along with Maxwell or Epstein or both. This was not helping his extreme position, but it didn't hurt as much as it would if he answered by admitting to Virginia's credible account on those points.

In this credibility contest on the subject of Jeffrey Epstein, where Dershowitz expected the world to believe he was absolutely truthful and Virginia was a bald-faced liar, we had to assess the veracity not only of the statements Virginia had made regarding Jeffrey Epstein but also of the statements Alan Dershowitz had made. I pulled out an article citing a time when Dershowitz spoke to the press on behalf of Epstein. "Did you publicly make the statement that we have now put on the record, which is that Jeffrey Epstein did not have sexual-erotic massages or sex with any minors, and that the girl that accused him of forcible rape was lying—had a long record of lying—of theft and blaming others for her crimes?" I knew that he had made the statement because I was holding the article directly quoting him in my hands as I was asking the question. He paused before answering, "I have no recollection of making those statements. I was his defense attorney. I may have made statements in court that were quoted by the newspapers. But I have no distinct recollection of making that statement."

Dershowitz wasted no time calling the victims liars, including, if not especially, Virginia, but he was indignant if anyone questioned the truthfulness of anything he said. During the deposition, I reminded him that Virginia was not the only person who had questioned Dershowitz's loose affiliation with the truth at times. There was also Noam Chomsky, renowned "father of modern linguistics," who had publicly labeled Dershowitz "a dedicated liar." Dershowitz did not like this at all and went on another rant, this time about Chomsky.

Dershowitz took a play out of Epstein's book to make sure I didn't get out of the deposition with a clean record. Any chance he got to take shots at me personally, he did. His go-to was to adopt Epstein's claim that I had helped Scott Rothstein run the Ponzi scheme, even though by this point even Epstein's attempt at this claim had been disproven and dismissed. That didn't dissuade Dershowitz. In fact, he doubled down.

He claimed in his deposition that Scott Rothstein and I were "joined at the hip" and Rothstein didn't do anything without conferring with me. He went so far as to say that I was the "brains of the operation." I don't think he knew it at the time, but our special master, Ed Pozzuoli, had been heavily involved in the RRA litigation over the Ponzi scheme, so watching Dershowitz chase imaginary rabbits and explain how I was the real Ponzi wizard had to be particularly tough for him to bear.

We moved on to discussing topics on which Dershowitz had taken a public view that might be relevant to someone weighing the character qualities of the two participants in the "he said, she said." In fairness, I wanted to give Dershowitz a chance to respond substantively on some of the positions he had taken that were troubling to us. When I questioned him about a 2002 article that he wrote in which he suggested that viewing child pornography should not be a crime, he got angry and started attacking me. He said my question was putting his ideas on trial and thereby was putting the First Amendment on trial. He finished by threatening to have the ACLU intervene in the case and closed by calling me "un-American."

Before we concluded, I had to know whether the information I had heard about him skinny-dipping on Martha's Vineyard was true. Of course, public nudity does not mean he did what Virginia said he did, but it was a rumor that seemed inconsistent with his holier-than-thou front. If false, it was a rumor he should be given the opportunity to denounce as such. After some back-and-forth, he reluctantly admitted to skinny-dipping on Martha's Vineyard but was quick to make sure I knew that Eleanor Roosevelt had also done so (not with him, I don't think). I didn't leave without asking him about the lady from his condo building. He admitted to being accused of being a pervert peeking at topless girls on the beach near his Miami home, but insisted that she was a "complete nutcase."

We left the deposition feeling confident. Virginia's deposition was three days later. The substance is sealed, but the theatrics were undeniable. Virginia was who she has always been from day one—confident and firm. I didn't watch her much; I was sitting across from Alan, watching his reactions to her responses. Those were the last depositions taken in the case.

In March 2016, the case was settled.*

———————

Although the court had ultimately stricken the allegations and denied our motion to join Virginia in the CVRA, the order made it clear that the rights of Virginia and all other similarly situated victims would be afforded and protected without the need for formal intervention in the case. While the defamation lawsuit was nothing more than a time-consuming distraction, something positive did come of our tactical decision to file the motion. We were able to move forward in the CVRA action knowing that we were not only representing Courtney and Jane Doe 2, but that we stood with our clients in fighting on behalf of all victims of Jeffrey Epstein who were deprived of their rights in Florida during the negotiation of the 2007 NPA.

———————

Virginia was now ramping up her defamation case against Maxwell, filed in New York's federal district court. Maxwell's deposition was set for April 22, 2016, in New York. She was represented by Jeff Pagliuca and Laura Menninger of Denver, Colorado. For a variety of complicated legal reasons, I was

———————

*Dershowitz has consistently maintained that he is innocent of the allegations Virginia made against him. Among other things, he has pointed to records he relies on to establish he could not have been present when the events occurred, and he has suggested that Virginia may have mistaken him for someone else. Despite Dershowitz's strong denials, Virginia remained sure of herself. This dispute has still not died. In fact, in 2019 Virginia and Dershowitz sued each other for defamation.

not able to take Maxwell's deposition. Sigrid McCawley took the deposition and did a great job. To this day the deposition remains under seal.

---

After Maxwell's deposition, Jean-Luc Brunel was becoming increasingly important. His lawyer Joe Titone was still claiming to be having trouble serving Epstein and wanting our help. I told him that we had been hearing this for over a year but had yet to see Jean-Luc, and he had never produced those explosive photos he claimed to have.

By May 2016, we were well into the litigation against Ghislaine Maxwell and knew that Jean-Luc had important information about the role Maxwell had played in the scheme to recruit girls for Epstein. Joe Titone had carried several messages to Jean-Luc, letting him know we wanted to speak with him. Finally, Jean-Luc agreed to talk with us.

Preliminarily, Titone and I discussed some of the information that Jean-Luc was going to be able to provide, including events that occurred in New York that the U.S. Attorney's Office in the Southern District of New York was sure to be interested in. After receiving this information, as well as other witness accounts regarding illegal New York activity occurring at the mansion and at the apartments, we set up an appointment for a presentation to be made to the sex crimes division at the U.S. Attorney's Office.

Three of us—Pete Skinner, a Boies Schiller Flexner lawyer and former Southern District of New York AUSA; Stan; and I—went to the meeting. The AUSA acted confident that a case would be brought against Epstein for crimes committed against Virginia and others in New York. Of course, first she had to have facts, witnesses, evidence, and victims of a New York crime. We assured the prosecutor that the number of victims in New York far exceeded those discovered in Florida. The group walked out excited that New York was finally going to bring a case against Epstein. I said to David and Pete, "Don't hold your breath, the Southern District obviously doesn't know who they're dealing with yet."

On May 2, 2016, true to his word, Jean-Luc Brunel showed up to the Boies Schiller Flexner office in New York. He did so on one condition—

that I would not be there. He explained before he arrived that he did not like me. He somehow blamed me for the fact that he had skipped out on his original deposition. His reason for disliking me wasn't very logical, but this was his condition, so I lived with it.

I still believed that Jean-Luc was pretending to cooperate with us while really being there as a Jeffrey Epstein spy and told Stan, who would be meeting with Jean-Luc without me, as much. Jean-Luc was claiming, after all, that he now hated Epstein because his association with Epstein had ruined the reputation of the modeling agency. It was hard for me to imagine a decades-long friendship between the two of them having gone sideways because of the exact conduct that had brought these two men together in the first place. So, what was Jean-Luc's game? Was this voluntary interview being offered in hopes of getting our help to serve his bogus lawsuit on Jeffrey Epstein, or did he have other motives in mind?

Stan and Jean-Luc talked for hours. Jean-Luc put up a good front. He seemed to have several objectives. One was to convince Stan that he, Jean-Luc, was not the person he was accused of being. He explained how he had known Ghislaine since the 1980s and how she had introduced him to Jeffrey in the 1990s. He didn't speak well of Jeffrey or Ghislaine—these were once two of his best friends, but now he was willing to spill the beans on both of them.

Jean-Luc spun a story that even he was a victim of Epstein's operation. He was vulnerable when he met Jeffrey Epstein, he said, and yes, it was true that Epstein had gotten him back on his feet in the modeling industry and he was indebted to Jeffrey. But it irritated Jean-Luc because he would talk about models and Jeffrey would pretend that he had his own eye for modeling, while really, he was just trying to sleep with them. Epstein would put these girls in his apartments and say they were "models," but they never modeled. Maxwell basically did whatever Epstein wanted her to do. Brunel talked angrily about how his reputation had been ruined by Epstein, who took the modeling concept and turned it into trash.

Jean-Luc did seem to remember having met Virginia. And, certainly, he knew the names of many of the people whom Epstein lent his girls to for sex. Still, he identified only a few, and when pressed for names, focused only on one—Harvey Weinstein. Remember, this interview was happening in May 2016, more than one year before the world would learn about Harvey's unwanted sexual advances and attacks on women.

In later discussions, Jean-Luc described one incident in greater detail, which he said culminated in a heated argument between Epstein and Weinstein that terminated their relationship. Weinstein was at Epstein's apartment in France receiving a massage from one of Epstein's girls when he attempted to aggressively convert the massage into something sexual. The girl rejected his advances. As the story goes, Harvey then verbally abused her for rejecting him. Little did Harvey know, this was one of Epstein's favorite girls at the time and Jeffrey viewed the aggressive mistreatment as disrespectful to him. Jeffrey then came into the room, got in Harvey's face, and kicked him out of his house, delivering the message that he was never to come back.

Following the interview of Jean-Luc, I heard various versions of this story from others, including years later from Epstein himself, who referred to Harvey as a pig. Imagine that.

Even more interesting was Jean-Luc's knowledge and description of the current state of Epstein's operation. Epstein's new chief recruiter was a Russian-born twenty-something-year-old woman named Svetlana. According to Brunel, she was using her connections to import young girls into the United States under the pretense that they were models.

While many media accounts have hinted that a primary purpose of Epstein's enterprise was to attract young females and lend them out to powerful people in order for him to hold these sexual encounters over their heads as blackmail, that was not really the case. The primary, if not exclusive, purpose of the operation was Epstein's personal sexual gratification. If some of his friends liked what they saw and wanted to partake, Epstein would share with a select few. For those who participated, it incidentally provided ammunition for Epstein to hold over their heads if he ever wanted to, but despite all the speculation, there has been no recovered evidence that he actually used any of this sexual information against anyone in order to get something out of them. Maybe the knowledge that he could have done that was enough. Maybe it was also enough to influence his pals without his having to threaten them explicitly.

Either way, Jean-Luc verified what we thought was true: Epstein's so-called jailing in Florida had not changed the essence of who he was, only the way he operated. Jail had had no effect on the number of cult followers. The devotion of his past and current female followers was reminiscent of the Manson family at its peak.

Very seldom were we able to infiltrate Epstein's cult or "turn" anyone for even a period of time against the operation to reveal its hidden secrets and inner workings. Even those who had freed themselves and were no longer disciples were hypnotized by the power of their leader and reluctant to cooperate. For some, the resistance was driven purely by fear. For others, despite being severely damaged, their resistance came from their having felt indebted to Epstein as well as their unspoken oath to never betray him.

Here we were at this pivotal time when Jean-Luc, a long-standing, high-ranking member of the Epstein team, was divulging incriminating information about the leader and the "family." Why was he doing this? Before this in-person meeting, I believed he was really a planted infiltrator working for Epstein to learn what he could about our investigation.

After the meeting, I felt differently. If he was an Epstein spy, he had crossed the line in the amount of information that he had shared with us, including firsthand accounts of Epstein engaging in sex with minors both inside and outside of the U.S.—describing nothing less than an international sex scheme. At some point, Jeffrey had miscalculated something. Either he misapprehended his friend's allegiance, or if Jean-Luc was meeting with us at Epstein's direction, then Epstein had performed a poor cost-benefit analysis.

The ultimate test of which side of the fence Jean-Luc was on was to see where he wanted to go from here. Was he cooperating with our investigation or did he have other motives? Jean-Luc made it clear that his ultimate objective was to clear his name. We told him the best way to do that was to meet with the U.S. Attorney's Office and tell them what he knew. He agreed. Stan called that office that night and explained to the prosecutor that Jean-Luc was ready to meet the next day. The interview was set up for the following morning.

No surprise, Brunel "had an emergency come up" that night and had to fly out of the country with no immediate plans to return. Sound familiar? Needless to say, he did not meet with the U.S. attorney.

# THIRTY-SEVEN

# WITNESS AFTER WITNESS

Fter meeting brunel and finally confirming how expansive Epstein's operation had become, we hired a team of investigators and sent them after very specifically targeted individuals whom we had identified as former victims of, recruiters for, or close friends of Jeffrey Epstein. Some of these people fell into more than one of those categories. Our goal in this part of the investigation was to find victims who were now more mature and more likely to cooperate. We had a long list of people who fit the description, but many slammed doors in our faces. With persistence, though, some talked. Over time, some who originally refused to speak to us began to call. Those who cooperated filled in many gaps for us. Each piece of information led to another witness with more information. The multidimensional puzzle was coming together, one piece at a time.

We also began tracking down former employees including butlers, drivers, and housekeepers. Most expressed a desire to help but would not do so out of fear. Each cited a nondisclosure agreement they had signed while under Epstein's employ as preventing them from talking. One couple in California cried when our investigators were asking about things they had witnessed while working for Epstein. Still, they would not share details until they called the person they were designated to call in the NDA if ever approached by anyone. We were told by others that the NDA indicated that if anyone was approached by law enforcement, private investigators, or anyone, for that matter, they were to say nothing and call one of Epstein's trusted advisors immediately. Whatever clauses it contained, they are evidently draconian enough to make the signers think twice about telling their stories. The nice California couple called the lawyer listed in the NDA, which resulted in Epstein's lawyer calling the next day telling us they were now representing the couple and demanding that we never call them again.

Still, from Brunel, we knew that nearly everyone in Epstein's crew had been recruited by someone else to give a "massage" and had been elevated to some higher position. With each person who cooperated, we got the names of all those before and after who had any association with Epstein, some with years of involvement in, and thus knowledge of, the Epstein organization. During the next six months we were interviewing victims from Florida, as well as from New York, California, New Mexico, and many other places.

---

While working in the office one weekend, we got a call from a woman whom we will call Fantasia. Fantasia was nearly forty years old when she called and described how in 1994, when she was seventeen, she had been recruited by Maxwell to provide Epstein with a massage in Europe. She had then been flown to Little Saint Jeff's and his other fancy homes. She was introduced to other powerful billionaires. After having spent time with them sporadically for more than a decade, she had tremendous insight into the relationship between Ghislaine and Jeffrey. Fantasia believed that Ghislaine felt indebted to Jeffrey for taking her in right after her father's death.

Fantasia explained that Ghislaine's role in life was to please Jeffrey, a job that included telling Fantasia which sex outfit to wear to make him happy. The schoolgirl outfit was his favorite. Another time, while in London, Fantasia and Ghislaine encountered a very young-looking girl who Fantasia thought was innocent and should be left alone. She recounted Maxwell protesting and telling her that someone had to give Epstein a blow job and if this new girl didn't do it, then Maxwell herself would have to—and clearly, she did not want to. Fantasia explained that when underage girls were around, Epstein's desire to have sex with them was so overwhelming that he would physically shake. She reconfirmed that he couldn't survive without a constant supply of new girls. Fantasia even went so far as to tell us that she had known Epstein for so long and had seen enough of his "evil" side that she believed he wasn't beyond killing someone, especially if that was necessary to keep his sex addiction alive. Whether that was accurate or merely an impression he cultivated, Fantasia did not know, but she was wary.

There came a time when the case against Maxwell was on the verge of going to trial and Fantasia was strongly considering testifying with crucial information. As witness lists were being exchanged by the parties, she received a mysterious call in the middle of the night. The voice on the other end said, "If you care about your daughter, you will stay out of the litigation in New York." That was enough to make up her mind. She was out.

---

Another young woman named Johanna had given an interview to Sharon Churcher for the *Daily Mail*, which had been published in 2011, about her experience and the fact that she, like Virginia, was recruited by Ghislaine. Despite speaking with the police and this publication, she had serious reservations about going on the record again. This whole experience was something she had tried hard to forget. Still, she was too important for us not to try to get her to cooperate. Her time with the dysfunctional "family" overlapped with Virginia Roberts's. The two at one time knew each other, and Virginia remembered Johanna as a very nice person.

Johanna was one witness who could corroborate a large part of one of the most seemingly unbelievable parts of Virginia's story—her sexually charged relationship with Prince Andrew, the Duke of York. We contacted Johanna, but she did not want to be involved. Virginia was not taking no for an answer, though. She insisted on going to see Johanna herself.

Virginia called her and talked her into meeting in person. During that meeting, Johanna came around. She knew that Virginia's standing up to Ghislaine and Jeffrey was very brave. Plus Virginia's courage was contagious. Everyone who meets Virginia can't help but love her.

Johanna, just like the rest of Jeffrey Epstein's targets, looked like a natural-born model. She walked us through her story. While attending school at Palm Beach Atlantic University, she was sitting on a bench one day when Ghislaine approached and asked her if she knew anyone who would be interested in working for her as a personal assistant. Johanna said that she would be interested and went with Ghislaine to Epstein's house that day.

Johanna spent the next couple of years working for Epstein and Maxwell and remembered many details about her interactions with Virginia and the duo. She remembered going on a trip with Epstein, Maxwell, and Virginia to Atlantic City when Virginia was too young to enter any of the casinos, so the girls stayed outside and stuck together.

Perhaps most important, she vividly remembered an encounter with Prince Andrew at Epstein's New York mansion. She described that Virginia was sitting on one of Prince Andrew's knees and Johanna was sitting on the other. While the two girls were in his lap, Ghislaine took out a puppet figure of Prince Andrew and placed the puppet's hand on Virginia's breast, at which point Prince Andrew placed his hand on Johanna's breast. Everyone laughed.

Johanna was also able to confirm other elements that were important to our representation of Virginia, including certain famous friends that Jeffrey Epstein collected. David Copperfield was one. On numerous occasions, Johanna met Copperfield, who was clearly a close friend of Jeffrey's during that period.

Other witnesses that I had interviewed had also told me of the friendship between Epstein and Copperfield and how their private islands were located close enough for them to visit each other on occasion. For a young woman like Johanna, the fact that there were stars who were friends with Jeffrey and Ghislaine was an attractive bonus of the job. Even the King of Pop himself, Michael Jackson, had been enough of an Epstein acquaintance to pay him a visit in Palm Beach while Johanna was working there.

Ghislaine, Jeffrey, Prince Andrew, and Alan Dershowitz had all separately attacked Virginia's story from many angles, claiming that she was indulging in sensational fantasy when describing Epstein having various famous friends and acquaintances around. They also challenged the truth of this intricate system she described by which Ghislaine and other recruiters constantly searched for girls to entertain Epstein sexually.

One by one, we were disproving each of these defenses. Because of the careful attention that Epstein and Maxwell paid to keep the stratification of the enterprise intact, and to wall off the levels below from understanding how the system worked above, no one witness could give us everything. But more and more people were coming forward, allowing us to take tidbits here and nuggets there and piece the truth together.

Johanna had been around Epstein and Maxwell enough to have observed and experienced the "family" that operated like a vacuum cleaner, sucking up unsuspecting girls before spitting them out and replacing them with new ones. She was close enough for Ghislaine to have included her as one of her so-called "children," and to have referred to herself in front of Johanna as the "mother hen" over Epstein's girls.

In order to defend herself in the lawsuit, Ghislaine needed to plausibly deny knowledge of Epstein's sexual activity with minors. She could not believably say that Virginia was lying about having been recruited underage into this sexual enterprise. It also seemed laughable for her to deny having any knowledge whatsoever of the facts uncovered by the police and the FBI during their investigation in 2005. But she couldn't admit to knowing either. The approach Ghislaine decided on was to claim that she was no longer in Epstein's life between 2001 and 2005, when the crimes against the dozens of young children had been committed.

Remember, once their investigation had started, the police wanted to talk to her, but Ghislaine had disappeared from Florida and never spoke with law enforcement. Everyone knew she was the long-term girlfriend and closest partner of Epstein's, but we could not rely on widely disseminated rumors and newspaper articles to prove the obvious. We needed evidence of the kind you could admit in court. One witness at a time, we were getting it.

Johanna was an essential piece of the puzzle, because she put Maxwell front and center in the picture during the time when the police had accumulated concrete evidence of Epstein committing crimes against children on a daily basis.

In the summer of 2016, we were finally in a position where we had a more complete picture of Epstein's operation. We now understood the existence of a New York spiderweb of underage victims that was very similar to the Florida version. We also had a strong grasp of the ways in which Epstein had attempted to restrict himself from engaging in sex with minors after he was jailed in Florida. What we still didn't fully comprehend was how his sexual attraction to children all began.

The most coveted witness we were after was a talented performer whom we will call Kat. Kat was important to us because she was the earliest child victim that we knew about, and Epstein and Maxwell had groomed her before they started employing their "massage" routine. After many years of trying, I was finally able to reach her on the phone right in the middle of the Maxwell litigation. She not only confirmed Epstein's predatory sexual behavior but also provided insight into Maxwell's intricate role.

Kat explained to us that Epstein and Maxwell had recruited her in 1994 when she was only thirteen years old, while she was sitting alone on a bench outside her summer camp in Michigan—the same camp Epstein had attended twenty-seven summers earlier. (He gave money to the camp from 1990 to 2003 and occasionally visited the area.) Kat was an enormously talented singer, and Epstein promised to make her a star. Jeffrey and Ghislaine made Kat feel indebted to them by paying for her singing lessons, her private school education, and even the New York City apartment where Kat and her mother lived. Epstein often had Kat sing for him at his house.

As part of their grooming process, Ghislaine and Jeffrey would talk about sex with her frequently. By the time Kat was fourteen years old, Epstein was regularly molesting her and Maxwell was continuing to remind her of all Epstein was doing for her career. When Kat was seventeen years old, Jeffrey Epstein forcibly raped her, taking her virginity. Kat explained that Epstein referred to himself as her "godfather," and that he did everything he could to impress her with his money and his connections. During the time when she was being abused by Epstein, he introduced her to both

Donald Trump and Harvey Weinstein. This, like everything Epstein did for Kat, was a reminder of all that he could continue to do for her in the future so long as she complied with his wishes. Epstein's hold over Kat lasted for a long time: She still hung out with him and Ghislaine occasionally in her twenties, despite the years of abuse she had survived.

But her feeling of gratitude toward Epstein was not the reason for her reluctance to cooperate or tell her story. Her apprehension was driven by fear and hopelessness, explaining that "Fighting his endless supply of money is impossible. There is really nothing that will be gained and everything to lose." I disagreed with that conclusion because I thought her account was so damning to Epstein that the authorities would have no choice but to act. However, given Epstein's ability to escape responsibility in the past, I could not convincingly counter her pessimism.

While this victim was always polite and had a powerful story to tell, she wouldn't go on record without being forced to do so. It was a difficult balance to strike between representing our current clients and keeping promises not to involve those who bowed out for one reason or another. This one was the toughest thus far. Had she come forward years earlier, so many children would have been saved. Here we were decades later, more young women being abused, and still she would not speak up. But out of respect for her desire to stay out of it, I kept my promise not to drag her in.

Either way, she told us enough to confirm that Epstein's sexual predation upon children went back to the early 1990s, at least. Her experience made it clear that Epstein's scheme had been fine-tuned over the years. This well-oiled machine of sexually explicit massages did not begin that way. In the 1990s, Epstein and Maxwell had not yet fully developed their routine. Instead, Epstein's sexual predation upon young children was initiated through more traditional grooming tactics. This information allowed us to gain a better understanding of exactly when and how Epstein's compulsive sexual abuse of children likely began, or at least what his recruitment scheme looked like early on.

THIRTY-EIGHT

# THE CULT

OUR INVESTIGATION WAS LONG, EXTENDED through the United States and beyond, and accumulated information from the early nineties through the mid-2010s. The Jeffrey Epstein cult, which had evolved to some degree over time, was coming into clear focus. It was far more complex than the media would ever report. There was no one-size-fits-all perspective from those who entered through the Epstein/Maxwell world, even among the victims.

Some believed their experience with Ghislaine and Jeffrey followed a sexually free, philosophical rule of law. Unlike many of Epstein's victims who suffered from extreme depression, eating disorders, drug use, nightmares, loss of self-esteem, and other serious psychological trauma, some thought their experience was beneficial and carried on Epstein's philosophy. This cultish operation was openly discussed within the inner circle, and Epstein and Maxwell mandated that everyone follow it in order to be elevated into that higher status.

Sex was central to the deeply held and guiding philosophy of Jeffrey Epstein. He thought female sexual availability should be determined by biology and not established by arbitrary social norms—or the law. He demanded that each of his recruiters be on the lookout for new sexual partners all the time. As for the target age, "the younger, the better," according to Epstein. Under his law, science was all that mattered. Prepubescence, therefore, was where he drew the line.

According to Epstein, the age of consent, if dictated by anything other than biology, was arbitrary—which was a word signifying that it should have no application in any aspect of his life. How could a female whose body was able to bear children not be given the choice to perform the acts necessary to give birth? Society, through the years, had created these concepts of marriage and monogamy that not only contradicted human nature, they unbearably constrained and killed people's freedom. Sexual freedom. The fact that a female can have multiple orgasms and a male only one was evidence that females were meant to have multiple partners—again, law according to Jeffrey Epstein.

These teachings were masterfully discussed by Epstein at just the right time in order to indoctrinate his new followers. Some of this information was disseminated early in the recruitment stage. Even some witnesses who were infrequent visitors in Epstein's massage rooms knew his philosophy in general. The idea that a man with an abundance of money and resources should be sexually free to engage with multiple partners was a basic tenet of Epstein's worldview, and anyone drawn in for even a brief period of time needed to tacitly accept it. Epstein's regulars not only had to be familiar with his philosophy, they had to live by it.

---

Ghislaine so adored Jeffrey that she would do anything for him, including bringing him other girls. She was powerfully persuasive and influential in making the girls like him, too. Jeffrey's brilliance was at the center of her pitch. For her, recruiting vulnerable girls like Virginia was an easy sell. Epstein had powerful friends. On his private island, he hosted his own personal scientific conventions attended by the most brilliant minds in the world. His impressionable young female followers watched in awe as he participated in high-powered group discussions about evolution, artificial intelligence, and cell regeneration.

The sell was even easier because Epstein was obviously very rich. Whatever the pitch had been to get some young girl to the home, it appeared to be true when she got there, which always helped him seal the deal. The allure of Jeffrey Epstein was even more attractive to the regular harem of girls brought to give him a "massage," because he was always available to them. Many people are rich, of course, but most of them still have regular lives to maintain—calendars, meetings, and the need to be in certain places at certain times. Not Jeffrey. He had no children. No office he needed to visit. No work he needed to tend to. He could wake up every day and decide to jump on his private jet and go anywhere, at any time, with anyone. He could get three, even four massages a day. And he did just that.

It had taken years, but I had finally talked to enough witnesses to understand what really drove him. For the most part, it was simple. His philosophy was not something he shied from. Epstein accumulated disciples, like Ghislaine Maxwell, who could help grow his network of girls in each location he frequented into a massive web that included young children, just as he had done in Palm Beach, to serve his sexual addiction.

After meeting Ghislaine, his sexual appetite for new, and young, females became insatiable. He designed several different "systems to get girls," as he would call them, and was always looking for new ones. To understand the systems and the progression of his operation, it is important to understand the different relevant time periods, as we learned. The first period began in the mid-1990s and lasted through Epstein's Florida "incarceration" in 2008. The next began while he was on work release and continued upon his release from the Florida jail system through the time that he was arrested in 2019. This time period was important because jail had a real impact on Jeffrey Epstein. It taught him that he was not completely invincible and would not last long in any real jail.

Once released from his "jail" stint in 2009, Epstein "disciplined" himself, as his lawyer Marty Weinberg would earnestly characterize Epstein's behavior modification at his bond hearing in federal court in New York on July 15, 2019. That just meant that he tried harder not to have sex with children after getting in trouble in Florida, making sure that each of the females recruited to his house was at least eighteen years old. His appetite did not diminish at all, and the harm he was causing to these barely legal females was significant. In some ways, his schemes to lure the girls into his homes became even more insidious. He targeted vunlerable young women with immigration problems, medical problems, or lofty professional ambitions and promised to make them legal, get them treatment, or make their educational or professional dreams come true. They just had to do as he said. Which, whether they liked it or not, was all about sex.

# THIRTY-NINE

# PADUCAH AND BEYOND

KNOWING NOW THAT EPSTEIN WAS actively pursuing minors for sex in the 1990s, when Maxwell was widely known to be with Epstein every day, I looked back at my files to locate witnesses I knew were also around the pair during that time period. Maria Farmer had a star by her name in my notes. I had been told by a source that she had been assaulted by both Epstein and Maxwell. In fact, she was the very first victim to ever come forward and report the duo to law enforcement, in 1996.

It was June 2016 and I really wanted to meet with Maria in person. She was someone I had known about for many years and had tried to track down in the past. I had good reason to believe she had information on Ghislaine's role in recruiting girls for Epstein. This type of information was becoming more crucial than ever, because it was at the center of Virginia's defamation lawsuit against Ghislaine Maxwell.

I called every number for Maria that I could find. I had my investigators call every number that they could find. Finally, Maria called me back and left me a message saying that she knew I was trying to reach her. I returned her call immediately. She started off by telling me that she had spoken with Vicky Ward from *Vanity Fair* a long time ago but her experience was not included in Ward's story, which was devastating to her, and that she really didn't know whether she should talk to me. She had already suffered more than she could handle from her experiences with Maxwell and Epstein. She didn't know me, and she certainly didn't trust me.

Maria eventually agreed that she would talk to me, but only in person. She gave me her address in Paducah, Kentucky. This was a town and region of the country that I knew nothing about. I told her I would go there and spend as long as I needed for her to have the opportunity to tell me everything. By the end of the phone call we had built a rapport.

Later that month I flew up to meet with her. To get there I had to fly to Nashville and drive over to Paducah. I stayed in the only hotel that I could find within ten miles of her house and planned to meet with her the next morning. By the time I arrived for our meeting, Maria had hundreds of photographs sprawled across her floor. She had also dug out her old diaries, telephone books, and Rolodexes. It looked like she might have spent the whole night before digging things out of boxes in her closet.

We chatted for only a few minutes before she launched into everything that she thought I had come to Paducah to hear and see. Unlike other witnesses who were cagey and reluctant to share, Maria was grateful that I had come so far, and she was ready to tell me everything she knew. She had researched me before I arrived and knew about all the work that I had done to shed light on the case. She admired that I had given a voice to the victims of people whom she felt were the most evil human beings on the planet. I didn't fully appreciate how much my commitment to seeing her in person meant to her until I understood her background and how Maxwell and Epstein had affected her life and her career.

Additionally, she had been fearful about what Epstein might do to her when Vicky Ward had discovered her in 2002, and she still felt some of that worry now. When she decides to do something, Maria is one of these people who is all in. She either trusts you or she doesn't. After *Vanity Fair* broke her trust, it took a long time for her to open up again. But she took a chance with me.

She thinks fast. And talks fast. She's an eccentric artist who certainly doesn't think like a lawyer, which allowed her to share her whole narrative rather than only the specifics that a lawyer would need to know. Maria and I spent hours that day going through photos and other mementos she had collected from her time with Epstein and Maxwell.

Maria was in her early twenties when she met New York socialite Eileen Guggenheim (unrelated to the Guggenheim Museum). Eileen recognized Maria's extraordinary artistic abilities. While Maria was in art school, Eileen got her a job with her sister, Barbara Guggenheim, who is married to the successful entertainment lawyer Bert Fields. Maria was hired by Barbara and Bert to perform mundane tasks around their home in New York. Wanting to help her find a job in her chosen field, Burt or Eileen spoke to Epstein because he was known as an art aficionado who could no doubt advance Maria's artistic career. Sure enough, Epstein called Maria and offered her a job at his mansion in New York City. Which, in turn, led to Maria's introduction to Ghislaine. Maria told me all about her work with the duo and the impact that it had on her life.

Relevant to my purposes, Maria had numerous examples of Ghislaine's role in recruiting girls for Jeffrey. Even then, nearly ten years before the Palm Beach investigation, Epstein had an unquenchable appetite for young girls, and Ghislaine had a knack for finding them. Maria described how sometimes she would be riding in Ghislaine's chauffeured car when Ghislaine saw a girl, stopped the car, got out, and lured her to Jeffrey. Other times, when Maria and Ghislaine would walk through Central Park, Ghislaine would approach a girl minding her business on a park bench and, within minutes, convince her to give up her phone number. All the girls came to the house under the false belief that this rich man was going to help them out or further their careers, whatever they might be.

Maria was working on the ground floor of the mansion, checking contractors and visitors in and out of the property, with Maxwell hovering in the vicinity while different girls came in every day. There was more than one occasion when a young girl would show up in her high school uniform—Jeffrey's favorite "look"—and go upstairs only to return sometime later in tears. When Maria asked Ghislaine why, she was typically told that Jeffrey was working as a model scout for Les Wexner, owner of Victoria's Secret, and had probably just told that girl that she was not good enough to be hired by the company.

As Maria became better acquainted with Jeffrey, his and Ghislaine's promises about her career became more enticing. Epstein had many connections in the art world. Everyone who was anyone knew Epstein and Maxwell. They both constantly made it clear that they had a real ability to give opportunity to talented people such as Maria. They flew her to an art school in Santa Fe, during which time she visited the nearby Zorro Ranch—the twenty-one-thousand-square-foot New Mexico estate owned by Jeffrey Epstein sitting on nearly ten thousand acres of land.

The more time Jeffrey and Ghislaine spent with Maria, the more they learned about her. At one point, Epstein became intrigued when he discovered that Maria had a sister named Annie ten years younger than she. He insisted on seeing pictures of her. Maria thought it was odd, but she adored her sister and wanted to help her. She regarded Annie, a young teen, as the most pure and beautiful person on the planet and, of course, described her as such. Now, twenty years later, here in Paducah with pictures strewn across the living room floor, she still described Annie that way.

———————

Maria recounted how Jeffrey looked at the photos of Annie that she shared with him and asked what Annie's plans were for her future. Maria said that Annie wanted to go to an Ivy League college but didn't have the money and, despite her many talents, would likely never be able to do that. Epstein seized on this opportunity and in his best philanthropic voice told Maria that he could make that happen. But Annie would first need to come to New York so that he could meet her personally and vouch for her qualifications.

Annie was fifteen when she was flown from her home in Arizona to New York City. She was driven from the airport to Maria's apartment by Epstein's driver and taken to see *The Phantom of the Opera* on Broadway with her big sister, courtesy of Epstein. The following day, Epstein made arrangements for the sisters to come to his mansion on East Seventy-First Street so he could meet Annie. He was his normal charming self, explaining matter-of-factly that he was willing to make all of Annie's dreams come true. If she wanted to get into an Ivy League school, he could make it happen. And, in the meantime, he would pay for her to enter any education program she wanted, worldwide.

He told Maria and Annie that he was going to go with them to see *12 Monkeys* that night. The sisters sat in the movie theater with Jeffrey between them. Maria's eyes stayed glued to the movie; she was giddy that her baby sister was with her in New York with the chance to be catapulted into everything that she deserved: an education and the type of career she was intelligent and beautiful enough to attain.

They all left the movies together. Epstein had the girls dropped off alone at Maria's apartment. Annie flew home the next day and Maria went back to work at Epstein's house, where Jeffrey agreed with Maria about Annie's special qualities. He told Maria to have Annie pick a program that she wanted to attend that summer and he would pay for it. Annie picked a program in Thailand.

Ghislaine contacted Annie's mother and told her that before Annie could go to Thailand, the students that Epstein was putting through school were reporting to his home in New Mexico. Epstein's assistants made arrangements for the now sixteen-year-old Annie to travel to New Mexico for what she believed would be a gathering of students her age to learn about the programs they were attending overseas.

When she got there, Annie was picked up from the airport and driven to the 7,500-acre Zorro Ranch compound, where she was greeted by Ghislaine and taken into the house. Much to her surprise, she was the only student there. Before she could question why, Ghislaine and Jeffrey told her that they had a big day planned for her: they were taking her shopping. As it would any girl her age, this made her feel special.

While in town near the ranch, Annie commented about a pair of cowboy boots that she saw in a store window. Ghislaine and Jeffrey took her to try them on. They bought her the boots, which she loved, before taking her back to the ranch. While out that day, Jeffrey periodically grabbed Annie's hand and held on to it, rubbing it affectionately. This made Annie uncomfortable, but it wasn't the first time it had happened. While she was in New York at the movie theater with Maria and Epstein, he had reached his hand over and quietly held hers during the second half of the movie.

Annie had not told this to her sister. She thought she shouldn't. This guy was her sister's boss and she didn't want Maria to be fired from her prestigious position. He was also helping Annie achieve the education that she wanted. But she did wonder about it. Was the hand hold to convey that he saw her as a friend? Was it done as a demonstration of the type of affection a mentor has for a talented kid? Or was this as weird as it felt? Regardless, his doing it again while out on the town in New Mexico caused Annie's mind to race.

Annie concluded that he was a very friendly older man who showed his affection for people in an odd but nonthreatening way. The first time had been more troubling to her because it was sneaky and in the dark and made her feel he didn't want anyone else to know. This time, though, Ghislaine was there. Epstein was holding Annie's hand in front of his girlfriend or wife or whatever she was. For that reason, she decided it could not possibly mean something bad. Besides, this was a necessary trip before Annie got to have the experience of a lifetime attending a summer program in Thailand—a stepping-stone in her life and an opportunity she could never have had otherwise.

After they returned to the ranch with her new cowboy boots, Ghislaine told Annie to put them on and model them for Jeffrey. Jeffrey then told her that they looked really good and that she deserved a massage. She felt uncomfortable because Ghislaine made her get naked before covering her with a sheet. Ghislaine then massaged Annie herself. At one point, Ghislaine pulled the covers off Annie, exposing her breasts before beginning to massage them. When the massage was over, Annie stood up and realized that Jeffrey had been watching them the entire time.

Annie went to sleep in her own bed and woke up to find Epstein lying in her bed under the covers, cuddling with her. She didn't know what to do, but thankfully she was scheduled to leave later that day. She packed up her things. Before she left, Epstein and Maxwell told her that they couldn't wait to see her again when she got back from Thailand.

---

Realizing that Maria was the witness I thought she was, I called the team at Boies Schiller Flexner from my hotel room near Paducah and told them that someone needed to come out and meet Maria to get a firsthand appreciation of her importance. David called me back and told me Stan was getting on a plane and would be there that night.

We needed to make decisions on how we were going to prepare for this trial and how Maria fit into it. There had been this philosophy at the time that because the years that Maria was with Epstein did not overlap with Virginia's, Maria could only be marginally relevant to Virginia's case against Maxwell. (Maria's Epstein interlude ended four years before Virginia's began.) The rest of the team believed that because she was a twenty-five-year-old adult and not a minor at the time of her interactions with Epstein, and because Virginia had not known her, a court might not see her information as relevant to Virginia's case. With what I had learned that day, I believed she was very important.

Stan flew out that night and got a room in the cheap hotel. We spent the next day at Maria's house, going through photos. By the end of the day, Stan appreciated how Maria's knowledge was important to explaining how Ghislaine fit into the story. It was Ghislaine who interacted most with Maria. Maria described Ghislaine and Jeffrey as Bonnie and Clyde. It's funny, several witnesses used that exact description. Maria could explain how there was nothing that Epstein did that Ghislaine didn't know about; in fact, she personally facilitated almost every aspect of his life. Ghislaine was the main person bringing Epstein girls. Her specialty was making them feel comfortable before handing them off to Jeffrey. It was Ghislaine who'd dished out most of the pickup lines; in fact, she made most of them up herself. Ghislaine was also the one who had cozied up to Annie to make her feel special.

During the summer of 1996, while Annie was in Thailand, Maria's relationship with Epstein and Maxwell took a major turn. Maria was sent by Epstein to live at Les Wexner's home in New Albany, Ohio, just outside Columbus, so she could finish some artwork she had been contracted to do for the James Brooks movie *As Good As It Gets*. Maria's younger brother had come from Kentucky to join her in the guesthouse on the Wexner complex, a sprawling property owned by the wealthiest man in Ohio and one of the richest people in the world. Ghislaine and Jeffrey flew from New York to Ohio to pay her a visit one day.

Ghislaine called Maria into Ghislaine and Jeffrey's bedroom and asked her to get onto the bed so they could talk. Jeffrey was lounging there watching television, so Maria, fully clothed, got into the large bed with the two of them and watched. Talking was not on the agenda. Ghislaine was the first to reach out and grab Maria's breast, followed instantly by Epstein, who did the same. Maria panicked, jumped up, and ran out of Jeffrey's room into the one where her little brother was sleeping. She called the local police, got no help, then called her father in Kentucky to drive to Ohio to pick her up.

After a standoff at the gate of Wexner's estate between Maria's father and Wexner's guards, Maria and her brother were finally permitted to leave.

Back home in New York, Maria wasted no time calling the FBI and the New York City police to report the sexual assault by Epstein and Maxwell.

Not long afterward, Maria told us she received a phone call from Ghislaine Maxwell, who said, "If you report us to the police again, I will have you killed."

After that telephone call, Ghislaine and Jeffrey worked together to besmirch Maria's name in the art community in New York. With their connections, they easily managed to falsely discredit her and her work to the point that she was forced to leave the city. What's more, taking Ghislaine's threats to heart, Maria felt the need to go into hiding. The scenario was very similar to Virginia's dramatic escape to Australia. Stan did not need to listen to Maria long in order to understand the significance of her story.

That trip was really the beginning of my relationship with Stan. The way he asked questions of Maria and evaluated the evidence was impressive. It was very conversational. Before that trip, Stan and I had not spent much time talking beyond discussing the facts and strategy behind the various cases that had sprouted. I left Paducah impressed that David had sent someone as savvy as Stan to Kentucky, within hours, and even more impressed by Stan's quick study of the situation.

During our three-hour drive back to Tennessee, I learned that, like me, Stan had been a quarterback in high school. I loved that. I learned that he grew up in Dayton, Ohio, which had many cultural similarities to my hometown of Jacksonville. I liked that, too. He went to Harvard for undergrad and law school, then had his storied legal career highlighted by his years in the Justice Department, which naturally meant to me that he was brilliant. But what I really wanted was to understand why Stan was David Boies's go-to guy. He seemed like David's trusted secret agent, for lack of a better term. I came to see that Stan is like the character "the Wolf" from *Pulp Fiction*—he can handle any situation for anyone at any time.

Stan has this diplomatic quality about him that makes him able to blend into any situation in any country, with very little background information at hand, and accumulate knowledge. I asked him if David had hired him out of the CIA to be his operative because of his former high-end government connections and knack for traveling around the world to handle mysterious business meetings.

He said he and David had become friends while playing softball on Sundays in Bedford, New York. "I couldn't pitch, and he couldn't hit," he said, "so when a game was over, we were pretty much left alone to talk to each other."

This sounded like a cover story to me. So I asked, "But are you in the CIA or are you not?" He laughed hard enough to make the question sound ridiculous and said no, he was not, but I'm sure he didn't expect me to believe him. He then said, "If I'm a James Bond, I sure am a poor man's version of him." Which, of course, is exactly what a real James Bond would say. We both started laughing, and I honestly wasn't sure if we were laughing because it was funny or true. I guess I still don't know for sure. Either way, he has stuck to the softball story as the origin of his relationship with David Boies.

# FORTY

# TWO MORE FOR THE GOOD GUYS

S HORTLY AFTER RETURNING TO FORT LAUDERDALE from Kentucky, I got a tip that I needed to track down Rinaldo Rizzo, a former housekeeper for one of Epstein's ex-girlfriends, Eva Andersson.

Rizzo and his wife were the housekeepers for Eva Andersson-Dubin and her husband, Glenn Dubin, from 2002 to 2005 and again from 2011 to 2013. Glenn is a billionaire investor and Eva is a doctor and former model who once boasted the title of Miss Sweden. More interestingly, we already knew that Eva was a former girlfriend of Jeffrey Epstein and still one of his best friends. They were so close that Epstein was godfather to at least one of Eva and Glenn's daughters, a fact that Epstein often bragged about.

As housekeepers for Eva and Glenn, the Rizzos were privy to copious amounts of information about Epstein just by the natural consequence of being around the Dubins, who talked often about Epstein and their frequent visits to one another's homes. The Rizzos were exposed to so much that, in 2005, they stopped working for the Dubins because, they explained, they had "seen too much" of Epstein. They only returned in 2011 because Rinaldo believed that the Dubins had cut ties with Epstein since Epstein had gone to jail for abusing children. He quickly learned that the Dubins had not parted ways with Epstein at all.

Rinaldo Rizzo was an upstanding guy, fearful of his ex-boss and also justifiably scared of Epstein. Still, his genuine heart and the fact that he was too good of a person to stay quiet about what he knew made him give in and speak to me. We spent a lot of time talking. After I would gather information, I would then cross-reference it with other intel I had from other witnesses.

As I asked questions, Rinaldo, an honest person just trying to do the right thing, began sharing many stories about what he observed when in Epstein's presence. He told me about a time when he took the Dubin children to see Epstein, whom the Dubin kids referred to as "Uncle Jeff," at his Palm Beach mansion. Rinaldo saw nude pictures everywhere around the house, which made him understandably uncomfortable. Out of curiosity, he wandered around a bit, until Maxwell walked up behind him and told him to go back outside because Epstein did not like it when someone snooped around.

On another occasion, Rinaldo had been asked to make lunch at the Dubins' house in New York for Epstein and his bevy of female followers, including Epstein's then girlfriend, Nadia. At one point, Nadia kissed Epstein, then Epstein made Nadia kiss one of the other girls while she and the girl danced with each other. Watching this unfold, Rinaldo and his wife concluded that something was very wrong with Epstein.

According to Rinaldo, Epstein was a major point of contention between Glenn and Eva. Glenn did not really like Epstein much. But Eva did. Rinaldo recounted that the couple would argue whenever something involved Epstein. But Eva was unwavering in her loyalty to Epstein. When Jeffrey was released from jail in 2009, Eva wrote a letter to his probation officer which read, "We are the parents of three children . . . They are all under the age of 18. I am aware that Jeffrey Epstein is a registered sex offender and had plead guilty to soliciting for prostitution, and procuring a minor for prostitution. I am 100% comfortable with Jeffrey Epstein around my children."

Rinaldo Rizzo was an important witness, but if he had this much information about Epstein, a household staff member who worked for Epstein himself would have even more. Alfredo Rodriguez had been released from prison, but I learned he had died of mesothelioma shortly after getting out. I'm not sure he would have talked to me anyway, although I believe that in his heart he was a good man who knew his bad decisions, and not me, had led to his unfortunate prison stint.

I turned my attention back to former housekeeper Juan Alessi, since he had a long history of working at the Palm Beach house. Alessi had started working for Epstein in approximately 1990. They had met through Les Wexner—Alessi had done maintenance and repair work for Wexner and began to do the same for Epstein. During his depositions, he had given us useful information.

Alessi had started working for Epstein during a time when Eva had been the lady of the house. Alessi liked Eva because she was well-mannered, considerate, and respectful of the household staff.

Eventually, that relationship ended around 1991, and Alessi was introduced to Epstein's new girlfriend, Ghislaine Maxwell, who was placed in charge of taking care of the house. Maxwell introduced a handbook to the staff that they all had to read, explaining that they would now be following royal practice in England. Among the rules Ghislaine implemented was a requirement that the staff never look the master, Jeffrey Epstein, in the eye.

Ghislaine was deeply controlling and did things Juan did not appreciate. When Eva was in charge, Alessi said, there weren't other females, including young girls around the house. He remembered that as soon as Maxwell took over the house, there were female visitors there who were referred to as "masseuses," but who did not look professional and appeared too young. Alessi also recalled that Maxwell loved to take nude photographs of girls, which she stored in a big album at her desk.

Alessi testified that after the novice "masseuses" performed massages, he would go upstairs to clean up the massage room. While there, he found recently used dildos. He put on his gloves, picked them up, rinsed them off in the sink, and returned them to a laundry basket filled with similar sex toys Maxwell kept in her closet. Alessi connected more dots for us as we pieced together how the sex scheme started and progressed. He also confirmed Virginia's account of her time with Epstein and Maxwell.

---

We weren't the only side investigating and setting depositions. Maxwell's attorneys set one for Tony, Virginia's long-lost boyfriend, whom she'd left behind when she escaped to Thailand. She had not spoken to Tony since she fled, and there was no way of telling what he would say. He was definitely not happy with the way Virginia had left him, and we assumed Maxwell had been in touch with him.

Tony knew as well as anyone that Virginia was telling the truth about Epstein and Maxwell. He'd had direct interaction with Epstein and personally participated in Epstein's operation by bringing high school girls to Epstein after Virginia had escaped to Thailand and left Tony. Still, why would Maxwell's legal team take Tony's deposition and put him on record unless they thought he would give them favorable testimony?

It was now 2016, and Virginia hadn't spoken with Tony since she fled in 2002. While she knew the truth, she didn't know what Tony was going to say. Had Maxwell gotten to him? Was Tony being paid to lie? Of course, if he was, we would be stuck in the untenable position of trying to prove that he was paid, which would be difficult. What was certain was that Tony's deposition was going to be taken and he wasn't happy with Virginia about the way their relationship ended. I didn't blame him.

Virginia had been the love of Tony's life. They had lived together from the time she met Maxwell until she ran away to Thailand. She had not told him that he would never see her again. She didn't even call him. She'd gotten married and gone with her new husband to Australia. Tony had every reason to hold a grudge. But all we needed from him was the truth. Nothing more, nothing less.

We decided that our best chance to keep Tony honest was to have Virginia attend his deposition in person. She had the legal right to be there.

He would have a much harder time seeing her for the first time in fourteen years and telling lies. But we did not want Tony to be caught off guard or to think that Virginia had been in the country without making her presence known before magically appearing at his deposition. That might make him more mad, if that was possible.

I decided that I needed to contact him before he walked into the room. As expected, he was pissed. I didn't need to say more than that I represented Virginia Roberts when he lashed out at me. "F*** this" and "F*** that" and basically "F*** her." Even fourteen years later, he was still upset. Before I could say anything, he wanted me to know how she had broken his heart and left him with an apartment he couldn't pay for, a car he couldn't afford, and a bunch of friends he lost almost immediately because he seemed like the biggest liar of all time trying to explain his live-in girlfriend's whereabouts when he had no idea where she was. He had worried about her. He didn't even know if she was okay.

I was genuinely sympathetic. But rather than trying to explain the complicated psychology that had led to Virginia's "abandoning" him (to use his term), especially since there was no way he was going to give me the time necessary to even attempt that—I decided to take a different route in. I told him: "I don't represent Virginia for the sake of trying to prove that everything she has ever done, including her relationship with you, was done right or that she was in the right. You may have a problem with her, and it may be justified. All we need from you is for you to tell the complete truth to the best of your memory."

He said, "I'm not doing shit until I talk to Virginia. I need some explanation about why she f***ed me over."

I tried to explain that one really had nothing to do with the other, but that if he told the truth I would make sure he had an opportunity to speak with her. Instantaneously, he went from hyperaggressive babbling to calm agreeableness. "Is she here?" he asked nicely.

I said, "She will be at your deposition, yes." Then I asked, "Have you spoken with Jeffrey Epstein or any of the lawyers from the other side?" But this, I quickly learned, was definitely not the right question.

Tony went on another tirade about how inconvenienced he had been over the years by people trying to serve him with subpoenas and by investigators hunting him down. So I opted for a more direct route. "Do you remember any relationship between Virginia and Jeffrey Epstein, and if so, what do you remember about it?" As it turned out, he remembered a lot.

He remembered things that would be helpful to the issues in our case—although he had no idea what those actual issues were and had no interest in knowing. I didn't even try to explain. He also remembered things that wouldn't be helpful to us. I let him rant about whatever was on his mind and did not try to stop him from venting. He eventually ran out of steam and calmed down. The more wound up he became, the more calm I remained. At some point, it made no sense for him to keep yelling. In the end, I think his realization that he was actually going to see Virginia gave him the possible closure he wanted and deserved.

He explained that Virginia had taken a job at the Mar-a-Lago Club, that she had been fifteen years old at the time (she had actually been sixteen), but he couldn't really recall the year, and who could blame him for that; it had been many years of heartbreak, which he had tried desperately to forget. This lack of precision didn't concern me. In fact, it was the subject of scrutiny by Maxwell's team and debate in our own. When Virginia was first located in her hiding place in Australia and forced to resurface, she'd said she'd been fifteen when she was recruited by Maxwell in 1998, and that is what went into the complaint filed by her lawyer, Bob Josefsberg, on her behalf—*Jane Doe 102 v. Jeffrey Epstein.*

That rendition of the chronology didn't make mathematical sense. In the summer of 1998, Virginia would have been fourteen years old. And she didn't even meet Maxwell until the summer of 2000, when she was sixteen and about to turn seventeen, something we learned after comparing Virginia's memory with police reports, school records, and finally her Mar-a-Lago employment file, which we obtained six years after her 2009 complaint was filed.

The fact that Tony was not exact in his recollection on the date that Virginia was recruited was immaterial. He was now trying his best to remember something that he had also tried his best to forget. However, certain facts he did clearly recollect. Within six months after Virginia was approached by Ghislaine, Virginia started traveling with Jeffrey Epstein.

Initially, Tony didn't know what was going on between Virginia and Jeffrey, but it didn't take long before he realized sex was involved and confronted her, and she admitted it. Whenever she returned to Florida from her trips, she carried handfuls of cash, and she and Tony lived in a brand-new apartment paid for by Jeffrey Epstein. She was on call to go over to his house at virtually all hours of the day and night and dropped everything in a split second when the call came in. She would sometimes leave town for weeks at a time.

When she finally confessed to Tony that she was being paid for sex, he didn't freak out for long. Her "work" for Epstein was supporting a lifestyle to which he had quickly grown accustomed. Plus, when Virginia was home, she was devoted to him, which he liked.

When she was not at home, she was experiencing a world that Tony couldn't provide for her, then or ever. He rationalized that this whole thing was working out best for everyone. During discussions, though, something even more challenging came up. He learned that Virginia was made to sexually perform not only for Jeffrey, but for some of his friends. Then he learned that she was also with women, including Ghislaine.

Tony even remembered Virginia calling him when Ghislaine fixed her up with Prince Andrew in London and explaining over the phone how she did not want to have sex with him, but it was part of what she needed to do to continue their lifestyle.

In addition to telling me what he remembered about Virginia, he also filled in many blanks to questions Virginia herself did not know the answers to. That included what happened with Epstein after Virginia left for Australia. While she'd believed Jeffrey Epstein had forgotten about her in 2002, after she had called him to tell him she was not coming back and he hung up on her, apparently that was not the case.

For months after she left, Epstein or someone on his behalf contacted Tony asking where she was. Tony, of course, really didn't know. And

Epstein, who was a human lie detector, knew from their conversations that Tony was telling the truth. They had something in common, Jeffrey and Tony. Virginia left both of them, at the same time. Epstein pounced on that common ground. Tony's financial source was gone, yet he was still accustomed to a lifestyle that required money.

"Do you want to make some cash?" Jeffrey asked him. "If you have any girls, bring them over and I'll pay you." Tony began to do just that. He picked up girls from the high school, from parties, from friends, from friends of friends, and anywhere else he could find them. He knew there was only one requirement: they had to be young. Epstein told him so.

But Tony quickly ran out of girls. He was getting older. By this time, he was almost twenty-one and no longer hanging out with sixteen- and seventeen-year-olds. This excuse didn't work for Epstein, though. The calls he made to Tony were increasingly aggressive. Sometimes they came from Epstein directly. At other times, it was a British-accented female voice on the other end of the line telling Tony to bring new girls for Jeffrey. At one point the woman identified herself as Ghislaine Maxwell.

When I got off the phone with Tony, it was even less obvious to me why Maxwell's attorneys wanted Tony to testify and wanted it badly. Maybe it was because they knew he was still mad at Virginia, and that was enough. What's more, I had no way of locking him into what he had told me on the phone. So even though it seemed unlikely he would change his story and lie, we stuck to the original plan and took Virginia to his deposition. If he thought she was going to be there and she didn't show up, that was certainly something that could trigger an angry fake story.

While the substance of his deposition is under seal, I can say this: Virginia showed up, Tony showed up, and Tony told the truth. It was strange being in the room. Virginia had a husband and a family whom she loved, and Tony had a life she wasn't part of, but it was obvious to me that merely seeing her was what Tony needed to put this chapter behind him. To this day, I have no idea why Maxwell's attorneys worked so hard to get Tony under oath, but I'm glad they did.

Piece by piece, we were tightening the attack on Maxwell through these different witnesses. Our chessboard was looking pretty good and more witnesses were popping up, almost daily. While the focus of this particular lawsuit was Maxwell, our investigation was uncovering pieces of the bigger puzzle, which was dangerous for Epstein.

# FORTY-ONE

# RANSOME

THE MAXWELL CASE WAS GETTING more public attention as we got closer to our May 15, 2017, trial date. We were constantly chasing leads. Often witnesses cold-called us out of nowhere.

In October 2016, Paul Cassell got an interesting call from a woman who said her name was Sarah Ransome. She began by telling him she, too, had been victimized by Jeffrey Epstein with Ghislaine's help and she wanted to assist Virginia in any way she could. Paul told her that there was a sizable legal team working for Virginia and he didn't want to make Sarah repeat to them what she was telling him on the phone. He would arrange for everyone who needed to hear her story to be on the phone with her at the same time. He told her that in the meantime, we just needed to know the time period in which she was involved with Epstein so we could check our records and cross-reference her history with the evidence in our possession.

She told Paul that she was with Epstein and Maxwell from 2006 into 2007. I had reviewed Epstein's flight logs so many times that I nearly knew them by heart at that point. I recognized her name from the logs immediately.

Brittany and I went over to the Boies Schiller Flexner office in Fort Lauderdale and sat at the end of the grand conference room table surrounded by floor-to-ceiling windows overlooking everything between downtown and the ocean. There was a conference phone separating us from Sigrid; another brilliant Boies Schiller Flexner lawyer, Meredith Schultz; and her paralegal, Sandy Perkins. We had copies of flight logs, message pads, photographs, and the black book lying around the table for everyone to cross-reference as we heard the details of Sarah's story for the very first time.

Sarah was in Barcelona, Spain, and the phone connection between us was bad. It also took me at least five minutes to familiarize myself with her South African accent well enough to understand her. She explained that she had been following Virginia's story and had wanted to call us for years, but she had failed to do so out of a deep-seated fear of Epstein and Maxwell.

Sarah had grown to admire Virginia's coming forward after all these years, though, and sympathized with her story. Sarah had googled Virginia to get in touch with her and discovered the Victims Refuse Silence Facebook page. It told her what Virginia was trying to do for other victims, so Sarah knew she wanted to help.

She started her story long before a time we needed to know about, but we didn't want to interrupt her. It was hard enough to establish a rapport with her across the Atlantic without trying to redirect the thoughts of someone who clearly needed an open forum to express herself. She explained how she had moved to New York to pursue a modeling career and had been living the New York City high life before she met Jeffrey Epstein.

During that initial call, she explained that she had been to Epstein's island on multiple occasions in 2006 and 2007. She even claimed to have photographs of herself on the island with Epstein, Maxwell, Brunel, and other women. Any time a witness had photographic evidence, it bumped that person up on our priority list because no matter how many high-paid lawyers Jeffrey Epstein and his gang hired, photographs were hard to deny. That didn't mean that they wouldn't try, of course.

Sarah then told us about an incident when she had gotten into a situation in New York and needed legal advice. She said Epstein had referred her to a lawyer named "Ellen" in his office in New York City. Sarah kept going on and on in a very rapid, thick accent about her troubling experiences with this lawyer named Ellen, then suddenly shifted to a new subject.

One of us stopped her and said, "Wait, this was the lawyer Ellen that you had met with before?"

Sarah replied, "Yes, Ellen Dershowitz."

At that moment, I looked straight at Sigrid. Sigrid looked up and we realized that for the last ten minutes, she had been talking about *Alan* Dershowitz. We told her to stop talking. "Are you saying that the lawyer you have been talking about is Alan Dershowitz?" I asked. Sigrid and I kept asking the same question in different ways. I think Brittany and Meredith each even took a shot at clarifying the story. Finally, Sarah yelled, "Yes, you idiots, the lawyer Alan [still sounding like "Ellen"] Dershowitz!"

By this point in the conversation, Sarah was corroborating so many different parts of Virginia's story that we knew we needed to see her in person. Before figuring out how to orchestrate a meeting with her, I inquired about other evidence that she might have had. "Do you have any emails from anyone in Epstein's organization during that time period? What do we need to do to get the photographs that you say you took back in 2006 or 2007?" She told us they were in storage in London and she was in Spain with no money to get to them.

Sarah swore that the photographs were there. She had the address of the storage facility. We told her we would pay her to go get the photographs. At the same time, we had all heard from witnesses before about magical photographs and evidence that often failed to materialize. Sometimes the photographs would turn up, and most times they wouldn't. Nonetheless, we worked with her over the next month to retrieve boxes of documents from storage. When the London Boies Schiller Flexner team delivered the boxes to her, none of the photographs were there. She was very frustrated. But she eventually found them on her old computer and started sending them one at a time, including photographs of her with Jeffrey Epstein, and his crew, including Ghislaine Maxwell. The photographs had been taken in December 2006. Sarah was twenty-two at the time.

These photographs were a big deal. In December 2006, Epstein was under federal investigation. The case against him that was initiated by the Palm Beach Police Department had already been transferred to the FBI. At that time, Epstein's dream team of lawyers, including Alan Dershowitz, was speaking frequently with the U.S. Attorney's Office, telling them one way or another that Epstein's accidental misbehavior was now a thing of the past and that he was living a good, wholesome life. Yet while his lawyers were negotiating a plea deal over his receipt of sexual massages for money, he was also traveling to his island to receive sexual massages for money—from Sarah Ransome and others.

Based on those facts alone, it made sense that if Sarah Ransome had a legal problem in early 2007, Jeffrey Epstein would have introduced her to his friend and lawyer at the time, Alan Dershowitz. Plus, we knew from flight logs that Sarah was traveling with Epstein to New York and his island at a time when Epstein had to be in regular contact with Dershowitz.

We couldn't, of course, get a picture of a relationship between Epstein and Sarah based only on finding her name written on a flight log or in an email. Photographs, though, are different. Once Sarah started sending the photographs of Sarah Kellen, Ghislaine, Jean-Luc, and Epstein on the private island, it became obvious that she had spent enough time with them to know more about how the organization worked, and who was involved in what.

The photos also revealed that Maxwell was still very much a part of Epstein's traveling sex circus in 2006 and 2007. At a time when most defendants would be on their best behavior, or hiding, Epstein was frolicking with young females on his private island. Was he thinking their adult ages protected him now? Was he thinking no one would find out? Could he really just not help himself?

This was all happening amid Maxwell's concerted effort to make herself a ghost in Florida after the search warrant had been executed on Epstein's home in late 2005. Yet there she was, too, front and center in the pictures confirming Sarah's account. This didn't jibe well with her defense that she was no longer part of Epstein's life during that time.

To evaluate Sarah's importance any further, we needed to pay her a visit. I was going to go to Barcelona and needed a partner for the trip. This was a mission for Stan, being the 007 that he was. On January 4, 2017, we flew to Barcelona and went to the hotel where we had arranged to meet Sarah. We had seen her in photographs, but those were taken in 2007 and here we were ten years later, not really knowing what to expect. I saw her walk in.

Of course, the thought crossed my mind that this could be an Epstein setup, which is why we took the extra precaution of flying across the world to meet with her in person. Sarah was extremely paranoid. She was probably thinking that somehow, *we* were the ones working with Epstein. Those who crossed paths with him believed he was able to do anything, at any time, to anyone. I don't think I met a single witness who didn't believe they were being followed or investigated by him. And what made their paranoia reasonable was that, many times, they were right.

Sarah didn't want to talk in public at all, not even to give greetings in the lobby. She told us that she was checking in to her room and would find us in the meeting room that we had reserved. Once she joined us, we spent at least eight hours straight with her. She had a lot to say. The time period when her life intersected with Epstein's was not very long—less than a year—but she had emails to prove it and she had more photographs. As suspected, Epstein was getting "massaged" as usual while his legal team was negotiating a deal with prosecutors on his behalf. The pictures were enough to reveal that, even then, Epstein had no concern that the federal government was ever going to do anything to him.

The email communications between Sarah Ransome and Jeffrey Epstein, Sarah Kellen, and Jeffrey's assistant Lesley Groff were even more powerful than the photographs. In 2007, Epstein had paid for Sarah Ransome to go back to South Africa, in part with the mission to retrieve a new young model for him.

I knew Jeffrey Epstein's scheme. While in his presence, each girl was expected to be on call for a "massage," which, of course, meant sex. Every time. When not in his presence, everyone was expected to be looking for the next girl to bring to Jeffrey for a massage. In exchange, he made promises, and Ghislaine made promises, and others made promises on his behalf. Sometimes the promises were kept; other times, they were not. Jeffrey was very calculated in that way. He made sure that the small promises were kept so that his girls always believed that he would make good on that one big promise that in all reality he never intended to fulfill and instead used as a carrot to dangle.

For Sarah, Epstein had promised to get her into the Fashion Institute of Technology (FIT), a fashion design school in New York, if she continued to grant him sexual favors. Sarah knew that Epstein had the ability to get her in, but with Jeffrey, there was always a catch, always a negotiation, and nothing was ever as it seemed. To Sarah, it was simple: she had to do as Jeffrey and Ghislaine and his other associates demanded and, in turn, Jeffrey would get her into the school of her dreams.

Once she was back in South Africa, Jeffrey told her to write an essay that he would submit to FIT as part of her admission application. He also told her that she needed to weigh less than fifty-two kilograms (114 pounds) before he would help her. It seemed he had made this requirement intentionally unattainable, or just didn't care how much anyone suffered to meet his needs. Sarah was five foot ten, she weighed more than 114 pounds, and she was twenty-two years old, which by his standards was too big and too old. He preferred teenagers but would settle for young adults who resembled children in ways that mattered to him. Given that he was being investigated, he couldn't run the risk of getting caught with a minor, so he had no choice but to find older girls and try to make them look as young or as small as possible. But even with all the power, coaxing, promises, and dictates he used on them, it was not easy to achieve.

The body type that he liked most—one that was not completely developed, or one with small breasts, narrow hips, few curves, and the "purity" of having had little or no sexual experience—did not exist among twenty-two year-olds in the same frequency it did among teens. This frustrated Jeffrey. He had a lot less patience with someone Sarah's age.

Still, without quite achieving the lower weight he required, she returned to the United States without having recruited any girls abroad, and lived in one of Epstein's apartments at 301 East Sixty-Sixth Street. She stayed there only a few months before she left the United States in May 2007, after realizing she was never going to reach Epstein's weight requirement and he was never going to get her into FIT.

Sarah was very convincing, and she had the evidence to support all major aspects of what she was saying. Even the parts where she didn't have absolute proof were generally supported by the circumstantial evidence that we had gathered from other sources.

After our two-day debriefing with Sarah, Stan and I headed for the airport. We split up because we were going different places on different flights.

I had a connecting flight in Frankfurt, Germany, on my way home from Barcelona where I had to get off the plane, walk out onto the tarmac, and board one of the buses that would take connecting passengers on a short haul over to the terminal. When I got off the plane, I saw that the bus I was about to board had a long line of people waiting to get on, and there was another one—without a line—about a hundred feet in front that was about to shut its doors. I ran for it, got on just before the doors closed, and rode it to my next gate.

After boarding my flight, I was sitting in my seat looking over my notes when I realized the plane was taking an unusually long time to take off. It didn't concern me, though; I knew I had a long flight ahead of me anyway and figured it wouldn't make a big difference.

Suddenly, an airline official appeared on the plane looking very concerned. She came directly over to my seat and asked me my name. I told her Brad Edwards and she asked me if I was okay. I said, "Yeah, I'm fine." She kept asking me if I was sure I was okay. As she was saying this, the only thing that made any sense at all was that I must have been followed by someone who was trying to do something really bad to me.

She said, "Were you on the plane from Barcelona?" I told her that I was. She asked me how I got from the plane to the terminal, so I told her I'd boarded a transport bus, like everyone else. She said she needed to talk to me about that because something I was telling her didn't make sense.

When I asked her what she meant, she brought me up to the front of the plane and told me in private that the bus I was on had been hit by a huge luggage transporter and knocked upside down, killing three people and seriously injuring more. She asked me how I had managed to be on this airplane in one piece.

Having gotten the picture, I explained that I had not boarded the bus I was supposed to take but got on another one in front of it and didn't even know anything that had happened to the one behind. I wanted to ask her if the driver of the luggage transporter worked for Jeffrey Epstein, but I didn't, I swear. This was a surreal experience. By some miracle born of impatience, I had escaped a disaster.

Even more surreal was that there was a mass shooting at the Fort Lauderdale airport on the same day, which caused a panic for everyone who knew I was flying home. Thankfully, I had flown into Miami instead of Fort Lauderdale, which in and of itself was odd because I almost never fly into Miami. When I landed, I had dozens of text messages from people who knew I was flying home that day and were worried. Not knowing about the shooting, I thought the text messages were asking if I was okay because of the bus accident in Germany, when in actuality no one at home even knew about that. In one day, I discovered twice that I was lucky to be alive.

Fast-forward a year and a half to 2018 and I was representing the victims from the Fort Lauderdale airport shooting.

# FORTY-TWO

# THE BODYGUARD

O N MY TRIP HOME, I thought about a story that Sarah Ransome had shared with us where she explained that she was so desperate to escape, she attempted to swim off Epstein's island. She explained that Epstein's bodyguard witnessed the whole thing and would corroborate her story. When I returned, I called the bodyguard right away. He told me to meet him at the Starbucks.

This former bodyguard was a Russian mixed martial arts fighter hired by Epstein to provide security. With this type of background, I mistakenly assumed he was a coldhearted tough guy who protected whomever he was hired to protect, and who would never share details. By all appearances, he truly seemed like a movie character who was meant to defend someone evil. The bodyguard seemed like someone whom Russian mobsters would hire. But he didn't sound like a bad guy when I called to set up our meeting.

He had a secretive way about him, like a robot that was put on earth not to gossip about anyone or anything. But he wasn't the heartless character whom I had previously believed him to be. Don't get me wrong, he wasn't excited to meet me, but he had agreed to do so.

When I got to the Starbucks that night, I was early, as usual. It was nice out, so I picked a table outside. He had no idea who I was or what I looked like, even though we had crossed paths outside of depositions and meetings

I'd had with Epstein several years before. He arrived within minutes, walked inside to grab a coffee, then looked around until our eyes met. He didn't hesitate before walking in my direction, knowing somehow that it was me. He didn't want me taking any notes. I put my pen down and prepared to listen.

I asked him how he got started with Epstein and what he saw during his employment. He was hired initially because Epstein was worried that some girl's dad would try to kill him. While I had never heard anyone say that Epstein had this fear, I had often wondered how it never happened. He continued to talk in a low voice, primarily on the subject of the young females in Epstein's life. He confirmed what many others by this point had said—that Epstein's entire life, from the time he woke up to the time he went to sleep, revolved around young women.

As soon as Jeffrey got out of jail in 2008, there were girls at his house all the time—the only thing that changed was the target age of his victims. They were all promised something that Jeffrey would do for them, and at some point, this bodyguard expressed his concern to Jeffrey about his misleading them. He said, "You just got out of jail, you can't keep doing this with these girls." He made it clear that Epstein was engaging in the same conduct that landed him in trouble in the first place but with a slightly older age group, focusing his attention not on rounding up high school kids, but on the modeling industry as his recruiting playground.

These were girls who believed they were there—wherever "there" was at any given moment—for a legitimate reason, not illicit sex. But Jeffrey's purpose with them was sex and only sex. His bodyguard watched as dozens of young aspiring models were lured into Epstein's world before being discarded, more broken than before. When this bodyguard told Epstein that he shouldn't keep doing this with girls, he said Epstein responded, "Don't act like my grandma or you will be fired."

Yes, he confirmed that Sarah tried to swim off the island, but her attempt showed no greater level of distress than he'd seen in other girls throughout the years. The rest of our meeting had little to do with girls, and much to do with the danger he saw me putting myself in with Epstein.

He was himself a real-life tough guy, yet I could tell he was frightened by Epstein. And he stressed that I should also be frightened. He had no precise information; it wasn't as if Epstein had told him I was a target. He simply made it clear that I was somebody Epstein had talked about, and not in a friendly way. But of course, I already knew that.

As we got to know each other, he increased the seriousness in his voice. "You don't know who you're dealing with. I worked for him for years and *I* still don't know who you're dealing with. He knows everybody who's powerful in this world." He went on to explain that Jeff's connections were not just to the local police, who were "definitely in his pocket," and from whom "when he was in jail and on house arrest, he got so many favors." He elaborated that Epstein "made very clear that the federal government would never prosecute him."

He also snuck stories in to give me examples of how scary Epstein was. On one occasion, a lawyer was found at the bottom of a swimming pool. Epstein asked him if he thought people would believe it was a suicide, as if it wasn't, and suggested that he, Epstein, had something to do with the woman's demise. It wasn't someone I had ever heard of during my years of investigating Epstein, so I had no reason to believe it was a connection to any case I was working on, but the purpose of the message was clear.

He went on to tell me that when Epstein was in jail, he still had extraordinary power, even within our own government. This bodyguard had been sent by Epstein to Virginia to CIA headquarters. Nervously telling me the story, he said, "I didn't know why I was there, but he told me they would take care of me. I attended a class for a week. At the beginning of the class, everyone had to introduce themselves. There were forty-five people. Forty-four people were in the CIA or some other government unit with top secret clearance. I was the only private citizen. Everyone introduced themselves and the instructor saved me for last. He did not let me introduce myself. Instead, he just introduced me as what he called a 'special operative.'" He explained that he then attended the classes for the week before he was given a book with a personalized note and told to deliver it "to Jeffrey." He took the book to Jeffrey's seldom-occupied county jail cell and delivered it without reading the contents of the note.

"Anything else give you any other hints as to who Epstein is?" I asked.

"I can only tell you where we went and what I observed, but he goes out of his way not to share any real information," he replied. "He spends most of his days doing what you know he does: hanging out with his girls. Getting massages. The rest is traveling with very specific missions; most don't last very long. The girls he trusts come along."

He told me, for instance, about a prince or a sultan (he didn't recall which) whom they would meet all over the world. Epstein also often met with Ehud Barak, the former prime minister of Israel. Barak frequently visited Epstein in New York as well, and on extended stays took residence at Epstein's 301 East Sixty-Sixth Street apartments.

In fact, not long before my meeting with the bodyguard, Alan Dershowitz had confirmed Epstein's close relationship with Barak. Dershowitz testified that during his personal, non-privileged conversations with Epstein, he and Jeffrey discussed the Middle East. Dershowitz further described an in-person discussion that he had observed between Barak and Epstein at Epstein's New York town house wherein the two were drawing up resolutions to Middle East conflict on a blackboard. It was clear that Epstein was exactly as powerful as we always thought he was. But, there was this air of mystery surrounding his connections to international dignitaries like Barak that always begged the question of who Epstein really was.

Before we split up, there was one more story he shared. On one occasion, after returning to New York just after completing his Florida "jail" sentence, Epstein yelled to this bodyguard that they needed to leave in a hurry. It was clear to him that whatever the reason, it was important and Jeffrey was pissed. Even to his professional bodyguard, when Jeffrey was pissed, he was scary. On that occasion, Jeffrey demanded that the Suburban be brought around quickly. Jojo, the driver, also understood this was an emergency in Jeffrey's world. Jeffrey didn't talk during the car ride from the mansion to the Wall Street office of a major league hedge fund manager whom the bodyguard couldn't (or wouldn't) identify.

They got to the office building and Epstein got out of the car with purpose, walking briskly to the front door of the high tower. His bodyguard was trying to keep up.

They headed to the elevator and Epstein didn't stop to tell the front desk that he had arrived. When he got up to the floor of the hedge fund, Epstein, still on a mission, walked straight toward the back of the office complex to what his bodyguard referred to as the "president's" office.

Epstein opened the door without knocking and barged in. He walked to the chair side of the desk, leaned over to the "president," and said, "You need to get that money to Israel immediately. Like f***ing yesterday."

As the story was relayed to me, the man on the receiving end of Epstein's demand was shaking. This man was another Wall Street billionaire who made his own rules. With his voice quivering, he responded to Epstein, saying, "I wired thirty million dollars today. It's already there. You can check." Without a word to him, Epstein turned around and walked out, leaving the building the same way he'd come in.

His bodyguard had no idea what that conversation was about, but he knew it was important. He also believed that it epitomized what Jeffrey did for a living, when he was not getting "massages."

The point of telling me the story was not just to convey that Epstein was powerful or scary or controlling, even over other powerful and scary people. To me, the point was that no matter what I knew about Epstein, there were many more layers to peel back and not many people who understood what lay at his core.

Before finishing our meeting, I asked the bodyguard what Epstein did with his days after being released from house arrest in Florida. "Girls. Always girls. I don't know the ages. I think they are nineteen, twenty, twenty-one. They are mainly models or something. Different girls all the time. Coming from everywhere. He tells them he can make them something. Then they do whatever he tells them to do. I don't think they are as young as the girls he got in trouble with before, but the damage he's done to these models is worse than what he did to the girls he went to jail because of in 2008. He controls them, then destroys lives."

Before we left, he made it clear that he was scared for my safety. He looked at me across our small round table, giving me a stern final warning: "Jeffrey Epstein is not someone to mess with. You know this, but you keep messing with him. Be careful."

"I will," I assured him before thanking him for meeting.

I got in my car and tried to scribble as many notes as I could, since I was not able to do so during the meeting. Then I thought about what he had said the whole hour-long ride home.

Until this meeting, I didn't really appreciate all that Sarah had been through. Nobody did. She was clearly damaged, and it took tremendous courage for her to come forward to help Virginia. She hadn't been a minor child when she was with Epstein, but what he had done to her was harmful and wrong. He promised to make her professional dreams come true in order to lure her in, then groomed her into having sex.

Was what he did to Sarah a crime? While the answer didn't jump off the page to me, it seemed criminal, especially after listening to his former bodyguard. Was it something Sarah could sue Epstein for? It seemed like the answer should be yes. I went back and looked at the statutes that were listed in the seven-page non-prosecution agreement, as surely Epstein and the government had studied Epstein's lifestyle to make sure he received immunity for his way of life. Looking through the crimes in the NPA one at a time, I came to 18 USC § 1591—one of the main federal statutes the U.S. attorney in the Southern District of Florida and Epstein's attorneys listed.

That statute designated as a crime the recruiting, enticing, transporting, or soliciting of someone by means of fraud, force, or coercion for sex. That is exactly what he had done to Sarah. Epstein had made false promises, which Sarah Ransome reasonably relied on to her detriment—the definition of fraud—in order to cause her to engage in sex. The civil counterpart of section 1591 was in section 1595, which allowed for a civil action for any criminal violation of 1591.

It was the second week of January 2017 when I was reading through this statute and quickly realized there was a ten-year statute of limitations. Had Sarah's claim already expired? Not yet. But I realized that it would expire in a few days, and even though she was just a witness whom I did not yet represent, I advised her of this fact. She wanted justice and wanted a complaint filed against everyone involved in the commission of any aspects of these acts immediately.

So, we filed the lawsuit on her behalf on January 26, 2017, against Epstein for his violation of the sex-trafficking statute; Ghislaine Maxwell for her role, which included instructing Sarah how she must perform various sex acts on Epstein; and Sarah Kellen and Lesley Groff for their role in facilitating the acts, which included carrying out the fraudulent promise to get her into FIT. While not filed on behalf of a child victim, as the others had been, it was another lawsuit filed on behalf of a brave victim that would help uncover other aspects of Jeffrey Epstein's abusive world.

# FORTY-THREE

# "YOU CANNOT BE SERIOUS"

H AVING FILED SARAH RANSOME'S CIVIL lawsuit, we turned back to Virginia's case against Ghislaine Maxwell, which was heating up for a trial set to begin on May 15, 2017. Our witnesses were lined up, our exhibits were ready, and we had already booked our hotels in New York for a month, including a large war room at the hotel across the street from the courthouse. The defense strategy had to be to try to exclude as much of the testimony and evidence as possible. They didn't really have more to hang their hats on.

There was one last deposition that we were going to take—Maxwell's, again. Because she refused to answer certain questions during her previous depositions, her next deposition was set to take place in the court-room with the judge serving as a special master. This deposition was set for the week before the trial, so it goes without saying that we were prepared.

While the protection of other victims was and always will be our main priority, our witnesses were ready to testify, and the truth about Epstein was finally going to become public. After decades, the justice system was going to expose Epstein's sex-trafficking operation.

In the week leading up to Maxwell's final deposition, hearings had also been scheduled by the court to address last-minute legal issues. Amid the chaos, a final mediation was scheduled so that the parties could take one last

312    BRADLEY J. EDWARDS

shot at a resolution before embarking on what was sure to be an explosive and costly legal battle.

Without consideration for the mediation, Sigrid and I continued to prepare for trial. We had more than one thousand exhibits to get in order and countless witnesses to line up. It was a massive event to put together, with our team working around the clock to get us ready. In my mind, there was no chance the case was going to settle. As a formality, nonetheless, Virginia arrived in New York early for mediation that was set to take place May 3, 2017. Sigrid and I didn't have time to be at mediation, so Stan and David went without us.

To this day, it pains me to think about this next part. I got a surprising late-night call from Stan. It was over. The case had settled on the eve of Maxwell's deposition, just days away from our arrival at the courthouse steps.

Because the details of the settlement had not been finalized and we knew by now that anything could happen, Sigrid and I continued to prepare for trial. We boarded our flights to New York for the hearing that was set to take place before Maxwell's final deposition. By the time we landed, the paperwork was signed, and the remaining obligations were canceled. Rather than turn around and go home, Sigrid and I met David and Stan at Cipriani in New York to discuss the events that had unfolded in the last few days. Sensing what I'm sure was my obvious frustration, David said to me, "I know that this is not the ending you were hoping for, but it's a great resolution for Virginia." He wasn't wrong. Virginia was happy, although she is a fighter and she was a little torn as well. Her perseverance had already caused the Epstein/Maxwell wall to crumble and she didn't need a trial to continue speaking her truth. She had proven herself. She had already won that round. Big time.

On the other hand, there was still a feeling of emptiness. I couldn't bring myself to say more than a few words the whole dinner. I left the restaurant uncertain where to go. I don't think I spoke a word until I got back to Florida the next morning. There were still unresolved issues for me. Jeffrey Epstein was still free.

The universe must have been sensing my inner turmoil because on June 9, 2017, while I was still sulking about the trial that never happened, the Florida Supreme Court resurrected my personal case against Epstein. This was huge for so many reasons. We had been about to go to trial back in 2013 when that chance was stolen right out from under me by some crazy legal opinion that turned the tables, creating a real risk that Epstein would be a massive creditor of mine with every incentive in the world to destroy me. Rather than bail on the case when I had the chance, as nearly everyone had encouraged me to do, I risked it all hoping that one day the court would rule in my favor and give me a chance to finish what I started. Today was that day.

We were going back to the trial court with my case against Epstein for the malicious prosecution that he had instituted against me in 2009. At least with my case, I could control the client. I *was* the client. The difficulty was that I didn't get to be the lawyer in this case. I did learn that, for me, it was much easier to be the lawyer. However, being the client in two very contentious cases has allowed me to better understand the vantage point of my own clients. It's not an easy position.

Between Sarah's case, and now my personal case, I had legal reason to continue my investigation of Epstein. This helped me get over the fact that he slipped out of the exposure that would have come from the Maxwell trial.

# FORTY-FOUR

# JULIE

O N JULY 27, 2017, an investigative reporter for the *Miami Herald* named Julie Brown reached out to me. Up to that point, more than one hundred reporters had done the same, all asking for information about some aspect of the cases against Jeffrey Epstein. Some had inquired about the criminal investigation, others about the federal process that had resulted in the non-prosecution agreement, but few had dug deep to try to understand the case we had filed for victims under the Crime Victims' Rights Act.

There was a fair amount of arcane legal stuff in the CVRA case, which meant most reporters were understandably not interested. Still, the case highlighted a two-tier system of justice that worked differently for the rich than it did for common people. That was something we had now proven and that the public deserved to know.

Part of the reason for the case's low profile was probably me. For the most part, I don't speak much to the media, particularly during litigation. Sometimes it is unavoidable, but my general philosophy is not to do so unless it gives my client an advantage of some kind, such as the likelihood that helpful new witnesses might come forward. There were times, for instance, when we were looking for witnesses that I would speak to reporters and give them enough information that might prompt new witnesses to call our office or law enforcement. But speaking needlessly about an active case to the media just to get a story out there has never interested me.

When the email came in from Julie Brown, my initial instinct was to ignore it. I knew she was an investigative journalist for the *Miami Herald*, but it was also evident that she knew nothing about the case. So much had transpired over the past nine years that for her to catch up and write a meaningful and accurate piece—one that wasn't a regurgitation of previous stories—was, I thought, unlikely. It would also take a lot of my time, which forced me to ask, to what end? What would my clients get out of my taking time to become her source and shape her reporting?

Before I dismissed her altogether, I read the email out loud in the conference room where my team was preparing another matter for trial. Brittany told me, "You should really think about talking to Julie. I read some of her work on abuse in Florida prisons and it was good. She really investigates before she writes." Brittany was working on multiple high-profile civil rights cases at the time, so she had paid close attention to those articles.

I started to rethink ignoring Julie's email. I looked at her other projects online and it was evident that she was not half-assed in her reporting. Unlike a lot of others, she also appeared to have the patience to cover a story from multiple angles, and not rush to publish too quickly.

What's more, there was something bothering me about the case, something that a reporter willing to put in the time could help remedy. From the first cases filed against Epstein, the media had grouped our victims together and treated them as one collective identity whose voices didn't merit being heard. Even the few girls—now grown women—who had tried to speak were silenced by the bullying lawyers who represented the "misunderstood," politically connected philanthropist Jeffrey Epstein. Anyone who was identified as one of Epstein's victims was labeled as nothing more than a prostitute, because the charges that had been conjured up by Epstein's camp, the federal government, and the Palm Beach State Attorney's Office allowed him to plead guilty for "soliciting prostitution or procuring a minor for prostitution." Those prior reports lumping the victims together added to their suffering, making them seem like faceless, voiceless, meaningless objects—exactly as Epstein had wanted.

By this stage of the case, when I'd spoken to more than fifty victims, these characterizations of "the victims" as not having individual identities or being real people bothered me a great deal. I knew the backgrounds of the survivors, and who they were before they'd met Jeffrey Epstein. I had learned a lot about their early lives, what problems they had faced, what vulnerabilities they had displayed, and what had happened to them after they'd been abused and had tried to move on. I had known some for years and considered them friends. They deserved an identity, for the world to understand how brave and strong and special they were.

Was Julie the reporter who could help me breathe personality into the empty stereotypes that had been given to the public about the Epstein victims? While I was giving as many clients as I could a voice through the legal process, was Julie someone who could understand the facts well enough to help elevate those voices beyond the legal arena? If the answer was yes, was it worth the risk and the enormous amount of time it would take to help Julie catch up? Above all, I wanted to do what was best for my clients, which I knew might mean meeting with Julie.

I decided to at least respond to her email and invite her over to the office. In many regards, our first meeting was like all the others I'd had with reporters who claimed to want to do what Julie was saying she wanted to do. I had accumulated all of the evidence in these cases and done all of the work. Unable to imagine the scope of that decade-long task, or how voluminous the materials were and how complicated piecing it together really was, Julie, like other reporters, wanted to start with my just spoon-feeding her everything and making it simple.

I wasn't about to do that. Not because I didn't want to help, but because that approach wouldn't get her or me where we wanted to go. Her goal, she said, was to give the public the chance to hear from the victims themselves and to expose how the legal system and the media had failed them. Sure, I could have just let her interview several of my clients and put it into a story. But she would not have put any time into the story herself, so she wouldn't appreciate the necessary complexities. In turn, the result wouldn't be very good. Before she left my office, I told her I would help.

I made a list of things that she could review to understand the facts as well as the defenses that had been lodged against us, the labels that had been attached to the victims, and the bullying tactics that had allowed the bad guys to control the message in the past.

With my list as a guide, I told her where to go to find each public filing and piece of the case against Epstein on her own. I told her who to serve with Freedom of Information Act (FOIA) requests and where to get the pleadings that contained information she would find useful. Most reporters, I think, would have decided to focus on a short-term aspect of the story or begged for blind victim interviews. To Julie's credit, she didn't fall into that trap. She followed the road map and stayed on course.

At the beginning of her investigation, Julie was shocked by what she was finding. At other times, she was amazed. She would call me to ask questions, and her questions were good. She cared about getting the answers right. When I told her where to look to cross-check something, she would typically call back the same day to verify what I had told her. Often during that process she would, of course, discover other information that I had known at some point but had forgotten. As much as I was helping her with her story, if the end product was half-decent it would be enormously valuable to my clients' pursuit of justice.

# FORTY-FIVE

# COIN TOSS

AROUND THE TIME THE MAXWELL case ended, the partners in my law firm—Farmer, Jaffe, Weissing, Edwards, Fistos & Lehrman—were going in different directions.

All of us had risen from the ashes that Scott Rothstein had left behind and built a respected boutique law firm in Fort Lauderdale. Over eight years, we had created something that every one of us was proud of. But now, it was clear, it was on its way out—dying not for bad reasons but for good ones. Gary Farmer was now a Florida state senator with a life devoted to Florida politics, spending much of his time in Tallahassee. Steve Jaffe was ready to move on from the national networking in the class action area to the next phase of his career as a mediator. One way or another, changes had happened for us all.

We were all still friends, but I wanted to run my own firm my own way. It was bittersweet for me when we decided to split up—I was sad to see it end, but excited to start my new firm.

By this time, I was representing crime victims in high-profile cases around the country and trying a wide variety of civil cases. I felt that my core trial team was the best at what we did. As we were organizing the new firm, I got a crazy idea, one of those ideas you have to run past other people you trust before you act on it. Brittany was in the conference room with

Maria Kelljchian, our exceptional paralegal. Maria was the other person in our legal universe I trusted. Neither Brittany nor Maria was shy about giving me her opinions, especially if they were criticizing my ideas. So I asked, "What do you think about the idea of us having a New York office and asking Stan Pottinger if he wants to be my law partner?" Both reacted almost immediately with reasons why they thought it would be a great fit.

But look: Stan, in my view, was David Boies's personal 007. Not that either of them would put it that way, but I did. I thought that there was a pretty good chance that my proposition could make Stan laugh—though he'd be too diplomatic to do that out loud. I mean, who was I kidding? But I didn't have much time to game the idea. My old firm was winding down fast and I was trying to do a million things to get the new one started.

It took Stan no time to say, "I'm in." David Boies, he said, had told him long ago that forming a small firm had many appealing advantages and tempted virtually all lawyers at one time or another. But there was that inescapable problem to solve, and Stan brought it up: "Now we have to decide whose name goes first." I told him that I really didn't care, and I meant it. He said he felt the same way. He took out a quarter and said, "Heads or tails?"

I said, "Heads, of course."

He flipped the coin, put it on the back of his hand, and said without showing it to me, "You win, Edwards Pottinger it is." I still wonder whether the coin landed on heads or tails. He knows, of course, but he'll never tell me. He did once say, though, "The future belongs to you, m'boy, and the name of the firm should show it."

In December 2017, our new firm, in both Fort Lauderdale and New York City, was off and running.

---

We turned back to my ongoing malicious prosecution case against Epstein, knowing that the trial date would be here in just a few months. To win, we had to prove that Epstein knew that he had made knowingly false allegations in the complaint he filed against me many years prior. One of his allegations was that I took the depositions of his pilots and aggressively sought the flight logs of his private planes even though he said I knew that no underage girls had been on his plane. The wacky conclusion he drew in the complaint from this assertion was that I could only have been in aggressive pursuit of the pilots and logs because I wanted to further the RRA Ponzi scheme.

This, of course, was all untrue. Epstein knew there were underage girls on his plane and that I had the proof. On top of the flight logs, Epstein knew I was now Virginia's attorney, something he didn't predict happening when he made the false allegations. Virginia could conclusively establish that Epstein's premise was knowingly false because she was one of the minors who had traveled on Epstein's plane for the purpose of being sexually victimized.

Once the Florida Supreme Court ruled in my favor to let my case proceed against Epstein, Epstein's attorneys asked immediately to take Virginia's deposition. I guess they thought she might resist a deposition because her case against Maxwell had just settled and she was safely back in Australia. Who—even Virginia—would now want to get involved in this Epstein-Edwards saga? The answer was . . . Virginia. Epstein's team's hope that her commitment had dwindled could not have been more wrong. Over the years, she knew that I was not only her lawyer but also the subject of Epstein's bullying and intimidation. If there was a fight in which she felt her voice could make a difference, she was all in. I had stood up for her, and she would be there for me. Epstein and his team had underestimated us.

In October 2017, Virginia flew from Australia to the United States for her deposition in my case against Jeffrey Epstein. Once Epstein's attorneys realized that she was going to show up, and after she was already on the ground in the United States, they canceled her deposition. Epstein was no idiot; he knew Virginia too well. He, too, knew this was not the testimony he wanted.

We had already flown up to New York for Virginia's deposition. Even though it was canceled, we weren't simply going to put Virginia on a plane and send her back to Australia. Instead, Stan, Brittany, Sigrid, and I took her out to dinner at Trattoria Dell'Arte in midtown Manhattan. The whole group was on a high. Virginia's life was finally settling down in Australia after the media attention and spotlight had been on her for at least six years. We had just called their bluff on wanting to depose Virginia. My lawsuit had been revitalized. Stan and I were starting our new law firm. We were discovering new witnesses with new details about Epstein's sex-fueled organization all the time, which would allow us to one day do something with that information. Everything was falling into place.

Anyone looking at the table from outside would never know what we had all been through together, or the serious subject matter that had brought us there that night. We looked like a bunch of friends who had known each other forever, cracking jokes and telling stories. While Brittany was playing her normal role of asking Stan a million questions about whether he was in the Secret Service or MI6 or the CIA or some such thing, Stan was busy putting on a show for her amusement. With an unseen party behind him, he accidentally backhanded a glass of wine off the table and into the lap of the gentleman sitting behind us.

Stan apologized profusely, and the well-humored man at the other table was totally cool. The story we were telling at our own table was so funny that the flying wineglass became part of it. Everyone at our table and the other one was laughing uncontrollably. Mid-routine, Stan realized that he knew this guy—of course he did—from some prior life. He was David Letterman's announcer, Alan Kalter. No wonder, we thought, that he was so funny and good-humored. He'd endured ribbings from Letterman for years.

The scene that we were causing in the restaurant now was nothing short of a spectacle. Brittany, without missing a beat, left the table and disappeared. We thought she was looking for someone to clean up the spilled wine, but shortly after her return, three different birthday cakes were carted out to our table with massive sparklers shooting fire and flames out everywhere.

Everyone at the table was looking around, trying to figure out what was going on, until all three cakes were placed directly in front of Stan. Brittany began to sing "Happy Birthday" to him, even though, of course, it was not his birthday. But it was a smooth way on Brittany's part to handle the wine-spilling situation. Stan turned around and gave Kalter a whole birthday cake with a sparkler still fired up. Kalter had been fabulous from the start, and now he was even more so, joining into what was a fake birthday celebration but a celebration nonetheless. Everyone at both our tables sang "Happy Birthday" to Stan as the rest of the restaurant took a New York glimpse.

This fake birthday celebration started a ridiculous tradition we have followed ever since. Brittany has never gone to a restaurant with Stan without celebrating a fake birthday. Whether in New York or in Florida, in Ricky's, our favorite chicken wing shack (my choice) or a great restaurant in the city like Cipriani's (Stan's), it is always Stan's birthday and there is some celebration that inevitably draws in the other people in the restaurant. Funny how that works, but it does. And no matter how many times it happens, Stan is still caught off guard (or pretends to be). If he had birthdays as often as we celebrated them, he would be two hundred years old.

At the end of that night, I knew this was going to be a great partnership. The craziest part is that neither Brittany nor I have any idea when his actual birthday is. We figure it doesn't really matter since we celebrate it every time we see him.

# FORTY-SIX

# BRING IT ON

IN LIGHT OF THE UPCOMING malicious prosecution trial, Epstein changed his legal team, yet again. In the background, he still had the same lawyers advising him at the top: Marty Weinberg, Darren Indyke, the lawyers at Steptoe & Johnson, the lawyers at Kirkland & Ellis, and a handful of other firms. There was no end to the lawyers he could afford, and no end to his tactics to delay the trial. His lead trial counsel now was Scott Link and Kara Rockenbach from the Florida firm Link & Rockenbach.

As an aside, proving that we live in a small world, Kara Rockenbach had recently divorced Bard Rockenbach, whose firm had served as my appellate counsel and helped me win my case at the Florida Supreme Court. Link & Rockenbach was a brand-new law firm that had started up with one big client—Jeffrey Epstein. They spent every waking hour on this case, knowing that Epstein wouldn't have had it any other way.

Judge Hafele was quick to set the trial in my case for December 2017 with a strict instruction that there would be no continuances. Despite that and despite the judge's authority, I knew right away that his ruling was never going to stick because the system just wasn't prepared for a litigant like Jeff Epstein and his extraordinary ability to manipulate everyone and everything. Still, by this point, Judge Hafele knew that he was the one who'd sent the case up on appeal and that the longer he let it sit around, the better the chances were that Epstein would use his money and resources to keep the case languishing forever. So the judge was very stern.

Link & Rockenbach, brand new to the case, first explained that they needed to take my deposition. This would not have been a big deal if this were the first, or second, or even third time that my deposition had been taken, but this one would be the fourth. Scott Link was asking for seven hours with me, and since so much time had passed since my last deposition, the court allowed it.

In 2017, the deposition landscape was different from before for many reasons. In a way, I was now much more comfortable and accustomed to being in the witness chair. But the case had begun eight years prior, and had been on appeal for so long that the passage of time itself had become an issue. A deposition should be easy, right? Just tell the truth. But it wasn't humanly possible to remember every single detail of a litigation that had spun off into many related cases, from the CVRA case to dozens of cases against Jeffrey Epstein on behalf of victims; to my defamation case against Dershowitz; to representing Virginia against Ghislaine Maxwell; to representing Sarah Ransome against Epstein, Maxwell, Kellen, and Groff; and to this personal battle with Jeffrey that had itself spanned the entire range of directions that any case could travel.

In this case alone we'd had multiple claims, multiple counterclaims, the dismissal of the original claim, the dismissal of the counterclaim, Epstein's retention of at least five different law firms, and movement of the case from the trial court to an appellate court to the Florida Supreme Court and back down to the original court for trial.

Nobody knew the details as well as I did. But there were many details that I didn't know as well in 2017 as I had in 2009. I also didn't know Scott Link. I knew he'd been hired with the singular purpose of getting as much ammunition against me as he could and to attack me from every angle possible.

Before this deposition, I reviewed the prior three. Reading those transcripts brought me back to the first one. It had been taken March 23, 2010, just four months after I'd been served with Epstein's complaint alleging my partnership with Rothstein in the Ponzi scheme. Epstein was trying to show maximum intimidation that day. The deposition had been held in Jack Scarola's office and we were told that Bob Critton, Epstein's lawyer at the time, was going to take it.

Jack and I had walked into the conference room where the deposition was to be held. There was a large video camera at one end shooting down toward the other end with a blue backdrop and a chair where the witness would sit. I had never been in that witness seat myself, but I had seen many other people there. I never until that day really appreciated the feeling of being a deponent. That seat is much different from every other seat in the room.

I was confident, of course, because the facts were on my side, but that doesn't stop good lawyers from tripping up truthful witnesses. It happens all the time. Still, when I sat down, I thought it was simply going to be a deposition by Bob Critton. Critton was someone whom I knew well by this time through my cases representing Epstein's victims, and I couldn't understand why he'd agreed to represent Jeffrey against me. He didn't seem like the kind of person who would sell his soul for money.

But there we were. He was stacking up boxes of documents behind him when his associate Michael Pike came in and sat at the other end of the table. Darren Indyke, Epstein's virtual in-house counsel, also sat at the table. Jack Goldberger then walked into the room, another familiar face. Finally, Jeffrey Epstein and Alan Dershowitz filed in, with Dershowitz sitting closest to Critton, who was closest to me.

While I had wanted to take Dershowitz's deposition in the past, I had never been able to do so, which meant we'd never been in the same room until now. As he sat down and looked at me, I smiled and said, "Wow, for you to be here, I must be really important." He didn't laugh, he just stared straight-faced like a mad shar-pei. I said, "That's too bad, you can't even laugh at my jokes." Again, he still didn't crack a smile. Jeffrey did, though.

The deposition started with Critton straining to imply through his questions that I was in the know during my five-month employment at RRA. He had nothing, though, so he got nowhere. At one point, he tried to insinuate that because Rothstein wore nice suits and owned various properties, which I did not know about, I should have known that he was running a Ponzi scheme. Every point he was trying to make was unconnected and problematic for him.

The last quantum leap was a truly laughable stretch. It really didn't take more than five minutes before I settled in and realized that it didn't matter what quality of lawyer was taking the deposition, or that Dershowitz was madly passing notes to Critton, covertly asking most of the questions. Epstein's lawsuit against me was a contrived pile of trash. Jeffrey stacked half a dozen lawyers up to conceal the falsity of the allegations.

Reading that first deposition, I realized that I had been highly confident because the facts had been so fresh in my mind. Every detail that could possibly be relevant was new or recent back then. After that first one, quite a bit of time had passed before Epstein's lawyers had taken my next depositions, which were on May 15, 2013, and again on October 10, 2013.

Reading the second deposition, in May of that year, I was reminded that it had been nerve-racking for a different reason. It was taken by Fred Haddad, who was a legend in our local courtrooms. He looked unassuming but was for years involved in nearly every high-profile case in town. He was the guy who would walk into hearings wearing jeans, an old jacket, and shoes with no socks. He was constantly making jokes and pretending not to know what was going on while really having mastered every fact in every case. His shtick was a scary one because he could ease the opposition into thinking he was a friend only to chop their heads off with the next question.

In my own deposition, he rightly tried to stick to the case. But we had a history between us, so the banter would quickly devolve into personal stories of his clients whom I had prosecuted as a state prosecutor years before, or to his taking shots at me for supposedly overprosecuting those cases. At one point, I came back at him for his familiarity with divorce lawyers in town because he had hired one himself a time or two. We both had a laugh. The other lawyers in the room really didn't know what to do with us. Jeffrey had his army of serious attorneys over there and it was really just Fred and me firing back and forth and having a little too much fun.

Fred had a hard time accusing me of what Jeffrey was accusing me of. At the time, Fred was representing Russ Adler in the criminal case that the U.S. Attorney's Office was then prosecuting against him for his activities in the Ponzi scheme and RRA. Russ's name was on the firm's door, and the best that the government could come up with was to stick him with a charge for an illegal campaign contribution. Fred was confident in his representation of Russ, knowing that he was not an intricate part of the Ponzi scheme or any of the serious crimes that went along with it. So, accusing me of being involved, given that I was many levels under Russ while at RRA, was way too far-fetched for Fred.

Rather than attempt to attack me for being involved in a Ponzi scheme that he knew as well as anyone I had nothing to do with, Fred instead took the high ground and sought to dismiss my case on grounds that I had suffered no damages from Epstein's malicious allegations.

To prove this point, Fred presented me with my various legal commendations. He wanted to get me to admit that after Jeffrey Epstein sued me, my status as a trial lawyer had only continued to elevate. He made me admit that the various awards I had received were not any I had applied for but were distinctions I had received as a result of recommendations and recognitions by my peers. He then went through a list of settlements and large jury verdicts I had won for clients despite my allegations that Epstein's lies had hurt me.

He had a point. I saw where he was going but couldn't do much about it.

Next he went back to 2009, when the Ponzi scheme had destroyed the RRA law firm. When Jeffrey Epstein attacked me with false allegations in 2009, my reputation as a lawyer on a national scale was virtually unknown, a fact I could not deny.

Fast-forward four years, and by all objective ratings my profile had increased exponentially. His whole argument was that, even assuming Jeffrey Epstein intended to harm me with a false complaint against me, I had to concede that it had not worked. I had not, he said, suffered any damages. He stated on the record that I not only had to prove Epstein's malicious intent, but also that his falsehoods had caused provable damages to me. Without them, I simply had no lawsuit.

Before that point, Epstein had hired wind-up-doll lawyers that would march ahead in lockstep, carrying out his orders by attempting to prove the unsupportable false allegations he had filed against me. That strategy made my life easy. Fred's strategy did not. His quick change in focus on different elements of the case—causation and damages rather than liability—caught me off guard.

Fred took my deposition twice and gained some ground in each. I left the third deposition thinking that if I was on their side and had to try this case, I would admit to the wrongdoing of filing the false complaint and put all my eggs in the no-damages basket.

---

Here we were, on November 10, 2017, and I was about to have another deposition, my fourth, taken. Epstein's side of the table was filled with lawyers, as always. Darren Indyke, who was a staple at every Epstein event, was situated in his normal spot at the far end of the table in order to monitor and report back to Epstein everything that happened. Next to him was Jack Goldberger. But this time, there were some unfamiliar faces, too. In the next chair was a sandy-haired woman, wearing glasses. I later learned that she was the paralegal. Next to her and closer to me was a lawyer whom I did not know at the time but came to know as Kara Rockenbach. Closest to me was Scott Link, the main litigator now holding the Epstein reigns.

Scott was a longtime insurance defense lawyer with a reputation for being fearless in the courtroom. He and his legal team had at least ten Bankers boxes of material in the room. Every piece of material was marked and all of the lawyers on their side seemed to have reviewed every document in every box. They still had to work with bad facts, given that their client had falsely and maliciously attempted to ruin my business and professional reputation, but throughout the seven hours of examination Scott chipped away and scored points where points could be scored.

He picked up where Fred had left off a few years before. By that point, I was running a successful law firm and had many well-publicized settlements and trials. I went into that deposition thinking that Epstein had hired a new lawyer who would be ill-prepared and might try to prove what was false and unprovable. I left knowing that he had a legal team that was dedicating 100 percent of its time to this case and was intent on disproving my damages claim.

This was problematic, and Scott was taking the point further than Fred had taken it. Scott was saying not only that since Epstein's malicious complaint had been filed against me in 2009 my career had improved, but also that many significant and high-profile cases I had handled had come to me as a result of Epstein. In short, he was saying that Jeffrey Epstein's malicious action against me was the best thing to ever happen to me. Scott was very good, and his approach effective, a fact I realized while in the witness chair. But I couldn't do much about it. This move made our case much more complicated.

The case was set to go to trial on December 5, 2017. Unsurprisingly, Epstein again moved for a last-minute continuance, which the judge granted despite having guaranteed that there wouldn't be any additional continuations. He set the new trial date on March 13, 2018. Epstein's team was filing new motions nearly every day in an effort to limit the scope of the case and ensure that the jury would see less and less of the evidence we had accumulated on Epstein and his sexual misconduct.

Judge Hafele was meticulous and thoughtful about striking a fair balance between allowing enough of the underlying information about Epstein's sex activities to create a context, but not allowing so much that it would be prejudicial to Epstein. Of course, it was our position that the jury should hear everything.

It was only after a full presentation of all the available evidence of Epstein's crimes and his large number of co-conspirators that, we argued, the jury could assess the degree of maliciousness of Epstein's false claims about me.

Jeffrey Epstein's team took an extreme view in the other direction. From their standpoint the case should have been limited to only the information that was available to Jeffrey Epstein about the RRA Ponzi scheme. That was all the jury needed in order to determine whether Epstein had any basis for believing I could have been involved. All of the allegations of sexual crimes he committed should be kept out.

Judge Hafele took hours of arguments and presentations before ruling on what evidence the jury would and would not hear. Ultimately, he ruled that in the summer of 2009, when I was working at RRA, I was the lead attorney in charge of litigating cases against Jeffrey Epstein on behalf of three individuals—Courtney, Lynn, and Marissa. The discovery that was being sought during that time was related to those cases. Therefore the jury would be able to hear from those three victims and could assess the validity of the discovery I took. However, Courtney, Lynn, and Marissa's testimony was going to be restricted significantly. They could testify about their ages when they were recruited and say that the illegal sexual conduct had been committed against them on multiple occasions. However, the play-by-play and gruesome details of that conduct, and the extraordinary way in which it had damaged their lives, was going to be excised from this trial. The court felt that this type of testimony would be more prejudicial than probative, or, said differently, more harmful to Epstein than relevant to what the jury had to decide.

Virginia Roberts would also be allowed to testify, but only in a limited capacity. She was directly knowledgeable of the falsity of some of the allegations Epstein had made in order to justify his claims. Judge Hafele was going to allow her to testify about the fact that she had traveled on Epstein's plane while underage, for example (despite Epstein's insistence that no underage girls were ever on his plane), and a few other very narrow points, but nothing else.

The dozens of other victims who could have explained in horrid detail the factory of abuse that Epstein had created were not going to be allowed to testify in this trial. For Epstein, this ruling from the judge was a huge win.

In every trial, there are these types of legal arguments about what the jury should get to hear or see. I watched as Judge Hafele carefully decided. While I had not agreed with some of the comments he had made many years prior, I believe he treated both parties fairly and that his rulings on what would be admitted into evidence made sense. He was letting us admit enough evidence to prove that Jeffrey Epstein had filed a false complaint against me for the purposes of extortion and intimidation, but he was not letting us admit evidence that might lead a jury to find in my favor based on the serial nature of Epstein's sexual abuse. While this was not the case we wanted to present, it was fair.

# FORTY-SEVEN

# MY HERO IS GONE BUT NEVER FORGOTTEN

MORE IMPORTANT TO ME THAN any case was the fact that Papa was not doing well. He had played tennis until he was almost ninety years old, at which point he had a total knee replacement. He thought that after the operation he would be serving and volleying again. I did, indeed, take him out on the tennis court, but he never played competitively again. It sounds kind of funny to say that a ninety-year-old not competing was a big deal, but up to that point it was hard to imagine his not making it to the club every day for at least a few games. To give you an idea of how much tennis and competition meant to Papa, I'll tell a story. The last match he played before his surgery was against my father-in-law, Manny, who was forty years younger. While not a lifelong tennis player, Manny was a good athlete and was determined to beat my octogenarian grandfather. Papa started serving and on the first point, tripped over his shoe lace and fell on his face.

I ran to help him up, "Are you okay?" "Did he return my serve?" Papa immediately responded. "Yeah, he did." "Then I'm not okay," Papa said, making clear that the result of the point was all that really mattered.

Papa got up. And Papa won. Unfortunately, that would be his last singles match.

After his surgery, I watched as his health slowly declined. We talked four or five times a week about sports, the kids, my law practice, politics, and whatever else came up. But it was still sad watching his final days come.

My mom called and told me he was in the hospital and that he didn't look well, so I flew to Jacksonville to see him, taking my wife and oldest son with me. We had decided that our two younger sons were too young for that experience, so they stayed home with my in-laws. It was December 22, 2017, and we visited with Papa in the hospital. He was ninety-six. The doctors had diagnosed him with acute leukemia and given him only a few more days to live. My cousin and I went to his house and made up his bed so that he could come home for those final hours.

Papa was too weak to get out of bed, but never too weak to crack jokes. He was still challenging my oldest son to tennis matches on his deathbed. "Blake," he called out to my son, "come here." Blake approached the bedside thinking his great-grandfather may need something. "You want to get our rackets and go play? You might have a shot at winning today." He told Terry how pretty she was and how lucky I was that he hadn't met her first. He remembered so many things even I had forgotten, and all day I sat and listened as he still commanded the room.

He talked about his old stick-shift Datsun that he taught me to drive when I was thirteen years old. He blamed me for losing a doubles match he and I had played when I was twelve against two ladies at his club. This, of course, prompted me to remind him of the first time I had beaten him, later that same year. We laughed together about all our good times.

I had to get back home for Christmas, so I was trying to tell him goodbye. But I knew that it was a different kind of goodbye from others, and of course he knew it, too.

Terry was hugging him on one side of the bed, with my son on the other. When they left the room, he sensed that I was trying to tell him a deeply felt and final goodbye. He wouldn't let me do it. Instead, he said, "Don't do this, I am going to be fine."

I said, "I know you are, and I can't wait to see you again, but if anything happens and I don't, then just know I already miss you."

Flying home, none of us on the plane talked to each other. When we woke up the next day, on Christmas morning, my kids were happy to see that Santa Claus had come during the night. We were hosting Terry's family and I called to check in with my mom.

Shortly after we hung up, Papa died. Christmas was always his favorite day of the year. I decided to assume that since he never wanted anyone to be sad, he had chosen to die on Christmas when we would all be forced to be happy, that day and for all the Christmases to come. According to the doctors, he should have died days before, but he held on until it was the right time.

Any time I ever had a difficult decision to make, I would call Papa and ask what he would do. Whether I had been leaning that way or not, I nearly always went with the advice he gave me. He had never steered me wrong.

That didn't change after he died. I would think about what he would do and hear his advice as if he were still alive. Even though he was ninety-six, I was still heartbroken that he was gone. He had shaped my life and guided me in so many ways, it was impossible to add them all up. I flew to Jacksonville, gave the eulogy through my tears at his funeral, said goodbye, and sadly flew back home to Fort Lauderdale.

I needed a new focus after his death, a way to dedicate myself to something in the way Papa had dedicated his life to his family. With our first trial coming up under the new Edwards Pottinger name, I turned all of my attention to the client who needed our help the most at that time, certain that this was what Papa would have told me to do.

In January 2018, we represented a young woman who'd been sexually assaulted while working as a steward aboard a 150-foot private yacht docked in a Fort Lauderdale marina. After a long and hard-fought trial, the jury returned a verdict in favor of our client for almost $71 million, which we were told was the largest verdict in a single-plaintiff sexual assault lawsuit in

U.S. history. I sensed Papa was proud looking down. It was justice for our client. Unfortunately, it also added to Epstein's primary defense in my lawsuit against him because it allowed him to argue that my results as a lawyer continued to improve, and thus I hadn't been damaged by anything he'd said in his complaint.

Trade-offs are always part of law practice. This was the ultimate example of that.

# FORTY-EIGHT

# THE FUN NEVER STOPS

W HILE I WAS TRYING THE yacht assault case, Epstein, through his lawyers Link & Rockenbach, was busy taking last-minute trial depositions in my personal case.

Jack Scarola sent me the transcript of the deposition of former RRA attorney Bill Berger, during which Bill was asked questions that told me Scott Link had in his possession certain emails that were attorney-client privileged and never should have been turned over to Epstein. I told Jack that Epstein's having gotten hold of them was not just a hunch, it was a fact. Jack, not totally convinced, said, "We'll see." Because of this transcript, despite being overwhelmed with the other trial, I paid close attention to the exhibit lists that were being exchanged in anticipation of the Epstein trial.

On March 2, 2018, just before the trial was set to begin, Epstein's counsel filed a pleading that included at least forty-nine privileged emails spanning more than one hundred pages. The emails had never been lawfully provided to Epstein or his counsel. They were emails where I was discussing my client with other lawyers from my firm in 2009. The emails included information on the strengths and weaknesses of our cases as well as our legal and tactical strategy—the exact type of information that would give an adversary an unfair advantage, and which an adversary is prohibited from obtaining. Jack was shocked that Epstein had them and that the privilege had been violated. I myself was not surprised. I had told everyone years before that this was going to happen. Epstein always got what he wanted, especially that to which he was not entitled to have.

I knew from experience that laws and court rules never stood in the way of Jeffrey Epstein. His manipulation permeated everything he did. The nature of the emails forced us to do something about it, though, because the attorney-client privilege is sacrosanct. It is a privilege belonging to the client that can't be waived by the attorney. When the stolen emails were written back in 2009, I was the attorney working on behalf of Courtney, Lynn, and Marissa. Now, I was the protector of them and their private information. My being the client in this other case did not make it okay for protected information to be disseminated to Epstein.

We raised the violation with Judge Hafele that same day, which happened to be the Friday before trial was set to begin. The court ultimately ruled that these newly listed privileged exhibits could not be used at trial and would not form the basis of a last-minute continuance—a delay we all knew was one of Epstein's objectives. True to form, Epstein had his lawyers file a last-minute emergency appeal of the judge's ruling protecting the documents. My appellate lawyers at Burlington & Rockenbach were confident that the Fourth District Court of Appeal would not take the appeal from Epstein's lawyers at Link & Rockenbach. I was not so sure.

About three hours after we had left the courtroom and Epstein had filed his appeal, the appellate court ruled that his appeal had been accepted. Epstein got his emergency continuance yet again. Everyone on our side was mad as hell and trying to call me to give me some crazy explanation as to why this happened. I was at the movies with my kids and my phone was going off like a slot machine in Vegas. I silenced it. By the time I got out, I had more than twenty messages about how surprising it was that the Fourth had taken Epstein's emergency appeal. I wasn't as upset as they were, simply because I was used to Epstein getting his way and had always believed this was going to happen. We did everything we could and eventually we would get our day, but until then, if a delay of this kind could be won, Epstein would win it.

I looked at the glass as half-full. As much as I wanted the trial and as prepared as we were, this was March and we were overloaded with work trying to secure our client's judgment in the yacht case. This delay allowed both sides to figure out exactly how Epstein had come into possession of privileged materials he had never been given. It didn't take me more than a second to know how this had happened. From the moment I read the questions in the deposition of Bill Berger, before the leaked emails had even been filed, I'd told Jack that Epstein had obtained them from Fowler White, his former law firm in Miami.

On March 7, just days after the initial filing of the emails as trial exhibits, my suspicions were confirmed when Scott Link delivered a flash drive to Jack "duplicating the disc [he] located in Fowler White's files." The thousands of emails on that disc included an internal stamp indicating that the files had been last modified on December 8, 2010—the precise day that Special Master Carney's copy of the RRA emails was delivered over our strong objection to Fowler White, with an order by bankruptcy Judge Ray to make a hard copy of the privileged emails and "not retain any copies."

As we had forewarned everyone in 2010, allowing Fowler White to have the documents was truly allowing a fox to guard the henhouse. And now, here we were in 2018 learning that the fox had eaten the hen. We filed a legal motion to hold Fowler White in contempt in federal court in front of Judge Raymond Ray, who had presided over the entire RRA bankruptcy matter and who had signed an order on November 30, 2010, specifically directing that:

> The law firm of Fowler White Burnett, P.A., will print a hard copy of all of the documents contained on the discs with Bates numbers added, and will provide a set of copied, stamped documents to the Special Master and an identical set to Farmer [my law firm], who will use same to create its privilege log. . . . *Fowler White will not retain any copies of the documents contained on the discs provided to it, nor shall any images or copies of said documents be retained in the*

*memory of Fowler White's copiers* [emphasis added]. Should it be determined that Fowler White or Epstein retained images or copies of the subject documents on its computer or otherwise, the Court retains jurisdiction to award sanctions in favor of Farmer, Brad Edwards, or his client.

Fowler White had the disc the order directed them not to have. And now, Epstein had it.

Outside the courtroom all of the lawyers were talking about the fact that the violation was obvious. Judge Ray let us take the sworn deposition of a Fowler White representative to get to the bottom of how the CD of emails came into Epstein's possession. That representative testified truthfully that the disc now in Scott Link's possession had been located in the bottom of one of the Fowler White boxes and, as such, had been transferred to Scott Link when he took over representation of Epstein. The representative confirmed that the disc had been last modified on December 8, 2010, a date on which the documents were in the possession only of Fowler White. While he personally was unsure of what happened to the disc afterward, he was sure there was an inventory in 2014 that had listed the disc as being in Fowler White's possession before all of the boxes had been sent to storage. This testimony established the Fowler White breach.

We went to a final hearing and, from an outsider's point of view, there were very few disagreements between the parties. Epstein now had in his possession a copy of the exact materials that Judge Ray's 2010 order expressly precluded him from having. Despite knowing that we should win, I never got the feeling that Judge Ray saw it that way. As sad as it was, it came as no surprise to me when Judge Ray found a way to rule against us. Epstein called me the day the ruling came out to laugh at Judge Ray's ruling. "It's a funny ruling, isn't it, Brad. My lawyers kept the disc and still got a ruling in their favor. I wonder how that happened," he said, tongue in cheek. I wasn't going to let him get to me.

This already extraordinarily complicated case, where everything had been determined and yet nothing was certain, was set for a month-long trial now in December 2018. We began to prepare our mock trial, where Jack would represent me in front of a room full of three mock juries composed of approximately seventeen people total. I decided that in the mock trial, I would be the one to assume the role of Jeffrey Epstein's attorney.

For my entire trial career, in mock trials I always represented the defense. I had paid very close attention to the problems in our case and the defenses that scared me most, and no one knew Epstein better than I did. Certainly, no one knew my case's weaknesses better than I did. We had to make sure that the mock juries did not know the real identities of the lawyers and whom we really represented, otherwise they would realize who I was in the scheme of things and it would naturally bias the outcome.

On Epstein's side, I had put together all the defenses I would present if I had been representing Epstein, including all those defenses his various attorneys had cooked up over the years, particularly the "no damages" argument Scott Link had developed by this time. The liability case was tough to defend on behalf of Epstein. It was undeniable. The evidence demonstrably proved the falsity of the allegations he had made against me in his complaint.

His bad motive for making those allegations was equally transparent. At the time he had exploited the Rothstein debacle, I was the one calling him out most for the crimes he believed he had otherwise gotten away with, and the CVRA case was a huge thorn in his side that he couldn't remove. The posture in 2009, when he filed the case, was one where I was on the offense, eating his chess pieces one at a time, triangulating him, and leaving him with nowhere to go. He was already desperate, and when Rothstein happened, he seized on an opportunity.

We held the mock trial and, playing the role of Epstein's lawyer, I argued that no matter what Epstein's intentions were when he filed his complaint against Brad Edwards, nobody believed the allegations. In fact,

Edwards's profile had risen. Edwards had received eight jury verdicts in a row over a million dollars, and he'd recently won a record-breaking $71 million verdict. Ultimately, Edwards had suffered zero damages.

The results of the mock trial are confidential, but I can say that we left knowing two contradictory things: that a jury would likely find in "Edwards's" (my) favor, but would likely not assess the damages very high.

# FORTY-NINE

# MISS YOU, JOE

THERE WERE SOME PEOPLE JUST as excited as I was that Jeffrey Epstein was finally going to be forced to go to trial. One of them was Detective Joe Recarey. He put together a solid investigation back in 2005. He was one of the first good guys to be attacked by Epstein and his legal team. Still, for more than ten years he had taken my calls and was always there to help any of Epstein's victims who needed it at any time.

I still remember our first conversation, in 2008. When I told him who I represented, he tried to pitch the idea of bringing new charges against Epstein on behalf of my clients. He didn't hold back his frustration with State Attorney Barry Krischer, who had declined to bring the charges against Epstein that Joe had recommended. Instead, he told me, "Look, do not give up on this case. We are all pulling for you." I had no idea at the time where this advice would lead me.

Over the ensuing years Joe would periodically call me to check on the status of matters. He had been off the case for years but wanted to see justice done one day. I wanted him to see that, too. Unfortunately, he died suddenly on May 25, 2018, before he could see resolution. I was in New York on another case when his funeral was held. I was hurt that I couldn't be there to say goodbye to this man who had become my friend over the years. The one thing that I know for sure is that Detective Recarey did an outstanding job on his investigation and beyond. For that, my clients and I will always be grateful.

# FIFTY

# THE CALM

IN APRIL 2018, BRITTANY AND I went to visit Courtney at the work-release correctional center up in Palm Beach, where she was completing a three-year sentence for a drug offense. She was happy to see us. I felt like I had watched Courtney grow up. While it was painful for her to be in jail, she was one of the few people I've known who grew in a positive way while there. (And the good news is she was released later that year.) She had in my view always been a decent person, but she is particularly special when she is sober. I had told Brittany many stories about her, but she didn't realize what I was talking about until that day.

On the one hand, Courtney has this natural harshness about the way she sees the world and the way that the world has treated her. On the other hand, she has a mature understanding of life and doesn't dwell on the negative or look back. Regardless, no matter how serious a story might be, she can tell any part of it in a way that will make you laugh, not at her, but with her. And not just chuckle quietly but crack up. Somehow, she made her description of getting into a jailhouse fight a whole stand-up comedy routine.

Over the years, I talked to my kids about Courtney. They knew she was special to me, and that I was sad that she was in jail. But they were fascinated by her—both the fact that I thought she was an amazing person and, at the same time, the fact that she was in jail. This duality is not always easy for kids to absorb, but in time, they got it. They wanted to ask her some questions in the next letter I wrote to her. So, I added a section of questions from my kids. They asked her what she did for fun, whether she got to play any sports, and if she did, whether she won. She had never met my children, but she wrote back answering all their questions.

When Brittany and I sat with her that day, she told us how my kids' questions had made her smile. She had a five-year-old boy of her own, and he was her motivation to do right and get out as soon as possible and join him again. We would have visited with her longer, but the corrections officers were watching us laugh and probably listening to the conversation we were having from the other side of what was meant to be soundproof glass.

We got into the car as Courtney walked across the prison parking lot to pull out the new bicycle that she was so proud to show us. Once a day, she was allowed to ride her bike off the property and go to work. The bicycle represented the only freedom she'd had in the past three years. We smiled and waved at her as we drove away. The second my car left the property, my phone rang. In the caller ID field a familiar set of numbers appeared: 0000000000.

It was almost funny, because it played right into this conspiracy theory that Brittany had developed. While I was sure that it was impossible, she was right about the repeatedly uncanny timing of Epstein's calls. There were so many times when we would be talking, debating, and bouncing ideas off of each other around the office about my case and she would say, "Hey Jeff, call Brad really quick so that y'all can chat about this." Within minutes, sometimes even seconds of that, he would call. 0000000000.

It had been odd before, but this time it was eerie. This was the first time we had ever gone to see Courtney, and yet, after not having heard from Epstein for a long time, within seconds of the visit we got a call from him.

The substance of the call was not unusual. He was still looking for a fair way to get a "divorce" from me. But, of course, he still had a distorted version of fairness. As usual, we couldn't resolve any of the issues between us, but this particular call ended with him changing the topic to his relationship with Bill Clinton. He commonly name-dropped during our talks, but usually there wasn't much of a point. After each anecdote about him hanging out with someone famous, he would answer a couple questions I had to complete the conversation. It was rarely about anyone who mattered to any case.

However, since he chose Clinton to boast about during this call, that led me to ask him why he would drop the name of someone he had been hanging out with during the same time period as Virginia. He acted like he had no idea what I was talking about. The conversation ended with the two of us making a bet and agreeing that whoever won it would sign a crisp dollar bill and send it to the other. I bet him that I could prove that he was with former president Clinton in Africa while Virginia was in Thailand, at his direction. He bet I didn't have the evidence to prove that, although he didn't deny it. Later that day, I proved it, with evidence.

He immediately called back. I said, "I want you to write 'Dear Brad, you won.' And sign your name." He instead changed the facts and pretended not to have understood the bet. Classic Jeff. Regardless, I said I'd be waiting for my dollar bill, knowing even then I'd never see it.

As the summer of 2018 was coming to an end, I was juggling too many things while trying to get my own case ready for trial. I was still trying to play sports and coach my son's football team. While hitting tennis balls one night I suffered another severely herniated disk in the same part of my spine that had been operated on previously. I needed urgent surgery.

The timing is never good for these things, but this time it was especially bad. I was four months from the Epstein trial. Regardless, I had no choice but to take a break, rehab my spine, and recover. Quickly, I hoped.

Following the very first hearing after the surgery, Jeffrey called to ask me about my back. I had not told him about the injury, and in fact had tried to keep it a secret from everybody. This was his way of reminding me that he knew everything. In fact, the day after my follow-up appointment in New York, where I had traveled to undergo surgery with one of the best spinal surgeons in the country, I got a call from Epstein. He told me that he had heard I'd just returned from New York, a fact that I had obviously not told him. He then said, "I wish I had known; I would have had you arrested."

I thought I hadn't heard him right, so I said, "You would have had *me* arrested?" and he said, "Don't worry, I would have made them let you out after a few hours." He was laughing, and maybe it sounded funny, but the comment said a lot.

That wasn't the only time we talked about my surgery. Just before our case was set to go to trial, he called to tell me he was having back pain. Naturally, identifying me as the expert on back surgery, he wanted to know whether I liked my surgeon in New York. He went on to explain that he experienced pain after sitting for too long or after flying on an airplane. He said it was constantly nagging him, and he just couldn't figure out how to get rid of it.

Finally, after listening to him complain for a while, I said, "I know exactly what you need." He thought I was being serious because I was listening pretty intently to what he was saying, but I paused for a second and said, "A massage."

He reciprocated my long pause before saying, "F*** you."

We both laughed. But not for long.

# FIFTY-ONE

# THE STORM

BEFORE THE TRIAL STARTED IN my personal case against Epstein, we were ordered to attend another mediation.

On October 9, 2018, we all arrived to mediate with retired judge Howard Tescher. In one room were Jack Scarola, his associate David Vitale, Brittany, and me. In the other room were Jeffrey Epstein, Jack Goldberger, Darren Indyke, and Scott Link. I was annoyed. I knew Epstein was, too. The classic process simply could not work in this case. It never had. It would have been far more productive if Jeff and I had just walked into the hall and talked. After staying for about two hours—long enough to be polite—I left. I learned later that Jeff was not upset that I had left, only that he had not left first.

After years of fighting, we knew each other well. We were mortal enemies, yet at the same time, there was a mutual respect, perhaps even a measure of trust, that couldn't be understood by the lawyers or mediators whose job inevitably created the barrier between us. Jeff and I were, in our own eyes, very different people. My actions were often based on emotion, many times without regard to whether a decision was good or bad from a business perspective. Epstein was a numbers person who only cared about the financial bottom line, his ability to control outcomes, and whether a proposed solution made mathematical or scientific sense.

But after all this time with Epstein trying to solve this case in his customary fashion—with money—he knew that was not going to get it done. Not with me, and not now. In my steadfast opinion, there needed to be a public trial where a jury exonerated me for the false attack he'd made in 2009.

The jury could only award money; this was a civil lawsuit. Jeffrey reminded me of that many times. "Yes," I said, "but there is a message of vindication that comes with that monetary award that is not evident to the world with a settlement." He said he understood. And he did. Because while we were very different personalities in most ways, we had some similarities. We were both competitive to the core, principled to a point where abiding by our respective principles often risked personal harm, and stubborn. Once we had considered all angles and were satisfied that there was only one resolution in line with the principle for which we stood, we were both likely to be unmovable.

I had promised myself long ago that I would fight this case until the end. That was the only way I could make sure he would be held accountable.

Along the way of our litigation, he had almost escaped. And he had come close to getting a legal break that would have put him in a position to financially ruin me (and my family). Which in turn would have allowed him to spin a message that his victory was on the merits, real and deserved, and not merely technical.

Yet I had survived. He was out of ammunition. Even his last resort, the one he could always count on—his money—couldn't solve this problem for him this time. The trial was quickly approaching, and while it would present a watered-down version of his misdeeds, he could not confidently predict how it would come out. There was a national spotlight on the trial. Courtroom View Network had already been granted gavel-to-gavel live courtroom coverage of it. The whole country would be watching, and he knew it.

Even a fraction of the information that I could unveil at trial would cause the world to finally hear things he could not afford for people to know. The truth about his prior NPA immunity deal and the work I had done to try to unwind it would be exposed. The fact that there were over one hundred victims would be known. The other locations where he had committed crimes and did not have immunity from arrest and prosecution would be out there. The identities of some of his personal friends, business associates, and co-conspirators would be revealed. All of this and more would increase the risk of his being arrested one day. And that—the prospect of having to serve a real prison term—was his Achilles' heel. It was the only thing that really frightened him. He was not fit for confinement.

Of course, I still had significant risk on my side as well. Remember, he had filed a proposal for settlement for a significant amount of money, which I had rejected. If I got a verdict that was 25 percent less than his offer, the law said that even though I won the trial, I would be responsible for his attorneys' fees, which were in the many millions of dollars. It would be a financial disaster. And I knew this was possible because his argument that I had suffered no real damages from his smear was not without merit.

Trial was to begin right after Thanksgiving, on December 4, 2018. The two of us were still communicating regularly, and neither of us was budging.

More troubling to me than the stress associated with the upcoming event was the time it was taking me away from my family. For now, no matter how hectic things ever got, I made sure I did whatever I needed to do to spend quality time with my wife and boys. Most important, I was never going to miss one of my kids' games. In fact, from the time each of them was four years old, I was Blake and Austin's head football coach and Cashton's soccer coach.

If it meant that I needed to get to work at four o'clock in the morning every day so that I could be at practice by five p.m., I did it. I would never let the kids suffer because I was busy at work. Sometimes this was easier said than done, and this year, it was more difficult than ever. Still, up until this point I had managed to keep the norm no matter what.

On November 3, 2018, my oldest son, Blake, and I won our fourth youth football league Super Bowl with him as quarterback and me as head coach. He was named MVP of the game. Austin and I lost our Super Bowl game that year on a last minute touchdown, but he was also named the MVP, and I was named the coach of the year. There was nothing I enjoyed more than coaching my boys and teaching them the lessons my dad and Papa taught me.

But now we were running into soccer season and with around-the-clock preparation necessary, I was, for the first time, not able to devote the time I wanted to coaching Cashton's team. This was weighing on me.

Not only that but Thanksgiving was approaching. Thanksgiving is a holiday that carries so much tradition and meaning with my family, I wouldn't have wanted it interrupted for anything. As far back as I can remember, my family has gone camping in the woods on Thanksgiving. When I was small, it was only my immediate family, including my grandparents, Granny and Papa.

During most of my childhood, we pitched a single tent and slept in sleeping bags and on air mattresses. At least one of them would deflate the first night and leave someone sleeping on sticks. We had campfires every night where we roasted marshmallows and made s'mores. In the mornings, we would cook stick-biscuits, which literally meant wrapping biscuit dough around a stick and poking it into a fire. When the biscuit was finished cooking, we would fill the middle with butter, sometimes cinnamon, too, and eat it. I can almost taste one now.

During the days, we would ride bikes, fish, hike, and throw around a football. There were no cell phones. This holiday in the woods was a protected sanctuary. It was an especially great time for my brothers and me because we could play all day and no one made us shower. Besides, we didn't need no stinkin' shower, considering we swam in the nearby lake and tubed down the river.

I was always so fascinated by my twin younger brothers, Travis and David. I can remember when they were born, even though I was only four years old. I thought that their being identical twins made them the coolest people in the world.

There is a story that my mom would probably remember better than I, but I'll tell it just the same. One day she was pulled over for speeding with all three of us in the car. I sat in the back seat, crying and telling the policeman that he couldn't take Mom to jail because my brothers were only one year old and I was only five and I couldn't drive them home yet. The officer and my mom were laughing—she wasn't going to jail—but all I remember thinking was that I had to protect them. While we were as close as brothers could be all through the year, Thanksgiving was the holiday we loved the most, when we spent some of our best quality time together.

When I met my wife, Terry, she started going camping with us. By that point, the Thanksgiving camping tradition had grown to more than forty people who camped for five days, from the Wednesday before Thanksgiving until the Sunday after. Instead of tents, almost everyone was now sleeping in campers and fifth wheels.

Despite these luxury upgrades, my wife's Cuban culture wasn't really known for camping. I can't say she has ever really enjoyed it, but she always embraced it because of how special it was for me. Once we had children, especially as they got older, she grew to appreciate the importance of it all.

There is nothing better than getting to watch our three boys in the woods, doing the same things my brothers and I had done together many years before. It's a total detachment from the rest of the world. The moment they get up in the morning, they each grab an old bicycle and tear off into the trails through the woods. I get to sit around the campfire with my brothers, playing cornhole or cards together, like the old days.

Unfortunately for me, the timing of my trial could not have been worse. As much as I wanted to ignore it and enjoy Thanksgiving with my family, that wasn't an option. That year, I borrowed a camper and drove it seven hours north from South Florida to a campground just outside Jacksonville, Florida. Usually during car rides, we played music and talked and refereed the usual brotherly bickering in the back seat. This trip was different.

We hadn't only packed camping gear. I had packed five Bankers boxes of Epstein-related trial materials. My lawyers were back at the office also sacrificing their Thanksgiving with more than sixty Bankers boxes of materials accumulated over the previous decade. Instead of having fun, Terry and I were talking about the trial.

She knew what was at stake. Both of us had been living with this case for more than a decade, and it had a big impact on our lives. And she was understandably annoyed that now it was interfering with this important family time. She was also irritated because her birthday was on December 1, just three days before the trial was supposed to begin, and yet another life event of hers was pretty much going down the drain because of my battle with Jeffrey Epstein. She may not have known it then, and she still may not even know it now, but I couldn't have gotten through any of this without her.

I was trying to make Thanksgiving as normal as possible under the circumstances. Usually over this holiday I would leave my cell phone in the camper. I got almost no reception in the woods anyway, so doing that wasn't very challenging.

This year, however, I had to be available to my attorneys and needed to maintain contact with the various witnesses as we decided on their scheduled appearances. I still tried to limit the amount of time I spent on the cell phone; talking required me to ride my bike to the very front of the campground—more than a mile from our campsite—just to get one bar of reception. I could only go up there two or three times a day, and even that was pushing everyone's patience.

In between calls, I spent time riding bikes and playing football with my boys, but the reality was that my mind wasn't there. I spent every second thinking about the upcoming trial. Even at night, sitting around the campfire helping my youngest son cook hot dogs without getting burned, I couldn't help thinking about the last-minute preparations needed to make sure we won.

Similar to every other trial, I tried to analyze what defense I was most afraid of and how best to plan against it. In this case, the malicious claims

Epstein had made about me could now be proven without doubt as false. So that didn't concern me.

*What would I do if I were in his shoes having to defend the case?*

I thought back to the mock trial and how I'd defended him. It was late, the fire was burning out, and my uncle was telling me a story about a cruise he had been on where his bathing suit flew completely off when he tried the surf slide. It was funny. But I couldn't laugh. My mind was only on the case.

Just then, I got a call on my cell phone. 0000000000. I tried to answer but got no reception. I jumped on the bike and pedaled from the campfire to the front of the campground. I didn't have Epstein's number—so I had to wait for him to call back, which he did, within minutes.

The call was short, "Brad, Jeff here. I really don't want to hurt you. I have always fought fair. This is your last chance to end this. You have no damages. The trial will cause you harm and I won't be able to stop it. We need to find a fair way to stop this."

He paused, waiting for me to talk. I said, "It's not about money. You know that. It is about the truth."

"Fine, then if the truth comes out, the case will end. I'll work on that. Don't get fatigued at the end. You have better endurance than that. We have come too far to not finish this the right way," he said. Not totally clear where he was going, I stayed quiet. "Good night," he said before hanging up.

Playing his words over in my mind, I knew for sure now that Jeffrey Epstein was going to admit wrongdoing. I had thought this before. But now I knew it was true.

In any civil case such as this, the plaintiff—me—has to prove "liability," meaning prove that the defendant did something wrong. Also, as noted, I had to prove that I had been damaged as a consequence of that wrong. From the mock trial, I knew that the liability case against him was a guaranteed win, but the damages were a problem.

Epstein knew this, too. There was no way he was going to let us put victims on to testify about his serial molestation of children or the deep investigation I had conducted into it, an investigation that had culminated in his very attack on me that resulted in our case.

It would set in motion the type of unwanted national attention that would put Epstein at criminal risk as well. This phone call from him told me he had thought this through.

Over the years, whenever we got evidence proving that Epstein's attack had been made with malicious intent, I would get a call from Jeffrey, or a message from one of his attorneys, saying that I should just "walk away from the case" while I still had time. This mantra was designed to make me wonder if I had missed something.

Now there was no longer any time left for him to feign a position of strength. The trial was going to happen. He had run out of ways to stop it. But he did have one option. A good one. He could surrender. He could admit that he had filed a false complaint, thereby precluding me from introducing evidence of his bad acts and restricting the trial to my damages—the weakest part of my case.

I grabbed my phone from the camper and texted Jack, *I need to speak with you immediately*. It didn't matter that it was midnight on Thanksgiving Day, after most people had eaten turkey and gone to sleep.

Jack doesn't sleep much anyway. Over the years, I have talked to him at midnight and then communicated with him by email at four thirty in the morning. He responded by saying that he was up, so I called. "They are going to admit liability," I said, to which Jack responded, "What are you talking about?"

I laid it out for him. Surrender—or at least partial surrender—was his only option, and it was a good one.

He paused, clearly thinking about what this would mean for our trial. I explained at a rapid pace. "The trial will literally be reduced to three or four witnesses, including me and our expert, whose testimony will be limited to basically the small number of people who could have electronically seen this complaint that Epstein has now admitted to the world was false. If the number is tiny, so are my damages. At least, that'll be his argument."

Jack's initial response was "I do not believe they will do that. But I do agree we should start preparing in case they do." I left that call worried.

For the rest of the camping trip, I couldn't get my mind off this ploy. It occupied my time so much I didn't get to spend any real quality time with my aunts, uncles, or the rest of the family whom I only see this one time of the year, the only time we all come together to be thankful for what we have. I still feel bad about that.

Terry saw that I was uncharacteristically absent from the festivities. On Sunday, I packed up the camper and we began driving home. She encouraged me. "I've never seen you like this before. The trial is going to be great. This is what you've been wanting for years. Don't worry about us, it's all going to be over soon, which is all I want."

I responded, "That's not the problem. This isn't going to be the trial that I always wanted. He's never going to let that happen. He's too smart for that."

I told her what I'd explained to Jack the night before. Always cutting to the chase, she said, "You're still going to win. You are right. He is wrong."

As much as this last trick up Epstein's sleeve had me thinking about the downside, I still thought I was in a much better position than he was. The attention given to the trial would create risk for him that some other prosecutor, in some place outside of Florida, would prosecute him for the crimes he had committed elsewhere. Eventually, he would have to make another move to protect himself from this, and he was running out of time.

Almost as soon as I pulled the camper back into my driveway after a seven-hour trip home, I got an incoming call.

0000000000.

# FIFTY-TWO

# THE HANDSHAKE

EPSTEIN AND I AGREED TO meet in person one last time before the trial. He picked our usual place—Starbucks off Glades Road in Boca.

I was fifteen minutes early and yet he had gotten there first. Of all the tables available, he chose the outside corner table and the chair that I had sat in during my meeting with his bodyguard.

Was this his way of saying that he knew about that meeting? If he did, how did he know this was the table we sat at? Even the chair. We didn't talk about it, but when I walked up, the look on his face told me his location and positioning were no accidents.

As I approached the table, he leaned back in his chair. As soon as I sat across from him, he started talking. "What I did to you was wrong. I am sorry. I do not believe you have damages. I know you want my apology. I'll give it to you. It is sincere. Are we done?"

I said, "Okay, but for this to end the case, your apology will have to be as public as the false complaint you filed against me. And it has to be clear. Not a lawyered-up statement nobody can really understand."

He said, "Fine." He then apologized. I believed him.

I said, "At this late stage of the game, it has to be in the courtroom."

He said, "You want me to kiss your ass in Macy's window?" stealing the famous line from Lyndon B. Johnson. Before I could say anything, he said, "Done," and with that we worked out the other details of the settlement. When that was over, we talked for a bit.

"Did Stan tell you we used to work in the same office in New York?" he asked.

"Yes," I responded.

"Did he tell you about my date with the girl with two vaginas?"

"He actually did mention that to me at some point," I confirmed.

He got the biggest smile, before delivering his punch line, "I felt like I was dating a bowling ball."

I looked at him skeptically and with disapproval for his degrading commentary. Seeing that I was unamused, he pulled out his phone to validate the existence of the anatomical condition as if that would also cure the offensiveness of his joke.

This meeting, this settlement, did in certain ways actually change the hostile relationship between us. Maybe it should not have, but it did. Of course, I still did not like him. I couldn't. He had hurt many people I had come to care about deeply. It was also clear that he didn't like me for the way I had come after him, tooth and nail, for more than a decade. Strangely, though, our mutual dislike included a kind of begrudging mutual respect that at this end stage allowed us to talk without jockeying for leverage or advantage.

We had never been in communication without having underlying anger and hostility brewing beneath us. But, at the same time, in ten years of battles, we had grown to know each other almost too well. Sitting there in Starbucks, an outsider might have thought we were old friends. We weren't. But combat against a formidable warrior bears some form of camaraderie when the guns are finally down. And that's what this was.

It felt like we were touching gloves after a long boxing match and trading stories about maneuvers we made against one another after the opening bell.

He said, "You should write a book. Make it a movie. I still want to have some input on who plays me when you do a movie one day."

His biggest regret, or so he said, was that he never got to tell his side of the story. This was not the first time he had told me that, but it was the first time I did not laugh after he said it. I said, "If I write a book one day, I'll make sure to include your side."

Smiling, he said, "Maybe we can write it together. You write what you think happened and I'll write what actually happened."

"Deal," I said.

He brushed that off. I said, "Either way, the CVRA case is still going forward, so we're a long way from our final meeting."

"You'll lose that case soon enough," he said confidently. "Other than the CVRA, you and I are done with each other, right?" he confirmed. He then went on to explain that he and former Israeli prime minister Ehud Barak were close friends who loved to talk about problems in the Middle East. He explained that they also talked about the greatest advancements in the conduct of war, and about how those great war generals from history on opposing sides met after battle to discuss the tactics and defenses they'd used. Every great battle, he said, had the right balance between offense and defense, aggressiveness and passivity. Even the defeated general had not completely lost if he had learned lessons from his mistakes.

"When the CVRA is done, we need to get together," he said. "A meeting between war generals is necessary for both of us. You can come to my place in New York or I will come to your house, if you will have me. I owe you answers. And I have many questions myself. This has been a well-fought war, between you and me. We owe each other this meeting."

"Sounds good," I said. "I'll see you in New York one day then."

Despite the fact that there were details that still needed to be hammered out, I stood up and extended my hand. He said, "Because of germs, I don't usually shake hands."

I looked at him and said, "Come on, man, give me a break, I know where your hand has been and I'm still shaking it." I had clearly just taken a shot at him. Rather than take offense, he laughed and agreed to shake on it.

We had a deal.

On November 28, a week before my trial was set to begin, while Courtroom View Network prepared for live coverage and other national media were paying attention, Julie Brown released her story on the *Miami Herald* website. It included print and videos detailing the crimes Epstein had committed, the cover-up, and compelling video interviews of four of Epstein's victims, including Courtney, Michelle, Virginia, and Jena-Lisa, another client of mine. The story ended by telling the world that the Edwards-Epstein trial was about to begin the following week.

Julie didn't know that Epstein and I had just resolved the case. Nobody knew. Her story caused a frenzy. It generated headlines around the world. Media calls flooded our office, my cell phone, and the email accounts of everyone who'd had any involvement with the story.

The timing could not have been better. In fact, Epstein's lawyers believed that I had orchestrated it in order to maximize the attention on Epstein's public admission of wrongdoing and apology.

# FIFTY-THREE

# HIS SURRENDER

W HILE EPSTEIN AND I HAD reached a final agreement, nothing was ever final with him. There were only a few days between our Starbucks meeting and the trial date, which was when Epstein planned to deliver the public apology, but you never knew what could take the deal apart: the release of Julie's story, some aspect of the still-scheduled trial, something totally unknown and unpredictable. The trial was set to go forward on December 4, on my oldest son's birthday, and only a select few other people knew the trial was not going to happen.

The Epstein camp was fuming about the timing of the *Miami Herald* story. It was impossible to know for sure if this saga was really going to end. Even as Brittany and I drove to the courthouse the morning of the trial, I was waiting for a last-minute maneuver.

Driving north on I-95 from Fort Lauderdale to Palm Beach, I felt as if I were trapped in some alien territory in my own mind. Brittany turned to me and asked, "What's going on? I've seen you happy, mad, frustrated, anxious, but never like this." I really didn't know how to respond. I was conflicted between wanting this trial to proceed at long last, and knowing it was smart to settle it. Especially since it was settling on my terms.

After years of work, the first trial I could control completely was not going to happen. I had uncovered so many witnesses, put together Epstein's scheme, and had solid proof of the crimes he had committed throughout the country. While I knew how the judge had ruled on what would and would not be allowed into evidence, and I knew that much of the information I had accumulated would not be aired in this trial, this ending still felt deeply anticlimactic. I explained as much before we parked.

Brittany looked at me and said, "This has never been the case you cared about. Helping the girls through the CVRA has been your mission; making sure Epstein faces criminal charges, that's all that matters. That's all still alive. You've won at every stage of that case and you are going to win in the end. Today, Jeffrey is telling the world that you were doing the right thing all along and he intentionally tried to derail you. What more do you want?"

She was right. We parked next to Jack and walked into the courthouse together. The walls were lined with reporters waiting for jury selection to begin. When I entered the courtroom that morning, I didn't see Jeffrey. This was not a good sign, but also not a surprise. I never believed he would actually show up.

Judge Hafele took the bench and the parties informed the court of the settlement. I heard a gasp from the crowd. Scott Link faced the reporters from the well of the courtroom and read a document that was a statement from Jeffrey Epstein:

> While Mr. Edwards was representing clients against me, I filed a lawsuit against him in which I made allegations about him that the evidence conclusively proves were absolutely false. The truth was that his aggressive investigation and litigation style was highly effective and therefore troublesome for me. The lawsuit I filed was my unreasonable attempt to damage his business reputation and cause Mr. Edwards to stop pursuing cases against me. It did not work. Despite my efforts, he continued to do an excellent job for his clients and, through his relentless pursuit, held me responsible. I am now admitting that I was wrong and that the things I said to try to harm Mr. Edwards's reputation as a trial lawyer were false. I sincerely apologize for the false and hurtful al-

legations I made and hope for some forgiveness for my acknowl-
edgment of wrongdoing.

I never thought I'd hear those words or anything close to them. Even
after he had said them to me at Starbucks. But, he stayed true to his word
and delivered on his promise to publicly apologize to me.

After the apology was read to everyone in the courtroom, Judge Hafele
spoke. He tried to find his usual way of being even-keeled by thanking everyone for their professionalism along the way. I don't remember his exact
words, but he gave a special thank-you to the victims who were courageous
enough to come forward and stand up, like Courtney, Lynn, and Marissa.

It was difficult to reconcile his closing remarks with those that he spoke
at the hearing many years earlier when he had caused me to move to recuse
him from the case. But like everyone involved, I think he, too, had matured
and had developed a better understanding of the case over the years.

The press was ready for a trial and not sure what to make of what had
just happened. The words of the apology caught everyone off guard. It was
an extraordinary and powerful ending caught on tape.

Those in the courtroom who were set up with video cameras permitted by the judge were rewinding and replaying the apology over and over.
Jack Scarola spoke last before we left the courtroom, thanking the judge
and explaining to the court and the public, "This was no settlement, it was
a surrender."

Our team filed down the hallway, passing reporters who were shoving
microphones in our faces. We walked out the doors and across the street to
where Jack had stacked dozens of boxes of Epstein trial material and exhibits for everyone to see. He had prepared the display and organized a massive
press conference. He had not told me this was going to happen, but I was
impressed. He stepped up to the microphones and began to speak.

I had planned to be a good client and let my lawyer talk, but many of
the reporters' questions felt as though they deserved answers only I could
give.

I don't remember what I said, only that I spoke with pure, unlawyer-like emotion and rawness including whatever came to mind. Video cameras captured it, so there must be a record of it somewhere. I think at some stage during the press conference, I even told the somewhat embarrassing story of how I entered this fight by scribbling the word "Emergency" on the top of the first pleading that I ever filed in federal court. I wasn't there to pretend to be someone I wasn't. I tried to give an earnest account of what had happened beyond this particular case, and why I would continue to fight with the CVRA case.

The press conference had ended, but it wasn't really over. People had traveled from all over the country for the trial and were pulling me into unavoidable interviews. I was even filmed in an impromptu scene for a Netflix documentary where my legal team and I shared our thoughts on the settlement that had just occurred. When I finally left, I got home to see my family and celebrate what was left of my son's birthday. Just like that, it was over.

This was the first time in a decade when there wasn't personal litigation going on between Jeffrey Epstein and me. We were done. Or were we?

The public apology on the heels of Julie Brown's story got the attention of the U.S. Attorney's office in the Southern District of New York. They opened a highly secretive investigation knowing that if Jeffrey Epstein ever caught wind of it, he would find a way to shut it down. While they could covertly obtain information that our extensive investigation had uncovered, they could not talk to victims directly without risking it tipping off Epstein. However, by pure coincidence, or karma, they could catch a break.

# FIFTY-FOUR

# CHECK

O N FEBRUARY 21, 2019, I was walking out of a hearing in the Jacksonville courthouse when I got a call from a friend of mine in the press. Judge Marra had ruled that "there was a violation of the victims' rights under the CVRA." This was not a surprising ruling because the evidence was overwhelmingly in our favor, but you never know until you know. This was what we set out to prove in July 2008, more than ten years earlier. We had waited so long for this day. I called Courtney. She started crying instantly.

I read the judge's order quickly. The government had violated the victims' right to confer at three separate times: (1) on and before September 24, 2007, when the government was negotiating and signing the non-prosecution agreement; (2) in and around January 2008, when it sent letters not telling the victims about the previously signed NPA but, rather, falsely counseling "patience" while the government supposedly "finished" its already long-finished investigation; and (3) on and around June 30, 2008, when the government notified or attempted to notify the victims about the impending state plea, but still did not tell them that the plea would effectively extinguish their rights to ever see Epstein prosecuted.

A clear-cut example of the government's violating the victims' rights was its remarkable decision in 2008, well after the NPA had been signed by Epstein and the federal government, to send the victims (and, in some cases, their attorneys) deceptive and dishonest information that the case was "currently under investigation" and that "this can be a lengthy process and we request your continued patience while we conduct a thorough investigation."

Judge Marra's decision confirmed what I had said in July 2008.

When Courtney and I finished celebrating over the phone, she asked, "So what does this mean? Where do we go from here?" It was a good question. Judge Marra ordered us to confer with the government to decide what remedy was appropriate given the finding of a violation. We tried to confer but were told by the U.S. Attorney's Office that the Southern District of Florida was being recused, disqualified from participating in the formation of a remedy, and replaced in that task by federal prosecutors in the Northern District of Georgia, which was in Atlanta.

Now the press was all over the injustice of the NPA. Judge Marra's order was appropriately critical of the blatant violations instigated by the U.S. Attorney's Office for the Southern District of Florida, which, at the time the NPA was signed, was led by Alex Acosta. Acosta, no longer a U.S. attorney, had been appointed in 2017 by President Trump as the U.S. secretary of labor.

There were rumblings that there would be a congressional investigation into not only the plea agreement but any role Secretary Acosta and others had played in its creation. The press was constantly calling me for comment on Secretary Acosta or President Trump in an effort to bait me into providing them with quotable political commentary on information that was entirely irrelevant to our victory. I wasn't comfortable with speculation, and really had no interest in playing into the media's attempt to dilute our victory by turning it into some political conspiracy. So I took a pass.

# FIFTY-FIVE

# CHECKMATE

O UR FOCUS WAS ON WHERE to go from here. What would be the remedy for the violation? Our position was since the court had ruled that secretly signing the NPA behind the victims' backs was a violation, then the NPA was an illegal agreement that should be declared null and void. If the agreement was invalid, then so was the immunity protection it provided. This would mean that Jeffrey Epstein and his co-conspirators could be prosecuted for the Florida crimes committed many years ago.

Of course, the government did not agree with our proposed remedy, but the thought of it made Epstein very nervous. Sensing danger, he reached out to me again. He wanted to help settle the CVRA case in any way that would avoid the remedy of invalidation of the NPA that we were seeking. In early March 2019, Jeffrey and I began talking again, and meeting every so often at Starbucks.

The U.S. Attorney's Office in the Northern District of Georgia needed to speak with all of Epstein's victims again to get their view on what remedy they wanted to see for the violation of their rights. Epstein hated the fact that the government was now speaking directly with his victims, so he asked to formally participate in the case. As a result, we began working with the government and Epstein to set up a joint mediation. All the while, the government continued to interview victims. When he learned of the interviews through a statement made by the government in a pleading, he was annoyed, though he believed they were all related to the CVRA.

But at the same time, the U.S. attorneys from the Southern District of New York and the FBI had begun conducting interviews of their own, including interviews of my clients Courtney and Olivia. By coincidence, the CVRA was providing cover. While Jeffrey Epstein was worried about shutting down the CVRA case before we reversed his NPA and revitalized the possibility of a Florida prosecution, another investigation was building rapidly, and this time, it was Epstein who was in the dark.

Shortly after my clients and other victims were interviewed in the criminal investigation in March, I got a call from Julie Brown. She said she had a source that told her New York was investigating Epstein and that FBI agents were interviewing his victims. She needed me to be the second source so that she could report it. That would have destroyed the investigation and put many people in physical danger. I had to tell her that I had no idea what she was talking about and that any interviews being conducted were related to the CVRA. *Whew, that was a close call.*

It wasn't long after that Jeffrey called me again. He wanted to meet at our Starbucks. We met in May 2019. He was different. Nervous. Pacing. He seemed almost paranoid. *Did he know?* I couldn't tell, but he seemed frustrated by his inability to control the CVRA. We talked about ways of resolving things, but he equivocated, as usual, still unable to agree to all of my terms.

During the meeting, he went on an angry diatribe about Alan Dershowitz. Dershowitz had just done an interview on *The View* and made comments essentially saying Epstein was guilty.

"This guy was my lawyer, and he's talking about me like that?" he railed.

At one point, he got up from our outside table and walked to the end of the sidewalk with his phone to his ear. I could tell that he was yelling, but couldn't make out what he was saying. He walked hurriedly back to the table and sat across from me.

He crossed his legs, leaned back, placed his phone on the lap of his gray sweatpants, and lowered his glasses. "I can be nice, but I can also be real mean," he said referring to his call. "That was Alan. He's going to stop talking."

I have no idea whether he actually called Dershowitz or whether anyone was even on the other end of the line.

He looked right at me, "Brad, what is the end goal with the CVRA? Even if you win and the judge rules it's invalid, there is no way they will prosecute me. This will go all the way up to the attorney general. You know Trump was my friend and Barr is his boy. Let's end this CVRA thing and be done."

Name-dropping was part of Epstein's normal routine and I took every-thing he said with a grain of salt. He knew he could basically say whatever he wanted about his associations with powerful people and I had no real way to verify or disprove it.

Calming for a second, he thought out loud: "So what do you really want?"

"Courtney has been the driving force of the CVRA. She deserves to have her legacy preserved," I explained.

He quickly retorted, "I'm not going to disagree with you. What does she want, though? What if I put up a building in her name? The Courtney Wild Center for Victims? What do you think? Would that do it?"

"Look, this isn't just about her. This is about all of the victims. Court-ney wants to help others and you know that."

"Okay, Brad, so what's fair? What if I give them all health insurance? For them and their families? Sound good?" he responded, growing antsy with my refusal to immediately agree with him.

While he did show interest in solving this problem of his, it wasn't a real offer. It was just his normal creative pontification. He knew that I would have to share these ideas with Courtney and that she would get her hopes up. Just another move in the game that he was always playing.

We left without much further discussion other than an agreement to see if some alternative was possible to resolve the CVRA.

When we tried to set up a three-party mediation where the victims, the government, and Epstein would attend, Epstein backed out. Was he pulling the rug out at the last minute as a negotiating tactic, as he had done so many times before? Or had he suspected another investigation was under way and mediation might be a trap? Who knows.

We never spoke again.

In June 2019, while my son Austin and I were driving home from a day of fishing, a call came in—0000000000. I had always answered in the past. This time, I didn't know what to say. I didn't know what he knew or what he might have suspected. My knowledge alone of the New York investigation would have been treated by him as the ultimate betrayal. Consequently, it would have subjected me to the full power of his wrath.

After staring at the number for several rings, deciding whether to answer, the ringing stopped.

I felt my heart beating fast. I called Brittany and Stan on a three-way call. "If something doesn't happen soon, then it will never happen. I have this feeling he knows something. Or he is about to find out. And he will kill someone this time. Me. He will see me as the common denominator to his problems."

Brittany jumped in, "You didn't do this to him. He did this to himself."

Stan quickly assured, "If truth be told, he should be mad at me, not you, Brad."

"He won't see it that way," I explained recounting the details of the events that had unfolded over the past few months.

Shortly thereafter, we hung up.

Stan and I didn't talk until I was on my Fourth of July family vacation in Naples, at a bowling alley, waiting out a sudden thunderstorm. After letting Stan go to voice mail at least four times, I answered to hear him say, "I just got a call from the FBI. He's in handcuffs . . ."

# EPILOGUE

O N JULY 6, 2019, JEFFREY EPSTEIN was arrested on sex-trafficking charges. On August 10, 2019, Jeffrey Epstein was dead. He was so unique in his way of thinking that it was hard for anyone not to want to get closer to him. I understand why he had so many visitors when he was in jail the first time. I, for one, would have had a difficult time not showing up to visit him in jail the second time. I had a lot of questions for him and I know he had a lot for me.

While our meetings usually began with a struggle over who would talk first, I am sure he would have beaten me at that game if we'd ever met in his cell. I expect he would have tugged at his prison garb and wasted no time asking, "Did you have anything to do with this?"

The CVRA case, which he had dismissed as unimportant, led to more litigation, then more public charges, then more nasty press, and then, finally, the attention of the Southern District of New York's prosecutors. Once they were focused on him, the other knights and pawns also fell: there was a secret grand jury; an unforeseen airport arrest; a court decision not to grant bail; an awful case of detention shock; the prospect of a lifetime of more of the same along with his hard personal assessment of an impossible-to-accept future; and the profound conclusion he reached—the most profound personal conclusion any human being can reach: to be or not to be. And then, in the middle of the night, there was his final exercise of total control, the guiding principle by which he lived, and died.

The truth is, I struggled with Epstein's death. It is what it is, right? But really, it isn't. I couldn't figure it out. Maybe I still haven't. This is a man whom I despised. He had threatened me; he had threatened my family. He had harmed many of my clients. He had tried to ruin my career.

Yet somehow, every single time we stepped into the ring, he made me think that he was a *fair* guy. It wasn't until after he was gone that I finally realized he had read me like a book and fought me on my terms. Despite the years that I had spent explaining the ways in which he had exploited every single one of my clients, his victims, I never realized how incredible he really was at reading and manipulating his target.

Epstein tried to manipulate me the way that he manipulated everyone else in his life. He probably believed he had succeeded until he was handcuffed in New Jersey getting off of his plane from France.

But honestly, to a certain degree, he was right. I had one major miscalculation: the subjectivity of fairness. I have based my entire legal career on fairness. Maybe even my entire life. From the lessons that my father and Papa taught me as a kid to the way that Scott Rothstein purported to run his law firm, the concept of fairness always resonated with me in the belief that so long as you are fair, you are doing the right thing. Fairness was my moral compass. Fairness has always been a fundamental pillar of who I am.

Jeffrey Epstein was a master at figuring out what drives other people. Because he actually had no conscience and no allegiance to any ethical belief, he would latch on to his adversary's driving force and exploit it. He did that every time. It turns out he even did it to me.

As I sit here today, after all these years, I finally know how it happened. I can remember our first real conversation as clear as day. I was in my office, with my back against the wall and my feet up on my desk. It was our very first one-on-one conversation on the phone. Thinking about it now, I really can't believe how I didn't see it then.

He had called my office to see how he could resolve our personal lawsuit. "How much did you make last year?" he asked me.

"Why?" I responded.

He quickly told me that he would pay my yearly salary to settle our personal case.

Without even considering the idea, I said, "That's not *fair*."

Rather than disagree, he retorted, "Well, what does fairness mean to *you*?"

I thought about it for a few seconds and said, "You know it when you see it. I can't give you a universal definition, but at the very least, it means that you take into consideration all factors and not just one."

He surprised me again by inquiring, "Tell me all of the factors I should be considering."

From that moment forward, he would incorporate the concept of fairness into every substantive discussion that we would ever have. Not because he believed in it, but because he knew I did. Once he grasped the notion that my entire way of dealing with an adversary was in terms of fairness, he began to speak my language. Whether he was conveying an offer, a counteroffer, or just a general principle of life, he would couch his position in terms of what was fair or unfair.

It turns out that I left that same conversation thinking I had gotten somewhere with him, when in reality he was learning everything he needed to convince me that we both believed in fairness, even between adversaries. I didn't realize until after he was dead that the common ground that I believed existed between us was really a facade.

Not a single person could ever win the ultimate game against Jeffrey Epstein. If he were alive, I have no doubt he would say I came the closest. And I suppose looking *objectively* at our entire relationship, especially at the end, he would say I won. But while I got him in a way he didn't see coming when he stepped off of his plane in New Jersey, he was playing me all along in a way I never saw happening. We were both exploiting one another's weaknesses, each always sincerely believing the other had no idea.

In my current state of reflection, I've remembered a conversation that it would now be tough to forget. We got into a debate on the age of consent. I reminded him that according to the law, the age of consent is not negotiable. He said: "I can only assume you are couching this in terms of fairness, and if so, at this point are we talking about subjectively or biologically? And to whom? You do agree, right, Brad, that whoever is analyzing this should be fair to me, too, right? Shouldn't the real question be whether I treated everyone fairly? Before you answer, have you ever had a client say that I was aggressive to them when they weren't into it or tried to hurt them when they were saying no?

"My point is that no matter how uncomfortable the subject, some objective fairness should be applied all around. To everyone. Even to me, don't you agree? My lifestyle is unorthodox. But that doesn't mean it's wrong. I have improved many lives and injured, in reality, very few. I know you disagree with that, but your best argument is an arbitrary line in the sand. That line can't apply to every situation—you can't think the application of arbitrary rules is fair, Brad." He knew that I would agree that everything should be fair. He took each conversation and centered the driving principle around fairness.

Over the years, because I really didn't fully appreciate his exploitation of fairness and, more important, his ability to exploit the susceptibility of the concept to interpretation, he was able to extend this apparent mutual respect garnered after many conversations and several meetings one step further. Fairness naturally transformed into trust. Trust transformed into a strange relationship that, to someone looking at us talking through the window of Starbucks, might have looked like friendship, although knowing how things ended, it's obvious it never was.

During one conversation, he made a point to tell me he knew and very much respected that I prided myself on being fair. "I know you as someone who would never go back on your word or on your beliefs," he explained, adding, "so I want to make sure that when you evaluate what is fair to you and your clients, you also look at what is fair to me to make sure that the ultimate result is fair, because true fairness cannot only be fair to one side. By definition, that would not be actual fairness, right?" I agreed that fairness inherently required a mutual consideration of all positions. "We are on the same page. We have the same belief. You know, Brad, we're more similar than you think," he attempted to convince me once again that we shared common beliefs.

It was this idea of "going back on my word" that I couldn't really let go of after Epstein and I had finally shaken hands and formally agreed to settle our issues with one another and move on. In his terms, it was our official "divorce" from being adversaries.

Not long after, I was called by a new client to represent her against him. When I called Jeffrey to tell him about this new client, he said that my representation of her was inconsistent with our agreement to be done with one another. In some technical sense, he was right.

That actually made me second-guess things.

Just before we finished the conversation, he took it a step further and said, "I know you wouldn't go back on your word."

What he certainly didn't know was that by that stage, I was already deeply cooperating with the highly confidential criminal investigation against him being conducted by the Southern District of New York.

*I couldn't go back on my word.* He was right. I don't go back on my word. The concept of fairness was far too ingrained in my brain. But he was a criminal. He had destroyed the lives of so many people. People I cared about. *So why did I care?*

I couldn't explain, I still can't explain, why I felt compelled to stand true to my word, but what I knew was that Julie Brown, the *Miami Herald* reporter, had entered the picture at almost the perfect time. She had published her story at the same time that Epstein and I had reached our agreement to stay out of each other's lives forever. Julie Brown wanted her publication to mean something. And, no doubt, it was meaningful. Her timing of publishing—incidentally—to coincide with our settlement was impeccable. It meant that if I cooperated with authorities, Jeffrey Epstein would forever believe Julie caused the investigation. I saw this as a clear opportunity to do the right thing for my clients and the world while also never allowing Jeffrey to know that I had not kept my word to him.

The truth is, all I ever wanted was for the right thing to happen. In some messed-up universe, I didn't want the right thing to happen at the expense of compromising my fundamental principle of fairness. Even though it was right, it wouldn't be fair to go back on my word. Jeffrey Epstein had pinned me between rightness and fairness.

My two worlds were colliding—the idea of accountability for everyone who has done something wrong and the idea that you should honor your promise. It was impossible to reconcile those two things. But I ultimately managed to do it.

Maybe someone out there will fault me, but I think that what I realized in the end, while not fully understanding until now the ways in which he was able to manipulate me, was that everything paled in importance to getting the right end result. Whether the "agreement" that the two of us had reached was fair or not, seeing him in jail for the rest of his life was the only thing that was fair to me, to my clients, and to the world.

Still, I couldn't risk him learning that I had dishonored him. Isn't that funny? He was behind bars, and still, I was worried about what might happen if he found out that I had somehow betrayed him. He would have been so disappointed. *But why did I care?* Maybe I'll never know.

## ACKNOWLEDGMENTS

I owe this book to my wife, Terry. The life of a trial lawyer, especially one who chases bad guys for a living, can be trying on any family. Yet, no matter how much was at risk or how much danger was present, she kept our family together and safe while supporting me every step of the way. After the Epstein case was finally over, she encouraged me to write this book, even though it meant many long nights away. Thank you, T.

I also dedicate this book to my three boys, Blake, Cashton, and Austin, who were my constant reminder to never give up. As they grew older, the importance of the continued pursuit became increasingly evident. Boys—fight for what you know is right and never give up, no matter what stands in the way.

To the many victims and survivors of Jeffrey Epstein, those with whom I have met and those I have not, I am sorry for what you experienced. I hope our efforts helped ease the pain and that you know we have tried to do everything that we could to let you know that you mattered to us.

Brittany Henderson: I could not have written this book myself. In fact, I didn't. After talking about writing the book for years, you were the one who put your foot down and said, "Let's do it." We will get to look back on this book-writing experience and know we accomplished something as a team. When the workday ended, we started writing. I would stand in your office dictating (more like ranting) as you typed. Then I would look at the screen hours later and see that you had worked your typical magic, editing, rearranging, fact-checking, and generally writing the book. My Ratatouille. In truth, you deserve more credit for the final product than I. After storytelling for hours, I would be done (sometimes in the wee hours of the morning) and you kept going. (I'm sure you would insert an age joke here.) You are not only one of the very best lawyers I know but also my most trusted friend, and now my coauthor. Yes, I will keep my promise—the next book we write together, your name will go first.

Courtney Wild: You are my friend. Thank you for always keeping it real. Your perseverance and resolve are unmatched. You overcome all obstacles and, to me, are the definition of an American hero. Dream big. Follow your dreams. You have so much to give this world.

Lynn: Thank you for never sugarcoating anything, always calling things like you see them, and staying true to yourself. Your perspective is fascinating and like I have always told you—you will be a star one day.

Marissa: I am sorry you have been through so much but am so proud of how far you have come. I am thankful for your trust in me and having the opportunity to represent you and help improve your life.

Virginia Giuffre: Nobody is a stronger force than you. In any war, you are the person I want by my side, mate. I am proud to call you my friend but by this point you are like a sister. Keep changing the world!

Sarah Ransome: Thank you for coming forward when you did. You made a difference in the lives of many.

Maria Farmer: You were the first to say anything. The world would have been a safer place had someone just listened to you. I am sorry they didn't. But thank you for staying with it and continuing the fight.

Chauntae Davies: From the day we met with you in California, we knew you were special. You helped to shed light on the fact that Epstein's victims were not all underage and that his strategy was often long-term and much more devious and calculated than most knew. I look forward to reading your book one day.

Anouska De Georgiou: Thank you for finally making the call to me. I know that was tough but from our first conversation you connected dots that we previously couldn't. It is an honor to have met and represented you.

Jena-Lisa Jones: You helped bring Epstein to justice by coming forward and fearlessly telling your story. That took guts. Thank you for your bravery.

Michelle Licata: Thank you for sticking with this when many people had given up hope.

Maria Kelljchian: Words cannot express how thankful I am for you putting up with me, listening to my crazy ideas (usually), and keeping our law firm running. Without you, these cases could not have turned out as successfully as they did, and this book wouldn't be the same.

Mike Fisten: No good investigation can be done alone. While I had numerous investigators along the way, you were in the trenches with me during crucial times. In addition to game-planning with me, tracking down witnesses, and coordinating surveillance on Epstein, you also guarded my house and my family when things got hairy, for which I am forever grateful.

Randee Kogan: In my view, you are hands down the best trauma therapist. You helped ease the victims' suffering.

Shelby Marin and Paige Murtagh: My longtime friends and trusted confidants. Thank you for taking the time to read this, for talking it through, and for your valuable ideas.

Jose Lorenzo: This book really could not have happened without you. This project took even more of Brittany's time than her crazy work life already does. Thank you for being an amazing husband to Brittany. She could not be the incredible lawyer and person she is without you. And thanks for being such a wonderful friend to me.

Jesse Smatt: Thank you for always being a sounding board and helping to protect my family.

Chad Mayes: My lifelong best friend. When there was nobody else I could talk to, you were there. The same way you have always been and the same way it will always be.

Janet Rodriguez: My secret weapon. Until now. Your opinions and ideas helped win many trials and got me through some of the toughest times in the Epstein saga. I'm not going to let you retire from cutting forever.

Marie Villafaña: My biggest regret with this book is that I was not able to completely explain the unfair position in which your former office placed you. I am hopeful you will one day tell that story. Until then, thank you for believing in the victims and trying, with both hands tied behind your back, to bring down Jeffrey Epstein. I know the truth—you were a hero to this case who had to hang out there as a scapegoat. Anyone who knows you knows you are a kindhearted prosecutor who tried to do right.

Jim Hill: Nobody stuck with the story longer or worked harder to get it right. Your dedication did not go unnoticed by me or any of Jeffrey Epstein's victims for whom you clearly showed compassion and integrity in journalism.

Michele Dargan: You were the first reporter to expose the truth as it was happening. Anyone who does their homework would find that the "news" of Epstein's abuse was not recently reported for the first time. You did it years ago, before it was a popular cultural topic.

Julie Brown: Thank you for having the courage to finally publish what other major publications would not. You made the public listen when all other journalists were scared.

Paul Cassell: For those who know you, you are the Wizard of Oz, the most brilliant legal thinker and writer. Without you, the CVRA case would not have made it very far. You were the not-so-secret weapon. If anyone must litigate against the United States government and a billionaire at the same time, they either need a large team of lawyers or simply Paul Cassell. My friend, forever.

Jay Howell: You were not only an inspiration for this book, but also for my career. Thank you for all that you do and all you have done representing the rights of crime victims.

Stan Pottinger: Thank you for encouraging me to write this book. I would have never done it without you convincing me that it needed to be written. Even though I am pretty sure that you are not (at least any longer) in some special investigations unit, you will always be our 007. I look forward to the next bad guy we get to take down together. Thank you for your dedication to bringing Epstein to justice and for just being a great friend. We are looking forward to celebrating many more birthdays with you.

Seth Lehrman and Matt Weissing: Thanks for always standing by me from the very beginning. There are few people I can always count on, but I know I can always count on you.

Steve Jaffe: From the first day we met, you believed in me. Your encouragement played a big role in the outcome. Thanks for that.

Jack Scarola: At my most vulnerable point, you volunteered to defend me so that I could continue my pursuit. I appreciate you more than you will ever know.

Earleen Cote: Sorry to always make you so nervous for me. But thank you for caring. Especially given that you know worrying isn't going to stop me. I owe so much to you, including the courage (or insanity) to finish what I started.

David Boies: You selflessly jumped into this fight full steam ahead and never cowered at any time. I was honored to have been in the trenches with you and look forward to the next fight.

Sigrid McCawley: You live up to the Superwoman name. Your passion and commitment are unparalleled. We will always be there when you need us because you are always there for everyone else.

Meredith Schultz: While you may not have received the credit you deserve, your contribution was undeniable. Another genius behind the curtain to whom we all owe so much.

Mike Satz and Broward County State Attorney's Office: Thanks for giving me the opportunity to become a trial attorney. You provided me with the foundation. I hope I have made you proud.

Mom: Thank you for keeping me in line, teaching me what is fair, and making me believe there is no limit on what can be done if you put your heart into it. I love you.

Dad: Thanks for being tough on me, and spending time with me fishing and playing sports. Thanks for coaching me and teaching me that there is no substitute for preparation and hard work. Winning is fun. Losing is not. So, winning isn't everything as long as you are okay being unhappy. Most of all, thank you for teaching me how to be a good father. And to never be scared of anyone. The bigger they are, the harder they fall.

Travis and David Edwards: From the day you were born, I would jump in front of a train for you. That is still true today and I know it goes both ways. While we don't live close, you are both always in my thoughts. Love you both.

Granny: You are the most selfless person I know. You deserve credit for everything and expect it for nothing. You are a role model whose lessons will live forever. The fact that you were able to put up with Papa and his antics for so many years is nothing short of amazing. I miss him with you every day, but I am so happy to still have you in my life.

Jennifer Bergstrom: Mel's first call was a good one. I thought when you heard we put the book together in a month that you would run scared. Thanks for giving us a shot.

Aimée Bell: Without you believing in me, Brittany and I could not have done this. Your encouragement (and strict deadlines) always kept us going.

Mel Berger: The best agent in the world. From the first day we spoke, I knew you were the one. Looking forward to our next one together.

Max Meltzer: The same way I couldn't do it without Brittany, we appreciate you being a part of the team with Aimée. Thank you for the hours that you put into this for us.

Sally Marvin: You were a real pleasure to work with, especially getting me to pay attention to publicity—the part of the process that is outside my natural comfort zone.

Elisa Rivlin: Your legal precision was greatly appreciated.

The New York assistant U.S. attorneys, FBI, and NYPD joint task force agents and victim advocates: From beginning to end, you handled every aspect of the investigation and prosecution perfectly, with professionalism and appropriate delicacy. You will never know how much you meant to the lives of so many people, not only the many victims but also to parents, attorneys (including especially me), and the public. You helped to restore faith in the criminal justice system and upheld the Crime Victim's Rights Act.

Dera: My trusted man's best friend. Through thick and thin, you were there. You listened when nobody else would. There was never a run you would not go on, and not a trial room you would not watch guard over. Because of you, I was always safe. To the greatest dog to live—thank you for being with me, until your end.

Epstein might have had a dream team of lawyers, but we had a legal dream team as well. Nothing could have been possible without an extraordinary legal team. It was an honor and pleasure to have had the opportunity to work with those who also tirelessly fought for the victims tirelessly refusing to give in. That team consisted primarily of Paul Cassell, Sigrid McCawley, Brittany Henderson, David Boies, Stan Pottinger, Meredith, Jay Howell, Jack Scarola, David Vitale, Karen Terry, Pete Skinner, Dan Crispino, Tom McCawley, Matt Weissing, and Bill Berger. Anyone in the legal profession knows, no legal team can be successful without an excellent support staff. Ours included Maria Kelljchian, Beth Williamson, Shawn Gilbert, Christina Fitch Escobar, Maria Cardenal, Iris Zambrano, Sandy Perkins, Linda Carlson, and Julius Williams.

To my many other clients, I would like to thank you individually and for some of you I have a lot to thank you for but understand and respect your desire to maintain your anonymity. Still, you know who you are. I am honored to have represented you and am always here for you if you need me.

Finally, a special thanks to Annie Farmer, Josh Roberts, Manny and Terry Perez, Clara Moran, Shawn Gilbert, David Keller, Raymond Robin, Bob Josefsberg, Adam Horowitz, Heather Riley, Amy Robach, Jorge Font, Chuck Lichtman, Meg Garvin, Gary Farmer, G. Michael Keenan, Bruce Rogow, Dave Parello, Janette Perez, Nikki Perez, Tracy and Don Henderson, Brandon and Tyler Henderson, Ginger Oliver, Police Chief Michael Reiter, and Detective Joe Recarey.

# RESOURCES

Many people have asked what they can do to help support victims—both of Jeffrey Epstein and his associates as well as of sexual assault in general. Two nonprofit organizations that Brittany and I are affiliated with are working toward this goal.

**Victims Refuse Silence** is the organization founded by Virginia Roberts in 2014. It is a nonprofit organization designed to help survivors break the silence associated with sexual abuse all around the world.

More information can be found at the organization's website, https://www.victimsrefusesilence.org/ or on its Facebook page, https://www.facebook.com/victimsrefusesilence/.

**Stand with Epstein Victims** is the nonprofit that Brittany and I founded in 2019 to raise money to help victims of Jeffrey Epstein. Jeffrey Epstein spent many years victimizing young women who have spent their lives recovering from his abuse. During those same years, institutions of higher education and research accepted financial donations from Mr. Epstein despite his involvement in publicly known sexually abusive conduct. We started Stand with Epstein

Victims to provide those institutions and individuals who accepted such donations a nonprofit organization that will make sure the funds are used exclusively to make a difference in the lives of Epstein's many victims. Recognizing the great need for financial assistance, we are now accepting donations from the public in general. In order to ensure a fair and transparent distribution of funds received, an independent volunteer oversight committee will equally divide all proceeds among confirmed victims of Jeffrey Epstein.

More information can be found at www.StandWithEpstein Victims.com where donations can also be made.

Additionally, we'd like to call attention to two incredible organizations that victims of sexual violence can turn to at any time.

**RAINN** (Rape, Abuse & Incest National Network) is the nation's largest antisexual violence organization. RAINN created and operates the National Sexual Assault Hotline, which can be reached by phone at 800.656.HOPE (4673), or through a confidential online chat system at https://www.rainn.org/get-help.

**The National Human Trafficking Hotline** connects victims and survivors of sex and labor trafficking with services and support to get help and stay safe. The hotline can be reached at 1-888-373-7888, by text at 233733, or through a confidential online chat system at https://humantraffickinghotline.org/chat.